THE DIMENSIONS OF QUANTITATIVE RESEARCH IN HISTORY

History Advisory Committee of MSSB:

Forthcoming volumes in the MSSB series *Quantitative Studies in History*:

Slavery and Race in the Western Hemisphere
The History of Legislative Behavior
The New Urban History
International Comparison of Social Mobility in Past Societies
International Trade and Internal Growth: The Variety of Experience
Quantitative Studies of Popular Voting Behavior
Government and Education: Policies, Expenditures, and Consequences
Studies of Political Elites

Published:

The Dimensions of Quantitative Research in History (Princeton, 1972)
Essays on a Mature Economy: Britain after 1840 (Princeton, 1972)

The Dimensions of Quantitative Research in History

EDITED BY

William O. Aydelotte ✦ Allan G. Bogue

Robert William Fogel

CONTRIBUTORS

William O. Aydelotte - Allan G. Bogue - Philip Dawson

Robert William Fogel - Ellen Jane Hollingsworth

J. Rogers Hollingsworth - Gerald H. Kramer

Susan J. Lepper - Jack L. Rutner - Gilbert Shapiro

Jeanne C. Fawtier Stone - Lawrence Stone

Stephan Thernstrom - Charles Tilly

PRINCETON UNIVERSITY PRESS

L.C. CARD: 75-166370

ISBN: 0-691-07544-1

Printed in the United States of America by
Princeton University Press, Princeton, New Jersey

TO

Lionel W. McKenzie

AND

Frederick Mosteller

who were instrumental in

launching the MSSB program in history

Preface

THIS IS the introductory volume in a series sponsored by the History Advisory Committee of the Mathematical Social Science Board in order to encourage the application of mathematical methods to historical analysis. Princeton University Press will publish the series under the general title "Quantitative Studies in History." This volume lays stress on the scope of the quantitative methods that are today being applied in history and on the variety of issues to which these methods are germane. Each of the subsequent contributions will focus on a major historical problem. Other volumes in the series are listed on p. ii.

The Mathematical Social Science Board (MSSB) was established in 1964 under the aegis of the Center for Advanced Study in the Behavioral Sciences "to foster advanced research and training in the application of mathematical methods in the social sciences." The following fields are each represented on MSSB by one member: anthropology, economics, history, geography, linguistics, political science, psychology, and sociology. The three methodological disciplines of mathematics, statistics, and computer science are also represented. Members of MSSB are appointed, subject to the approval of the Board of Trustees of the Center, for a term of four years. At the present time the members of MSSB are:

Richard C. Atkinson, Department of Psychology, Stanford University (Chairman)

Preston S. Cutler, Center for Advanced Study in the Behavioral Sciences

Michael F. Dacey, Department of Geography, Northwestern University

Roy G. D'Andrade, Department of Anthropology, University of California—San Diego

Robert William Fogel, Departments of Economics and History, University of Chicago and University of Rochester

Leo A. Goodman, Departments of Sociology and Statistics, University of Chicago

David G. Hays, Program in Linguistics, State University of New York—Buffalo

Harold Kuhn, Department of Economics, Princeton University

R. Duncan Luce, Institute for Advanced Study, Princeton, New Jersey

Allen Newell, Department of Computer Science, Carnegie-Mellon University

Roy Radner, Department of Economics, University of California—Berkeley

William H. Riker, Department of Political Science, University of Rochester

Patrick Suppes, Department of Philosophy, Stanford University

MSSB has established advisory committees to plan its activities in the various substantive fields with which it is concerned. The current members of the History Advisory Committee are listed on page ii above.

Supported by grants from the National Science Foundation, MSSB has organized five major classes of activities.

(1) *Training Programs*, which last from two to eight weeks during the summer, are designed to provide young pre- and post-Ph.D.s with intensive training in some of the mathematics pertinent to their substantive field and with examples of applications to specific problems.

(2) *Research and Training Seminars*, which last from four to six weeks, are composed of both senior scientists and younger people who have already received some training in mathematical applications. The focus is on recent research, on the intensive exploration of new ideas, and on the generation of new research. The training is less formal than in (1); it has the apprentice nature of advanced graduate work.

(3) *Advanced Research Workshops*, last from four to six weeks, but they are almost exclusively restricted to senior scientists and are devoted to fostering advanced research. They afford the possibility of extensive and penetrating contact over a prolonged period, which would otherwise probably not be possible, of men deeply steeped in research.

(4) *Preparation of Teaching Materials.* In some areas, the absence of effective teaching materials—even of suitable research papers—is a very limiting factor in the development of research and teaching activities within the university framework. The Board has, therefore, felt that it could accelerate the development of such materials, in part, by financial support and, in part, by help in organizing their preparation.

(5) *Special Conferences.* Short conferences, lasting a few days, are organized to explore the possibilities of the successful development of mathematical theory and training in some particular area that has not previously been represented in the programs, or to review the progress of research in particular areas when such a review seems warranted.

Robert William Fogel, CHAIRMAN
History Advisory Committee, MSSB

Chicago, Illinois
November 1971

Acknowledgments

THE AUTHORS have benefited from the criticism and suggestions of many scholars. Some are indicated in the footnotes to the individual essays. Others are listed in the Appendix.

Many of the administrative burdens connected with the production of this volume were borne by Mrs. Marilyn Gore. She was in charge of the arrangements for the June 1969 conference described in the Appendix; she was the conscience of both the authors and the editors in the struggle to meet the various deadlines; and she typed parts of the manuscript.

Mrs. Babu Jones served as an efficient and diligent editorial assistant. Susan Leibundguth aided in the herculean task of checking and correcting the footnotes.

Contents

THE DIMENSIONS OF QUANTITATIVE RESEARCH IN HISTORY

Introduction

WILLIAM O. AYDELOTTE, ALLAN G. BOGUE,

AND ROBERT WILLIAM FOGEL

THIS COLLECTION of essays, dealing with the applicability of mathematical methods to history, is designed as a teaching vehicle. Its purpose is to show by some examples the way in which quantitative methods can be used and have recently been used in historical research. The object is to demonstrate the advantages and limitations of these methods for historical purposes, not by an abstract discussion of methodology, but by a series of essays that attempt to apply such methods to a wide range of concrete historical problems.

The decision to emphasize substantive research, and to refrain from including any papers devoted primarily to questions of method, was considered and deliberate. It does not imply any disparagement of methodological or theoretical presentations, which are at times necessary and can be most useful. It seemed, however, that, at this point in the discussion of quantitative techniques, an emphasis on the actual problems of research would be more helpful. This is partly because books that offer guides on various kinds of technical problems are already available, and others are in the process of being published. More important, however, is the point that a judgment of the advantages of an innovation must ultimately rest upon what is done with it: whether research along the lines indicated has been undertaken and carried through, and whether it has produced results of interest. There has been a good deal of controversy over the value of quantitative methods, and misunderstandings on the subject have arisen. A few examples of different kinds of quantitative research now under way may help to clear the air and to indicate, more precisely than would be feasible by other means, both the possibilities and the limitations of this approach. The essays that follow, though they make use of methodological innovations, are all addressed to specific historical problems. This does not mean, of course, that technical matters are ignored since, in the formal study of substantive questions, it is often necessary to say a good deal about method and about research strategy. In these papers, however, these matters are treated as the means to particular ends rather than being discussed in general terms.

The object of this collection of essays can also be described in a broader context. The book is a response to, and an attempt to aid and stimulate, one of the most interesting developments of recent historical scholarship. In the last generation there has been a growing concern among historians with large analytical questions, and with studying these questions by formal methods including, when the evidence permits, quantitative techniques. Historians have increasingly come to appreciate the effectiveness of statistical tools in coping with the problem of finding uniformities in the data at their disposal, and in providing the means of making inductive inferences by logically defensible procedures. These methods have proved valuable, not only because they serve as powerful instruments of analysis, but also because they give access to reservoirs of important historical information that could hardly be exploited effectively without them. A number of members of the profession have come to hope that a variety of different kinds of historical problems, heretofore discussed only in rather general terms, can by such means be treated more effectively and brought closer to a solution on the basis of ordered knowledge. The considerable amount of experimentation by historians along this line has produced results that have already attracted a good deal of attention.

The methods that have demonstrated their value for historical purposes vary greatly in level of complexity. A mere summary of the data or a reclassification of them in a relatively simple manner can sometimes bring to light important uniformities, or demonstrate the absence of expected uniformities, in a way that makes possible significant revisions of earlier views. In the course of time, however, historians using such methods have become bolder and more far-ranging in applying them. They have passed from a mere summary of the characteristics of a group to the development of indexes by which different degrees of the same characteristic in different individuals could be measured. They have attempted not only descriptive statistics, where all members of a population are examined with regard to the points in which the student is interested, but also statistics of inference in which the attempt is made, with proper safeguards, to deduce from the study of a sample something about the attributes of the larger population from which the sample was drawn. Some scholars, notably the econometricians, have attempted to recombine primary data into constructs that conform to rigorously defined concepts. While some statistical presentations can be followed by almost anyone, others are so technical and abstract that they leave most members of the history profession, except for the handful with mathematical expertise, far behind.

There are differences, also, not only in the level of complexity but in the kinds of techniques used. The choice between these will depend on the interest of the student and on the kind of problem he wants to study. If, for example, he is interested in establishing the existence of blocs of voters in a legislature, he may want to make use of cumulative scales; if he is primarily concerned with the explanation for such group behavior, regression analysis may be more to his purpose. Statistical devices can also bring to light different features of the evidence in which different scholars may be interested. For a student concerned with prediction, with ascertaining what is the likeliest outcome of a set of circumstances, the value of the statistical method is its ability to normalize. A student may, however, for good reasons, be more interested in deviations, in the extent and range of departures from the usual pattern. For him, statistical techniques can not merely provide the context, the norm from which these individual cases departed, but can also be used to measure the extent of the deviations and to summarize, in whatever categories prove most convenient, the number of cases at each level of deviation.

An attempt has been made, in the choice of the papers commissioned for the conference and reproduced here, to illustrate the wide range of intellectual concerns and technical approaches that has appeared in recent quantitative research. Although it is scarcely possible, in a volume containing only nine essays, to reflect the full extent of this variety, the editors feel that, within this limited scope, this effort has been reasonably successful. The nine rather dissimilar papers in this book deal with a number of different problems, in different areas of study, and employ different techniques and classes of evidence. Though it cannot be pretended that they cover the whole field, they do go some distance toward indicating the diversity of historical problems to which mathematics can be applied and the diversity of the methods that can be used to study them.

To assist in the preparation of these essays, two conferences were organized.[1] The first, which was held at Harvard University in June 1966, brought together the authors of the papers and a small group of historians, other social scientists, and statisticians. This conference was convened after the authors had clearly formulated the objectives of their papers, but early enough to permit them to take advantage of the suggestions of the social scientists and statisticians with respect to the formulation of behavioral models and the development of appropriate estimating procedures. At the second conference, convened in Chicago in June 1969, the penultimate versions of the papers were reviewed. Approximately sixty historians, social scientists, and statisticians par-

[1] The participants in these conferences are listed in the Appendix.

ticipated in this meeting. The discussion of each paper was initiated by three predesignated commentators. The papers were criticized and challenged both by statisticians, on formal grounds, and by specialists in the field, on general grounds. An attempt was made, in selecting the three commentators for each paper, to include at least one of each: an individual qualified to make technical criticisms and to appraise the soundness of the formal procedures; and also a commentator who, though not necessarily a statistician, and preferably not a statistician, had a recognized preeminence in the field the paper dealt with and could appraise the value of its findings in terms of the general state of scholarship in the area. These interchanges were often stimulating. Many of the criticisms were acute and well founded, and raised important and difficult questions. Statisticians were sometimes able to suggest more effective or simpler means of accomplishing certain ends, or to raise points that necessitated some revision or recasting of the formal claims made in a paper. Historians, by raising wider issues of interpretation, indicated some of the contexts in which the new findings would have to be examined if their value were to be properly appraised, and also called attention to facets of the problems studied that were not covered by the detailed research but that would have to be taken into account in any general description or interpretation.

The editors considered at one point including the comments in the book, but this proved not feasible. A principal obstacle was the fact that many of the speakers took these criticisms to heart and incorporated them, or at least took account of them, in making their final revisions. The comments, though highly relevant to the preliminary versions of the papers presented at the meeting, would not have been appropriate as critiques of the later drafts reproduced here, and we could hardly take further advantage of our guests by asking them to write a new and entirely different set of criticisms expressly for this book. It should be added that the comments have also been most useful to us in preparing our introduction in which we have tried to reflect, even if only indirectly, a few of the questions raised and the arguments pursued in the discussions.

This isn't quite the whole story. The experiment of including non-statisticians among the commentators on a set of statistical papers, though it still seems to the editors to have been a courageous effort and one well worth making, also created some problems. This confrontation brought sharply to the surface, to an extent that may have been surprising to both parties, the difficulties that the quantifiers and the non-quantifiers had in communicating their ideas and concerns to each other. Neither group, apparently, found it easy, in all cases, to get the other to understand what it was driving at. Some of the commentators were troubled by a certain "deafness" on the part of the speakers, a failure to catch the point of what they were saying. They felt that their objections, though courteously listened to, were not fully understood and did not receive satisfactory answers. On the other hand, some of the speakers were disappointed in the nature of the criticisms they received. It was not that the commentators were overly sharp. On the contrary, everybody was terribly polite; and, in any case, the whole purpose of inviting the commentators was to elicit criticisms from them. It was more the other way round. A commentator would sometimes fail to notice the real weaknesses of a paper, the points on which it was most vulnerable, and on which he could have given the speaker a rough time if he had seized the opportunity. In some cases a commentator who was expected to prove a formidable critic would apparently not even grasp the central argument of the paper he had been asked to discuss and would, instead, make observations that were friendly but uncomprehending, insightful in general terms but not directly relevant to the matter at issue.

This is still not the end of the story. There appear to be, to judge from the proceedings of the conference, two problems of communication and not one. Those using statistical methods in history sometimes find it hard to establish a common basis for discussion, not only with their fellow historians, but also with statisticians. Statisticians are powerful and helpful critics of the technical procedures. They sometimes, however, seem to have difficulty in following or display a lack of interest in the theoretical, often non-mathematical inferences that historians may try to extract from the findings. From the historian's point of view, the value of technical research consists in and is determined by the light it can cast on general problems of historical interpretation. Statisticians, as is perhaps to be expected, tend sometimes to be less interested in such problems and less knowledgeable about them. Nor were the practical suggestions of the statisticians invariably useful with respect to the pursuit of the matter in hand. Proposals were occasionally made for the employment of new techniques and devices of analysis which, though they might provide some interesting exercises, did not seem likely to advance the intellectual purposes of the research in any way that was immediately apparent. Quantitative historians sometimes find themselves occupying a delicate middle ground, a kind of no man's land, between statisticians and traditional historians, in which they are trying to apply the technical devices developed in one field to the substantive problems that have been raised in the other. A historian who tries to bridge this gap is sometimes left dangling in between and has trouble in making effective contact with the specialists in either direction, with exactly the two professional groups who should, properly, be able to help him most.

The failure of some historians to catch the issues of the papers might in part be attributed to their lack of technical knowledge. The problem, however, seems to go deeper, and to relate to misunderstandings about the basic objectives of this kind of research: what purposes it can serve, and what may or may not be reasonably expected from it. Though quantitative methods in history have now been practiced for a while, there still appears to be, even at this stage, a real problem, not only in making their findings acceptable, but also in making their purpose understood. It was disturbing to some of the speakers to find that their objectives, their attempts to achieve more precise and reliable knowledge on limited but carefully defined questions, were not recognized as valid and sometimes, apparently, not even perceived by some of their most distinguished colleagues.

One barrier to communication between quantitative and non-quantitative historians may be that some of those who have not attempted quantitative research cherish unrealistic expectations of what it can do: what can be claimed for it or, perhaps, what they think is wrongly claimed for it. The uninitiated tend to expect a breadth of scope and a degree of certainty from statistical investigations which it is not in the nature of the method to yield. They demand, for a statistical presentation, that its arithmetical findings should be indisputable, that it should present a complete explanation of the events it covers, and that it should contribute to the establishment of a general or universal law predicting that certain consequences will invariably ensue from certain conditions. Such expectations are the stuff that dreams are made of and would not be seriously considered for a moment by those who have any considerable experience with this kind of research. The folklore that has grown up around quantitative methods has not only impeded their use but has also worked to prevent a clear appraisal of the results they have been able to produce: the limited but significant tasks that can be performed by using them and that could hardly be performed in any other way. It seems desirable, then, to stress several points here, not to show that the statistical method is too limited to be of use, but rather to indicate the kinds of uses to which it may be put and the kinds of results it can produce.

The belief that the use of quantitative methods will result in universal laws or complete explanations of the circumstances with which they deal rests on a misapprehension of the nature of the approach. Historians have in any case not been notably successful in establishing universal laws or complete explanations. The achievements of the system-builders have, on the whole, not been accepted by the majority of the profession. It is worth pointing out, also, that most of these constructions have not been based on quantitative analysis: the system-builders, for all their claims to be at the forefront, have tended to be methodologically conservative. In any case, a resort to quantitative methods is more likely to restrict than to broaden the focus of a particular inquiry. Attempts at precision limit what can be covered. It is sometimes surprising how small an area it is possible to examine when one is making a conscientious attempt to be exact. In quantitative research it may be hoped that, if the work is successful, some uniformities, some larger simplifying generalizations may make an appearance, as they occasionally have, but these are likely to be within a rather narrowly defined range.

This restriction of focus, however, is not a disadvantage of the method but, properly considered with all that it implies, its principal merit. What is attempted in this approach is to take more effective advantage of selected parts of the evidence: to seize on those parts of the data that can be handled more strictly, by mathematical means, and to subject them to a more refined analysis. The procedure consists in applying close and exact attention to the limited elements of the general problem under consideration that are capable of being handled in this fashion. Restriction of focus is the price that must be paid for being more sure of one's ground. If this resulted in trivialities, the price might be regarded as too high. This objection is, indeed, occasionally made against formal methods: that they can be applied to only a narrow range of problems, which are often not the most important ones. Certainly it is true enough that not all topics of historical investigation lend themselves to mathematical analysis. Nevertheless, the use of formal methods does not necessarily imply and has not in fact implied the neglect of major problems of historical interpretation. For one thing, quantitative methods, though they limit the historian's reach in the manner just described, greatly extend it in another respect. They make it possible for him to examine the characteristics of and variations in great amounts of data, and to test quickly various alternative strictly formulated hypotheses about them. The method permits easy control over large, in some cases extremely large, masses of information that would be difficult to handle by other means, so difficult indeed that in many cases it would scarcely be practicable to attempt the task.

Furthermore, a concrete finding on a limited point, attained by a systematic marshaling of the evidence, may prove to have important implications for a much larger question. The findings, when their full implications are considered, may provide valuable new insights and permit reformulations and advances in the discussion of considerably more general problems. Fogel has pointed out elsewhere that the questions now being attacked by econometricians are, despite the novelty of the method, the classical issues of American economic history. In political history it has also proved possible to develop detailed projects of systematic research that bear directly on major issues, much studied and disputed, and that make contributions that clearly advance the argument. The papers included in this volume, though each describes a specialized and limited inquiry, are all directed, as will appear from the discussion of them below, to general issues the importance of which can scarcely be doubted.

It is also quite mistaken to expect that the results of quantitative research, even on the limited points they cover, will be or may be expected to be conclusive or final. This is partly because quantitative research in history—though quite a bit of it has now been done—is still a relatively new venture. The paths are not yet well trodden and future directions are not wholly clear. It is still not certain what kinds of problems will prove most rewarding to study, or what technical devices will be most effective in coping with them. A good deal of further experience may be needed before guidelines on these matters are well established. Much more is involved here, however, than the novelty of the approach. It is not in the nature of the statistical method, or of any other research method for that matter, to produce definitive answers to major questions. Though the lack of finality of research results is an old story, unrealistic demands in regard to quantitative research are sometimes made by the uninformed, and it is not always appreciated that quantifiers also suffer from disabilities.

It is wrong to suppose that a resort to numbers affords the student a kind of security unattainable by other kinds of evidence or that a set of papers that use figures will, for this reason, be definitive. The accuracy of the computations by no means betokens a similar precision of knowledge regarding the substantive matters described. There may be errors in measurement and tabulation. In some fields, in research involving the study of social classes for example, it may prove extremely difficult to set up categories so clearly defined that there can be no question which individuals should be assigned to which. Furthermore, statistical results are seldom conclusive since it almost never happens, in an enterprise of any scope, that all the evidence points in a single direction. Most important, statistical manipulations merely rearrange the evidence; they do not, except on an elementary level, answer general questions, and the bearing of the findings upon the larger problems of interpretation in which historians are interested is a matter, not of arithmetic, but of logic and persuasion. It is always arguable whether the results of an investigation have been correctly interpreted. The interpretations presented may arouse controversy, and there may be legitimate disagreement as to how far certain inferences are warranted in the light of all the evidence at our disposal. Anyone who believes, with regard to a large statistical project, that the categories will be wholly unambiguous, that the results will point conclusively to a single position, and that there can be no doubt about what the findings mean, cannot be well acquainted from experience with the practical problems of this type of research.

In recent controversies some of those who attack the new procedures have tried to show in a series of books and articles, a number of which are quite able, that final explanations cannot be achieved in history even with the aid of formal methods. The point may be at once conceded, but it is irrelevant to the discussion of the merits of formal methods, for this is not what formal methods do or what they are supposed to do. Those who use such methods do not, if they know their business, pretend to have achieved finality. Far from this, such a claim would be rejected as absurd, not only by anyone with experience in historical research, but also by anyone who had made a careful attempt to use quantitative techniques to describe and study social, economic, or political phenomena.

What is attempted in quantitative research, as in other research, is not full knowledge of reality but an increasingly closer approximation to it: what has been described, in a mathematical metaphor that is entirely appropriate, as the asymptotic approach to truth. The value of statistical techniques, in the cases where they can be applied, is that they make possible a highly effective deployment of our limited information. They provide means of coping systematically and efficiently with the obstacles in the way of making general statements and afford powerful assistance in the search for uniformities, in the face of the varied and confusing data with which historians are ordinarily confronted. They provide also an accurate means of seeing where we stand, how far the emerging generalizations require to be qualified and how significant are the exceptions to them. These techniques, even if they cannot produce the ultimate, can at least bring us increasingly closer to a position that we can urge with a certain amount of assurance.

This is the kind of task attempted in the research projects described in the following papers. These enterprises are not directed toward the illusory goals of universality and finality. They may more properly be regarded as conscientious and responsible efforts to tackle problems of some moment and to advance our understanding of them through the examination of new classes of information and through the study of these materials by techniques of analysis as refined as the evidence permits. The essays published here do not, of course, constitute the last words their authors will ever say on these various subjects. They are, on the contrary, a set of reports on extensive projects that are still under way, a number of which, perhaps all, are likely to result later in presentations of book length. For most of these investigations there are still gaps in the information and unresolved questions, the examination of which may well raise further problems. The hypotheses adumbrated in these papers are tentative, and additional research may produce neater and more satisfactory conclusions. In view of the difficulty of the tasks undertaken it would be surprising if, in the course of time, some revisions of the conclusions of these papers, and of the theoretical frameworks in which they are cast, were not in order.

These statements are also, inevitably because of their brevity, incomplete. It is impossible in a short paper to deal adequately with the whole range of problems entailed in an extensive investigation, and for the most part the contributors have wisely limited themselves to a single question or set of related questions. The extent of the substantive findings that could be included has also been restricted by the need, in a set of technical papers, to spend a certain amount of time on necessary preliminaries: identifying and clarifying the historical problems to which the research is addressed, and indicating the main lines of the scholarly apparatus that has been set up to deal with these matters.

The editors wish, finally, to offer a few remarks about each paper. No extensive discussion is needed. The statements of the arguments may be left to the authors. Nor would it be appropriate in this place to offer an appraisal of each piece and to enter into argument with the author about it. It may be useful, however, to attempt to put each paper into perspective in terms of the kinds of questions it has tried to come to grips with, the approaches it has used, and the technical and analytical problems that the investigation raises.

These essays, despite their variation in method and in subject matter, are addressed to a limited number of broad historical problems that can be roughly identified, and this general classification has been used as a basis for their arrangement in this book. The first two are concerned with the structure of society and the nature of social mobility, though one treats a restricted elite in England over a period of several centuries and the other a large urban population in a modern American city. The next two deal with the relation between social conditions or social change and the development of radical or violent protest. Both use materials drawn from French history, though one is concerned with the late eighteenth century and the other, primarily, with the mid-nineteenth. The fifth essay discusses patterns of voting in the American electorate. The sixth and seventh are both concerned with legislative behavior in the mid-nineteenth century, though they deal with different countries and different problems: one takes up alternative research strategies for identifying the location of political power; the other treats the patterns of voting and of political choice incident to the breakup of a major party. The last two papers deal with the factors shaping certain aspects of government intervention in the economy, one on the local level and the other on the national level. Certainly none of these general topics can be dismissed as unimportant. All of them have, on the contrary, been matters of central concern to scholars for some time.

The fact that some of these essays are, in this general way, related in theme does not, however, mean that exact comparisons can be made of their findings. Comparative studies can be useful and fascinating, but they need to be planned in advance: similar questions must be asked of similar data. The general problems on which these investigations bear are many faceted, and they have been approached in these essays in rather different ways. A more appropriate way of looking at these contributions is to regard them as illustrating the complexity of major issues of historical interpretation and the variety of different kinds of investigation that can aid in the study of them.

To give only one illustration of this point, out of several that could be offered, the first three papers are all concerned, in part at least, with social mobility. They treat three different countries: Lawrence and Jeanne Stone deal with England, Stephan Thernstrom with the United States, and Gilbert Shapiro and Philip Dawson with France. A comparative study of this problem in these three settings would be most interesting, but it cannot be attempted on the basis of these materials. The Stones and Thernstrom are traveling quite different routes. It is not only that the Stones deal with a far longer span of time, or that they consider the period before 1879 and Thernstrom, as it happens, the period after 1880. More important, the Stones are concerned with the penetration of men of new wealth into a restricted governing elite while Thernstrom deals with the social structure of a large American city. The authors also use quite dissimilar classes of evidence and techniques of analysis. The focus of the Stones' paper might seem closer to that of the paper by Shapiro and Dawson, who are also interested in the upward mobility of a middle class into an aristocracy. The central concerns of the two projects, however, are different. It is not only that Shapiro and Dawson deal with a single year, and the Stones with three centuries, or that their principal body of evidence is the *cahiers*, whereas the Stones' is primarily architectural, though they use more conventional sources as well. There is an even greater disparity in objectives. The Stones are collecting evidence regarding the existence and extent of mobility. Shapiro and Dawson, on the other hand, are interested in the effect of opportunities, or the lack of opportunities, for upward mobility upon the development of radical protest against the *ancien régime*.

1. Lawrence Stone and Jeanne C. Fawtier Stone, "Country Houses and Their Owners in Hertfordshire, 1540-1879"

The structure of British society and the composition of the British social and political elite have been, from various angles, central concerns of scholarly investigation for some time. The subject has aroused brisk controversy, and on a number of points vigorous disagreement still persists. The fierce debate over alternative social interpretations of the political events of the seventeenth century, though some of its fury is now spent, has by no means wholly subsided. Accounts of modern British history in class terms have attracted a good deal of criticism, and a number of those who have written on the subject have doubted whether rigorous class definitions are feasible at all and have suggested that it may be unprofitable to attempt to make use of such categories.

The concept of social class has been, for the last century and a half, one of the principal devices used to make political and social history intelligible. It is clear now, however, that historians have not always used this concept to good advantage. Early formulations were crude and gave an inadequate idea of a complex reality. They have not proved such useful summarizing devices and have not provided such convincing explanations of events as once was hoped. It is to be regretted that much of the theorizing about social classes was done before there existed any considerable accumulation of the results of systematic research on social stratification. Vague and naïve concepts on this subject, though we now know that they have little relation to the facts, still survive in the clichés and assumptions of a good deal of historical writing to confuse and to plague us. The assumption that some writers appear to have made, that classes could be easily defined and identified, has broken down as a result of more careful work. We have now, thanks to research over the last generation both in history and in other fields, a clearer picture of the complex nature of social stratification and of the kinds of research questions that it may be profitable to ask about it. A number of recent historians have tried to take advantage of these insights and have sought to develop social categories that would be less vulnerable, trying to derive them not from abstract theory but from what has been observed about the trends of the evidence. The first four papers in this volume, though they deal with quite different subjects, are all concerned to some extent with this problem and all make efforts in this direction.

One figment of the historical imagination that has particularly irritated some modern students is the supposed "rise of the middle classes." This phenomenon, located by A. F. Pollard (writing in 1907) in Tudor England, identified by Piers Plowman as occurring in the fourteenth century, and assigned by other writers to other periods, has been used to account for a variety of things and has indeed, as J. H. Hexter says, tended to serve "as the ultimate solution of all the problems of explanation in European history from the eleventh century on." Such interpretations of British history have, however, become increasingly unacceptable to historians, particularly as a result of research and discussion over the last several decades. It is hard to show, on closer scrutiny, that the "middle classes," whoever they were, rose, or at least that they rose all that much, at the times when their rise was supposed to have made all the difference. Arguments couched in these terms can be supported, as Hexter has shown in his witty and acute contribution to the discussion, only by employing class definitions so loose that they will not bear scrutiny.

In the light of recent evidence one is apt to be more impressed by the extraordinary retention by the British landed class of a large part of its social prestige and political influence until quite recent times. There is ample testimony to its continued predominance even in the nineteenth century and, to some extent at least, in the twentieth century as well. This eminence of the landowners lasted even into a period when the political and economic bases of their power had to a large extent been undermined or eroded. The most striking social event in modern British history, Hexter has argued, and the one that most needs to be accounted for, may be not the rise of the bourgeoisie but its conspicuous failure to rise, and the survival of the landed class which, by a series of adaptations to new circumstances, successfully maintained its power through all the vicissitudes of three-quarters of a millennium. We do not yet, however, know the whole story, and debates over the rise and fall of major social groups in England still have a certain unreality, and will continue to until enough research has been done to give us a more reliable account of the principal lines of the evidence.

Lawrence and Jeanne Stone, in the project described in the first essay, are attempting to make a concrete contribution to the discussion of this slippery and elusive topic by supplying some hard data. In order to measure the degree to which members of the business and professional classes could and did move upward, they propose to use the ingenious device of a study of the ownership and transmission of large country estates. By examining the extent to which these big country houses changed hands, and by assembling and analyzing biographical information about the owners and purchasers, they hope to provide some definite information on the penetration of members of the so-called middle class into the ruling elite. Though the analysis may not tell the whole story of this penetration, it will at least make use of materials that have not been systematically exploited for such a purpose before and that are of unquestionable importance.

Research on the history of the landed class in Britain has of late been much aided and stimulated by the opening to scholars, particularly since World War II, of increasing numbers of private archives of landed families. It is a particular interest of the Stones' research, however, that they use, in addition to these more conventional sources, architectural evidence as well. The value of such evidence for social history has occasionally been noted by others. H. J. Dyos, for example, in his book (1961) on the suburb of Camberwell in the Victorian period, took account of the relation between architectural structure and social structure and made a number of interesting suggestions. The pursuit of this intriguing line of inquiry may, however, be even more rewarding for a rural community than for a suburban one. This is because of the central role that the country house has played in British life, a subject to which a number of scholars, such as H. J. Habakkuk and F.M.L. Thompson, have already given some attention. The landed estate in Great Britain has, over the last several centuries, had a social and political significance far transcending its economic value. The great country house served as the basis of its owner's weight in the community, provided a physical expression of the standing of a family, and also, once the development of the strict settlement had made it possible to use the estate as a vehicle of family purpose, afforded a sense of the identity and continuity of the family from generation to generation.

In this investigation the Stones hope to cover an extended time span, 1540 to 1879. Lawrence Stone has already made a massive and widely acclaimed contribution to the study of the British elite in the first century of this period, in his book *The Crisis of the Aristocracy, 1558-1641* (Oxford, 1965), and his intimate acquaintance with the social history of the late Tudor and early Stuart periods gives him an impressive initial advantage. The Stones now propose to extend greatly the coverage in time, though dealing with a much more restricted topic. They intend to make comparative studies of three counties: one, Hertfordshire (with which the present essay in large part deals), immediately adjacent to London and presumably, for that reason, atypical; one further removed from the capital; and one at a considerable distance.

This paper is an early report on an extended project of research, the data for which have not yet been fully assembled or analyzed. The findings presented cover only a part of the story that the Stones hope eventually to tell. They have described the broad outlines of the changes in house construction that their investigations have so far revealed. They had given much less space, however, to the identity of the owners and purchasers of these houses. This topic, though it is of course central to the main question raised in the research, is a large subject, and the Stones have preferred to reserve a full discussion of it for a later presentation. Their paper deals also with certain central problems of method to which careful attention must be given at the outset: the nature of the evidence, how far it lends itself to their purposes, and the kinds of categories, both of houses and of men, that can be set up on the basis of the available information.

A research enterprise of this kind faces substantial difficulties, both technical and conceptual. Although the Stones have found the sources of information extensive, especially for Hertfordshire, they have not always been adequate to their purposes. The data vary in reliability, and certain gaps in them have presented difficulties. On the whole they have found evidence about the houses less comprehensive and less easy to get than evidence about their owners. The complexity of the data and the variety of the purposes for which they wish to use it have also created coding problems, though work on these is by this time well advanced and a satisfactory codebook has been prepared.

In this research, the Stones must deal with formidable problems of taxonomy. The task of drawing lines of social demarcation, though in a project like this it is inescapable, is one of the most difficult and disheartening in the study of modern English history. It is not easy to devise class definitions that are precise enough to permit tabulation and analysis but that also reflect traditional class concepts to an extent that is sufficient to make them relevant to current historical controversy. The Stones have, actually, two sets of problems, since they need to classify both houses and individuals. The solutions, they argue, must inevitably be to some extent arbitrary. Their evidence so far seems to indicate that, both in the size of houses and in the social significance of their owners, there exists a smooth continuum in which there are no obvious breaks. Hence any cut-off point must be artificial. This, in turn, raises the difficult question of how far a segment of society, necessarily defined by an arbitrary cut-off point on a smooth continuum, can justly be regarded as an identifiable social group.

The Stones' candid and informed discussion brings out how many policy decisions must inevitably go into the rules adopted for tabulating the figures, and to how great a degree subjective judgments are unavoidable in working with social definitions and lines of demarcation. It is perhaps an advantage to them that their sample is relatively small, 151 houses and about 1,500 houseowners, which permits an intimacy of knowledge of the details that may provide some guidance in the final determination of the groups to study. Readers will examine with interest the ways in which the Stones have endeavored to cope with these matters and the kinds of categories they have been able to set up. The value of their contribution will consist not only in the results they are able to produce but also in the kind of headway they can make against some of the intractable problems that have been a recurring source of trouble to students working in social history.

2. Stephan Thernstrom, "Religion and Occupational Mobility in Boston, 1880-1963"

The paper by Stephan Thernstrom contributes significantly to the body of findings on population mobility at the local level which have been accumulating since the 1930s. So early as 1933 James C. Malin published the first of his series of reports on settlement patterns and the turnover of farm operators in Kansas, thus becoming the first American historian to make major use of the population and agricultural census manuscripts of the federal and state enumerations. Malin was interested in the persistence of farm operators and their descendants, in the age structure of the farmers and their wives, in their nativity and subsequent residence and in many aspects of the farm business. He reported that the usual settler was older than the Turnerians believed, that the age patterns of frontier adults probably approximated those in older areas, and that a particular frontier region did not in turn serve as a major source of population for the frontier which developed immediately beyond it.

Malin discovered that the flow of population out of frontier communities was not greatly different in good years and bad years but that inflow diminished sharply during periods of depression. In his population research, Malin concentrated on sample townships in the various rainfall belts of Kansas, analyzing the persistence of the members of each cohort of new settlers found in each census through subsequent enumerations down to 1935. He reported that the dramatic changes in physical environment experienced in moving westward across Kansas apparently did not much influence the turnover of settlers. Rather, the members of each new group appearing in the manuscript census behaved very similarly to the new cohorts of earlier and later censuses. All groups experienced a considerable loss of members in the period immediately following arrival and then showed a definite tendency to stabilize, losing cohort members more slowly thereafter. Although primarily concerned with native-born settlers, Malin noted that the foreign-born residents identified in his research were more persistent than the natives.

Although the contemporary implications of Malin's work on population persistence inspired an economist of the U.S.D.A. to attempt a replication study, its immediate impact upon historical scholarship seems to have been less than we now know that it deserved. More attention was attracted during the 1940s by the work of Frank L. Owsley and a number of his students at Vanderbilt University, who used the data in the 1850 and 1860 manuscript censuses in an attempt to reconstruct the economic and social structure of areas in the antebellum South. They documented to their satisfaction the existence of a "yeoman" population large enough to destroy the stereotype of a monolithic slaveholding South—a yeoman population moreover that might have served as the seed bed of the humanitarian democracy necessary to end the slave system. In this research Owsley and his students were primarily interested in the aggregate picture of the social and economic structure which they could develop rather than in the mobility and economic fortunes of the individual Southerner. In retrospect it is unfortunate that the Vanderbilt scholars did not systematically identify the members of the census cohort of 1850 in the 1860 census data and analyze the changes that had taken place in their social and economic status. Such work might have provided some extremely interesting evidence as to the "openness" of Southern society.

Although a number of scholars were using Malin's methods during the 1950s and early 1960s, it was particularly Merle Curti's study of the settlement process and the development of democratic institutions in Trempeleau County, Wisconsin, published in 1959, which emphasized the utility of research based upon the manuscript census rolls of the nineteenth century and related materials to a new generation of historians. *The Making of an American Community* reflected not only Curti's interest in areal mobility as studied by Malin, but also Owsley's concern with social structure. Curti correctly noted the important relationship between the two. His study provides an analysis of settler turnover, and also attempts to show the general distribution of property and the degree to which individuals improved their economic position from one census to the next. In a particularly interesting section of the research, Curti ascribed social status to both rural and urban occupations and then tabulated the totals of those who had risen or declined in status between 1870 and 1880.

Curti published his study of Trempeleau County in 1959, after a decade of work upon it. In 1964 there appeared the first book length study in which an author using similar methods concentrated upon eastern urban dwellers, Stephan Thernstrom's *Poverty and Progress: Social Mobility in a Nineteenth-Century City.* This book is a painstaking study of the members of the laboring class in Newburyport, Massachusetts, based primarily on the manuscript census rolls of the years between 1850 and 1880. Although using some of the same analytical techniques as had Curti, Thernstrom developed various ingenious methods of his own. He was able to show that, while considerable numbers of Newburyport's workers improved their status by acquiring property, the number who improved their status by moving into more highly regarded occupations was much smaller. Thernstrom's findings allowed him to refute various of the preconceptions of twentieth-century social scientists who had studied aspects of social mobility. Well written and persuasive, *Poverty and Progress* has been of major importance in attracting a considerable number of young scholars to the study of social mobility or related topics in various American towns and cities.

Thernstrom's contribution to this volume of essays is drawn from a larger study of occupational mobility in Boston during the late nineteenth and twentieth centuries. Carrying his concerns beyond the problems treated by Curti and those considered in his earlier research, Thernstrom examines the degree to which members of various ethnic groups in Boston were able to enhance their occupational and social status and to maintain improvements in these respects into the succeeding generation. His data suggests that young blue-collar Catholics in Boston were as proportionately successful as the scions of Protestant working-class families in finding their way into white-collar occupations. But a larger percentage of the Catholics had blue-collar fathers than did the Protestants. And once they had improved their positions, the Italian or Irish workers were more apt to lose them or "skid" than was the Protestant or Jew. Catholics from working-class families experienced less upward intergenerational mobility than did Protestants and young Catholic men from middle-class families were less successful than young Protestants of comparable origins. After considering the possibility that discrimination, peasant background, confinement in the ghetto, differential fertility rates, or institutional completeness accounted for his findings, Thernstrom suggests that cultural values provide the most likely independent variable. His materials, however—he explains—leave unclear the question of whether religion or national origin contributed most strongly to those cultural values. But in conclusion he notes that his findings are congruent with Weber's great thesis linking the "Protestant ethic" to the rise of capitalism in Europe and more specifically the corollary to this thesis, holding that "exposure to 'the Protestant ethic' would continue to predispose Protestants to success in the market place in later historical periods, and that Catholicism would continue to inhibit the worldly aspirations of its adherents."

Thernstrom has faced formidable problems in this piece of research. None of his data, of course, were compiled initially with answers to his specific kinds of question in mind, and he had to "manufacture" his data from several different sorts of records, a situation that always complicates the construction of time series or the analysis of periodic observations. Some of the data were incomplete and the numbers in his various ethnic groups differ considerably, his sample understandably yielding a much smaller number of Jews than of Roman Catholics or Protestants. Like others doing comparable research he has had to satisfy himself as to the size of sample which can be considered adequate for his purposes and the relevance and meaning of significance tests. In all these respects Thernstrom has made an honest effort to face up to the issues involved and, although in retrospect he might have preferred to have drawn larger samples, his defense of his methods carries the ring of conviction and common sense. But the methodological issues raised by the paper run deeper than mere problems of data retrieval and sampling. There has been a tendency in this type of research, as in the newer political history, to engage in "number smashing" unrelated even to middle range, let alone grand social or political theory. Thernstrom's comparative analysis of the conclusions in related research, his emphasis on the fact that modern findings must not be assumed to apply to earlier time periods, and his careful use of Weberian theory all give encouraging evidence of the rewards that historians may find in the judicious and explicit use of theory.

At the Chicago Conference, Donald J. Bogue described this paper as being a "very important" contribution to the literature of historical demography. Quite aside from the substantive findings it is notable for the thoughtful manner in which Thernstrom has considered alternative explanations of the data. This research also emphasizes the success which the new historians of urban social processes are having in utilizing data sources long disregarded or undiscovered. In its contingency tables and probability analysis the paper also reflects the growing statistical expertise of the modern scholar as contrasted with the raw scores, percentages, and averages used by the authors of antecedent research.

3. Gilbert Shapiro and Philip Dawson, "Social Mobility and Political Radicalism: The Case of the French Revolution of 1789"

The third and fourth papers also involve questions of social analysis but in a different context, since they are primarily concerned with the relation of social and economic circumstances to political attitudes and to political action. The discussion of the relation between socio-economic conditions and political events has, of course, a long history, going back well before Marx, and has received attention from many distinguished historians since, both Marxists and non-Marxists. The issue has unquestionably been a major one in the modern study of politics.

On this subject, as on others, the enthusiasm of some scholars would appear to have overreached itself. Social theories have sometimes been used to explain historical developments in ways so careless as to provoke a substantial amount of deserved criticism. A number of historians of the present generation have called attention to the crudeness of prevalent class concepts, to their weakness particularly on the psychological side, and to the obvious presence of other elements besides class interest in political motivation. Some critics have seriously questioned whether class concepts have, or can have, much explanatory power. Hexter identifies, as one of the notions that has played a considerable part in his own thinking and writing, the view that: "The only way you can fit history into what is roughly described as the economic or class interpretation is to leave out half or three-quarters of what happened and not ask any very bright questions about the remnant."

So categorical a dismissal would apply, one might suppose, more to a rigid and obsessive application of such theories in the teeth of the evidence than to careful research in which an attempt was made to weigh and appraise the effect of various determinants. In any case, in view of the results of recent massive investigations of the American electorate, it is difficult still to maintain that social backgrounds and political attitudes are in all cases wholly unrelated. The point must be stated cautiously, for the relationship between the two has proved to be far from consistent, not only because of the complexities of most systems of social stratification which preclude the easy identification of class groups, but also because other things besides social background have been shown to be related to political choice: religious and ethnic differences, regional loyalties, rural-urban conflicts, sex, age, and the political attitudes of one's parents. Even so, the trend of the evidence is strong. Seymour Martin Lipset attempted in his *Political Man* (1960) to bring together the results of many research studies on political behavior. His conclusion, regarding the relation of political to social conflicts, was that, while political parties may renounce the principle of class conflict, "an analysis of their appeals and their support suggests that they do represent the interests of different classes. On a world scale, the principal generalization which can be made is that parties are primarily based on either the lower classes or the middle and upper classes." Whether this means that the concept of class has explanatory power can, of course, be argued, since it is elementary that a correlation doesn't prove a cause-and-effect relationship. Yet the correlations are impressive enough to merit study and promise to be helpful in attaining some greater understanding of the nature of political behavior. Whether such further research would result in a general or sweeping "class" interpretation, or whether it would suggest that this line needs to be played down and that other matters may be more important than previously realized, remains to be seen. It is worth mentioning that a certain amount of recent work points in the latter direction.

This general issue, the relation of social and economic circumstances to political attitudes and events, has, as might be expected, engaged a considerable part of the attention of those interested in the history of the French Revolution. Class interpretations, almost Marxist in character, have been put forward by some of the most distinguished scholars in the field. Lefebvre describes the French Revolution as "the crown of a long economic and social evolution that made the bourgeoisie the mistress of the world." Soboul holds that "the revolution is explained in the last analysis by a contradiction between the relations of production and the character of the productive forces."

Attempts have been made over the last few generations to accumulate systematically organized information that would help to test generalizations of this character or that would at least make it possible to assign them a more concrete meaning. These include, for example, Crane Brinton's pioneering study of the Jacobins (1930), and Donald M. Greer's statistical monographs on the victims of the Terror (1935) and on the emigrants (1951). Such books have had considerable effect on the development of scholarly opinion even though, in the course of time, qualifications have been expressed both about the ways in which they summarized the evidence and also about the inferences that they presented. The theoretical implications of various kinds of social definitions have been extensively explored by other scholars, for example by Alfred Cobban, who held that historians needed sharper tools than the Marxist ones and that some of the most famous Marxist concepts such as "bourgeoisie" and "feudalism" were too imprecise to be useful for the discussion of eighteenth-century society. Cobban dealt, in a series of books and articles, with problems involved in the interpretation of the evidence we have on these matters and reached a thoughtful and carefully argued position which, though not all scholars in the field accepted it, still commands respect. These are only examples for purposes of illustration: there has been much further work. The discussion of the French Revolution in these terms has produced so huge a literature that no brief recapitulation could do anything like justice to it.

In general, the more modern approach, the innovation that seems to be of value, is not to argue whether classes exist, or who were the bourgeoisie or the aristocracy, but rather to look for social indicants of various types and to consider what conclusions may legitimately be drawn from the correlations they produce. Both the third and fourth papers reflect this line. Both of them, instead of rearguing the old Marxist thesis or discussing empty questions of abstract class definition, try to define the social concepts they use in empirical terms and to see what can be made of the evidence.

Gilbert Shapiro and Philip Dawson, in the third paper, express the view that, despite the long argument over the social interpretation of the French Revolution and the various conflicting opinions that have been put forward, there has not been available, up to now, much concrete evidence on which a judgment could be based. They attempt to cast some light on this general question by presenting information on a point which, though it is narrowly defined, they regard as important. Their paper, which is deliberately restricted in scope, takes up the single question of the relation of political attitudes to expectations of opportunities for entrance into the nobility or, on the other hand, to the lack of such expectations, in France in 1789. The matter is of considerable interest since major theorists have disagreed on whether radical sentiment is more likely to be the consequence of opportunities for upward mobility, with the disorientation that arises in such a situation, or whether radicalism more generally ensues from the frustration of hopes for upward mobility. Shapiro and Dawson have in particular considered the hypothesis, classically formulated by de Tocqueville, that the former of these two suppositions may be correct and that revolutionary feeling may be strongest in the regions of a country that are most advanced economically and in other ways and where, presumably, there were the most considerable opportunities for men to move up in the social scale.

In testing such a hypothesis what matters most, one might suppose, is not facts but beliefs: not what happens but what people expect, not the real incidence of ennoblement but the judgment of contemporaries regarding the possibilities of ennoblement. It is the second of these, expectations rather than facts, that might be expected to influence men's attitudes. This distinction must be drawn, and Shapiro and Dawson are careful to draw it. Unfortunately, however, it is difficult to see into men's minds, all the more so when they lived nearly two centuries ago. The authors have therefore been compelled, as the only means of handling the subject rigorously, to take as their independent variable not the second alternative but the first, not the social expectations of their subjects, which cannot now be ascertained with accuracy or in detail, but rather what in the existing circumstances their subjects might reasonably have been entitled to expect: what the authors refer to as the perceptible opportunities for advancement. The paper attempts to examine the relationship, in various communities, between opportunities for entry into the nobility, as measured by the number of saleable ennobling offices, and the degree of middle-class radicalism, as measured by the evidence of the *cahiers*.

The project brings up several classes of problems. There can be some technical argument about how much may legitimately be inferred from the figures and how important are the differences they reflect. Beyond this, the principal variables involved in this study, social mobility and political radicalism, are both difficult to measure. Another point, on which there was some emphasis in the discussion of this paper at the conference, is that the authors have centered their attention on a single type of mobility, ennoblement through the purchase of offices, and it is possible that other avenues to ennoblement should also be taken into account, as well as other paths to advancement that may have been open under the Old Regime. Also, since a man could get ahead not only in his own town but, in certain circumstances, elsewhere, there may be some doubt whether the number of ennobling offices in a single community can properly be regarded as the whole story of the expectations of a resident. It could be argued that claims regarding the importance of the independent variable analyzed in this study cannot be accepted unless a number of other possible variables are properly controlled in making the tests. There is also the question whether it was the men who expected to get ahead, or the men who didn't, who wrote the *cahiers*.

The authors have by no means shirked or ignored these problems. They have grappled with the ambiguities of both their central concepts, mobility and radicalism, and have devoted a considerable part of their exposition to problems of definition. They have sought, for example, to distinguish between the possible reactions of someone who had a chance to be ennobled and someone who didn't but was merely a spectator of the process, perceiving the upward mobility of others and drawing his own conclusions. They have also presented an interesting discussion of the kinds of radicalism reflected in the *cahiers*, of which they have made an extensive systematic analysis, giving attention to the circumstances in which the *cahiers* were produced, and considering various alternative ways in which the degree of "radicalism" of a *cahier* could be intelligibly measured. They have dealt with the problem of Paris which might be expected to be a special case and atypical, by presenting two sets of figures, with Paris and without.

The writers of this paper are modest in their assertions about their results. They claim, not to have resolved a major scholarly controversy, but only to have produced evidence that, so far as it goes, appears to tell in a certain direction. It tells, interestingly enough, for the de Tocqueville position and against the Taine-Dollot position. This finding, if further investigation continues to confirm it, is a valuable one and adds something important to our understanding of the period. The present paper, however, gives only a partial account of the extensive research on which it is based. It is, of necessity, largely devoted to an exploration of some of the general questions involved in this research and to the rationale of the technical apparatus that has been set up to deal with these matters. A fuller exploration of the statistical materials will be needed before it is possible to tell how far the inquiry has contributed to a reinterpretation of the history of the period. For the present, the authors have conscientiously laid out the evidence as they found it, and further discussion of the subject can proceed from there.

4. Charles Tilly, "How Protest Modernized in France, 1845-1855"

In the fourth paper Charles Tilly explores the relation between social and economic change and political action in a much wider context. He addresses himself to the question of how far and in what way structural changes in French society, such as industrialization and urbanization, have produced and shaped violent conflict.

The general issue on which this topic bears, the impact of industrialization upon modern society, has long been a central concern of scholars and has precipitated controversies that are, even now, by no means resolved. The blistering indictment by the Hammonds of the social effects of the industrial revolution has been much qualified by revisionist economic historians such as Sir John Clapham and T. S. Ashton, though it has in recent years been vigorously reasserted by, among others, E. P. Thompson and E. J. Hobsbawm. There are many things to consider in making a judgment on this large question and perhaps, with the limited amount of information we have, no final judgment can be made, though the subject was well worth investigating and the conflicting shifts of scholarly opinion have brought to light much that was interesting.

Another way of getting into this question, however, and the line that Tilly pursues in his study, is to examine the relationship between industrialization and mass violence. That such a connection existed, at least for Great Britain, has been argued by E. P. Thompson (1963) who holds that the industrial revolution witnessed the emergence, roughly in the period from 1780 to 1832, of a distinct working class. This group, he states, came to feel an identity of interests that resulted in an increased amount of organized protest from 1780 on, and especially after 1800. This protest, according to Thompson, was a direct result of the consciousness of the workers that the industrial revolution presented a threat to them and of the realization by different groups of workers that they had common interests. Their resentment was expressed in the Luddite riots, among workers whose skills were being rendered obsolete by machine production, in the increase of trade-unionism, and in the development of political pressure groups culminating in the emergence of Chartism in the later 1830s.

In more general terms, one of the most widely accepted views, which Tilly considers at the outset of his paper, has been the thesis that industrialization is, in its social effects, a process of quick disruption followed by slow stabilization. According to this scheme, the relative social quiescence of the preindustrial period gives way to a phase of intense social unrest as the great changes of industrialization and urbanization make their impact, which is then succeeded by a period of greater calm as the industrial society becomes mature, and more sophisticated and efficient techniques are worked out for dealing with the disagreements that arise. This is the familiar model of the hump-backed curve of the growth of violent protest in an industrial society that shows in graph form the relation between civil violence and the stages of economic development measured by such indicants as economic prosperity or the increase of the gross national product. In this model, the incidence of mass violence is low in a society with a primitive economy, increases with the increase of industrialization up to a certain point, and then slopes downward as the economic system becomes more highly developed. Tests of the model have been made by comparing the present state of affairs in a number of different countries that are in different stages of industrialization, and much of the information gathered from contemporary international comparisons of this kind appears to support the hypothesis.

It is Tilly's contention, however, that this hypothesis cannot be accepted until it has been tested, not only for different countries at one time, but also for one country at different times, so as to get some evidence on change over an extended period. He has tried to do this for France. He has gathered and tabulated an immense amount of data on outbreaks of violence in France over the last century and a half and has summarized a section of his findings in his contribution to this volume. In his paper he surveys changes in the incidence and character of collective violence in France over a considerable span of years and then presents a more detailed account of the mid-nineteenth century and particularly of the decade 1845-1855, which he thinks may be a turning point. He has kept in mind the twentieth-century comparison, and in many tables the figures for the three decades 1830-1860 are matched by figures for the three decades 1930-1960. His principal interest, however, is in the 674 disturbances that he has identified as occurring in France from 1830 to 1860, a disturbance being defined as an interaction between at least two formations, in the course of which some person or property was damaged or seized, and in which at least one formation included 50 or more individuals.

Tilly's first conclusion, out of which much of his later argument develops, is that, for modern French history, the model of the hump-backed curve breaks down at once. The history of violent protest in France, according to the data he has been able to assemble, affords little or no support for the traditional view of the relationship between industrialization and violence. The model is entirely inadequate and has so little relation to the course of events that it must be discarded. Tilly has, in fact, been unable to discover any clear connection between industrial or urban growth and the development of turbulence. On the contrary, apart from minor occasional fluctuations, the frequency of disturbances did not greatly change throughout the period of industrialization. Following the lines indicated by this basic finding, Tilly has raised a number of questions that entail some novel ways of looking at the central problem with which he is concerned.

He suggests, for example, that the main currents of collective violence may flow much more directly from the political process than scholars have been accustomed to admit. The yearly fluctuations he has observed seem more closely correlated with political change than with social and economic change. Tilly has come to be concerned, as a result, less with the direct impact of major structural changes and more with the political processes through which these changes may possibly have operated. Nor is he willing to allow that structural changes of an economic or social kind were necessarily the sole origins of political tensions leading to violence. He deals also, for example, with the resistance to centralization: the protest against the imposition by the central government of its powers of taxing, conscripting, and judging in communities that were already accustomed to the exercise of these powers by the agents of smaller, provincial governments. The resistance to central authority, he points out, recurred regularly whenever it had been weakened by war or revolution. Waves of protest against the collection of taxes by the central government, for example, occurred after the revolutions of 1789, 1830, and 1848. Also, the information Tilly has been able to assemble on the objectives of collective violence, though he is aware of the ambiguity of evidence on motives and the caution with which it must be interpreted, appears to reinforce his position regarding the decidedly political character of these outbreaks.

Tilly suggests, however, that, if no change in the frequency of collective outbreaks with the progress of industrialization can be observed, it may be profitable to look for change of another type, and he deals particularly with the possibility of there having occurred significant alterations in their character. He believes that he has found substantial evidence pointing to this. He holds that in the course of time such outbreaks became bigger and briefer. In the 1840s and earlier, he finds, the predominant forms of collective violence—the invasion of fields, the tax revolt, the food riot, the anti-conscription rebellion—were somewhat disorganized and uncontrolled: a type of violence that he describes, in one of the two general categories he has set up, as "reactionary." By the 1860s these forms of protest had almost disappeared and had been replaced by strikes, demonstrations, and similar complex, organized actions—the type of collective violence that he describes, in his other general category, as "modern." The change is from communal contenders (religious groups, villages, members of local markets) to associational contenders (industrial firms and trade-unions). The former type of outbreak was localized and uncoordinated; the latter was disciplined, scheduled and organized in advance, tended to be on a large scale, and was apparently instigated by more highly organized groups. Tilly's paper deals with how this change took place. He suggests, though he has not yet been able to establish this with certainty, that the change began in the 1840s and was largely completed by the 1860s so that the decisive point, at which transition was occurring most rapidly, appears to be the middle decade of the nineteenth century, the decade to which he has given particular attention. The change, as he describes it, was not immediate or absolute: the old forms, though fading away, still showed themselves powerful in a last outburst around 1848; the new forms, though taking over in the middle of the century, became predominant only after long previous cumulation in the most advanced sectors of French society. Tilly does not suggest there were no associational groups before 1845 and only such groups after that; he is trying, rather, to indicate what patterns were general or usual.

Following out this line of argument Tilly proposes the hypothesis that the impact of large structural changes was not direct but indirect: that these changes, though they did not in themselves generate collective violence, may nevertheless have contributed to change its character. The impact of these changes, he suggests, was upon the number, identity, and organization of the contenders, which in turn helped to determine the predominant forms of collective violence as well as the places in which it erupted. The effect of industrialization and urbanization was to bring about a decline in the communal bases for collective violence and an increase in the associational bases. The transition to an industrial society involved a temporary uprooting and disorganization, a state of affairs in which collective violence was less feasible and less effective, but which led ultimately to a new kind of organization among the discontented. Urban-industrial life massed men together in groups and eventually promoted the formation of special-interest associations of which trade-unions are perhaps the most conspicuous example, though there were other kinds as well. Tilly suggests that this organizational process, which transformed the character of the outbursts, may be the basic link between industrialization and collective violence.

These views, if they prove acceptable, are clearly of great interest. We do not, however, as the author points out, have the whole story yet. Tilly's group has already been working for years on assembling and tabulating the data. He insists, nevertheless, that he has as yet arrived at only a primitive stage of numerical description, verification, and comparison, and that he has only scratched the surface in making tests and drawing inferences from this body of materials. Some of his generalizations are, as he has indicated, not yet conclusively established. Furthermore, in this project as in others, basic problems of interpretation arise about which there may be some argument. The argument depends in large part upon the definitions and classifications adopted, and regarding some of these there may be controversy.

It is not easy, for one thing, to be definite about the occupations and social positions of the participants in the disturbances, in view of the complexity of the French social structure and the inadequacy of the police dossiers on certain points on which we should much like to have more information. Tilly has made some effort to compare the characteristics of participants in the disturbances with the characteristics of the population as a whole, but feels that this attempt has not been wholly successful. He found it difficult to reach secure ground in ascertaining the occupations of participants. Nor is it clear that Tilly's two general categories for describing disturbances, "reactionary" and "modern," suffice for the complexity and diversity of the evidence. There was some controversy on these matters in the lively discussion at the conference that followed his presentation. It may be possible that each category includes a variety of activities sufficiently dissimilar so that to group them under one heading can be misleading. It is also possible that the use of such general categories may obscure features of the evidence that might provide simpler and readier explanations of the phenomena described. There are also, as the author is well aware, exceptions to the general trends he has identified. Associational or "modern" conflicts can be observed before the mid-nineteenth century, and even before the industrial period, while communal or "reactionary" conflicts have occurred in the twentieth century. The extent and importance of such exceptions is a serious matter, for they raise questions not only about whether the mid-nineteenth century was a turning point, in the manner suggested in the paper, but also about the hypothesis that the character of these outbreaks was related to economic change. Tilly has made it clear that he is not wholly satisfied with the evidence supporting the view that the turning point in the change of the character of collective violence was in the middle decade of the nineteenth century: one particular obstacle to reaching firm ground on this point is his finding that disturbances were infrequent in the 1850s, which makes it difficult to get a clear picture. There was, apparently, relatively little collective violence during the reign of Napoleon III. Fascinating though these preliminary results are, there are clearly basic problems of historical interpretation as well as of mathematical analysis that will require further thought and attention in later and more extended presentations.

5. Gerald H. Kramer and Susan J. Lepper, "Congressional Elections"

The effort of Gerald H. Kramer and Susan J. Lepper to obtain more precise information regarding the determinants of voting in Congressional elections, the only paper in this volume on electoral behavior, stems out of and carries forward a reassessment of the methods and objectives of American political history that has been in process for some years. So early as 1949 Thomas C. Cochran in his famous denunciation of the "presidential synthesis" gave expression to a growing concern, shared also by others, that the work of American political historians had far less explanatory power than was desirable. Though a number of historians expressed approval of Cochran's statement we can hardly argue, some twenty years later, that they rushed to provide the sociologically sophisticated and state-oriented political histories that he demanded. Yet there has been a gradual shift of focus in the writing of American political history, and it seems reasonable to suggest that much of the quantitative or behavioral work going on now is actually in the spirit of the Pennsylvania professor's manifesto, even if it is not precisely in the form that he originally suggested.

It was Lee Benson who most significantly pointed the way to new directions of research in this field. We sometimes do injustice to forelopers or to "slow publishers" when we suggest that the work of particular scholars has broken new paths. Yet it seems clear, in retrospect, that Benson's long essay "Research Problems in American Political Historiography" in Mirra Komarovsky's *Common Frontiers of the Social Sciences* (1957) was the first important contribution to a "new" American political history, dealing with popular voting and related institutional developments. In this paper Benson suggested that historians could move to a more sophisticated level of analysis if they used popular voting data systematically, comparing the results of different elections in terms of time, space, and rate of change. We could, he maintained, successfully tackle the problem of explaining election outcomes only after we had first shown "who voted for whom, when." In a series of illustrative case studies he showed how the numerical election returns, simply processed and analyzed in terms of change through time, in terms of differences from area to area, and in terms of differences in the rate of change in time or space, gave us additional understanding of the Presidential contests of 1824, 1860, 1884, and 1896. In the course of this article Benson described a number of specific determinants of popular voting behavior—sectionalism, urban-rural differences, and class and ethnic group distinctions. Thus Benson, in 1957, not only proposed a method of analysis but also identified, in a manner that has proved most fruitful for further work in this field, a number of independent variables that might in certain circumstances shape the results of elections in the United States.

The substantive evidence which Benson used in his article of 1957 was essentially illustrative and, as he explained, derived to a considerable extent from the research of others. In *The Concept of Jacksonian Democracy: New York as a Test Case*, published four years later, he presented an elaborate research monograph dealing with political behavior in New York during the Jacksonian Era. One of his more striking conclusions was his contention that membership in ethno-cultural groups was a much more efficient predictor of party allegiance in New York during the 1830s and 1840s than was class affiliation or economic interest. On this point he flatly contradicted a major assumption that can be found, either expressed or implied, in most of the previous treatments of Jacksonian Democracy. Benson went further and speculated that the propensity of particular ethno-cultural groups to affiliate with either the Whigs or the Democrats reflected a commitment to particular life styles or values—those groups subscribing to a Puritan ethic tended to be Whig in political affiliation, he believed, while non-Puritans showed a preference for the Democratic Party.

The Concept of Jacksonian Democracy has had an extensive influence on historical thinking in the United States and has inspired a number of other scholars to undertake similar projects, and to make increased use of quantitative tools. Another contribution of Benson's, however, which has also been of the greatest importance, is his work in organizing the Committee on Quantitative Data in History of the American Historical Association. This committee has cooperated with the Inter-University Consortium for Political Research, under the leadership of Warren Miller, in assembling a data bank of county-level voting returns for major political contests in the United States from 1824 to the present, as well as other types of information relevant to the study of politics. The impact of this vast accumulation of data upon research in American political history may well prove to be of revolutionary proportions.

Another line of research that has contributed materially to the development of new approaches in American political history is the series of efforts made by political scientists to discern underlying patterns in the aggregate data of national election returns. This is a rich field where much has been done, but one particularly interesting example may be cited as an illustration. In 1955, V. O. Key, Jr., in "A Theory of Critical Elections" suggested that certain national elections, occurring periodically, reflected basic adjustments in voter allegiance that were destined to stay approximately the same for a considerable period of time, until another critical election occurred in which the electorate was again wrenched into a markedly different alignment. In the "critical election" Key provided the historian with a concept that—in company with more elaborate election typologies—has proved a more useful basis for periodization than the Presidential administration.

A number of the new insights of political scientists have been derived from survey research on Presidential elections which, on an academic basis, dates from 1940. In particular, scholars of the Survey Research Center of the University of Michigan began, during the presidential contest of 1952, a continuing series of panel surveys of national elections. As administered, described, and interpreted by Angus Campbell and his associates, this research has provided historians and social scientists with challenging concepts and theories. Core voters, marginal voters, surge, decline, realigning elections and other phenomena identified by the Michigan scholars helped to inspire Charles Seller's effort to document a two-party equilibrium cycle throughout the course of American Presidential elections. Dean Burnham's challenging article, "The Changing Shape of the American Political Universe" is an interesting effort to argue that the national electorate in the nineteenth century was far different in its partisan commitments from the political universe described by Campbell, Converse, Miller, and Stokes.

The degree to which scholars can succeed in fusing the political world of the present day, as displayed in the results of survey research, and the political phenomena of the period between 1787 and 1936 is still a matter of debate. A growing number of historians foresee considerable dividends to be gained from efforts to test hypotheses derived from one period by the available data of another. This is not, however, always easy to do. The survey researcher has certain advantages since he extracts his data from the individual voter, whereas a student of an earlier period must usually infer the motivation of the voting of individuals from aggregate voting statistics, newspaper accounts of political campaigns, and the personal papers of politicians. The historian's analysis of the voting of various groups in the electorate—ethno-cultural, social, demographic, or economic—must in general rest on inferences from aggregate data. This raises a problem about the reliability of the correlations on which rigorously quantitative historical studies of electoral behavior must heavily depend.

Researchers have approached this problem, the so-called "ecological fallacy," with varying degrees of sophistication. Even with aggregate materials it is sometimes possible, by careful work and the exercise of ingenuity, to make some headway against this difficulty. At the heart of almost all investigations of this type is the effort to identify groups whose collective needs shape the voting of their members significantly more toward one party than toward another. Theories designed to explain a particular election outcome are generally attempts to identify the factors in the political milieu that may have caused the members of various reference groups to change their allegiance. It seems reasonable to assume that, in any given election, such determinants may include both long-run and short-run factors.

Students of popular voting recognize that some forces playing upon the electorate may be so general in their operation that they produce direct correlations, or correlations that may be revealed by a more refined analysis, with election returns over an extended series of contests, even though they may influence some groups in the electorate more strongly than others. The authors of the fifth paper, "Congressional Elections," set out to determine the effects of certain identifiable and measurable factors on the course of elections over the 68 years from 1896 to 1964. Assuming for the purposes of the analysis that voters behave rationally, in the sense that they support the party in office as long as its performance "is 'satisfactory' according to some simple standard," Kramer and Lepper set forth a series of variables that may have influenced the outcome of Congressional elections. These include the underlying basic partisanship of the electorate, the effect of incumbency, the extent to which the party in power has satisfied the economic expectations of the electorate, the influence of the "coattails" of strong Presidential candidates, the distribution of the electorate between farming and non-farming occupations, the extent of seniority of an incumbent, and the leadership position of an incumbent within Congress.

The central problem confronting Kramer and Lepper was the devising of a model that, on the one hand, was consistent with *a priori* views regarding the behavior of the electorate but that, on the other hand, could be tested by the severely limited relevant data at the historian's disposal. The conflict between theoretical considerations and the restricted availability of data led inevitably to certain compromises both in the formulation of the model and in the estimation of its parameters. Thus, for example, the satisfaction of the electorate with the incumbent "team" is made to focus on economic performance. This is not because Kramer and Lepper were unaware of the importance of the behavior of incumbents on political and social policies but because of the great difficulty in formulating measures of the performance of particular parties on such issues as foreign policy and desegregation. Similarly, at one point they were forced to use, as a measure of the total income of farmers, the Department of Agriculture series on "Realized Net Income of Farm Operators," thus omitting wages paid to hired hands and income to farmers from non-farm sources.

The model was examined on three levels. Kramer and Lepper first applied it to the total Congressional electorate. They found that increases in per capita income significantly helped members of the incumbent party, while increases in prices hurt them. These, and the other factors they considered, explained from 48 to 64 per cent of the variation in the Republican share of the Congressional vote.

By disaggregating the total electorate into farm and non-farm sectors, it was possible to shed light on the long-term decline in the Republican share of the Congressional vote. The two-sector version of the basic model revealed that among non-farmers the index of Republican partisanship was only 43 per cent; but in the farm sector the index was 79 per cent. Thus the decline in the farm share of the population, from 32 per cent in 1914 to 7 per cent in 1964, by itself explains much of the long-term shift away from the Republicans. It also appears that while the non-farm electorate responded quite markedly to annual fluctuations in per capita income and prices, farmers did not. As for incumbency, it helped candidates obtain support from farmers but had little effect, or hurt candidates, with non-farm voters. The variables employed in the two-sector model explained three-quarters of the variation in the Republican share of the votes in 21 Congressional elections.

The variables singled out by Kramer and Lepper were least successful in explaining electoral behavior at the county level. Of the four counties that they examined (two in upstate New York and two in central Pennsylvania) there was only one county in which they were able to explain over 40 per cent of the variation in the Republican share of the vote. This was to be expected, both because of the poorer quality of the data and because of the greater importance of unmeasured idiosyncratic factors at the county level. Nevertheless, it appears that basic partisanship was more influential at the county than at the national level. Changes in per capita income and prices, on the other hand, at least for non-farm areas, made more difference at the national level than at the county level. Perhaps the most surprising finding was the lack of significance, for popular voting, of seniority and leadership in Congress.

The contribution of Kramer and Lepper is important not because it represents the final word on the explanation of changes in the make-up of Congress since the turn of the century, but because it is a prototype for future work. Their paper reveals how much light can be cast on the course of Congressional elections by the careful application of simple statistical models to available data. Refinement of their results may be obtained by considering alternative measures of the influence of economic variables. For example, Kramer and Lepper assume that all (or most) of the response of the electorate to changes in economic variables is focused on the year preceding the elections. While this may be a reasonable assumption in non-agricultural areas, it seems less plausible in the agriculture sector where random factors dominate year-to-year movements in income and prices. But perhaps the most important refinements will be made by the inclusion of social and political indicators of the performance of the governing party as explanatory variables. That advance must, however, await the construction of measures of social and political achievement.

6. Allan G. Bogue, "Some Dimensions of Power in the Thirty-Seventh Senate"

The sixth and seventh papers deal with the analysis of legislative roll calls. The interest of historians in these materials extends back before the beginning of the twentieth century. So early as 1896 the American historian Orin Grant Libby called attention to the possible value of an intensive study of roll calls, and from the 1890s to the present, historians have regarded the Congressional debates and journals as indispensable sources for the study of United States politics. Yet in their handling of these materials, particularly of roll call data, historians have on the whole been unsystematic, often using Congressional votes as illustrative material rather than as an integral component of their research. Actually, of course, the amount of detail provided by legislative roll calls was overwhelming when viewed in the perspective of the statistical methods and the processing facilities available to both social scientists and historians prior to the late 1940s. Advances in data processing and in statistics had changed the situation drastically by the mid-1950s, and some historians followed the lead of social scientists in adapting new methods, such as the Guttman scalogram, to their own research.

By the mid-1960s some specialists in American political history were familiar with a considerable arsenal of statistical tools applicable to research in the history of legislative behavior, including not only cumulative scales but also cluster blocs, factor analysis, the index of cohesion, the index of likeness, and a variety of other measures. Use of the computer in processing information on roll calls was becoming routine. Although one eminent historian denounced the scalogram as a device that obscured voting patterns rather than clarifying them, this device and other statistical methods have allowed historians to describe the voting patterns of individuals more precisely and to identify the voting blocs that reflect underlying determinants of voting more objectively than was possible before. As a result of the work of historians or historically oriented social scientists such as Charles D. Farris, Duncan MacRae, Jr., William O. Aydelotte, Joel Silbey, Thomas B. Alexander, Gerald Wolff, Edward Gambill, Glenn M. Linden, Jerome M. Clubb, Howard W. Allen, Aage Clausen, and others, we have a considerable and growing body of detailed information concerning the determinants of voting behavior and their relative strength in various eras of the history of the United States Congress. Much more research of this sort needs to be done, however, and historians have made only a bare beginning in developing a comparable approach to state legislative behavior.

Useful as has been the work on voting in Congress and the identification of major voting blocs there, such historical studies thus far have left a number of important problems relatively untouched. What for instance has been the effect of seniority and other institutional factors upon voting at various times in our Congressional history, and to what degree have the attitudes of legislators concerning the legislative role changed through time? One question that most historians have ignored, or perhaps simply taken for granted, is the subject of power, its *locus*, and its uses in the legislative process. The concept of power is, of course, a difficult one to operationalize, and one social scientist recently has likened it to phlogiston. But if the term did not exist we would no doubt have been obliged to invent it, and during the last generation a few scholars have produced interesting assessments of the Congressional power structure during the nineteenth century.

In his study of the historiography of the Kansas-Nebraska Act of 1854, Roy F. Nichols pictured a senate controlled by the Democratic party which was, in turn, controlled to a considerable extent by members of the F Street Mess. In the absence of strong executive leadership, this small group of Southern senators used the power of their seniority and their positions as chairmen of key committees to enforce party loyalty and to shape one of the most important pieces of legislation of the nineteenth century, the Kansas-Nebraska Act. Nichols's article is a classic illustration of the application of traditional historical methods to a decision-making situation, but much of the author's proof rests on inference, and the reader remains uncertain as to whether the incident was typical of the system of power in the Senate during 1854. Did the F Street Mess exercise similar authority in matters that were unrelated to the sectional crisis?

In his study, *The Washington Community, 1800-1828* (1966), James Sterling Young pictured a central government, "thrice handicapped," by a lack of civic attachment, by the tendency of rival governmental subsystems to develop around the nuclei provided by the separate branches of government, and by the attitudes of the government leaders toward power, "attitudes which rationalized a government community which denied dominant power to any subgroup and enduring leadership to any position in Washington. Antipower attitudes justified artlessness in politics and stifled the impulse toward that state craft . . . essential for the effective management of conflict in a government designed to insure conflict." Within Congress, Young argued on the basis of some roll call analysis, the dominant determinant of voting behavior was the boardinghouse group or mess. But in the Jackson period, he maintained, there emerged "incentives and rationale for the development of organized parties—incentives and rationale which popular indifference withheld from the Jeffersonians. Serving the needs of an aroused and demanding citizenry would relieve power-seeking from the onus of self-seeking at Washington, and would provide incontestable justification for leadership initiatives in a governmental community deeply committed to the representative principle."

During the same year in which Young published his study of the Washington political community in the early nineteenth century, David J. Rothman published a monograph, *Politics and Power: The United States Senate, 1869-1901*. By the end of the century, Rothman argued, a highly disciplined Republican Party strictly controlled the Senate, though this party was in turn rigorously disciplined by a small group of Republican senators who managed the Republican caucus and also determined the order of business in the Senate. The influence of these men was based upon their interlocking control of the Steering Committee, the Committee on Committees, and other important committees. Their power, particularly that of William B. Allison, was sufficient to force the rank and filer, who wished congenial committee assignments or who sought to move particular legislation through the Senate with dispatch, to make his peace and play the good soldier. Most of Rothman's evidence is drawn from the correspondence of various senators, or based on the events surrounding the passage of particular bills. He also, however, presented tabulations showing that relative party cohesion in the final votes on major legislation was higher in the Senate at the end of the century than during the 1870s. He interpreted this finding to mean that the power of the party leadership and party discipline had increased in the interim and indeed, he believed, it was greater than ever before.

In his paper in this volume, Allan G. Bogue takes a somewhat different tack from that of Rothman, Nichols, or Young and considers the possibility of deriving more precise measures of the individual's power by using roll-call analysis. This is an extremely thorny problem, and although social scientists have accumulated a body of relevant theory and statistical methods, particularly as a result of their efforts to analyze community power structures and legislative behavior, most of the work must be regarded as suggestive rather than definitive. Focusing on the Senate of the Thirty-Seventh Congress, one of the most productive Congresses in American history, Bogue draws first upon literary materials to compare the "power" or legislative influence of William Pitt Fessenden, Charles Sumner, and John Parker Hale, as reflected in decision-making incidents, in reputation, and in formal positions, modified in the last case by the individual's unique legislative style. After some discussion of the power indexes or measures of legislative effectiveness developed by Donald R. Matthews, Robert A. Dahl, and William H. Riker, Bogue compares several different types of indexes of "power," using votes on Southern issues during the second session of the Thirty-Seventh Senate, with each other and with the results of the analysis of the traditional sources.

Bogue does not claim that the indexes developed in his paper allow him to evaluate the legislative influence of the members of the Thirty-Seventh Senate definitively. Power relationships among individuals must inevitably change; he is aware of this and indeed suggests that it is one of the reasons why the use of power formulae have in the past proved to be rather unsatisfactory predictors for subsequent time periods. He has used comparative methods in both sections of his paper, rather than depending only, for example, upon—say—a reputational approach to his analysis of literary sources or upon a game theory index alone in treating the quantitative data. Convergence in the findings within the two parts of the paper, as well as between them, suggests that the better of the quantitative measures might be used alone if proper caution is exercised in interpreting the results, though the author's preference would still be to compare the results of several measures.

The paper makes novel use of the memorial addresses found in the *Congressional Globe.* It also presents, as earlier writers have not done, a comparison of the quantitative results of a set of different power or influence formulae, all of which are computed upon the basis of the same fundamental data. The MacRae and Price critique of Dahl's power index is itself, in this paper, subjected to criticism. Substantively, the paper sheds new light on the legislative roles of Senator Fessenden and Senator Sumner and provides the first precise comparison of the legislative effectiveness of all of the senators in the second session of the Thirty-Seventh Congress. In this respect the power indexes emphasize the importance of two senators—Clark of New Hampshire and Doolittle of Wisconsin—whom historians have not ordinarily considered seriously in their study of the Civil War.

7. William O. Aydelotte, "The Disintegration of the Conservative Party in the 1840s: A Study of Political Attitudes"

In the seventh paper, William O. Aydelotte raises, in the small compass of a single set of events, a large and controverted question: the relation of political factions to issues. Students of politics and of political history have generally acknowledged the immense importance of political parties. These organizations have played a central role in the operation of parliamentary systems, certainly in the twentieth century, probably also, as many would argue, in the nineteenth, and possibly even further back, though their structure becomes more shadowy and their significance more a matter of controversy as we retreat in time. Despite the admitted significance of parties, however, there is much that we still do not know about them, particularly for party systems before 1900. Further work needs to be done on their institutional roles and functions, and also on their composition and the groups from which they drew their main support, both in the legislature and the electorate. On the attitudes of parties to issues, the subject with which this paper is concerned, there is, at least for British party history before 1900, a dearth of studies that assemble the relevant information. It is still not possible to say, for most of the nineteenth century, how far the principal parties in Great Britain did or did not differ from each other on major questions of the day.

It may seem curious that this should be so, for the history of Parliament has been, over the last couple of generations, a central concern of British scholarship. The potentialities of intensive research on this subject have been perhaps most brilliantly demonstrated by Sir Lewis Namier in his two great books published in 1929 and 1930. Many others, however, have also made investigations along comparable lines. With this monographic work, and with the monumental set of studies undertaken by the History of Parliament Trust, parliamentary history has become a major scholarly enterprise, and much new and valuable information has been brought to light. Yet the kind of research designed to show party attitudes on issues has not been extensively pursued. In part this is doubtless due to the fact that the kind of information needed for effective study of this question, the division lists, are not available, or at least not available in sufficient quantities, before the nineteenth century. Namier, though he was alert to the possible value of analysis of the division lists, could do little of this kind of work for the period he studied because of the paucity of information. Most of the others who have worked in parliamentary history, even in more recent periods, have not extensively exploited these materials, though a few have, and have produced some results of real interest.

On the whole, however, it is in the United States rather than in Great Britain that the path-breaking work has been done in the systematic analysis of political attitudes. American scholars have studied, not only roll calls in the United States Senate and House of Representatives, but also, and with even more dramatic results, the political attitudes of the American electorate. The pioneering monograph *The People's Choice* by Paul F. Lazarsfeld, Bernard Berelson, and Hazel Gaudet, which was first published in 1944, has been followed up by a series of other massive investigations undertaken under the auspices of a number of distinguished scholars including not only Berelson and Lazarsfeld but also, among others, Angus Campbell, Philip E. Converse, Warren E. Miller, and Donald E. Stokes. As a result of this impressive body of findings our knowledge of the political behavior of the American electorate has, in a relatively limited period of years, been placed on a new footing. Much has been established that was not previously understood, and scholarly discussion of the subject can now proceed on a far firmer basis of ordered knowledge and dependable information.

The approaches used in this research on electorates, its substantive findings, and the insights it has produced have also been stimulating to students of legislative behavior. The author of the present paper, in particular, has gained much from the study of this literature. It should be added that, since information on the behavior of legislatures is more abundant, it is sometimes possible, in the pursuit of such lines of inquiry, to attempt a more refined analysis. Lazarsfeld in his groundbreaking work dealt principally with the single dependent variable of party choice: he found that, for the study of an electorate, the attempt to consider issues as well did not add appreciably to the analysis. This is not the whole story, for later students of electoral behavior have been able to make some headway, in general terms at least, with issues too. In the study of a legislative body, however, it is often possible to carry the analysis of attitudes on issues a considerable distance. Far more detailed information is available, for members of a legislature as compared to members of an electorate, about the attitudes of individuals on subjects to which they had perforce paid some attention and on which they had, in many cases at least, acquired enough knowledge so that their voting preferences represented significant choices. The richness of the materials, for Britain in the mid-nineteenth century, makes it possible to examine in some detail the relation of parties to issues and to attempt to suggest, on this subject, a position that can be supported by extensive documentation.

The general question raised in this paper is whether opposing groups in a political system stand for and support different policies or whether there is, on most important matters, a consensus between them. The theory that a consensus on basic issues exists, and must exist, between the opposing parties in any smoothly running parliamentary system has won wide acceptance. It was a commonplace in the utterances of informed political observers in the nineteenth century, and indeed in the eighteenth century as well, and it is a commonplace in our own age in the writings of many of those who have studied and discussed party voting and party behavior. In an earlier paper, however, Aydelotte argued that this generalization was incorrect for British politics in the 1840s. He presented the results of a study, based on the use of cumulative scales of the Guttman type, of the ideological differences between the two opposing parties in the British Parliament of 1841-1847 and, on the basis of this evidence, reached the conclusion that the two major parties did differ from each other substantially on a series of significant questions.

The present paper represents a second stage in this investigation. Although it raises the same questions that were raised in the earlier paper and replicates the tests, these tests are now applied not to two opposing parties but to two factions within a single party, the two groups into which the British Conservative Party split at the time of the repeal of the Corn Laws in 1846. An attempt is made to ascertain how far these two wings of the Conservative Party disagreed on other matters as well as the Corn Law question, and how far the break in the party in 1846 can properly be described as a general ideological split. Information has also been included on a second question that proved to be closely related to the first: at what point in time these two wings of the party began to oppose each other and became clearly differentiated by their votes.

The findings of this investigation of the two segments of a single party are in striking contrast to the findings of the earlier study in which the two parties were compared. The break between the two parties was clearly related to a number of important questions. The division within the Conservative Party, on the other hand, except for the Corn Law issue over which the break occurred, was apparently not ideological in any way that is now clearly recognizable. Although members of the two sections of the party did disagree on several other matters, it is difficult to fit these into a single conceptual scheme. Of course, there may have been connections between these other matters that were obvious to a contemporary but are no longer apparent to us. Whether a set of questions are related is a matter of opinion, to be determined by a judgment that is inevitably in part subjective. It is, however, a standard assumption in building cumulative scales that the existence of a scale does not demonstrate unidimensionality of content: other explanations are always possible; and there must be supplementary evidence, ordinarily emerging from an analysis of the apparent content, before the view can be accepted that a given scale represented a single issue. It is also to the point that there appears to have been a realignment of Conservative votes on some questions: a number of Conservatives, at the time of the great separation, took up positions different from those they had held earlier. As it turned out, it was the chronological dimension, not the dimension of substantive content, that made the pieces fall into place: that made it possible to resolve this originally confusing evidence into a reasonably clear pattern. The information, so far as it goes, tells strongly against an ideological interpretation of the break in the party. The view, which has attracted some attention in the past, that the two wings of the party represented substantially different positions on a wide range of issues, so that the free traders or "Peelites" were in general much closer to the Liberals than to the other Conservatives, seems decisively repudiated by these findings. The contrast between the results of the two investigations, the comparisons of two parties and of two groups within a single party, furnishes an excellent example of the value of studying attitudes not only for the legislative body as a whole but also for the parties separately. A more detailed scrutiny of this kind can reveal points of some interest that would not come to light in an analysis of the entire legislature.

This paper differs from some others in the volume in that it is based on categories the definition of which is less controversial. It deals not with social classes, which are notoriously hard to delimit, but with votes in a legislative body and with party labels. On such matters disagreements about classification are less likely to arise and, for this reason, greater reliability can be claimed for the results of this paper than for the results of some of the others. The other side of the picture is that this restriction of the types of evidence admitted involves a corresponding restriction of scope. There are important matters, closely relevant to the issues of this paper, that are not taken up here but with which the author will be faced in later stages of his research. He has, indeed, already made a beginning on some of these points in other papers. Of the questions not dealt with here, perhaps the most important is the motivation of the attitudes described, the relationship of the party break to a variety of possible independent variables, both personal and political, that might account for it. Certainly the findings presented here, which do not include the independent variables, except insofar as time may be counted as one, are by no means adequate to furnish an explanation of the breakup of the Conservative Party, though they bring out certain features of this incident, less clear heretofore, that may contribute toward an understanding of it. The paper deals with only a limited part of the whole intricate complex of political events surrounding this major development.

It is also a restriction on the paper, though a scarcely avoidable one, that it treats only one event, the disintegration of only one party, and does not, and cannot, attempt to generalize from this to the disintegration of parties in general or to the circumstances that might accompany them or produce them. Even so, the results of the paper can be seen in a broader context in that they at least constitute one example of phenomena that could be studied more widely. The fact that the party break in this case seems to a large extent non-ideological is of some interest. It might be worth while to make similar inquiries for other party breaks as, for example, the disintegration of the American Whig Party in the pre-Civil War period, or the division of the British Liberal Party over the Irish issue in the 1880s. This last subject is, in fact, currently receiving some attention from another scholar.

With this paper, as with others, there are a number of problems of interpretation that must be given some attention before its implications can be correctly appraised. Even if its findings are accepted, there may still be some argument as to what inferences may be drawn from them and how far they justify the assertion that the party break of 1846 was not a break over issues. Certainly the split was widely advertised at the time, by both sides, as arising out of a disagreement on principles. Also, it was clearly related to one issue, the Corn Law question. Indeed, the two factions of the party have been defined in the paper by their votes on this question, and it is hard to see how they could have been defined otherwise. The unity or lack of unity of a group in a legislature is ordinarily determined by ascertaining whether it votes unanimously or not: a split in a party that did not reveal itself by a divergence in voting would not have much practical meaning. With regard to the Corn Laws the break in the party was indeed ideological, and the central importance of this question at the time might suggest that less attention need be paid to irregular patterns of voting on other topics. There is no need to push the argument further here. It is enough if it can be used as still one more illustration of how much remains to be done, in research of this type, even after the tests have been made and the figures assembled, and to what an extent the interpretation of the results of a quantitative investigation, no matter how secure the figures appear, may still be a matter of controversy.

8. J. Rogers Hollingsworth and Ellen Jane Hollingsworth, "Expenditures in American Cities"

One of the puzzling anomalies in American historiography has been the failure of significant numbers of professional historians to develop a keen interest in urban history until very recently. Occasionally the new breed of urban historian engages in recrimination on this subject, suggesting that Turnerians, in ceaseless incantation of the frontier thesis, diverted the attention of American historians from the urban nuclei which contributed significantly to the development of the nation, even during its most agrarian eras. Undoubtedly the agrarian values which persisted among Americans long after significant numbers of them had come to live in urban centers did somewhat obscure the promise of urban history. But even after the shortcomings of the frontier hypothesis became generally recognized during the 1930s, there was no rush to develop an urban history; rather, after 1945, ambitious graduate students made the field of American intellectual history their Mecca, and this specialty became a major offering in the curriculum of most history departments. Although he included a chapter on the Westward movement in the collection of essays which he edited under the title of *The Reconstruction of American History* in 1961, a leading member of the second generation of modern intellectual historians, John Higham, found no place for a chapter on American urban history; and the volume, *History*, in the *Princeton Studies on Humanistic Scholarship in America*, by Higham, Krieger, and Gilbert, shows but two references to urban history in the index.

This is not to say that urban history of a sort has not been long with us. Even during the nineteenth century hopeful town boomers, reminiscent city promoters, and local historians were manufacturing urban history, as were also the urban reformers by the turn of the century. But modern urban historians consider Arthur M. Schlesinger, Sr.'s volume, *The Rise of the City, 1878-1898* (1933) to have brought the city to the sympathetic consideration of the historical profession as never before. By the time it appeared, Professor Schlesinger's research seminar at Harvard had become a training ground for urban historians. Since the publication of *The Rise of the City* the stream of historical books dealing with urban life in America has grown steadily in size. Much of this literature, as Eric Lampard and others have pointed out, emphasized the impact of the city on various aspects of American life and institutions. Most authors concerned themselves particularly with the late nineteenth and early twentieth centuries, and in their work we can often detect the assumption, shared by many Americans during the late nineteenth century and the Progressive Era, that the city was essentially a harmful and disruptive force in American life.

In the years since 1930, also, urban historians have written city biographies, and a number of these, such as Blake McKelvey's history of Rochester or the study of Chicago by Bessie Louise Pierce, are impressive. Some urban historians have also tried to introduce a comparative element into urban biography. Two particularly distinguished contributions of this type are Bayard Still's interesting analysis of urban patterns in the cities of the lower Great Lakes during the first half of the nineteenth century and, at a much later date, Richard C. Wade's *The Urban Frontier: The Rise of Western Cities, 1790-1830* (1959), a book that is remarkable also because the author tries to relate his findings to one of the major theories of American development. A special variant of comparative urban history has been the studies of intercity competition, one example of which is Wyatt W. Belcher's *The Economic Rivalry Between St. Louis and Chicago, 1850-1880.*

It is possible that the failure of urban history to attract practitioners in great numbers between 1930 and 1960 was due to the difficulties which urban historians experienced in trying to find an attractive conceptual framework and a body of theory that would give urgency or a broader meaning to their findings. At the final conference in which the papers of this volume were discussed, Robert R. Dykstra castigated city biographers for following the "one-damn-thing-after-another" approach. Yet even so early as the 1950s there were portents of change. Enough good city biographies were at hand to allow the biographers themselves to think increasingly in terms of generalization, and the influence of new trends in the social sciences also became apparent.

Although they were concerned primarily with Western community building, rural and urban, Stanley M. Elkins and Eric L. McKitrick showed in 1954 how concepts borrowed from a study of modern urban development by Robert K. Merton and his associates might be used to reshape the historian's conception of Western community processes during the nineteenth century. In 1961 Eric Lampard published a penetrating critique of the historical literature on urbanization and urged the profession to adopt the conceptual framework of those urban ecologists who viewed community structure, "as the outcome of a changing balance between population and environment (including habitat and other populations) mediated by technology and organization"—four variables which, he noted, were all subject to quantification. Such an ecological approach, Lampard believed, was "especially suited to the analysis of those economic and social changes which are associated with industrialization." This article, published in the *American Historical Review*, calls both for quantification and for theoretical conceptualization of a kind quite different from the traditional methods and common-sense assumptions of the older generation of city biographers.

Since publication of Lampard's article, the concern of some urban historians with both quantification and conceptual theory has become increasingly evident. In a methodological note published in *The Cattle Towns* in 1968, Robert R. Dykstra criticized the Elkins-McKitrick model, as well as Lampard's formula, and urged a more eclectic approach which would make use of the theory derived from community sociology as well as of the considerable literature on community power structure emanating from a number of social science fields. During the mid-1960s historians were applying much more rigorous theoretical and quantitative approaches to city growth as, for example, in "The Conception of Cities," an article published by Eugene Smolensky and Donald Ratajczak in 1965, a case study of San Diego's early history viewed in the context of location theory; or in Jeffrey G. Williamson and Joseph A. Swanson's *The Growth of Cities in the American Northeast, 1820-1870*, an investigation of the relation of city growth and size to economic efficiency and economic growth.

New urban historians seem to have been particularly stimulated by the book *Streetcar Suburbs: The Process of Growth in Boston, 1870-1900* by Samuel B. Warner, and Stephan Thernstrom's *Poverty and Progress: Social Mobility in a Nineteenth-Century City*. The recent volume edited by Thernstrom and Richard Sennett, *Nineteenth-Century Cities: Essays in the New Urban History*, provides a good introduction to the concerns of a rather considerable number of energetic young historians of urban process. According to the editors, the essayists "all aim at deepening our understanding of the lives of men and women living in dense urban settlements undergoing explosive growth and structural transformation." The essays deal with class mobility patterns, residential patterns, elites and political control, and family structure. Quantification of some sort appears in all of the essays and the assumptions and the hypotheses of the authors almost invariably show the influence of research in related disciplines. Without exception the essays were case studies focused on one urban milieu.

We may also, however, examine patterns of urban development in a broader context and analyze information about them in a way that will deepen our understanding of political and social processes in general. It is in this spirit that Ellen Jane and J. Rogers Hollingsworth have prepared their contribution to this volume. The general question they raise, an important one, is the relative influence of political systems, as compared to social and economic systems, in shaping policy outcomes. In this paper they are particularly concerned with one phase of this question: the influence of industrialization or economic development upon the level of government expenditure. Research on this issue can focus on the nation as a whole, on state governments, or it can, as the Hollingsworths have done, use the city government as the unit of observation. The general problem is the same, whatever the stratum of government under consideration. This is one out of a number of major problems of political history that can be studied, to great profit, in a local context.

Obviously there are limits to the types of policies which political systems can implement, whatever the social and economic systems may be, and this paper is simply one stage of a more elaborate analysis. Here the Hollingsworths try to distinguish the relative importance of various socio-economic determinants of political behavior in decisions about the level of government expenditures in middle-sized American cities during the early twentieth century. The Hollingsworths plan, later, to assess the importance of political variables in shaping policy in the same urban centers and to determine by use of multiple regression analysis the extent to which the systems co-vary or overlap so that they can determine the unique contribution which each made to municipal expenditures in the period.

Research of this kind has already found critics who dismiss some of the statistical relationships discovered as being little more than formal statements of the obvious. This, of course, is a stock criticism of quantification in historical research. The answer to it is that the interrelationships of *all* the relevant variables involved are seldom obvious. In this case, as the Hollingsworths point out, there were pronounced regional differences in the explanatory power of some important variables in their study, as well as marked differences in some respects between their findings and those described in research dealing with government expenditures in a more recent era. The specification of variables to measure certain of the economic and social characteristics of city populations is extremely difficult. The standard problems that beset most attempts at social classification arise here too. One cannot always be certain that a given index measures what it is intended or believed to measure: though the figures may be clear enough, their interpretation can be a tricky matter. It may also turn out, on further analysis, that two apparently distinct indexes are actually measuring the same thing. The careful use and interpretation of multiple correlation and stepwise regression can reduce such dangers but hardly remove them. Of such pitfalls the Hollingsworths are well aware, and their paper should stimulate the urban historian to push beyond the case study approach and also provide additional evidence for the student interested in the relationships between socio-economic and political systems.

9. Robert William Fogel and Jack L. Rutner, "The Efficiency Effects of Federal Land Policy, 1850-1900: A Report of Some Provisional Findings"

Between 1785 and 1935 the government of the United States surrendered the title to the greater part of a magnificent landed estate into the hands of individuals or associations. Although we can detect reflections of changing attitudes concerning the exploitation of natural resources in our land policy from the late nineteenth century onward, particularly in regard to minerals and forest lands, the national government continued to divest itself of agricultural land in considerable amounts each year until the operation of the Homestead Laws was suspended under the terms of the Taylor Grazing Act of 1934, pending reclassification of the Western lands remaining in the possession of the nation. The central goal of American land policy during the nineteenth century, that of providing land for new farms, was clearly no longer an appropriate objective.

"Unfenced land," wrote Henry George in 1878, was a precious resource that had produced "all that we are proud of in the American character; all that makes our conditions and institutions better than those of older countries. . . ." Although Henry George was in a sense unique, American land policy was a subject of considerable public concern during the late nineteenth and early twentieth centuries, the same period in which the founding fathers of our modern historical profession were firmly establishing their discipline in American universities and colleges. Land reformers and Populists were charging fraud in the administration of the land laws and criticizing the accumulation of large holdings of land by corporations and wealthy individuals. And if some criticism was essentially negative, the suggestions and early successes of conservationists seemed a hopeful augury for the future. Whether they agreed with the critics or not, historians of the late nineteenth and early twentieth centuries must have found it easy to accept the importance of land policy. Although scholars have emphasized young Frederick Jackson Turner's dissatisfaction with the Eastern focus and political orientation of the history taught in institutions of higher learning, we must not forget that the Wisconsin scholar's major professor at Johns Hopkins, Herbert Baxter Adams, published a monograph dealing with the relationship between control of the Western lands and the ratification of the Articles of Confederation. And after Turner had so successfully proclaimed that "the existence of an area of free land" and its recession Westward before the advance of American settlers explained American development, no historian need apologize for studying the public domain during the next few generations.

Generalizing broadly we can say that the land historians concentrated their research for the most part on the background and passage of national land legislation during the Turnerian years, but by the 1920s a number of scholars were becoming interested in producing studies of land disposal in various states and in studying the policies of major secondary holders, particularly the land grant railroads. During this decade, also, Benjamin H. Hibbard published *A History of the Public Land Policies.* Still useful for some purposes, this book brought the insights of the institutional agricultural economist to bear upon the history of national land disposal and reflected a growing interest among scholars in the relation between land disposal laws and the agriculture that developed in the new-land regions of the nation.

The Turner hypothesis lost its allure during the 1930s but, for other reasons, the attention of a number of thoughtful historians remained focused on land policy, and their work continued to have contemporary relevance. Profoundly moved by the foreclosures, the dispossession of farmers, low agricultural prices, and the erosion of farm lands, which were so integral a part of the great depression, Paul Wallace Gates published the first of numerous articles and longer works depicting an "incongruous" and inequitable land system that had materially affected the character of the farming systems and the social structure of Midwestern America. At the end of a decade in which the struggle to survive in a deranged economy had been the dominant concern of millions of Americans, Roy M. Robbins published a major study of the shaping of American land policy, *Our Landed Heritage* (1942), in which he explained national land legislation in terms of the conflicting objectives of economic interest groups in American society.

Prosperity of course returned to American agriculture during the 1940s, but land policy continued to be a matter of more than theoretical interest. Agricultural policy remained a frustrating challenge, and user groups and latter-day predators squabbled over the management of the government's remaining natural resources. To some Americans conservation and environmental problems seemed to strike even to the national survival question. On a more practical level both Indian plaintiffs and the United States Department of Justice have strenuously recruited specialists in the history of American land disposal and commissioned considerable new research relating to the land sales policies of the United States government in connection with the many Indian claims cases, originating in the Indian Claims Act of 1946. The year 1968 alone was marked by the publication of three major books in the field of land history: Robert P. Swierenga's study of land speculation in central Iowa; Malcolm Rohrbough's monograph describing the early years of the General Land Office business; and a monumental survey of public land law development undertaken on behalf of the Public Land Laws Review Commission by Paul Wallace Gates.

As one recent writer has noted, the labors of the land historians have "entailed an exacting blend of muckraking, econometrics, and Monday-morning quarterbacking," and their efforts have produced a massive accumulation of articles and books, including some research showing perception and analysis of a very high order. But it is a literature which, according to Douglass C. North, is in "substantial confusion." And this in turn is attributable, he argues, to "the inability of the historian to come to grips with the problems without the systematic use of theory to examine the issues and the testing of resultant hypotheses by careful empirical research." Perhaps North overstated his case, but we do have in the essay presented by Robert W. Fogel and Jack Rutner an illustration of the way in which "cliometric" methods may be used to throw new light upon issues on which land historians have thus far failed to reach agreement. The paper deals with the years between 1850 and 1900, a period in which the number of farm units in the United States rose from less than 1,500,000 to more than 5,500,000.

Many historians of the public lands have certainly, implicitly or explicitly, criticized the policies of the United States government. Fogel and Rutner maintain that such criticisms fall into two main categories—equity and efficiency issues. Their paper deals only incidentally with the distribution of income, that is, with equity problems. They suggest that criticisms of the efficiency of government land policy may appropriately be evaluated by assessing the effect of such policies on the level of national income. More specifically they ask: did government land policy have the effect of attracting too much land, labor, and capital into agriculture? What were the effects of the distribution of land in the West upon agriculture or agricultural income in the East? What efficiency losses, if any, are attributable to the activities of speculators in the new land regions? These are the major questions to which Fogel and Rutner address themselves, using a combination of substantive research and theoretical analysis.

The authors argue that insofar as resources were misallocated in agriculture during the period under study, the fact seems attributable more particularly to the peculiar conditions of agriculture in the *post-bellum* South rather than to federal land policy. Indeed, they suggest that the addition of both more capital and more labor in Western agriculture would have been beneficial to American economic development during the last half of the nineteenth century. Some scholars have suggested that losses of income on discarded Eastern lands should be subtracted from the gain in national income attributable to the opening of new lands in assessing the general results of Western development. Fogel and Rutner deny that this contention is correct, although they admit that individual Eastern farmers or landowners may have suffered losses. Finally, the authors consider the possibility that the United States government released its lands at so low a price as to encourage speculators to hold them out of production, thereby reducing national income. Such losses, they argue, must have amounted to a very small proportion of the Gross National Product.

Some historians of public land policies may question whether Fogel and Rutner have understood the historical literature correctly. There is no doubt, however, that they do identify the major contributions to that literature and, at the Chicago Conference, the author of the most exhaustive modern description of our public land policies did not challenge them on those grounds. Others may hold that those historians who have criticized national land policy on the grounds of efficiency losses have been considerably less numerous than those who have dwelt upon equity issues, and one conference participant questioned whether it was indeed appropriate to relate land policy to the Gross National Product as a means of measuring its efficiency. Consideration of the literature does show, however, that a number of respected historians have introduced the efficiency argument in some form, and the relation of policy effects to Gross National Product by cliometric historians does represent an improvement on past practices.

The emphasis in the paper by Fogel and Rutner is upon theoretical analysis rather than upon the presentation of empirical evidence. In this respect the authors are upon firmest ground when they consider the subject of resource allocation within the nation and within the agricultural sector of the economy. In their discussion of the impact of speculation upon national income they draw empirical evidence from only one study, and their consideration of regional income and labor shifts is almost purely theoretical. Even so, and even though, as the authors admit, much research is required before we can accept their findings as definitive, the implications of the paper are important, and it promises to help materially in bringing order to a body of historical literature that is less than congruent at the present time.

In a paper of this sort, in which the theoretical formulation is itself a considerable contribution, we can hardly expect a definitive mustering of empirical evidence nor can we expect that all of the implications of the argument will be drawn out. The authors have not considered for instance the degree to which the operation of the Homestead Law may have modified the land market after 1862 or the impact of short-run variations in economic conditions on the system. At the Chicago Conference, Albert Fishlow suggested that the focus of the authors on broad regions of the United States rather than upon specific public land states may have obscured important variations within their data. Whatever the merit of such comment, this paper will require historians of public land policies to reconsider some of their basic assumptions rather carefully.

I

Country Houses and Their Owners in Hertfordshire, 1540-1879

LAWRENCE STONE AND

JEANNE C. FAWTIER STONE

The Problems

This essay is part of a larger study which is designed to apply statistical methods of analysis to data of varying quality, in order to test some subjective impressions and traditional assumptions about English social structure and social mobility in the Early Modern and Modern periods.* It is generally agreed that England was historically the first of the modernizing societies of the world, and in particular that she was the first to industrialize and the first to evolve a stable and broad based constitutional structure. For over a century it has been part of conventional wisdom that these phenomena can be partly explained in terms firstly of the slow growth of the middle class of business and professional men, and secondly of the ease with which this middle class could move upward through the social and political systems. So far, however, there is no reliable body of statistical information with which to check and evaluate the truth of this bold and far-reaching hypothesis. This particular study is narrowly focused on a single aspect, namely the degree of interpenetration of the landed and the merchant/professional classes as tested by the changing composition of the local rural elites. Samples will eventually be taken from three different areas at varying distances from London, in order to obtain some sense of the variety of the national experience. This interpenetration can best be studied by examining the ownership and transmission of the key type of property, namely the country house, which formed the residence of the family and was the main center of the family patrimony. The degree to which these buildings changed hands by marriage, by inheritance, or sale, and the origins of the families who acquired them, should throw a good deal of light on this process.

* Research for this paper was supported partly by a grant from the Mathematical Social Science Board, and partly by grant number GS 1559X from the National Science Foundation.

The second and relatively independent problem is concerned with the building and rebuilding of these country seats. It is safe to say that no other country possesses so many of these large country houses, built, rebuilt, and added to century after century. Their construction, together with that of the ancillary outbuildings, gardens, parks, plantations, and lakes, must have demanded very large capital investments, certainly larger than what was put into industrial development before the nineteenth century, and also must have employed a very large labor force. At present, however, nothing is known about the trends in the number, size, and phases of construction of these houses over time, and nothing about the motivation or background of the builders. If a quantitative study of building activity at the time could be made, it would then be possible both to construct a "house building investment index," and also to chart the number, size, and geographical location of houses at different periods of time. This information in turn could be used to throw light on the houseowners and thus on the size and composition of the local elite at any given time. A study of builders would also throw light on the life experiences that made it likely that a man would embark upon such an enterprise. This article is concerned firstly with describing the sources and methods of such a study, and secondly with providing answers about the houses and their construction. The owners will be the subject of a further article.

The Geographical Limits of the Sample

the county

The sampling unit has necessarily to be the county, if only because it was around the county that landed society tended to be organized. There were two reasons why the sixteenth century saw the slow growth of a sense of county identity among the gentry of the shires. The first was the decline of the family or household community of "good lordship," by which the late medieval gentry had been attached to the families of great magnates, crossing county boundaries, splitting counties, and creating personal rather than geographical loyalties. The decline of the aristocratic magnate household freed the gentry for new psychological and political orientations, and made way for new patterns of education at school and university. The second was the growing burden placed on the local gentry by the state, as it expanded its statutory social and economic controls without setting up a paid local bureaucracy of its own to handle them. The result was the development of county justices as administrators and judicial authorities, who slowly began to attach a political identity to their membership. This development was greatly fostered by the growth in numbers of the resident gentry in the countryside, and by marriage patterns showing a very high endogamy within the gentry of each county.

This local particularism was in part offset by a parallel growth of interest in national politics, as shown in increasing competition for a seat in the House of Commons; of loyalty to the national community, as expressed in increasing devotion to the Commonwealth and the Monarch; and of increasing involvement with London, as expressed by visits to the city and dependence on the city for supply of information and specialized services and commodities. This last was of course felt with a special force in Hertfordshire, which was probably more exposed to the pull of London than any other county except Middlesex and perhaps Surrey.

Close personal relationships between the gentry of the county were established at regular meetings of the quarter sessions and assizes, and local power struggles were focused on county offices such as Deputy Lieutenant, Member of Parliament, and so on. It must be remembered that there was an inverse correlation between status and wealth on the one hand and county particularism on the other. The baronets and knights had more contacts outside the county, were more involved in national affairs, and were more inclined to find their partners in a regional marriage market. The small parish gentry, on the other hand, were more narrowly locked into their county particularism by the restricted nature of their education, property holding, marriages, and aspirations for office. Despite these differences of emphasis, it is none the less true that by the early seventeenth century the county had become, even for the elite of the local gentry, the main area of administrative action, political conflict, social intercourse, economic investment, and marriage connections.

HERTFORDSHIRE

Hertfordshire is one of England's smallest counties, consisting of only 630 square miles between 10 and 40 miles to the north of London. It was chosen partly because of the excellence of its local records, and partly because it was thought likely to provide the most extreme case of mobility between land and trade, since it is already known that through all periods it has been a favorite area for the purchase of a landed estate by successful London merchants. It is situated very close to the capital, with good road communications, and yet even today much of it is rolling country of woods and fields of great natural beauty and offering an extraordinary sense of rural peace. The special quality of Hertfordshire was recognized at the time, and in 1704 Robert Morden wrote with pardonable hyperbole—"this County has an incredible number of Pallaces and fair Structures of the Gentry and Nobility. From Totteridge where the County begins and East Barnet to Ware are so many beautiful houses that one may look upon it almost as a continual street. The rich soil and wholesome air, and the excellence of the County have drawn hither the Wealthiest Citizens of London."[1] It has been this combination of proximity with rusticity that has made it so attractive to generation after generation of wealthy Londoners. It is no coincidence that the only regular coach service in the country in the 1630s ran through Hertfordshire from London to Cambridge, that the only three wagon-cum-coach services in the country ran between London and the Hertfordshire towns of Saint Albans, Hertford, and Hatfield, and that there were also regular carrier delivery services several times a week to four other Hertfordshire towns.[2] The ties that bound the county to the city were exceptionally close even before the middle of the seventeenth century.

Some clear evidence for the exceptional rapidity of turnover of land in Hertfordshire is available for the leading gentry of the county who took one side or another at the outbreak of the war in 1642. Less than 10 per cent of them had been settled in the county before 1485, compared with 18 per cent for Essex, 13 per cent for Suffolk, and 42 per cent for Norfolk. For all the gentry, large and small, the figures are 75 per cent for Kent and 40 per cent for Yorkshire and 25 per cent for Northamptonshire (see Fig. 1). Another test is the proportion of leading gentry who took sides on the war whose families had only settled in the county since 1603. For Hertfordshire, the figure is as high as 43 per cent, compared with 26 per cent for Essex, 18 per cent for Suffolk, and 14 per cent for Norfolk, while only 12 per cent of all Kentish gentry were newcomers.[3] Thus Hertfordshire had the lowest proportion of pre-1485 gentry and the highest proportion of post-1603 gentry of any county for which we have record so far (see Fig. 1).

Another indicator of the unusually mobile and open character of Hertfordshire society as early as 1640 is the degree to which its gentry was endogamous. Only 31 per cent of knights and baronets in the county married within the county, as compared with 28 per cent in Essex, 43 per cent in Suffolk, 44 per cent in Norfolk, and about 60 per cent in Kent. The figures for untitled gentry are even more

[1] R. Morden, *New Description of England* (London, 1704), p. 36.

[2] J. Taylor, *The Carriers Cosmographie* (London, 1637).

[3] C. A. Holmes, "The Eastern Association" (Cambridge Univ., unpublished Ph.D. thesis, 1969), App. III, p. 495, hereinafter referred to as "Eastern Association"; A. Everitt, *The Community of Kent and the Great Rebellion* (London, 1966), p. 36, hereinafter referred to as *Kent*; "Suffolk and the Great Rebellion, 1640-1660," *Suffolk Rec. Soc.*, III (1960), 20; *Change in the Provinces: the Seventeenth Century* (Leicester, 1969), p. 38; J. T. Cliffe, *The Yorkshire Gentry* (London, 1969), p. 13.

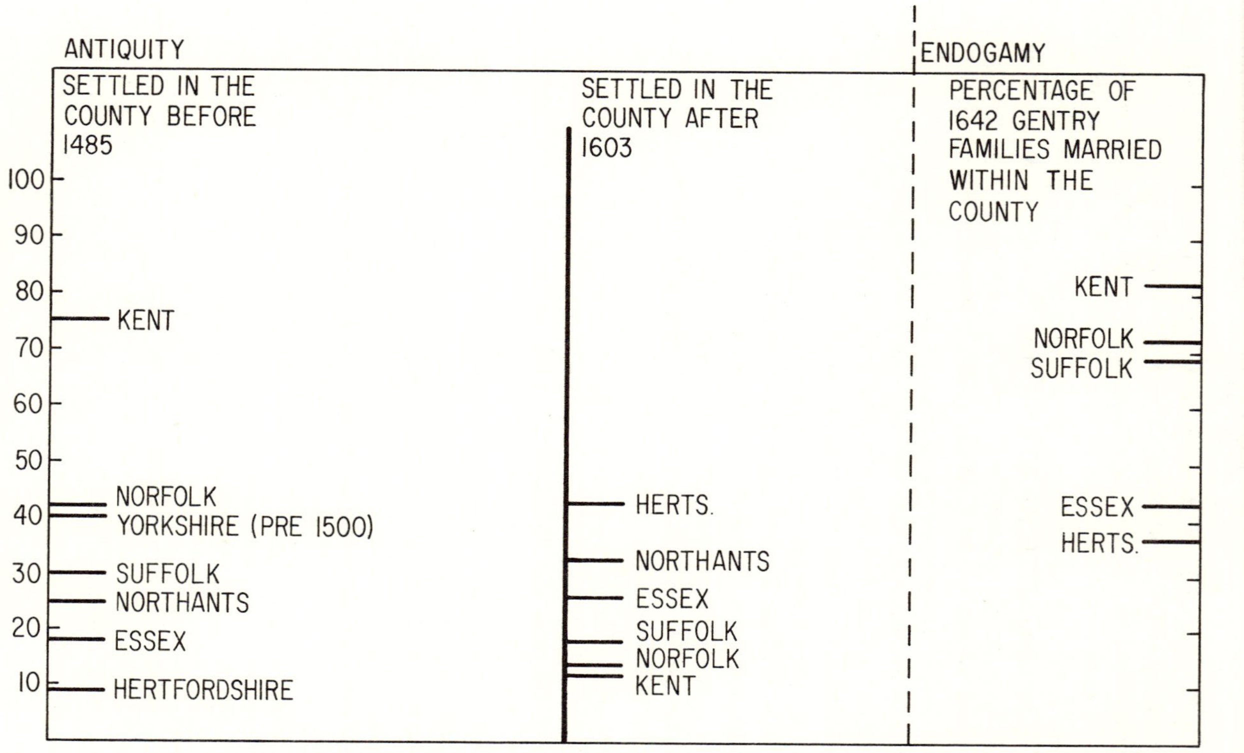

Fig. 1. Antiquity and Endogamy of Gentry in 1642

striking; 37 per cent for Hertfordshire, 43 per cent for Essex, 69 per cent for Suffolk, 72 per cent for Norfolk, and 82 per cent for Kent (see Fig. 1). Only Essex is remotely comparable on the scale, and the other counties are completely different in their marriage patterns, primarily because of the striking difference in their ties to London. Twenty per cent of Hertfordshire gentry married Londoners, as compared with only 3 per cent of Suffolk and Norfolk.[4]

A third way in which Hertfordshire is unusual is in the number of substantial country houses of which it could boast. This is demonstrated by comparing the number of houses assessed at 20 hearths or more in this and other counties in the Hearth Tax of 1662 to 1673,[5] which reveals a direct relationship between density of houses and proximity to London. Surrey, which is adjacent to London on the south bank of the Thames and also upriver toward Richmond, has the highest density of houses, closely followed by Hertfordshire. Calculated in terms of thousands of acres per house, the density in Hertfordshire is two and a half times greater than in Suffolk or Warwickshire, about four times greater than in Dorset, and about eight times greater than in Shropshire (see Fig. 2). Seventeenth-century Hertfordshire was thus a demonstrably atypical county in the extraordinarily large number of houses which it contained.

A rather similar comparison between Hertfordshire and other counties can be made 200 years later, in 1873.[6] It was then second only to Essex in the proportion of acreage (excluding waste) owned by small to medium-sized landowners. No less than 34 per cent was

[4] Holmes, "Eastern Association," App. I, p. 492; Everitt, *Kent*, p. 328.

[5] Hertfordshire: Public Record Office (hereinafter referred to as P.R.O.), E 179/248/23; 375/30; 375/31. Shropshire: W. Watkins-Pitchford, *The Shropshire Hearth Tax Roll, 1672*, Shropshire Arch. Soc., 1949. Somerset: R. Holworthy, *Hearth Tax for Somerset* (London, 1916). Suffolk: "Suffolk in 1674," *Suffolk Green Books*, Vol. 13 (1905). Dorset: A. F. Meekings, *Dorset Hearth Tax 1662-4, Dorset Rec. Soc.*, 1951. Surrey: "Surrey Hearth Tax in 1664," *Surrey Rec. Soc.*, XVII. Warwickshire: Hearth Tax Assessment for 1670 in Warwickshire County Record Office (we owe this information to Mrs. Judith Hurwich).

[6] The following figures are derived from the tables in F.M.L. Thompson, *English Landed Society in the Nineteenth Century* (London, 1963), pp. 32, 113-17.

LAND-HOLDINGS AS PERCENTAGE OF TOTAL ACREAGE IN THE COUNTY
(excluding waste)

	0-99a.	*100-299a.*	*300-999a.*	*1,000-2,999a.*	*3,000-9,999a.*	*10,000a.+*
Herts.	8	10	17	17	17	23
Rutland	7	5	5	8	18	53
Cumb.	16	22	16	12	10	19
Essex	10	17	20	15	19	9
Northants.	11	13	12	9	17	30

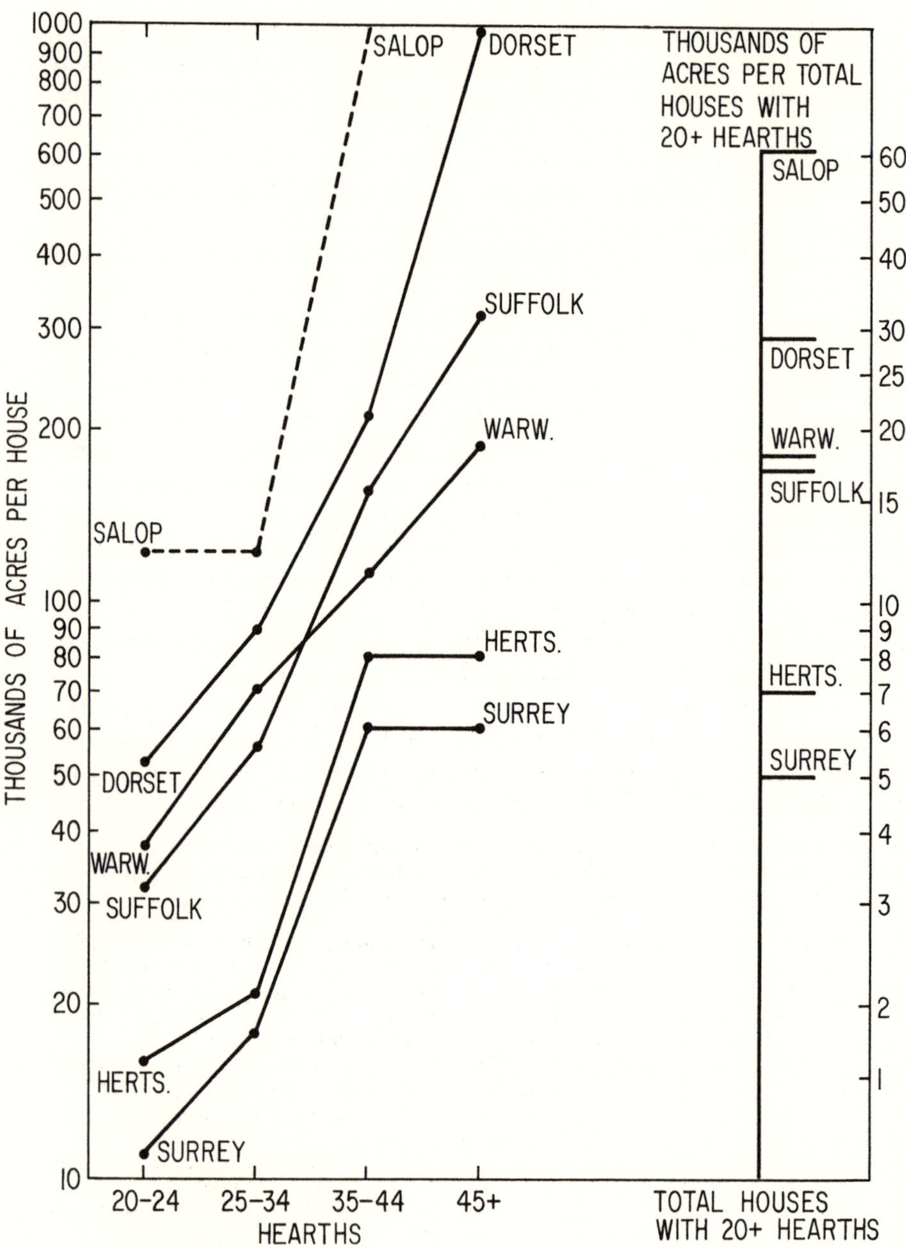

Fig. 2. Houses Assessed at Over Twenty Hearths: 1662-1673

owned by men holding between 300 and 3,000 acres each. In counties farther from London those in the 300 to 1,000 acre bracket would probably only count as yeomen, but in Hertfordshire they were usually small gentry living gentlemanly lives in gentlemanly houses, on the strength of an income derived partly from the high rental per acre in the county, but more from investments in business companies and in the Funds. The social structure of mid-Victorian Hertfordshire thus forms a striking contrast on the one hand with Cumberland, with its huge and dominant small freeholder population and its relative absence of gentry; and on the other with Rutland, the bulk of which was in the hands of the great magnates (see Fig. 3).

Despite these unusual features, it would be a great mistake to imagine that the landowners of Hertfordshire did not possess a sense of community. Although the degree of mobility and of access to non-landed sources of income may have been exceptionally great, the vast majority of landowners in the county were at all times resident on their estates and owned property exclusively within its boundaries. An examination of all the manors in the county in 1640 shows that 86 per cent of them were owned by residents within the county, and only 14 per cent by residents elsewhere.[7] This figure is much the same as those for Essex, Suffolk, and Norfolk, although it is likely that the causes are somewhat different in the more remote counties of Norfolk and Suffolk than in counties close to London like Hertfordshire and Essex. In the former the non-residents were probably mostly landowners with estates elsewhere; in Hertfordshire, and to some extent in Essex, very many of them were Londoners buying into the county with a view to later retirement.

This situation did not change significantly before the middle of the nineteenth century when the railways opened up the southwestern parts of the county as easily accessible weekend dormitories for London business and professional men, and when the suburbs of London began encroaching upon the southernmost edges of the county. But as late as 1873, of the 146 inhabitants of Hertfordshire houses who also owned over 2,000 acres of property and a rent-roll of over 2,000 pounds a year in or out of the county, only 19 (13 per cent) held a seat elsewhere, and only 36 (25 per cent) held more than 1,000 acres elsewhere (and this was usually in an adjacent county).[8] There are thus compelling historical reasons why the county should be the geographical unit of study.

[7] Holmes, "Eastern Association," App. II, p. 494.

[8] J. Bateman, *The Great Landowners of Great Britain and Ireland* (London, 1879).

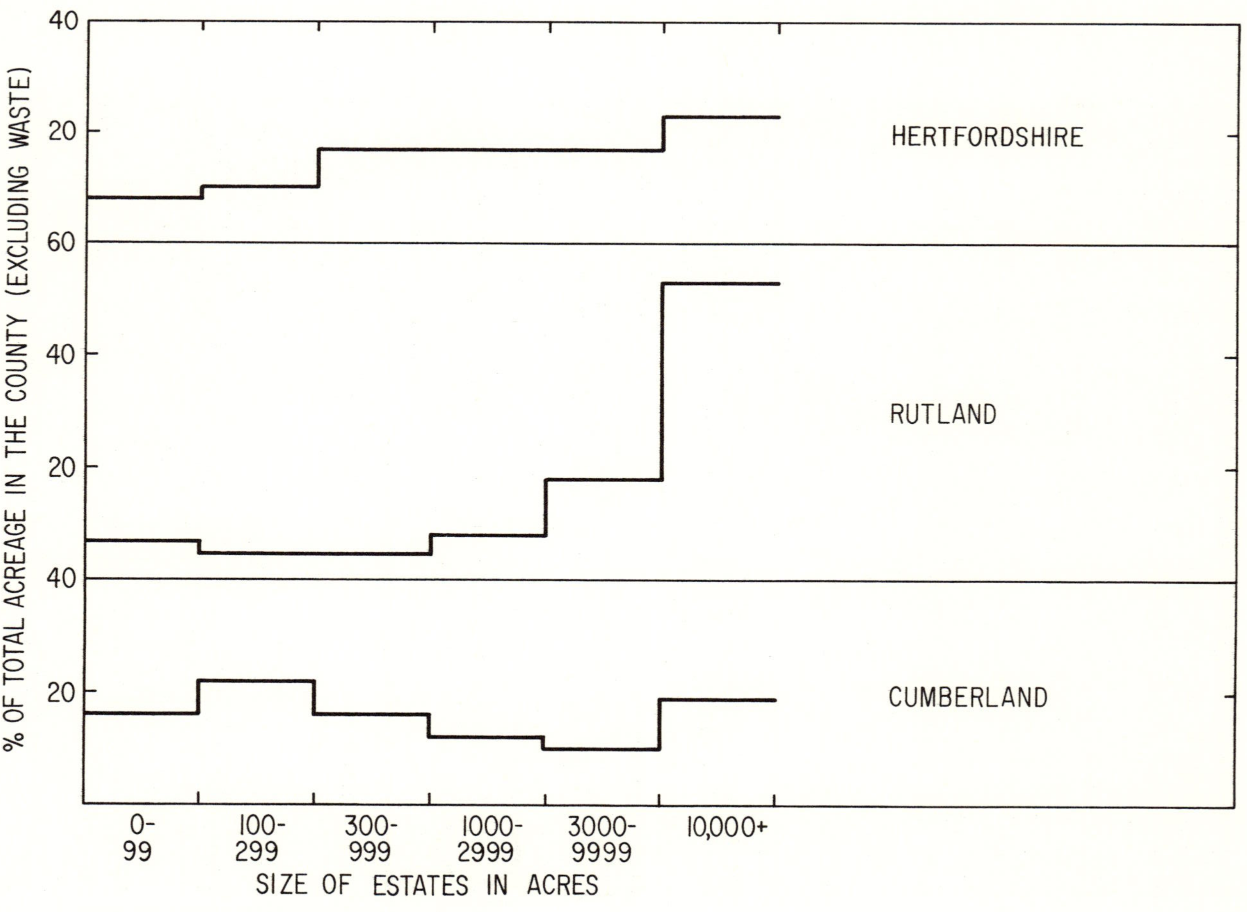

FIG. 3. Relative Distribution of Property in 1873

THE EVIDENCE FOR HERTFORDSHIRE

Hertfordshire has certain special advantages in respect to the wealth of its printed records. In the first place, the county is almost unique in possessing no fewer than five large-scale county histories published between 1700 and 1914.[9] These massive surveys in numerous folio volumes contain a huge amount of information about the owners of the houses and to a lesser extent about their building activities, particularly since two of the authors, Chauncy (1700) and Clutterbuck (*c.* 1820), were themselves minor gentry who enjoyed some familiarity with most members of this elite world. Several of these dedicated antiquaries went to the pains of transcribing and publishing *in extenso* the monumental inscriptions they found in the churches, many of which have now vanished, and which are often the only source from which can be traced the owners of seats and their genealogical connections. These nuggets of information are particularly valuable since the *Victoria County History*, in its myopic obsession with manorial descents, studiously ignores the history of all non-manorial properties, regardless of their size or the importance of their owners or the houses built on them.

England is extraordinarily, perhaps uniquely, rich in the records of the upper classes, partly because its archives, and particularly its private archives, have never suffered the disruptions and destruction of a social revolution, partly because the persistently aristocratic nature of its society has encouraged the collection of genealogies and family histories. It is not that the upper ranges of English society have remained impervious to lower-class infiltration. On the contrary, this widespread passion for genealogy has been stimulated precisely because of this infiltration, partly to establish degrees of antiquity in family origins, partly to trace the incorporation into traditional society of new elements, many of which were laying claims to ultimate gentry origins. If the historian is aided in his work by filiopietism, he is handicapped by the relative absence of helpful official records. Because of the perennial weakness of the central government, it is only at two widely separated points in time that comprehensive government surveys become of real value to him. These are the already mentioned assessments for the Hearth Tax of 1662 to

[9] H. Chauncy, *Historical Antiquities of Hertfordshire* (London, 1700), hereinafter referred to as *Historical Antiquities*; N. Salmon, *The History of Hertfordshire* (London, 1728); R. Clutterbuck, *History and Antiquities of the County of Hertford* (3 vols.; London, 1815-27), hereinafter referred to as *History and Antiquities*; J. E. Cussans, *History of Hertfordshire* (3 vols.; London, 1870-81); *Victoria County History of Hertfordshire* (4 vols.; London, 1902-14).

1673 and the *Survey of Landowners* of 1873.[10] By combining and collating the various returns, the Hearth Tax can be made to provide coverage of all but 6 of the 135 parishes in the county. The assessment, which was made to form the basis for a tax on chimneys, records the number of hearths of all houses in the county over a minimum poverty level and therefore should include all the country houses extant at that time. The tax lists only identify the taxpayer (who was the resident and not necessarily the owner) and the parish; the identification of the house has to be done from other sources. For houses of the size we are here concerned with, this represents little difficulty in most cases, although there are a few big houses listed whose residents cannot be identified, and a few big houses which are known to have existed but are missing owing to lacunae in the data.

A comparison of the number of hearths in the Hearth Tax with independent calculations of house size (excluding offices) based on extant building, old drawings, etc., shows a comfortingly high degree of correlation, with only a few unexplained anomalies on each side of the mean (see Fig. 4). This rough correlation gives one confidence in the reliability of the tax assessments to provide a rough indication of house size where no other evidence is available. This reliability is particularly important since for 32 of the 151 houses in the main sample the Hearth Tax assessment is the sole indicator of size which we possess for that period. It should be noted, however, that for the really large houses over 200 units the under assessment is greater than that for the smaller houses. It is clear that in the seventeenth century, as in the twentieth, the tax machinery favored the super-rich.

Another merit of the Hearth Tax is that it provides evidence of house size which can be correlated with contemporary lists of Justices of the Peace and with the near-contemporary map by Chauncy in 1700, thus helping to throw light on the most perplexing problem of all, namely where to draw the line between a minor residence and a country seat. Among the houses assessed at 10 or more hearths in the Hearth Tax, there are 101 definitely identifiable as country houses, even if minor ones, 10 probables, 7 doubtfuls, and 7 missing, making a total of 125. Some 58 past, present, or future Justices of the Peace lived in these houses, 54 of them in the country and 4 in towns. Apart from heirs who served on the bench in their father's lifetime, there were only 4 Justices who do not figure in the list of owners of

[10] P.R.O., E 179/248/23; 375/30; 375/31. *The Returns of Owners of Land in England and Wales, 1873* (London, 1875). Corrected and synthesized statistics for the wealthier landowners are given in J. Bateman, *The Great Landowners of Great Britain and Ireland* (London, 1879).

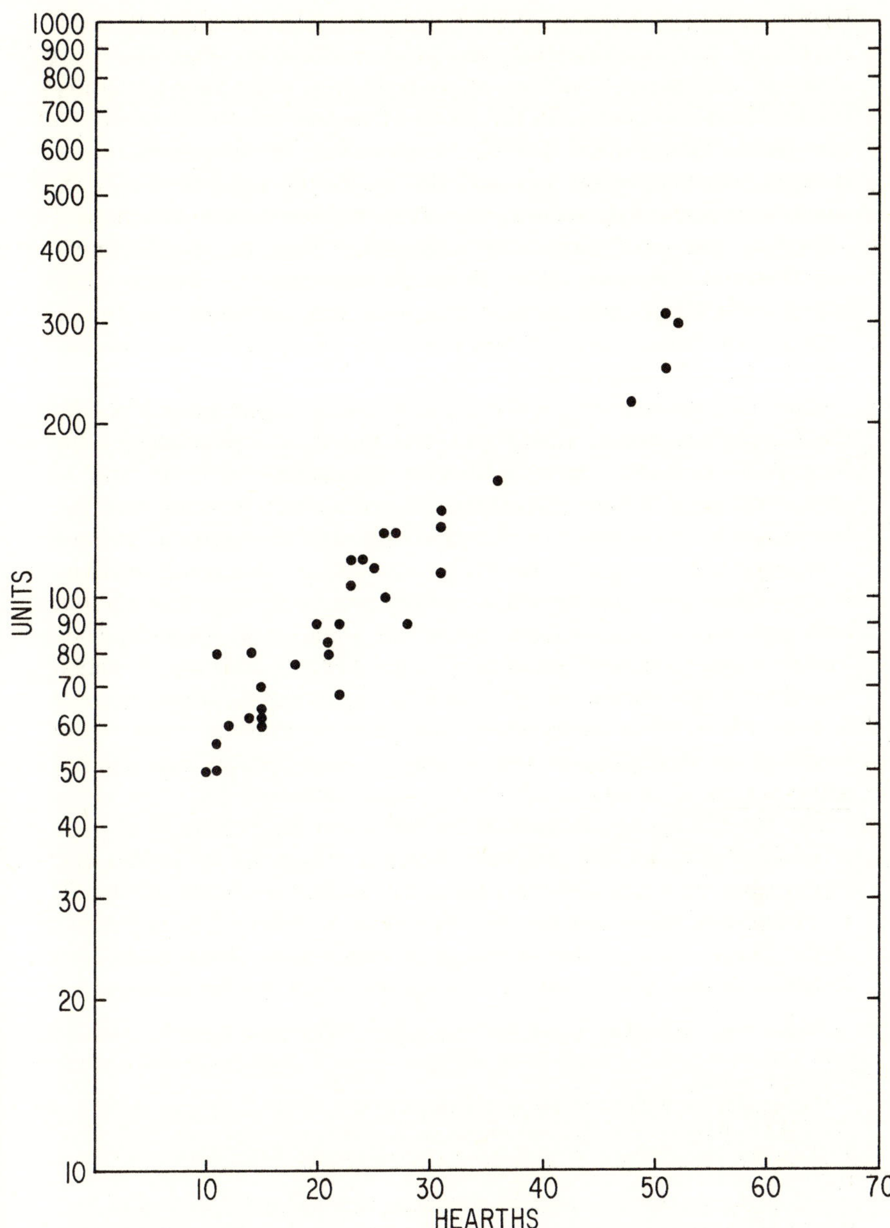

FIG. 4. Correlation of Hearth Tax Assessments and Estimated Size in Units: 1662-1673

houses with 10 or more hearths.[11] But it is not until the 15 hearth level is reached that houses which are lived in by other than the local elite tail off sharply, and we are left mainly with known country houses of known gentry. In the 10 to 14 hearth bracket there are 24 identifiable houses inhabited by town gentry; 40 houses in towns, some of which must be inns and the others the residences of merchants and professional people; and 40 in the countryside which must belong to substantial yeomen or innkeepers. There are also 3 identifiable inns and 9 rectories. At the 15 hearth and more level, however, one is left with 73 country houses, 1 certain inn, 13 houses in towns, most of which are probably also inns, and 16 houses in the country which cannot be identified.

The 1873 *Returns of Owners of Land*, which was carried out by the Local Government Board and was based on valuations for the Poor Rate, includes names, addresses, estimated extent of land in acres, and gross estimated rentals. All are subject to error, and the last excludes all income from London and also, of course, all income from non-landed property. By 1873, a number of enormously wealthy Hertfordshire residents owned a country seat in its own grounds but with only a few acres of land beyond the walls of the grounds. They therefore appear as very small men in the *Returns*, although in actual fact they were persons of great substance, living in large houses.[12] A few others were multi-county magnates, who were fairly small landlords in Hertfordshire but owners of huge estates and another major seat in a county more remote from London.[13]

The Hearth Tax assessments of the 1660s and the *Returns of Owners of Land* of 1873 are the two most valuable single lists of houses and owners, but they can and must be supplemented by many others. Of these the most important are the *Libri Pacis*, or official lists of Justices of the Peace, a reasonable coverage of which is available from 1558 to 1685.[14] From 1624 to 1833 it is possible to pick up the names of all

[11] Silus Titus of Bushey, Sir Henry Coningsby of The Weld (who is known to have been very poor), Thomas Took of Popes, and a Richard Crofts about whom nothing is known.

[12] Examples are William Stuart of Aldenham Abbey, Philip Longmore of Ardleybury, H.J.S. Bosanquet of Broxbournbury, R. R. Carew of Carpenders Park, H. J. Toulmin of Childwickbury, W. J. Blake of Danesbury, and W.F.J. Young of Heston Hall.

[13] Examples are Marquis Townshend of Balls Park and Raynham Hall in Norfolk (1,565 acres in Hertfordshire and a total rental of £22,560); Lord Rendlesham of Edge Grove and Rendlesham Hall in Suffolk (3,969 acres in Hertfordshire and a total rental of £25,024); and C. C. Sibthorpe of North Mimms Park (1,700 acres in Hertfordshire and a total rental of £10,300).

[14] 1558: British Museum. Lansd. MSS, 1218, f. 15.
1575: P.R.O., SP 12/104.
1579: P.R.O., SP 12/145.

the active Justices of the Peace from lists, published at the back of the various volumes of the *Hertford County Records, Sessions Books*, evidence which has been extended to 1879 by consulting the manuscript lists. Further evidence comes from two printed lists of J.P.s, which are composed of names of members of the bench stretching back over many previous years and added to as late as 1861 and 1887.[15] These, together with lists of sheriffs and Members of Parliament,[16] provide some of the raw material from which to begin the laborious process of identifying the local elite. Unfortunately, however, the Bench of Justices is never identical with this elite, and even the office of sheriff has its ups and downs.

To help in the selection process, other lists and other sources of evidence have to be scrutinized. For example, between 1786 and 1808, residents in houses may often be identified from the records of licenses to kill game.[17] Most helpful of all are the large number of maps and lists of principal houses, lists of prominent landowners, and handbooks and directories of the landed classes.[18] No single one of

---

1584: P.R.O., E 163/14/8, ff. 13-14.
1596: P.R.O., SP 13/Case F/11, ff. 16v.-17.
1608: P.R.O., SP 14/33, ff. 30v-32.
1621: P.R.O., C 193/13/1, ff. 36-38.
1626: P.R.O., E 163/18/12, ff. 45v-48.
1632: P.R.O., SP 16/212, ff. 28v-30.
1636: P.R.O., SP 16/405, ff. 30v-32b.
1650: P.R.O., C 193/13/3, ff. 30-31.
1652: P.R.O., C 193/13/4, ff. 43-45.
1656: P.R.O., C 193/13/6, ff. 39-41v.
1657: P.R.O., C 193/13/5, ff. 47-50v.
1660: P.R.O., C 220/9/4, ff. 36-38.
1662: P.R.O., C 193/12/3, ff. 44v-47.
1680: P.R.O., C 193/12/4, ff. 50-52v.
1685: P.R.O., C 193/12/5, ff. 61-65v.

[15] *Hertfordshire County Records, Sessions Books*, v, App. I (1624-58); VI, App. I (1658-1700); VII, App. I (1700-52); VIII, App. I (1753-99); IX, App. I (1799-1833); X, App. I (1833-43). We are indebted to Mr. R. W. Shorthouse for his kindness in compiling the post-1844 list of names from the original Order Books in the Hertfordshire Record Office (hereinafter referred to as Herts. R. O.). The two lists are also in the Herts. R. O. among the Quarter Session Papers.

[16] Lists of Sheriffs in Chauncy, *Historical Antiquities*, pp. 23-24; Clutterbuck, *History and Antiquities*, I, p. xxx; Cussans, *History of Hertfordshire*, III (2), Hundred of Cashio, Addenda, p. 311; Members of Parliament in Parliamentary Papers, *Returns of . . . Members of Parliament, 1213-1877* (2 vols.; London, 1878).

[17] *Hertfordshire County Records, Sessions Books*, VIII, App. VIII; IX, App. X.

[18]
1596: J. Norden, *Speculi Britanniae Pars* (London, 1598)	Owners & Seats
1695: J. Oliver, *Map of Hertfordshire*	Seats
1700: Chauncy, *Historical Antiquities*, map	Seats
1728: Salmon, *History of Hertfordshire*, map	Seats
1746: J. Warburton, J. Bland, and P. Smyth, *A New and Corrected Map of Middlesex, Essex and Hertfordshire*	Owners & Seats
1765: W. Dury and J. Andrews, *Map of Hertfordshire*	Owners & Seats

these many lists is even roughly comparable with any other, and every single one contains many unexplained omissions and unexpected inclusions. Only a very careful collation of them all offers any hope of establishing a definitive list of gentry and houses that may be regarded as candidates for inclusion in this study. Further aids to the identification and tracing of gentry and squires are the numerous genealogies and group biographies in which England is so singularly rich.[19] This wealth of published material is itself compelling evidence of an obsession with status and family ancestry which was kept alive by the irritant of that incessant injection of new wealth and blood which it is one of the purposes of this study to document statistically.

The evidence about the size, appearance, construction, and alteration of the houses themselves is less comprehensive and less easy to get at than that about their owners. For the size and shape of many of them, the most reliable evidence comes from the Ordnance Survey maps of 1867-1882, drawn on the gigantic scale of 25 inches to the mile. The scale of these maps is such that they include an outline

---

1797-98: List of Nobility and Gentry in Hertfordshire, in Bodleian Library, Oxford, Gough MSS, Herts. 4, f. 182	Owners & Seats
1801: C. Smith, *Map of Hertfordshire*	Seats
1820: Clutterbuck, *History and Antiquities*, map	Seats
1829: E. Moggs, 18th ed. of *Patterson's Roads*	Owners & Seats
1836: J. Burke, *History of the Commoners of Great Britain and Ireland*	Owners & Seats
1845: E. R. Kelly, *The Post Office Directory of the Six Home Counties*	Owners & Seats
1851: E. Churton, *The Railroad Book of England*	Owners & Seats
1852-55: J. B. Burke, *Visitation of the Seats and Arms of Noblemen and Gentlemen of Great Britain and Ireland*	Owners & Seats
1869: Cussans, *History of Hertfordshire*, map	Seats
1863: J. B. Burke, *Genealogical and Heraldic Dictionary of the Landed Gentry of Great Britain and Ireland*	Owners & Seats
1869-81: Ordnance Survey 25-inch-to-the-mile maps	Seats
1872: E. Walford, *The County Families of the United Kingdom* (London, 1872)	Owners & Seats
1886: *Kelly's Directory*	Owners & Seats

[19] The main sources for tracing genealogy of county families are: G. E. Cokayne, *The Complete Peerage* (London, 1910-59), and *The Complete Baronetage* (London, 1900-06); J. Burke, *Peerage and Baronetage of the British Empire* (London, 1839), etc.; *Extinct and Dormant Peerages* (London, 1831), etc.; *Landed Gentry of Great Britain and Ireland* (London, 1843-49), etc.; J. and J. B. Burke, *The Extinct and Dormant Baronetcies of England, Ireland and Scotland* (London, 1844); J. Burke, *The Commoners of Great Britain and Ireland* (London, 1833-38); Walford, *County Families of the United Kingdom*; W. Betham, *Baronetage of England* (London, 1801-05); T. Wotton, *The English Baronetage* (London, 1741); A. Collins, *The Peerage of England* (London, 1779); D.C.A. Agnew, *Protestant Exiles from France* (London, 1886); W. Berry, *County Genealogies: Pedigrees of Hertfordshire Families* (London, 1842); *V.C.H., Hertfordshire*, Genealogical Volume, and Chauncy, *Historical Antiquities*; Clutterbuck, *History and Antiquities*; Cussans, *History of Hertfordshire*.

plan of every house and therefore make possible a rough estimate of the square footage that each house covered at that time. Even this, however, is fraught with difficulties, since the map does not distinguish the lowly, often one-story, offices from the main block. This vital distinction has to be judged subjectively, usually on the basis of illustrations of the houses, although in most cases it is not too difficult to establish strong probabilities. For 50 houses we have scale plans and even some elevations, but these cover only the more important structures, together with a few supplied by the *Victoria County History* which covers some small manor houses dating back to the sixteenth century and still extant today. Scale plans of medium sized houses of the seventeenth, eighteenth, and nineteenth centuries are largely non-existent. On the other hand, exact measurements of the main reception rooms of a number of houses which have now vanished were included in the many "Books of Seats" and topographical works which were published in great profusion from about 1790 onward.

For a limited number of houses there have survived among the family records building accounts and correspondence which throw light on the date and cost of construction. The most useful collections are the Salisbury Papers at Hatfield, with very detailed records of the construction of Hatfield House; the Gorhambury Papers, with building accounts of Gorhambury; and the Panshanger Papers; both the latter collections being now on deposit in the County Record Office.

Some of the most illuminating material comes from three sets of drawings executed at different times, but all dating from before so many houses were changed beyond recognition by Victorian additions and alterations. The value of these three sets is greatly enhanced by the fact that each is the work of one man. This makes possible comparisons between one house and another at a given date, whereas individual stylistic peculiarities make it more hazardous to compare contemporary illustrations by different artists. In his history of the county published in 1700, Chauncy inserted some very elaborate engravings of 32 houses and grounds, all but 5 by J. Drapentier. Between about 1790 and 1799 a draftsman called H. G. Oldfield plodded around the county making drawing after drawing of over 100 houses. Although not very skillfully executed, and largely devoid of any sense of perspective, they are unimaginatively faithful to the original and provide the only coverage for many houses at that date. Altogether Oldfield took some 250 sketches of houses and churches in the hope of making up 20 duplicate sets of the hundred best and of selling them to the nobility and leading gentry at a handsome profit. But his plans went awry, and he landed in Hertford Jail for debt in 1799, with the drawings as his only asset and thus his only lifeline to freedom. Fortunately both for Oldfield and for posterity, one set was ultimately purchased by Lord Dimsdale and has been preserved.[20] Some 30 years later, in the 1830s, an infinitely more talented artist, William Buckler, followed in Oldfield's footsteps and recorded from many angles some 60 houses. Buckler showed meticulous attention to architectural details, a firm grasp of perspective, and a fine sense of composition.[21] His drawings, like the Drapentier engravings in Chauncy, are a pleasure to look at.

These three groups of drawings may be supplemented by large numbers of individual engravings and drawings, most of which date from between 1780 and 1840.[22] Finally, there are photographs of the buildings as they are today. Many houses were photographed in the 1950s, often only weeks ahead of the hammer of a demolition contractor, and many more of those which still survive were recorded by the authors in 1967-1969. What makes this wealth of visual material so important is the way in which each item supports the other, so that it is frequently possible to trace the changing appearance of an individual house in all its vicissitudes between 1700 and 1972.

On the other hand it must be admitted that the evidence for architecture varies considerably over time. Chauncy's personal knowledge of the county elite, and the engravings of Drapentier in his book, makes the period 1660 to 1700 a particularly well-documented one. On the whole the eighteenth century is far well less covered, although Georgian houses have a higher survival rate than Jacobean, and many have dated rainwater heads, etc. Between about 1790 and 1840, however, drawings, engravings, and written records multiply, so that this is the best documented period of all, much better than the forty years that follow. The uneven quality of the documentation suggests that caution should be used in making conclusions about the changing of building activity, since so much more is known about some periods than others.

The Chronological Limits of the Sample

As has been seen, the geographical limits of the county imposed themselves naturally, and the chronological limits also have caused little difficulty. The study begins in 1540, at the time when the Crown was throwing onto the market the monastic property it had recently

[20] Bodleian Library, Oxford, Gough MSS, Herts., 13, Vol. III, ff. 48, 58, 61. Herts. R. O., Dimsdale Collection of Oldfield Drawings.

[21] Herts. R. O., Buckler Drawings, Vols. I-IV. British Museum, Add. MSS, 36364-67.

[22] Herts. R. O., Extra-Illustrated Clutterbuck, Vols. II-IX; Herts. R. O., Gerish Collection; Herts. R. O., County Views; British Museum, Add. MSS, 32348-52; 9062-64; 33641; Bodleian Library, Oxford, Gough MSS, Herts. 11, 16, 17, 18.

seized from the church. This property was bought up eagerly and provided the site of many new seats and the economic foundation of many new families. It is from this moment that the county gentry begin to develop into a recognizable and identifiable social group, that their houses take on architectural pretensions, and that their activities and their genealogies can be documented with some certainty. The terminal date has been set at 1879, primarily because there is such a plethora of information in the 1870s and such a void later on. *The Returns of Owners of Land* was published in 1875 and refers to assessments of 1873. Secondly, between 1867 and 1882 the first (and last) large-scale mapping survey of the county was carried out by the Ordnance Survey, whose 25-inch-to-the-mile maps date from this period. Thirdly, the last great comprehensive history of the county was published by Cussans between 1870 and 1881; and lastly Edward Walford began publishing his remarkably catholic and comprehensive *County Families of the United Kingdom* in 1860. Walford was less of a snob than Burke and his volumes therefore provide the most complete survey of late Victorian landed society, new and old, commercial and aristocratic, that was ever undertaken.

Originally, it was intended to carry the story on to 1914 or even to 1960, but it has become clear that the evidence for this most recent period is more scanty and harder to dig out than that for any other in the last 300 years. Trying to find out what has happened to houses and their owners since 1880 is a baffling and bewildering experience, and one is left with the uneasy suspicion that it is perfectly possible for some vast late Victorian monstrosity to have been erected by some city plutocrat and to have been torn down again in the 1920s or 1930s to make way for building development, without leaving a trace of itself or its owners in the historical records. The other reason for cutting the study off at 1879 is that after that date the southern part of the county was becoming more and more built over, and more and more a daily commuting satellite of London.

The Social Limits of the Sample

The most difficult problem of all in a study such as this is to determine the boundaries of the sample. What is to be included, and for how long, and by what objective standards? Our purpose is to identify a county elite, defined not by any one criteria but by several: a) by social eminence, shown by ownership of a title or rank of honor; b) by style of life, shown by residence in a house with a certain amplitude of public rooms for entertainment and of pleasure grounds around it; c) by wealth, measured primarily by style of life; and d) by participation in the affairs of the county, shown by active membership of the bench or occupation of a local administrative or political office. No one of these criteria is sufficient in itself to justify admission to the ranks of the elite, though preeminence in one may sometimes compensate for weakness in another. But since the group under study is regarded as primarily a local status group rather than an economic class or a power elite, the criterion without which all else fails is life style as measured by the nature and size of the house in which the individual resides. This life style is itself evidence of wealth and is a necessary prerequisite for social status and for participation in local politics. To begin with, a list was drawn up of all houses in the county occupied by men mentioned in standard works on county families or identified as living in seats on maps or illustrations by draftsmen of the eighteenth and nineteenth centuries. There are 437 houses of which some record exists in one form or another at one time or another. They range from the huge palace of Hatfield, the residence of one of England's leading aristocratic families, down to the modest Victorian villa built for his retirement by a successful London businessman, about whom and his house we know virtually nothing. Both the size of the houses and the social significance of their owners lie on a smooth continuum without any clear breaks, so that any cut-off point is artificial and gives rise to nagging doubts about marginal cases and to a series of agonizing reappraisals that can have no end. But if we are to study the elite rather than an amorphous and shifting mass of people above a certain economic level, it is absolutely necessary to draw the line at a fairly high level. For one thing, it is not possible to discover sufficient information about many houses and their owners—particularly smaller houses with obscure owners—to present a coherent chronological record.

Where there are important lacunae in the records of a house and its owners, it is just not possible to use it or them, since the gaps would create serious distortions in the statistics. In quantitative studies of this kind one is peculiarly at the mercy of the evidence, since partial and incomplete data are almost impossible to use for comparative purposes. The documentation for this study is extraordinarily abundant in quantity, but it is variable in the degree of reliability and is rarely fully complete for any individual house. It is easy enough to eliminate those about which little or nothing is known—indeed this is inevitable and inescapable. But there remain very many houses for which the record is patchy, and it is here that serious problems of treatment arise. Since the more important the house, the better its documentation, there are compelling reasons for making the cut-off point fairly high.

Even if a high cut-off point were not imposed by the nature of the evidence, there are also strong historical reasons for such a decision. The inclusion of all the owners of the 437 houses in the sample would mean lumping together social groups which lived very different lives and had relatively little to do with one another. In the sixteenth and seventeenth centuries we find ourselves dealing with small "parish gentry," men whose property and influence were restricted to a single village, who almost never held the county offices of sheriff (which was still socially important at this period), Deputy Lieutenant, or Knight of the Shire in Parliament, and who only occasionally managed to get themselves put on to the Bench of Justices and then often more on account of their legal training than of their social status. The houses they lived in were appropriately small—E-shaped or oblong blocks consisting of the three basic units of a hall, offices, and withdrawing room, usually not more than 60 feet or so in frontage. In the late seventeenth and eighteenth centuries the social position of these minor gentry certainly did not improve, while their economic situation deteriorated as they were squeezed between stagnant rents and severe land taxes. Consequently the older families were exposed to attrition in their ranks as successful London merchants hastened to buy them out. Other new men bought modest estates and built themselves suitably modest villas, either as summer or weekend retreats within easy access of the city or as permanent places of retirement or residence. The process of converting farmhouses into country houses and villas was one which continued throughout the nineteenth century. The consequent proliferation of minor gentry or pseudo-gentry is hard to document statistically since no two contemporaries were able to agree upon where to draw the line. For example, 3 maps showing country houses in the eighteenth century marked 226 houses in 1700, 180 in 1740, and 138 in 1765. This might suggest to the unwary researcher a dramatic decline of the minor gentry in face of economic pressures, whereas in fact it only reflects the whimsical choice of the individual map makers. The first map, by H. Moll and published by Chauncy, clearly includes farmhouses which neither Chauncy nor anyone else thought worthy of mention in the text. The second, by Warburton and Bland, is a list of houses owned by persons sporting a coat of arms. At first sight this seems promising, until it is discovered that a number of the coats of arms are attached to town houses and name families otherwise unknown to the historians of the county, except possibly as the owners of manors long since separated from their houses. The third map, by Dury and Andrews, is on a huge scale, and marks at least as many houses as Chauncy, to only 138 of which are names attached. On inspection, there seems to be little or no logic behind the choice of houses to which these names are attached, and in any case the names are those of the residents and therefore includes many short-term tenants, so that it is not even comparable with the map of Warburton and Bland, which is mainly concerned with the owners of manors. It would be supererogatory to pursue the manifold objections to every conceivable listing of seats and owners which is available. Suffice it to say that no one listing is strictly comparable with any other, for the simple reason that no one has ever been able to set up clear rational criteria for inclusion or exclusion.

If the subject of study is the county elite and the country seats they inhabited and which offered visible proof of their political and social preeminence, it is necessary to draw the line a good deal higher. On the other hand any definition has to be modified slightly over time to account for changing social and economic circumstances. Lists of Justices of the Peace even in the sixteenth and seventeenth centuries omit some of the county elite and include many very minor gentry, while in the eighteenth and nineteenth centuries they are heavily diluted first by clerical and then by commercial and professional classes. Fortunately, however, although average house size increases steadily over the three and a half centuries under examination, the minimum size for convenient entertaining by a man of elite aspirations remains remarkably static.

What does change is the location of these houses. In the sixteenth century they were usually sited close to or on the edge of villages, with their grounds stretching away behind them into the fields. This is also true of houses built on monastic sites, some of which, like Hitchin Priory, were on the edge of towns. The main exceptions to this generalization for the early sixteenth century were houses in their own deer parks, but even in 1596 there were only 20 of these in the county.[23] Subsequently, however, the new-found taste for privacy, and the desire to be isolated from contact with social inferiors, resulted in more and more houses being built in the middle of nowhere, protected against the intrusion of the outside world by extensive grounds and parks, surrounded by high walls, and guarded by gates and lodgekeepers. By the early eighteenth century the number of walled parks had approximately doubled to around 40. During the eighteenth century this trend to isolation grew more and more pronounced as the elite tried to distinguish themselves from the *nouveaux riches*, who after about 1780 were establishing themselves in ever-increasing numbers in villas clustered on the outskirts of towns and villages. Those of the old elite who inherited ancient manor houses in villages tended to abandon them to little parish gentry and to move elsewhere.

[23] Norden, *Speculi Britanniae Pars.*

By 1800 the number of parks—no longer stocked with deer—had doubled again to 80, and by 1880 it had risen still further. The "great withdrawal" of the English elite from contact with the community often involved the diversion of public roads around the estate, for example at Panshanger, Shepalbury, or Edge Grove, and in exceptional cases (though none in Hertfordshire), in the total destruction and relocation of the village.[24]

The House Sample and the Owner Sample

This study is concerned with two closely related and at times overlapping fields of inquiry: the architectural history of a group of houses of a certain kind, with living quarters of above a certain size; their sequence of ownership and the relation of owners to houses; and the social history of some of their owners, who in turn constitute a group of men of a certain status, function, and power. It is therefore necessary to define very carefully and separately the criteria for inclusion of houses and owners into their respective samples. This is particularly important since in both cases it is necessary further to distinguish between the time span under consideration, according to whether houses and owners are being considered separately or in conjunction with each other. Thus a study of houses alone is only concerned with houses at times when they are over a minimum size, while a study of ownership patterns and purposes requires an earlier starting point in order to include purchase either of a smaller house to be enlarged or of an estate originally without a house. Similarly, when analyzing the group of owners in their role as houseowners, we are only concerned with them over the period during which they owned (or expected eventually to own) a house, whereas in a study of them as members of an elite their whole life span becomes relevant.

THE HOUSE SAMPLE

For a house to qualify for inclusion in the house sample it must fulfill *all* of the three following criteria:

i) *In size*, it must have a minimum of 50 units (as described below) of living space (i.e. excluding offices), which means a minimum, in the eighteenth and nineteenth centuries, of an entrance hall and 4 good-sized reception rooms, and for the earlier period a large hall *plus* 2 or 3 rooms providing much the same area of habitable space. It seems to be the case that although the average size of houses rises fairly steadily from 1540 to 1870, the minimum does not alter very greatly since there is an irreducible area of habitable space

[24] There are numerous applications for road diversion in Herts. R. O., Quarter Session Papers.

essential for the purposes of entertainment and display. The establishment of this minimum size effectively excludes the eighteenth- and nineteenth-century villas, which multiplied in luxuriant profusion in Hertfordshire, but which were designed for private domestic use rather than for public display and entertainment.[25]

ii) *In location*, it must stand in large grounds in the country, or on the outskirts of a town.

iii) *In possession*, it must belong to a man who *both*

a) inherits or acquires gentry status or above, and

b) uses the house as his main residence.

The only exception is that, provided that they fulfill criteria i) and ii), secondary houses are included in the sample of houses throughout if at some point they were used as the main seat.

Conversely, a house goes out of the sample:

i) If something happens to it (fire or partial demolition, etc.) which brings it below 50 units (though if it is a secondary house it may still figure for ownership purposes, but not for quantification of houses alone).

ii) If it is overwhelmed by urban expansion and becomes a town house. If it stands in large enough grounds to maintain its identity as a country seat, it still counts, even if, by the late nineteenth century it is enveloped by suburbia outside the walls (e.g. Hitchin Priory or Cassiobury).

iii) If it falls into the hands of

a) either the Crown or an institution; or

b) an owner or tenant below gentry status; or

c) if it is let by an absentee "owner not in sample" (see below) to a succession of tenants with no connection with the county.

All known houses which conform to these rules have been included, but there are a few which have had to be omitted since adequate documentation is not available for *both* houses and ownership. This has resulted in the exclusion of only 8 known houses, 2 of them because their sequence of ownership is missing. All of them are thought to be fairly marginal as to size, and most of them are nineteenth century in date.[26]

There are some 25 other houses marked on the Ordnance Survey of

[25] The differences in size and plan between a country house and a villa are well illustrated in J. Soane, *Plans of Buildings Executed in Several Counties* (London, 1788).

[26] Cumberlow, Edge Grove, Elmwood, Rossway, Serge Hill, Wallingfordbury, and Woodside.

the 1870s which by their ground plan seem to be possible candidates for inclusion in the sample. But they have been excluded since absolutely nothing else is known about either the houses themselves or their owners. This is partly due to the real insignificance of their owners in terms of status and local office, partly to the disappearance of some of the houses themselves by the time the *Victoria County History* was published in about 1900, owing to the rapid urbanization of the areas closest to London, and partly to the fact that in many cases—perhaps most—their apparent size is deceptive. In the Victorian period vast, gloomy, and rambling offices and servant quarters were stretched out over large areas of ground on a single floor, thus giving the impression of size on the scale maps which was belied by the modest proportions of the main living quarters of the family. These were therefore non-elite houses lived in by non-elite owners.

On the other hand, 12 poorly documented houses have been included in the sample, although the available evidence will hardly justify giving them 50 units at some period, usually in their early years. Of these 12, only 2 are thought to have failed at any time to reach or exceed 60 units, both of which stood in very large grounds, and one of which was a secondary house.[27] All the remaining 10 are almost certainly underassessed in their early years because of lack of documentation. Three of them were over 60 units by the time of the first Hearth Tax returns of 1662, which represents the nearest we can get to a good idea of their size at this time and one other for which we have no Hearth Tax, had exceeded 60 units by 1700.[28] Two are only rated at 11 hearths each in the Hearth Tax, but seem from other evidence to have been considerably larger.[29] This underrating may be a factor of age, early or mid-sixteenth-century houses tending to have a different distribution pattern of hearths from that of later houses. Three are not identifiable in the Hearth Tax returns while one lies in a parish for which the returns are missing.[30] All of these houses share the common disadvantage of having been pulled down (or totally engulfed in a major rebuilding) and only being known by one often fragmentary illustration or description, as a result of which they have been given the minimum units which this inadequate data will allow.

[27] Carpenders Park and Marchmont House.

[28] Aldenham Manor House, Bayford Place, Digswell, and Beechwood.

[29] Albury and Goldings.

[30] Gubbins, Little Court, Popes, and Stagenhoe.

Thus 8 houses are omitted for gross lack of information, and 12 are included because it is believed that inadequacy of documentation has resulted in their underassessment. These decisions are subjective and have to be accepted as the most reasonable that can be arrived at. The net result is a total sample of 151 houses extant at some period or another between 1540 and 1879.

THE OWNER SAMPLE

Owners are divided into two categories, only one of which, "Owners in sample" is subject to statistical analysis.

i) "Owners in sample." For a man to qualify for inclusion as an "Owner in sample," he must fulfill all of the three following criteria:

a) he must be of gentry status or above, by inheritance or acquisition;

b) he must own outright, or on long lease (i.e. a lease of 30 years or more) a house in the house sample;

c) he must either i) live mainly in the house, or ii) give some evidence of interest in the county. This can take the form either (1) of service as sheriff, active J.P. or local M.P. or (2) of responsibility for an addition or alteration to the house, even if his involvement in the locality is not otherwise recorded.

The justification for the admission of this last criterion, which is involved in only one case (that of Sir Robert Beachcroft at Gubbins), is that an addition or alteration, or a grandiose landscaping operation—which often precedes house-building or aggrandisement—can be taken as evidence of aspirations to become a resident country gentleman. Every known owner responsible for a building event is included in the sample.

It should be emphasized that in view of the basic proviso that an owner must live in a house of a certain kind and size, and in view of the known lack of correlation of elite status with local office-holding, the mere presence of a name in a list of sheriffs, active J.P.s or M.P.s is never a sufficient cause for inclusion in the sample; nor is it a necessary cause, except in the case of men (usually newcomers to the county) whose main base is or has been elsewhere—in the case of Hertfordshire, mostly Londoners.

In practice, the criteria established for inclusion of houses in the house sample, particularly as regards size and location, make for inclusion in the sample of owners of all known gentry and above who live in large houses, and all known baronets and above who live in medium or large houses, so long as their dates of ownership and the houses they lived in are reasonably well-documented.

ii) Owners not in sample. These consist of:

a) houseowners who are recorded for the purpose of maintaining historical continuity of the house but whose inclusion would have distorted the quantification of owners, since they do not fulfill all three owner criteria. These are people who either fulfill all criteria but are excluded on the grounds of infancy (died under age) or idiocy; or would qualify under criteria ia) and ib) but fail to fulfill criterion ic), their main base being a larger seat elsewhere and their involvement in the county in question being insufficient either to induce them to take any part in local affairs, or to make any alterations or additions to the house.

b) those institutions or men of non-gentry status who either sold or bequeathed property to an "Owner in sample" or were themselves the cause for taking a house out of the sample.

Sequences of ownership are much better documented than sequences of buildings, especially when, as in the majority of cases, we are dealing with manorial property, for which there is a wealth of printed sources. But a few houses were never attached to manors, and as time goes on an increasing number get separated from their manors by independent purchase and sale. Had it not been possible to fill most of the lacunae from ancillary evidence, the history of these non-manorial houses would have been extremely difficult to reconstruct. Even so, the ownership sequence of 6 houses is incomplete in one particular: the first owner/builder of Bonningtons, Danesbury, and Goldings, and 2 owners of a lease at Beechwood are identified on the basis of circumstantial evidence rather than known facts. The Crown lessee who altered Ashridge to make it habitable in 1578 and the residents at Belmont over a hundred-year span when it is assumed to have been on long lease, are altogether unknown.

If these rigorous tests are applied to create a universe of elite owners living in elite houses, what relation does the result bear to the more traditional ways of defining a local upper-gentry class? The inadequacy of local office-holding without corroborative evidence from other angles as the acid test of an elite status is best shown by the fluctuations in the proportion of office-holders who figure in the owner sample. In the sixteenth century the office of sheriff was almost wholly filled by "owners." During the reign of James I, there is a puzzling temporary intrusion of lesser men into the office and an understandable run of minor figures during the revolutionary years of the Interregnum (see Fig. 5). As early as the end of the sixteenth century the very high cost of the office was acting as a severe deterrent even to the wealthy, and many leading gentry were extremely anxious to avoid it, some going to the extent of offering bribes to be let off. Soon after the Restoration, Thomas Fuller described it as an "onus sine honore . . . , great persons by friends and favor easily escaping."[31] As a result, the status of the holders of the office declined sharply after 1680. By the early eighteenth century the proportion of sheriffs in the sample reached an all-time low of under 40 per cent. The office did not recover its prestige until the 1830s, by which time it had lost all but its formal functions, but had picked up those conspicuously honorific functions, which it carries today.

If even the office of sheriff is not a consistently reliable indicator of elite status as we have defined it, still less is the office of Justice of the Peace, whose social composition was always very much wider.[32] Total numbers on the bench rose fairly steadily from 25 in 1558 to over 40 in 1608, falling back to the low 30s in the 1620s and 1630s. They shot up to about 60 during the Interregnum, and stayed at that level until the evidence runs out in 1685 (see Fig. 6). Before 1640 well over 60 per cent of the Justices of the Peace are in the sample, but the number falls sharply to less than 40 per cent during the Interregnum (see Fig. 7). The postwar conservative reaction of the early 1660s drove it up again to unprecedented heights of social exclusiveness, with almost 80 per cent in the owner sample in 1662, but this was only a temporary situation. The proportion in the sample stays close to 60 per cent until the end of the seventeenth century, but it falls steadily all through the eighteenth century to 45 per cent, and then

[31] *Historical Manuscripts Commission, Salisbury MSS*, VIII, pp. 416, 464; X, 383, 386; XI, 486, 495, 498, 583; XII, 469, 496, 497; XVII, 332, 478, 519, 542; XVIII, 338, 339, 345, 348. *Calendar of State Papers Domestic, 1603-10*, p. 551. T. Fuller, *The Worthies of England* (London, 1662), p. 45.

[32] Sessions Books only include the Justices of the Peace who happen to get their names recorded in the Books, though there is reason to think that this listing includes virtually all the active members of the Bench. It omits those who, although nominally holding the office of Justice, did not in fact perform any of the functions of the office. These "sleepers" include out-of-county peers and politicians who were on the list mostly as a matter of courtesy, inactive in the county, and also prominent people in the owner sample who were too grand, or too preoccupied with national affairs, or too mobile in their residential habits, to bother with the local administration of justice. "Owners in sample" are taken to include sons of owners. For sheriffs after 1850 the graph includes in dotted lines the few men who would be in the owner sample if only something were known about the houses in which they lived.

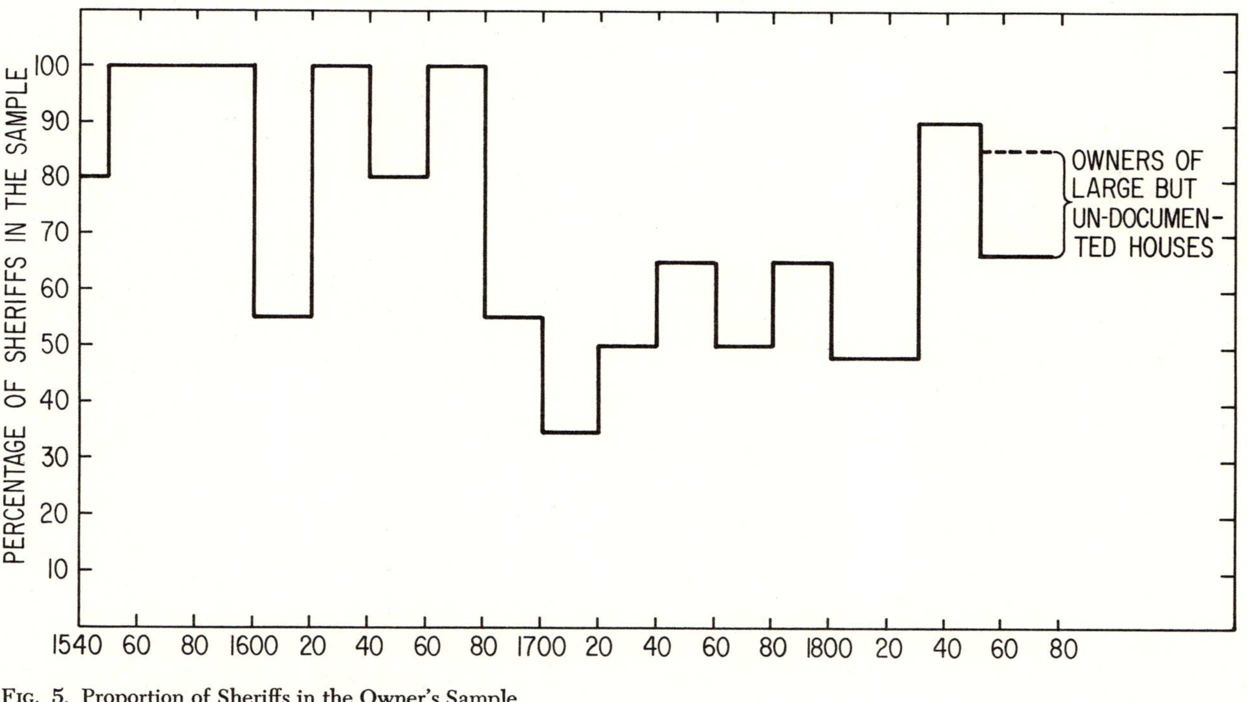

FIG. 5. Proportion of Sheriffs in the Owner's Sample

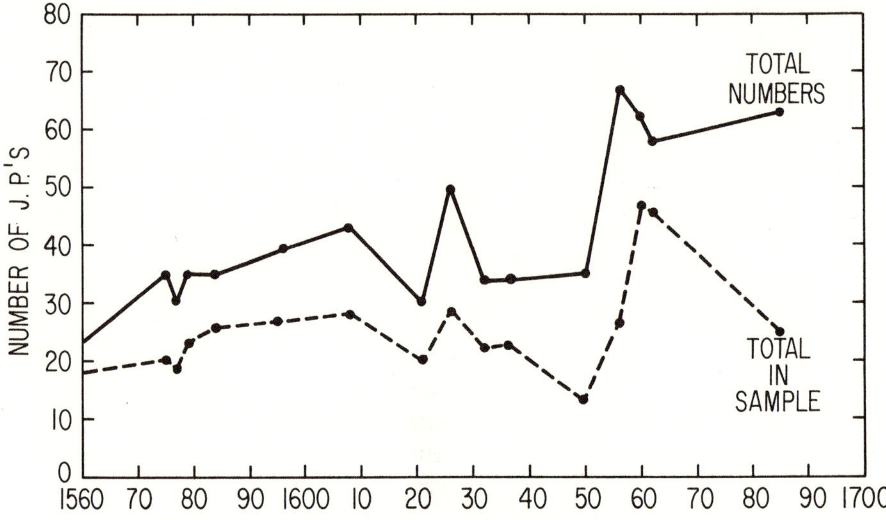

FIG. 6. Count of the Justices of the Peace in the *Libri Pacis*

drops again precipitously to the nineteenth century level of about 30 per cent.

An important cause of this fall is first the remarkable growth of clerical Justices in the late eighteenth and early nineteenth centuries, and secondly the later growth of urban and professional men in the mid- to late nineteenth century. The proportion of clergy among active Justices rose from zero in the sixteenth century to 2 per cent between 1635 and 1699 to 25 per cent between 1752 and 1799 and finally reached a peak of 33 per cent between 1800 and 1833 (see Fig. 8). Thereafter the clerical surge into lay administration subsided, falling back to 16 per cent in the 1850s and 4 per cent in the 1870s.[33] The graph of the rise and fall of clergy actively participating in the Hertfordshire Bench of Justices illustrates the secular trend of wealth, prestige, and political influence of the profession. In the late eight-

[33] The figures are taken from three sources: the *Libri Pacis* or lists of magistrates, from which there has to be eliminated the purely honorific presence of names of noblemen and leading politicians; Appendices A in Vols. VI-X of the *Hertfordshire County Records, Sessions Books*, which list those magistrates who are mentioned in the Quarter Sessions Books, 1624-1843, which means those who were active on the Bench over a given period of time; and two printed lists of magistrates of 1861 and 1887, which are in fact composite lists of all men appointed to the Bench over a long period of time running back some 20 years, and which include large numbers of purely honorific appointments. The latter are useful since they take care to distinguish active from honorary membership, and form an independent check on the Sessions Books.

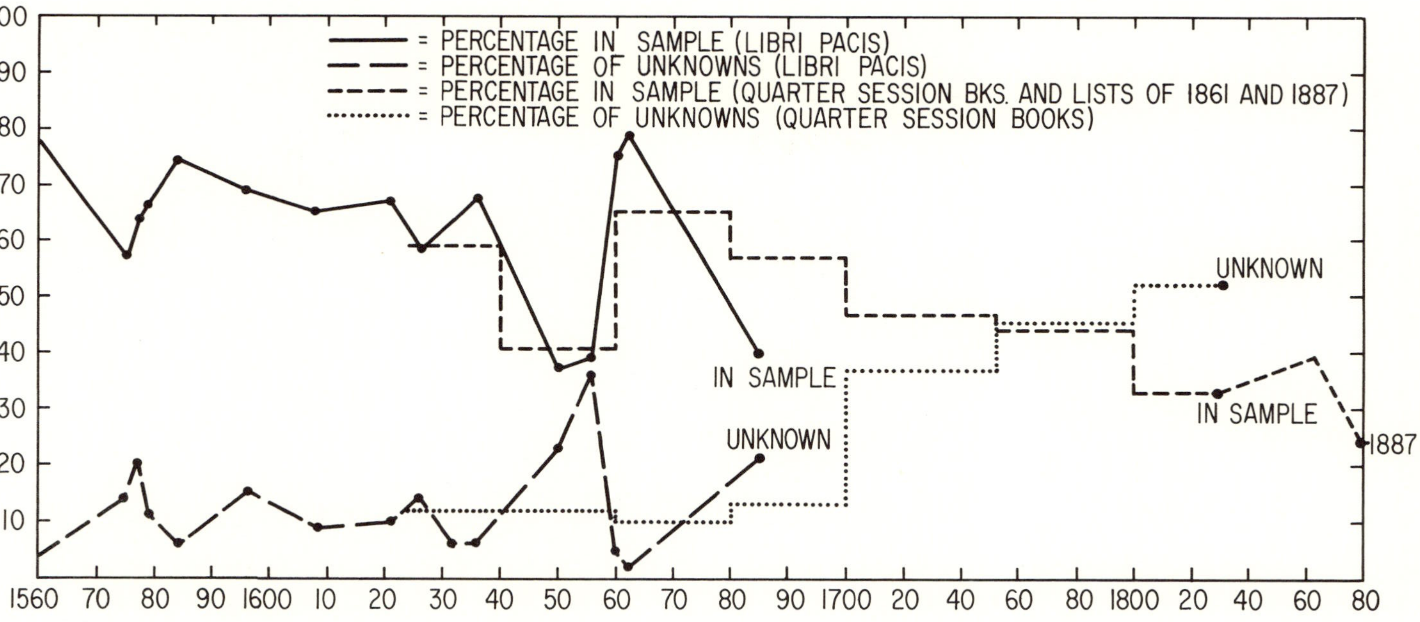

FIG. 7. Proportions of Justices of the Peace in the Owner Sample, and Unknowns

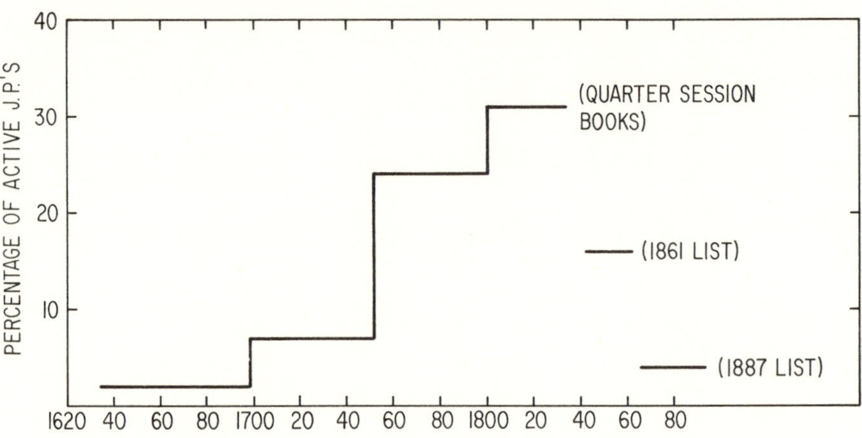

FIG. 8. Proportion of Clergy Among Active Justices of the Peace

eenth and early nineteenth centuries, the clergy rose to a position not much inferior to that of the lesser gentry (from which many of them sprang) only to decline in the nineteenth century in the face of the aggressive thrust of other professional groups and a rising bourgeoisie.

Before 1700 the proportion of Justices who, although not members of the elite, nevertheless lived in identifiable country houses, however modest, never fell much below 90 per cent. In other words, the Bench remained overwhelmingly gentry in composition, even if the elite of the county was being diluted with lesser men. Thereafter, however, because of the trickle of wealthy townspeople, especially from Hertford and Saint Albans, and also the flood of clergy, the local gentry never again comprised more than two-thirds of the active Bench of Justices in Hertfordshire.

It should be pointed out that by cutting the sample off at this point the elite of landowners is fairly effectively defined, but no light is shed either on the movement of lesser merchants, lawyers, and office-holders into the county by the purchase of a small estate and the erection of a small family house, or on the transfer of property by purchase and sale at this lower level. It is probable that both movements took place at a different rhythm than those affecting the elite properties only. For example, it can be demonstrated statistically that there is a clear correlation between the size of the estate in the county and the speed of transfer by purchase (see Fig. 9); the larger the estate, the more likely it is to pass by inheritance only, the smaller

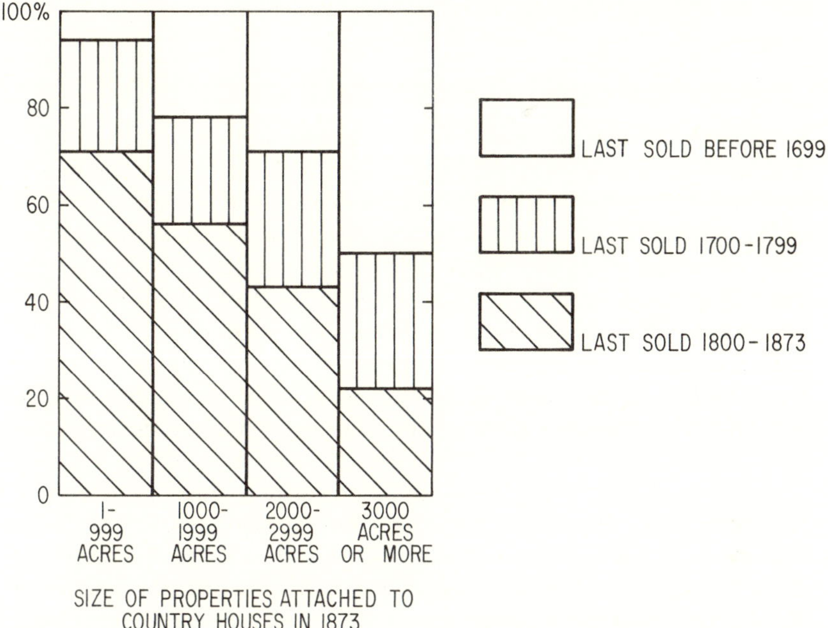

Fig. 9. Transfers of Houses by Purchase and Sale Related to Property Size in 1573

the estate the more likely it is to appear on the market.[34] The second variable which affected the speed of transfer of houses by purchase and sale is thought to be whether or not they were associated with manors. Houses on non-manorial property appear to have been far more skittish than those with manors, especially in the sixteenth and seventeenth centuries, and again in the nineteenth, when consider-

[34] The following table is based on *The Returns of Owners of Land, 1873* collated with data or sales taken mainly from the various county histories.

Transfers of Houses by Purchase and Sale Related to Property Size

	Size of Properties in Hertfordshire Attached to Houses							
	Under 1,000a.		*1,000-1,999a.*		*2,000-2,999a.*		*Over 3,000a.*	
Date of Last Sale	*No.*	*Per Cent*	*No.*	*Per Cent*	*No.*	*Per Cent*	*No.*	*Per Cent*
Before 1699	5	6	7	22	4	28	7	50
1700-99	18	23	7	22	4	28	4	28
1800-79	55	71	18	56	6	43	3	22
Total	78		32		14		14	—

able social prestige seems to have been attached to being a lord of a manor.[35]

THE OWNER SAMPLE AND LANDED SOCIETY IN 1663

Introduction. At one point in time, in one segment of the county, it is possible first to test the degree to which the owner sample is representative of the elite of the landed classes, and secondly to check on the reliability of the various other sources of evidence that can be used to make such a selection. This opportunity is provided by the survival of a list, hereafter called the Verulam List, of all those persons who in 1663 were assessed on their estates within the Hundreds of Cashio and Dacorum for the supplying of horses for military service.[36] These two Hundreds make up about one-third of the county and include the whole western section.[37] In all respects but one this area was fairly typical of the county as a whole. The exception, which is a very important one, was that before the Reformation these two western Hundreds were dominated by the Church, particularly the great monastery of Saint Albans, whose possessions included the whole of Cashio Hundred and much more besides. As a result, the impact of the dissolution of the monasteries on this area was quite exceptional and is reflected in the sample as a whole: of houses which were built on the site of, or were conversions of, houses seized from the Church, no less than 76 per cent (13 out of a total of 17) were in these two western Hundreds. Conversely, of the 13 houses of 55 units or more in the sample in 1540 which had been in lay occupancy since before the Reformation, only 3 lay in these Hundreds. Within ten years this disproportion had been made up, and indeed the rate of expansion continued to be swifter than for the county as a whole until about 1580. The void left by the Dissolution was filled by an influx of largely self-made men, the vast majority of whom had no previous connection with the county. This influx clearly upset the existing, already fragile, social superstructure, and by 1610, all three families whose estates antedated the dissolution had moved away to other counties. As a result, there lacked any strong local tradition of rule by a landowning class, both because for centuries the Church had been the chief landowner and because at the Dissolution what there was of an old

[35] Unfortunately it is often not possible to establish a clear connection between house and manor over the long haul, so that this hypothesis cannot be demonstrated statistically. It remains a hunch.

[36] *Historical Manuscripts Commission, Verulam MSS*, 1906, pp. 102-05.

[37] The only exception is the parish of Totteridge which belonged to Broadwater Hundred. There were also 5 outlying pockets of varying size, the only large one being formed by the parishes of Codicote and Saint Paul's Walden.

lay elite was displaced by a group of men who had little experience of ruling at this level, since the majority were either city-bred or very minor gentry. In any case, most of them were more interested in national than local affairs. This means that within this area the local power structure tended to go by default to lesser men, both in terms of wealth and breeding, than was the case in other parts of the county.

Since the evidence in the manuscript is confined to owners of land with a minimum rental of £100 a year, two large social groups are automatically excluded. These are rich men, predominantly townsmen, whose wealth was not primarily in land, and the large mass of those whose rental income was either too low or nonexistent. At the opposite end of the spectrum another tiny group is excluded, namely English peers, who were taxed elsewhere. There were only two in Cashio and Dacorum at this time, the Earls of Essex and Bridgwater, but their wealth was of such a different order of magnitude from that of other landowners in the area that their exclusion is more of a help than a hindrance.

The manuscript can be dated from internal evidence to the early part of 1663 and contains 118 names. With three exceptions, each name is followed by the parishes in which land is held, an estimate of the rental *per annum*, and the tax assessment. This information can be correlated, supplemented, and compared with that in other lists or sets of lists dealing with taxable income, social status, and local office-holding.[38]

The Contents of the List. For purposes of analysis, the 118 landowners in the list have been divided into four main rental categories (see Table 1). Only 15 out of the 118 cannot be identified at all, and all of them figure in the lowest income categories. Eighty-five were resident in Cashio and Dacorum, 55 of them in known houses; another 4 were clergymen, who may or may not have been resident, and must have been assessed on the basis of their Rectory or Vicarage lands. There are also 2 major landowners in the sample whose base was outside the two Hundreds, and another 4 persons whose residence in Hertfordshire is not clear, though their property connection is known or presumed. The list includes 7 identifiable Londoners (3 of them with known local connections) and 7 women, of whom the 5 that can be identified were widows, presumably assessed on their jointure lands if the heir was of age, or on the family property as the guardians of a minor. It should be borne in mind that the tax assessment is based on holdings in only two Hundreds and as a result in-

[38] This task was greatly helped by the work done by Mrs. Barbara Rothblatt in identifying names on the early Subsidy Lists.

cludes in its lower income categories, along with genuine small local men, a few magnates from further afield.

The Tax Assessments. The total extant rental of £24,538 on the Verulam List was reckoned capable of producing 48 horses, £500 in rental being taken as the equivalent of one horse in taxation.[39] Those with rentals below £500 were grouped together, usually with near neighbors, to make up a total of £500 or so for one horse. In the same way a man with a rental of £750 would be paired with one with a rental of £250 and the pair taxed for two horses. Between the £518

TABLE 1. RENTAL CATEGORIES

Rental (in £)	*Total Population*	*In Sample*	*Per Cent in Sample in 1663*	*Later in Sample*	*Unknown*	*Total Rental (in £)*	*Average Rental in Cashio and Dacorum (in £)*
500-1,600	16†	12	75	1	1¶	7,378§	614§
250-375	23	6	26			6,558	286
130-220	33	3	9	1	6	5,439	164
100-125	46	4‡	8		9	5,163	112
TOTAL	118	25	39	2	16	24,538	213

† Including 4 with no stated rental.[40]
‡ Including 2 whose residence and main holdings were in other Hundreds.
¶ Fairly firmly identified through her ownership of manors (see below).
§ Calculated on the basis only of the 12 whose income is stated.

and £700 mark there is a group of 7 people who are only taxed for 1 horse each and who therefore come off fairly lightly. The curious feature of this group is that 6 of them supported Parliament during the Civil War and might have expected to be overtaxed by their Royalist enemies, whereas in fact they are the only ones among the whole 118 who are undertaxed (with the exception of 2 people with rentals of £300 who together were assessed for 1 horse). There is no means of checking the reliability of the rentals given, but on the other hand there seems no point in an overestimate of the rental if this was to be followed by an underassessment of the tax, so it seems reasonable to assume that if not wholly correct the rental estimates at least approxi-

[39] These figures take account of the 3 horses assessed without rental. The number of horses adds up to 51, to which should be added between 2 and 4 more.

[40] All persons whose annual rental was £ 500 or over have an entry to themselves. Two persons have no rental but are assessed at 1 and 2 horses respectively; 2 more have no rental and no assessment, but since they have separate entries they must have been meant to be assessed at either 1 or 2 horses. All 4 are well known from other sources and 3 of them are in sample.

mate to the truth. One must conclude that as late as 1662-1663 the local authorities were being very cautious indeed in their handling of the not inconsiderable number of ex-Parliamentarian notables in the county. The tax burdens of the early 1660s are therefore likely to be especially fairly assessed.

If one takes into consideration the complexities of grouping those taxed together according to the place of their main holdings, the 1663 assessment seems a far cry from the inefficiency and gross favoritism displayed in the late sixteenth- and early seventeenth-century subsidy lists, which virtually ignored everyone at the top of the scale and bore down on those at the bottom. The difference is clearly shown in a comparison of the treatment meted out in these earlier assessments to the forebears of men in the Verulam List, according to whether or not they also figure in the sample.[41] Of 16 who were taxed in 1588, or in 1593, or in both years, only 4 are in sample; but the sample includes another 8, fully as rich if not richer, who were not taxed in either year, although their descendants became taxpayers in 1663. Although in the subsidy of 1625 more people were being taxed, in a less haphazard way, the main burden was still being borne by the yeomen and lesser gentry, and it still includes only 4 men from an, by then, enlarged sample. By way of contrast the Verulam List includes all members of the sample below the rank of English peer, which clearly reflects the efficiency and fairness in tax assessment which was a product of the pressures of Civil War.

A comparison between the Hearth Tax assessments and the Verulam List suffers from two limitations, in that residents of houses below 10 hearths were not noted when the returns were consulted in connection with the main sample, and that there are too many lacunae in the returns for Cashio and Dacorum for one to be able to argue *ex silentio* that all those whose names do not figure as residents of houses of 10 hearths and above necessarily lived in houses of less than 10 hearths. Thus, of houses in Cashio and Dacorum in the main sample, 2 are wholly missing, 1 is illegible, 1 is only available for 1672 when it had been partly pulled down, and 2 are only tentatively identified. In all these cases other data are available as to their size, which is why they figure in the main sample.

The most that can be done, therefore, is to get a rough idea of the difference between houses known to be lived in by people in tax categories I, and those in tax categories II, III, and IV (see Table 2). The average number of hearths of houses has been worked out by

[41] Cussans, *History of Hertfordshire*, II (i), pp. 157 and xx 160 ss.

counting as 11 hearths all those houses known to be over 10 hearths but missing in the return, and counting as 9 hearths all those houses which were not noted since they were below 10. It must be recognized that the former is certainly a gross underestimate and the latter probably a serious overestimate. As a result, the average tends to downgrade the larger houses and upgrade the smaller ones, so that any remaining difference must be very real.

TABLE 2. THE HEARTH TAX AND THE VERULAM LIST

Rental (in £)	Verulam List	Identifiable Domicile No.	Identifiable Domicile Percentage	Assessed in H.T. at 10+	Known from Other Sources to be 10+	Average No. of Hearths in Houses Taxed in H.T. as 10+
I. 500-1,600	16	16	100	12	2	23
II. 250-375	23	14	60	4	4	16
III. 130-220	33	15	45	6	1	12
IV. 100-125	46	13	28	6		15

The declining percentage of identifiable domiciles according to each category helps explain the unreliability of averages lower down the scale. But the difference in the number of hearths between the first and the other three categories is sufficiently large, particularly in view of the built-in tendency of the method of calculation to reduce differences, to suggest that there is a very clear social cleavage at about the £500 level in terms of life style. This greatly strengthens the argument for selecting the main sample in terms of ownership of houses above a certain size.

Manorial Ownership. Of the 57 owners of manors in Cashio and Dacorum at this time, 49 figure on the Verulam List and 6 do not figure on any known list and seem to be obscure men owning manorial titles either without land or with a rental below £100. Of the remaining 2 manorial owners, 1 was a minor whose known holdings correspond very closely to those of the only otherwise unidentifiable major landowner. She was a married woman, and it seems reasonable to assume that she was his mother and guardian (and therefore taxed in his name) who had remarried outside the county. The other, though technically resident in Cashio, lived in an enclave within Hitchin Hundred, where the bulk of his lands lay and where he must have been taxed, to judge by the way others were taxed whose lands were similarly situated.

At the top of the socio-economic scale, ownership of at least one manor, preferably near one's place of residence, was clearly still mandatory, while the lower one descends the income scale, the less important it seems to be (see Table 3). It is difficult to get a correct perspective on this subject since the bulk of the information is almost exclusively concerned with the transfer of manors, which are titles to legal rights which in this area were no longer necessarily attached to

TABLE 3. MANORIAL OWNERS AND THE VERULAM LIST

Rental (in £)	*Verulam List*	*Owned 1 or more Manors*	*Percentage Holding Manorial Property*
500-1,600	16	16	100
250-373	23	17	74
130-220	33	15	45
100-125	46	9	19

land. By the Restoration, the lordship of a manor may mean little save ownership of the manorial pew in the parish church and the attendant responsibility for the upkeep of the chancel. If these luxuries were available elsewhere, or were not deemed indispensable, a man might be content with a comfortable non-manorial estate in Hertfordshire. If he was a landed gentleman, he might be indifferent because his main base was in another, manorial, estate further afield; if he were a Londoner, he might be indifferent because his Hertfordshire house was merely a rustic retreat from the realities of life in London; or lastly, he might be indifferent because he was an agricultural entrepreneur primarily interested in farming, who would have few illusions as to his chances of success in attempting to climb the social ladder within the county where his business lay. The common feature of all three is their indifference to the trappings of status within the local community.

On the Verulam List there figure 7 men who did not own any manors in Hertfordshire but about whose non-manorial holdings something is known. Apart from 2 properties acquired by yeomen in the 1550s all are seventeenth-century acquisitions, 3 during the Civil War. None figure in the 1572 or 1634 Visitations, and the only 1 of the 7 who bothered to claim arms in the 1669 Visitation was a Saint Albans man who had made good in the City and established his main base in a manor in Kent. Another, the son of a London merchant, was to purchase more land and build himself a house, but he and his descendants seem to have remained essentially London-based. Both of these men come into the lower reaches of the sample. All seem to have been at least reasonably well-to-do, and the 6 whose residence we know about lived in modest to good-sized houses on the outer fringes of villages and towns. If these are the kind of people who have been described as "pseudo-gentry," the term appears somewhat inapposite. If they are occasionally confused with the gentry proper, this seems to be due less to efforts at protective social coloration on their own part as to a distorted vision on the part of historians owing to the nature of surviving documents. They themselves do not seem to have had such aspirations, if we are to judge from their indifference to status symbols such as the ownership of a manor.

Duration of Settlement in Hertfordshire. For 63 of the 118 individuals on the Verulam List the date is known at which at least some of their property, manorial and non-manorial, last changed hands by sale before 1663 (see Table 4). The extraordinary impact of the

TABLE 4. DATE OF LAST PURCHASE
(numbers and percentages of rental categories)

1663 Rental (in £)	*pre-1500*		*1500-49*		*1550-99*		*1600-49*		*1650-63*		*Total*		*Later Sold*	
	No.	*%*	*No.*	*%*	*No.*	*%*	*No.*	*%*	*No.*	*%*	*No.*	*%*	*No.*	*%*
500-1,600			6	37	2	12	5	31	3	19	16	100		
250-375	1	6	3	17	3	17	10	59			17	100	4	6
130-220	1	5	2	10	6	32	6	32	4	21	19	100	1	1
100-125					6	54	3	27	2	18	11	100	1	1
TOTAL	2	3	11	16	17	24	24	34	9	13	63	100	6	8

Dissolution in this area is reflected in Table 4. That continuous ownership of only 3 per cent of properties antedates 1500 is due to the fact that the few old-established gentry families had cleared out by 1610, as already noted. Of more general interest is the fact that of the 11 who acquired property between 1500 and 1549 over half were in the top rental category. In view of the very short time span (13 years instead of 50) the period of greatest activity was the last, from 1650 to 1663, which saw a great many changes at the top and the bottom of the economic scale. Like the unusual burst of house construction at the same period, which will be noted for Hertfordshire county as a whole, and which indeed it reflects, this spate of purchases is probably not typical of the country as a whole.

Table 5 illustrates very clearly how at different periods different classes of buyers dominated the market. There is a marked difference between the highest, who mostly acquired their estates in the early sixteenth or the early and mid-seventeenth centuries; the lowest, who

TABLE 5. DATE OF LAST PURCHASES
(percentages in each time period)

Rental (in £)	*pre-1500*	*1500-49*	*1550-99*	*1600-49*	*1650-63*
500-1,600	0	54	12	21	33
250-375	50	27	17	41	0
130-220	50	18	35	25	44
100-125	0	0	35	12	22
TOTAL	100	100	100	100	100

acquired their property mostly in the Elizabethan period; and the next to highest, whose acquisitive period was largely confined to the early seventeenth century. The wealthy, mainly office-holding, elite dug in during the period of the dispersion of monastic properties and received a transfusion of new recruits from the London business world in the seventeenth century. The lowest category of small landowners built up their estates by acquiring land sold off, often piecemeal, by the less successful among the original purchasers of ex-monastic property. The moderately large landowners consolidated their estates in the early seventeenth century, either by amalgamating properties of smaller men or by moving in directly with a fortune amassed in London.

Sixteen of the 63 individuals concerned trace their property holdings through inheritance by women, some of which go back to the early sixteenth century. It may be significant of a general trend toward smaller families and higher death rates that 5 of them were the husbands and another 2 the sons of heiresses or coheiresses—in other words that almost half the failures of the male line recorded in these property transactions over a 150-year period occur in the 40 years before 1663.

Table 6 indicates that 7 out of the 16 men in the wealthiest category were new men who had personally acquired their property. From a comparison with Table 4 it is clear that the buying phase went back to the period of 1600-1649 and was not a recent phenomenon. To the 19 purchasers in the Verulam List should be added two others who acquired their property by inheritance or marriage but also enlarged their holdings with additional purchases. Nine of these 21 had some previous connection with Hertfordshire, but no fewer than 12 are

TABLE 6. ACQUISITION BY INHERITANCE, MARRIAGE, OR PURCHASE

Rental (in £)	*Direct Inheritors*		*Acquired by Marriage*		*Purchasers*		*Total*	
	No.	*%*	*No.*	*%*	*No.*	*%*	*No.*	*%*
500-1,600	9†	14			7	11	16	25
250-375	13	20	1†	1	3	5	17	27
130-220	12	19	2	3	5	8	19	30
100-125	6	9	1	1	4	6	11	17
TOTAL	40	63	4	6	19	30	63	

† One of whom also purchased additional property.

known to have made their fortune in London. Some, of course, belong to both categories, but only 5 do not belong to either, so far as is known. Newcomers to the landed classes were mostly either rich migrants from London, some of whom were originally from Hertfordshire, the husbands of local heiresses, or local men, often in the professions. The 5 lawyers in Table 7 consisted of the Speaker of the

TABLE 7. OCCUPATION OF PURCHASERS

Rental (in £)	*Lawyers*	*Merchants*	*Merchants' Sons*	*Office-Holders*	*Landed*	*Not Known*	*Total*
500-1,600	2	3	2		1		8
250-275	2	1				1	4
130-220	1	1	1	1		1	5
100-125		2		1		1	4
TOTAL	5	7	3	2	1	3	21

House, 2 conveyancers, and 2 legal officers in the city; these last 2 do not seem to have been resident. Of the 5 merchants or merchant's sons in the top rental category, there were 4 baronets (if we include one who became one in 1665). They were still mostly men whose main interest was in overseas trade, but at least one of them was a government financier. The office-holders were rather different in kind, the one in the bottom category being a very minor royal servant, the other a rather more important personage with extensive estates in Bedfordshire. It is very much a sign of the times that office-holders, who a hundred years before formed the bulk of the wealthiest self-made men, had now been quite displaced by merchants, followed at a still respectful distance by lawyers.

Social Status. Table 8 shows a close correlation between rental income and titular rank at the higher levels. Although Esquires all

TABLE 8. SOCIAL STATUS

Rental (in £)	*Irish Peer*	*Bart.*	*Knight*	*Esq.*	*Gent.*	*Mr*	*No Label*	*D.D.*	*M.D.*	*Women*	*Total*
500-1,600	1†	7	3	4		1				1	16
250-373			1	13		7		1		1	23
130-220				10	2	7	12	1		1	33
100-125	1†	1†	3†	3	3	17	13‡		1	4	46
TOTAL	1	8	7	30	5	32	25	2	1	7	118

† Main base outside the two Hundreds.
‡ One of whom was later knighted.

seem to be armigerous, the same is true of only 1 out of the 5 gentlemen, while at least 5 of the 32 "Mr" and 3 of the 25 with no label at all appeared in the 1634 Visitations.[42] The list is not much help in explaining why some persons are called Gent., some "Mr" and others nothing at all. It may be worth noting, however, that the designation "Mr" seems to be used in two ways: specifically, of lawyers; and more generally, as a vague attribute, the logic behind which is elusive, given to some merchants, some parish clergy, and a very few yeomen.

Any attempt to compare the list with the Heraldic Visitations raises the question of how far the latter are a useful guide to social acceptability. Below the heading "Gardiner of Thundridgebury" and a description of arms and crest, the 1634 Visitation bluntly states: "These Arms and Crest . . . do not belong to this man." If that is the case, it must follow that in some cases presence in the Visitation is proof of aspiration to gentility rather than of gentility itself. On the other hand, absence from a Visitation seems to spring not merely from unsuitability or indifference, but sometimes from the possession either of a blazon originally registered with the Heralds in another county or of one of great antiquity. No firm evidence either way can be deduced from either

[42] *The Visitations of Hertfordshire 1542 and 1634*, ed. Walter C. Metcalfe, *Harleian Soc.*, XXII (1886).

presence or absence on a Visitation Return, so there is not much to be gained from any attempt to correlate the Verulam List with the Visitations. The most that can be said is that the Visitation of 1572 contains the names of three families one or more of whose descendants figure on the Verulam List, that of 1634 contains 28, and that of 1669, 18.[43] What is not at all clear is why 2 appear in all three Visitations, and why 10 appear in both 1634 and 1669. These figures do not seem to do much more than bear eloquent testimony to the greater diligence of Sir Richard St. George, who was responsible for the 1634 Visitation, as compared with his successor, Sir Edward Bysshe in 1669; but this should come as no surprise if the latter's lackadaisical Visitation of Oxfordshire in the same year was at all typical of his methods.[44]

Local Office-Holding. Table 9 lists all the offices known to have been held at various times up to 1663 by the men who figure on the Verulam List. Since 1 person could have held up to 2 or 3 offices in

TABLE 9. LOCAL OFFICE-HOLDING[45]

Rental (in £)	*M.P.*	*M.P. Inter-regnum Only*	*J.P.*	*J.P. Inter-regnum Only*	*Sheriff*	*Minor Offices*	*Total Offices*	*Total Officers*	*Population*
I. 500-1,600	4	2	7	1	3	1	18	12	15
II. 250-375	1	1	7	4	2	4	18	9	22
III. 130-220	1		7	2		7	17	12	33
IV. 100-125	1		6	2	1†	7	17	14	41
TOTAL	7	3	27	9	6	19	70	47	111

† Widow.

the course of his career, the table gives both the total number of offices held and of officers in the 4 rental categories. It confirms that by the Restoration local offices are no longer an exclusive prerogative of the elite. The Bench of Justices is now drawn from a much wider social spectrum than was the case earlier, particularly in the years immediately preceding the Civil War, and it is interesting to note that

[43] College of Arms, London, MS, D. 28.

[44] *The Life and Times of Anthony Wood . . .*, ed. Andrew Clark (Oxford, 1892), II, 152.

[45] Any discrepancy between the population on this table and other ones arises from the exclusion of women (except in the case of a woman whose former husband was a known office-holder) and peers. The names of minor office-holders come from *Calendar of Sessions Books . . .*, ed. William Le Hardy (Hertford, 1928-30), V and VI *passim.*

the minor office of county treasurer for hospitals and maimed soldiers and to a lesser extent that of chief constable of a Hundred, which were usually held for only one year, seem to have been used as a testing ground for possible recruits in the lower ranks of the Bench. Four of the 5 treasurers and one of the 12 chief constables on the list went on to serve as Justices, so that it is reasonable to conclude that service at this fairly lowly level was at least an indication of willingness to be part of the county establishment. The number of M.P.s fairly low on the rental scale is explained by the presence on the list of several M.P.s for the Borough of Saint Albans, some of whom were townsmen with only minor holdings in the countryside, others of whom were outsiders with only a token base in the area.

Although local office-holding was no longer the prerogative of the county elite, there is, nonetheless, a very clear correlation between wealth and the holding of major local office, as is shown by the fact that the only group where the total number of offices held exceeds that of its population is group I (see Table 9). It was still normal for a man in the next rental category to hold a major local office, but exceptional for a man any further down the economic scale, and there seems to be a very clear division at about the £500 level between the two groups.

The Verulam List and the Owner Sample. Of the 118 individuals on the Verulam List, 25 were in the owner sample in 1663 (see Table 1). Twenty-three had a residence in the two Hundreds and 2 resided outside them. Another 2 were to enter the sample at a later date, 1 in 1668, the other in 1682. All 10 men on the list with rentals of £600 or more are in sample, as well as 5 of the 15 with rentals of £300-£500. The postulate of a close correlation between the sample and landed wealth is not destroyed by the presence in the former of men who figure low in the rental category of the Verulam List. Of the 7 men in the sample with landed incomes in Cashio and Dacorum below £200, 6 already had or were about to inherit extensive holdings outside these two Hundreds.

Since the continuity of ownership of the houses forms the structural base of the owner sample, there are at all times a few men whose presence in the sample needs qualifying. They are mostly men whose families are on their way into or out of the sample, but they may include some whose death without male heir will bring in a possibly wealthier collateral branch from outside. Thus of 5 men in the sample in category II, 2 were to die out or sell out for lack of male heirs, 1 settled elsewhere, and 2 belonged to families that only remained in the sample thanks to continuing infusions of wealth from London trade.

One may conclude that £300 a year is the cut-off point below which no one is in the sample, while £600 a year is the cut-off point above which everyone is in it. The Verulam List confirms the assumption that the sample includes all the wealthier men in the county together with others the relative modesty of whose income is made up by other social advantages.

Conclusion. The most striking feature of the Verulam List is its comprehensiveness. Used in combination with other contemporary or near-contemporary lists, it enables us for once to look in depth at a broad segment of landed society. In comparison with other types of documentation for the period, the list correlates with the contemporary Hearth Tax assessment to a very reassuring degree. But it proves that inclusion of an individual in Elizabethan and Early Stuart subsidy lists cannot be used as an index of anything except lack of sufficient political influence to evade the tax altogether. It also indicates that the Heraldic Visitations are so incomplete in their coverage and ambiguous in their meaning as to be virtually unuseable by the social historian except as a source of genealogical information about such families as they happen to include.

Thanks to the list, it is possible to place the sample at one point in time in the context of the rural society from which it was drawn, and to assess its representativeness of the elite. To be placed in the rental category of £500 a year or over meant a tax assessment of at lease a full horse, which was presumably supplied from the owner's stable. This assessment level correlates well with the size of house (22 hearths on average, compared with 12-16 for all categories below); with the holding of a manor, which is absolutely universal; with the holding of a major local office (11 out of 15); with a title or at least the rank of Esq. (11 with the title of knight or over, 4 Esquires, and one rising lawyer called "Mr" by virtue of his profession). By way of contrast, of the 97 men who figure in the three lowest categories, only 6 had a title of knight or above, at least 3 of whom had their main base outside Cashio and Dacorum.

On the whole the conclusion of the comparison between the Verulam List and the owner sample is thus reassuring. Bearing in mind that those about whose houses we are ignorant are automatically excluded from it, the sample includes a majority (75 per cent) but not all the richest men in the area, a majority (69 per cent) but not all of the major office-holders, a majority (91 per cent) but not all of those with the title of knight or over. What this means is that the members of the county elite can be distinguished by their correlation not with one variable but with a whole series of them, some but not all of which are shared with persons lower down the socio-economic scale. A process of partial permeation appears to be taking place, as evidenced most strikingly in recruitment to the Bench of Justices, a process which in Hertfordshire may have been hastened by the temporary rise to local power of such men during the Interregnum. A possible explanation of this process is that it arose from a closing of the ranks as local society found itself harboring increasing numbers of outsiders whose main physical base or interests lay outside the narrow confines of the Hundred or county. Some of the latter seem to be prototypes of the "pseudo-gentry" that has been observed in eighteenth-century county society elsewhere[46] and which at this date may be a phenomenon common to counties contiguous to London.

Measurement of Building

In order to be able to calculate and compare the amount of extant old building and of new construction at different periods, it is necessary to adopt some uniform scale of measurement. In an ideal world it would be desirable to have both a measure of building costs per cubic foot, adjusted to some standard cost-of-living index so as to make possible comparisons over long periods of time, and also accurate measurements of size of all houses. Unfortunately, however, the number of building events for which we have financial records is very small, and the number for which we have full plans and elevations is certainly no larger. Moreover, even if we could measure cubic footage of the whole building in all cases, it would not tell us very much, for reasons which will be explained in a moment. Dreams of firm indexes of cost and size have therefore had to be abandoned, and attention has perforce been directed to devising some more imperfect but more workable measure of building activities.

The most perplexing problem is how to deal with offices. In houses of this social class, offices—meaning living quarters for servants and rooms for laundry, food storage, food preparation, etc.—bulk very large, since there was always a substantial retinue of living-in servants, ranging from about 10 up to 50 or more.[47] The only crumb of comfort is that the ratio of family quarters to offices does not vary very much according to the size of the house. The larger house certainly had a very much larger staff of servants, but this was almost entirely

[46] A. Everitt, "Social Mobility in Early Modern England," *Past and Present*, 33 (1966), pp. 70-72.

[47] Robert Kerr, *The Gentleman's House* (London, 1865), p. 383, gives a table of servants ranging from 3 to 32 and more, for whom accommodations should be provided by the architect, dependent on the size of the house.

offset by the fact that it also contained very much larger and more numerous rooms for formal and informal entertainment. Robert Kerr's figures for 1865 show that, depending on the size of the house, offices then comprised between 38 and 41 per cent of the whole in terms of square feet of floor space, and 27 to 26 per cent in terms of costs, which is a negligible range of variation.[48]

On the other hand, over time offices certainly changed their location and very probably also the proportion of building space they occupied. In the big courtyard houses of the sixteenth century, they are placed in one or two wings of the main block. In the smaller houses of the same period they may be straggling attachments, or altogether separated buildings. In the "double-pile" rectangular house of the late seventeenth and early eighteenth centuries, they tend to be crammed into attics and cellars, with the family quarters and entertainment rooms sandwiched in between on the two main floors. In the mid- or late eighteenth century, they are often in semi-detached blocks, linked to the family quarters by corridors. Sometimes they are tucked away discreetly on an obscure side of the house, and sometimes, in the larger houses, they are in wings which are openly displayed as integral parts of the architectural design. In the nineteenth century offices begin expanding, often on a single floor, wrapping themselves around the rear quarters of the main block and bulging out in all directions like a monstrous fungoid growth around the base of a tree.

Wherever they were sited, these offices were naturally spartan in their simplicity and cheap to put up—according to Kerr, they cost about half as much per square foot as the family quarters. Since the cost was relatively so little, since they vary so greatly in their loca-

[48] The following table has been calculated from *ibid.*, p. 892:

SIZE IN SQUARE FEET OF FLOOR SPACE

House Costs (in £)	*Quarters*	*Offices*	*Total*	*Offices as Per Cent of Total*
5,000	6,310	3,900	10,210	38
10,000	10,600	6,800	17,400	39
20,000	17,800	11,740	29,540	40
40,000	29,400	20,400	50,200	41
		(Cost in £)		
	3,639	1,365	5,004	27
	7,314	2,686	10,000	27
	14,774	5,237	20,011	26
	29,800	10,200	40,000	26

tion, since they are so hard to measure accurately, and since they add nothing to the display function of the house as a social unit, they have been ignored in the calculations, which are confined to the family quarters. This means that a judgment has had to be made of what proportions of the floor area a sixteenth-century courtyard house or of a Victorian house on the 25-inch maps of the 1870s was given over to offices. In the first case it has been assumed (in light of measured examples) that one-third of the floor space was taken up by offices. In the second, the proportion depends on the evidence about the appearance of the house derived from other sources, with a strong presumption that up to a half of the ground surface area and a third of the total floor space consists of offices. Where a seventeenth- or eighteenth-century house has a basement, it is assumed that the offices are there, and no deduction is made from the main floors; where there is no basement in a simple double-pile house, a deduction of one-fifth is made from the main floors, on the assumption (which is borne out by many of the known examples) that some offices were inside the main block, but that others were in a wing extended out of the back of the house, out of sight of the view of the façade.

Another difficulty is that it is virtually impossible to make allowances for the widely varying cost of internal decoration, primarily because in most cases we do not know what the cost amounted to, and also because we often do not know just what the internal decorations looked like. We are therefore obliged, whether we like it or not, to ignore what in the really grand houses was admittedly a very important factor in costs.

A third difficulty is that the construction and adornment of the house is only one part of the total expenditure on a country seat. Particularly in the eighteenth century, considerable sums were spent on massive stable blocks to accommodate coaches, horses, and stable boys, and even more went into beautifying the grounds. Park walls in brick could alone involve a very great expense if the park were large (they cost £1,100 a mile at Blenheim in 1722), while lakes, bridges, grottoes, fountains, temples, and so on were all important items of expenditure. Here again there is often no means of evaluating the cost of this type of work. All one can say is that when full documentary records are available, it appears the expenditure on grounds normally amounts to less than a third of the cost of the house. Robert Kerr estimated that for a substantial new house with 60 rooms, costing between £5,000 and £6,000 in all, there would need to be spent an extra £1,600 on stables and grounds.[49]

[49] *Ibid.*, p. 400.

Only in the case of the great house situated within enormous and spectacular grounds is the ratio of cost of grounds to cost of house significantly higher. In the 1790s George Richardson estimated that it cost between £500 and £850 to build a gateway and porter's lodge, £2,260 to build a stable for 20 horses and 3 coaches, and between £500 and £1,000 for a garden temple or a pavilion. When Mr. de Crespigny bought Colney Chapel House in 1775, he spent £5,000 on the purchase of the estate, £1,800 on the bare shell of the main block (without offices or internal fittings or decorations), £600 on the kitchen garden and walls, and £450 on the lake. In the few really gigantic grounds, costs during the eighteenth century were truly astronomical. At Blenheim Palace, it has been estimated that the Duke of Marlborough spent about £200,000 on the grounds between 1760 and 1820. King William III spent £74,000 on the gardens at Hampton Court between 1689 and 1699, while the Mausoleum alone in the grounds of Castle Howard cost £19,000. On the other hand, this disproportion only seems to apply to the very rare exceptionally elaborate grounds (of which there are none in Hertfordshire). Robert Kerr estimated that on a huge £40,000 to £47,000 house, there would only need to be spent £12,000 on the stables and grounds, which is not much different from his proportion for a much smaller house.[50]

Accepting all these limitations and deficiences, building has been calculated in terms of units, each of which consists of 100 square feet of floor space of living quarters. Each main floor of the main block is counted equally as a floor area. Attic floors with dormers or Mansard windows are counted at one-tenth of a unit per hundred square feet, and low third floors are counted at one-half of a unit per hundred square feet. Basements do not count at all, since it is assumed in all cases that they were used exclusively for offices. This computation, uncertain as is the data upon which it is often based, incomplete as it is in its omission of other important areas of expenditure, and approximate as it is in its neglect of ceiling height or building materials, nevertheless seems to give a rough evaluation of house size. The correlation of Hearth Tax assessments with independent unit calculations provides comforting mutual support for both. In terms of cost, it is less certain just what a unit means. In the mid-eighteenth century, plans and estimates of medium-size houses built by Robert Morris suggest a cost per unit of about £40, while by the 1790s

[50] G. Richardson, *New Designs in Architecture* (London, 1792), pls. xv-xxviii, Bodleian Library, Gough MSS, Herts. 13, ff. 64-65; D. Green, *Blenheim Palace* (London, 1951), pp. 199, 269; *Wren Society*, iv, 38. Kerr, *The Gentleman's House*, pp. 406-07.

prices quoted by George Richardson work out more like £55 per unit. The most elaborate calculations of all were made by Robert Kerr in 1865. He reckoned "the family department" cost (at London prices) £57-2/3 per unit for a £5,000 house, and £83 per unit for a £20,000 house, which is roughly the range with which we are concerned. Above this level, prices per unit soar up to the palace with 150 family rooms and 135 servant's rooms costing £80,000, for which the price per unit was estimated at £120.[51] The very valid point made by Kerr is that the price per unit rises directly proportionate to the size of the house, which means that the crude unit measurement is no more than a mean in terms of costs. Used as an indicator of expense, it underestimates the cost of large houses and overestimates the cost of small ones.

To sum up, therefore, the unit measurement system is riddled with imperfections, and in particular it underrepresents the real cost of the house and grounds of a great seat proportionately to that of a small villa. A possible way to adjust for this would be to make a correction related to unit size; say add 10 units to any house over 75 units, 20 units over 100 units, 30 units over 150 units, 50 units over 200 units. To do so, however, would introduce a hazardous degree of subjectivity into a statistical enquiry which is already sufficiently fraught with uncertainty, and the suggestion has been rejected.

Numbers of Houses

Before looking at the changes in the size and location of the sample houses, it must be stressed once again that entry into the sample does not necessarily mean a new house on a virgin site, and withdrawal from the sample does not necessarily mean abandonment. In the cases of 49 per cent of all the houses coming into the sample between 1540 and 1879, there was indeed no known house on the sites. But this figure is misleading since it is very probable that a considerable number of these new houses were in fact constructed on the sites of farmhouses or small late medieval halls. The highest proportion of these apparently new houses (17 out of 26) appear in the nineteenth century, and it is possible that in most of these cases they were indeed on genuinely virgin soil. Entry into the sample can mean either a completely new building, or passage from institutional or royal use into private hands, or the expansion or rebuilding on a larger scale by a man of increased wealth and power and status. Similarly, disappearance from the sample may indicate either its total destruction, or a decline in the status and wealth of the owner, or the deterioration of

[51] R. Morris, *Select Architecture* (London, 1755); Richardson, *New Designs in Architecture*; Kerr, *The Gentleman's House*, p. 892.

the house into an institution, a small manor house or a farm out on lease.

The number of houses in the sample rises rapidly and without interruption from 1540, when only 15 houses qualified, to 1669 when there are 93 in the sample (see Fig. 10). For almost a century after 1670

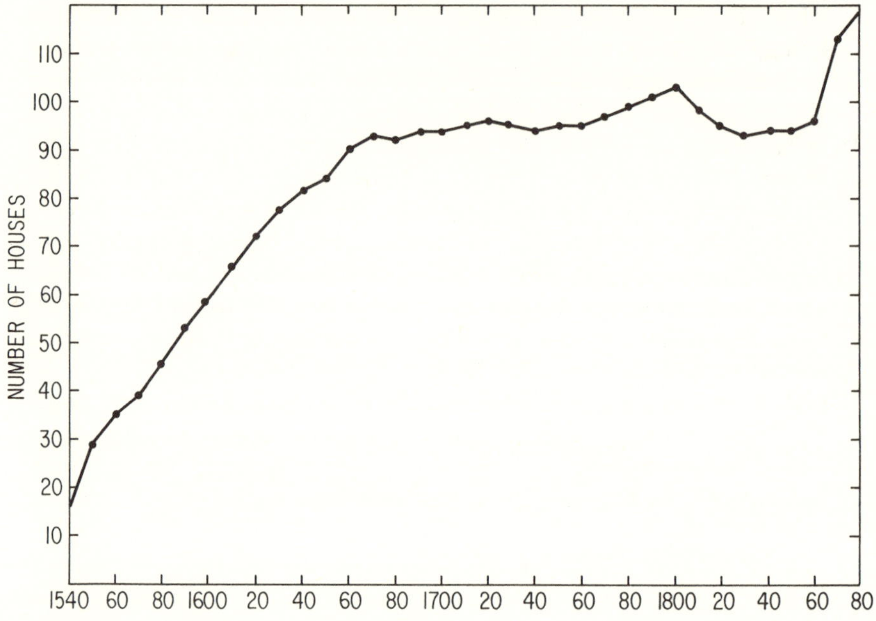

Fig. 10. Count of Houses in the Sample

the number of houses in the sample remains constant, but after 1760 there begins a long period of modest fluctuations. Numbers rise to a peak of 104 in 1799, falling back again to the old level by 1819. From 1820 to 1859 nothing much changes, but in the last twenty years of the period there is another sharp rise to an all time high of 108 in 1879, a peak which in reality may be even higher than it seems, since several of the 8 large houses omitted for lack of data probably fall into this period.

These changes in the number of houses in the sample are the product of two distinct movements, new houses entering the sample, and old houses going out (see Fig. 11), each of which processes must be analyzed separately. The phase of growth up to 1669 was caused by a very rapid increase in the number of houses built for the accommodation of residential upper gentry. The expansion of a farmhouse or a small medieval hall and solar into a substantial country house meant changing the social and political life of the community, which now became subjected to close supervision of a resident member of the county elite. It is also evidence of the growth in size of that elite as it settled ever more densely over the countryside. The growth phase is symptomatic of the creation of a county elite of wealthy squires during the century after 1540, a formative process which in Hertfordshire continued unchecked through the Civil War, Interregnum, and Restoration.

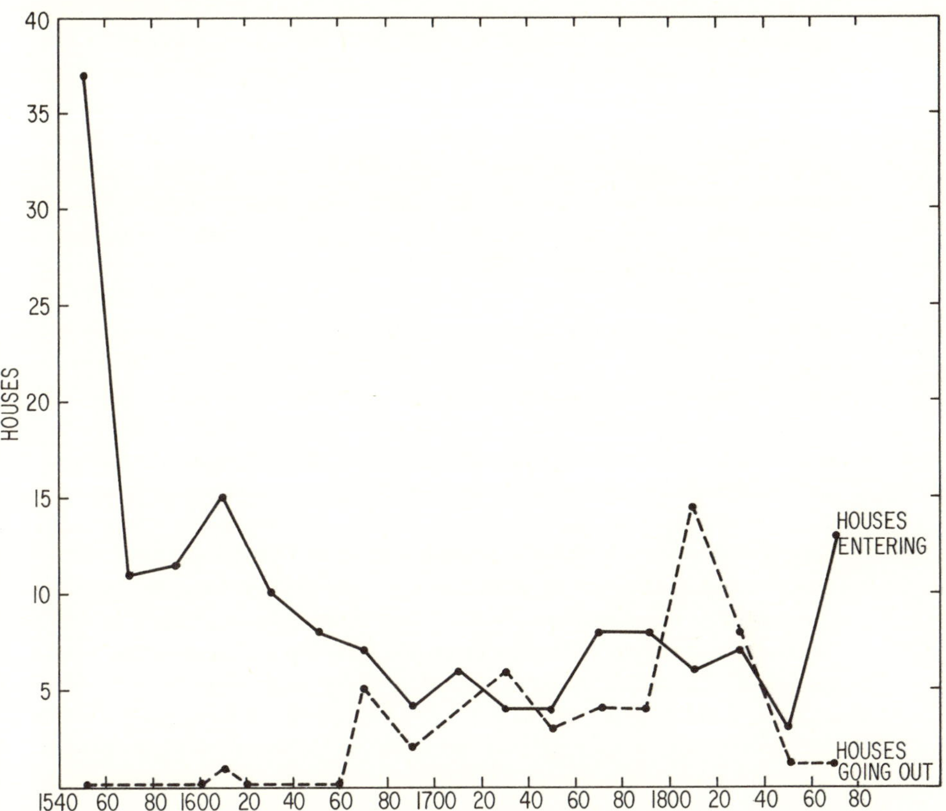

Fig. 11. Count of Houses Entering and Going Out of the Sample (20-Year Periods)

A vitally important cause of this growth was the dissolution of the monasteries and the subsequent distribution by the Crown by gift and sale of ex-Church and other royal property. No fewer than 7 of the first 15 houses in 1539 were converted monastic buildings, and 12 of them (80 per cent) were on recent Church or Crown land. Even as late as 1640, 43 of the 82 houses in the sample (53 per cent) were built on land which just over a century before had belonged to Church or Crown, 23 of them (28 per cent) on ex-monastic property. The importance of this redistribution of clerical property in the economic development of the upper-gentry class has long been assumed by historians, but these figures provide some precise evidence of the role it played in facilitating the formation of the new county elite and the erection of their houses. These houses needed large compact chunks of property on which to site themselves, and it was the throwing upon the land market by the Crown of its own and the Church's estates, together with the freeing of the private land market from its medieval trammels by the Statutes of Uses and Wills, which made possible the rapid acquisition of suitable holdings. It is interesting that in terms of new construction or substantial rebuilding, the major growth phase —easily the greatest of the last 400 years—was over by 1580, although there was a revival of new building, mostly by successful "new men," in the Interregnum of the 1640s and 1650s.

The 180-year period from 1580 to 1760 saw relatively little building on new sites or major rebuilding on old. This can be explained by the fact that the county was in a sense overbuilt, thanks to the excessive competitive enthusiasm of the Tudor gentry. Until 1670 the land market was still open, so that new men could easily buy a good house and estate, while a ready alternative was to buy a yeoman's farmhouse —of which there were also plenty—and to convert it into a house for a gentleman. In any case the number of elite gentry in the county did not grow any more for nearly a century after 1670, so that there was no great pressure on the existing stock of houses. Ninety rich squires was about as many as the county could hold. The beginning in 1670 of the period of stagnation in total numbers coincides with the leveling off of the prices of agricultural produce and therefore of rental income. It also coincides with the closing of the land market due to the exhaustion of Crown property, and with the decline of private sales caused by the spread of the strict settlement, which effectively prevented the dispersion of the family estates of the greater landowners. And so for almost a century after 1670, the stock of houses in the sample remains constant, the number of new entrants approximately matching the number of drop-outs (see Fig. 11).

The rise in numbers again after 1760 was caused by a second explosion of new construction in the late eighteenth century, partly by landowners enriched by the sharp rise in rents, and partly by businessmen profiting from colonial trade and war. The remarkable scale of this increase is largely concealed in the count of houses in the sample by the coincidental rise in the number of drop-outs (see Fig. 11). Between 1820 and 1860 there is a puzzling slump in both numbers and new construction, a lull which has been noticed by architectural historians, who have observed that the leading architects of the time devoted themselves to designing churches and commercial and public buildings rather than country houses. It was certainly a period of low rents and difficult economic conditions, but this hardly seems an adequate explanation. More easily explicable is the revived activity after 1860, when many new-made industrial and commercial magnates built themselves substantial, if aesthetically unattractive, new houses within easy access of London by rail or road.

As has been noted, changes in the total stock of houses in the sample are caused by the shifting balance between new entrants and drop-outs. Fifty-two houses disappeared from the sample between 1540 and 1879, 24 of which were destroyed. One suffered 2 major fires in 50 years and was not rebuilt until later,[52] but the other 23 were deliberately pulled down, often after a period of neglect. In 19 out of the 23 cases, the owner had another house within the county, so that the house destroyed was largely superfluous to his needs. Six of the houses had recently been purchased so that the grounds could be incorporated into the park of an adjacent house.[53] Only 2 were destroyed because accidents of inheritance had recently led to the acquisition of another and more attractive house.[54] One was torn down owing to a bitter family quarrel.[55] What is very significant is that the destruction of no fewer than 12 of the 23 houses took place between 1790 and 1829. What seems to have happened is that the elite had taken to living for longer and longer periods in London, or sometimes abroad, and were using their country seats less and less. The owners therefore tended to allow their houses to fall into neglect, and eventually they pulled many of them down altogether, a process upon which George Byng, Lord Torrington, repeatedly commented as he rode around the country in the 1780s and 1790s.[56] Furthermore, the rising interest in Gothic did nothing to increase respect or admiration for sixteenth- and seventeenth-century houses, which failed altogether to capture the imagination of the Romantics. It was not until the 1830s and 1840s that the growth of antiquarian interest began to extend the range of

[52] Benington Place.

[53] Gubbins, Tewin House, Hatfield Woodhall, Sopwell, Thundridgebury, and probably The Moor.

[54] Aldenham Manor House and Oxhey.

[55] Throcking.

[56] *The Torrington Diaries*, ed. S. B. Andrews and J. Beresford (London, 1934), I, 128, 333; II, 76, 87, 238; III, 33; IV, 9.

popular sympathy to the architecture of the Tudors. As a result of this change of taste, only 2 houses went out of the sample because of destruction between 1830 and 1879. It should be noted that these figures only include houses which were destroyed and not immediately rebuilt. If one were to include houses destroyed and immediately replaced on an adjacent site, like Gorhambury and Ashridge, the concentration upon the 40 years from 1790 to 1829 becomes even more striking.

The second major alternative for superfluous houses, other than pulling them down, was to lease them out. Eleven out of the 13 houses in this category were owned by men with alternative houses to live in, 6 of them within the county, the other 2 being owned by families which died out. Of these houses, 1 (Theobalds) was exchanged with the Crown in 1607 to become a royal palace and is an exception, both in date and the use to which it was put. Six of the others were leased out in the destructive period 1790 to 1829. Four became schools, 2 warehouses, 2 farms, 1 a hotel, and 3 were let to tenants as gentlemanly residences.

Destruction and leasing account for three-fourths of the total 52 drop-outs. Two others were early enveloped in suburbia and became town houses,[57] 6 were cut down to the size of villas in the eighteenth and early nineteenth centuries,[58] and the remaining 3 fell out of the sample since their owners declined in status.[59]

Geographical Distribution of Houses

Houses did not only change in quantity; they also changed in their geographical distribution. Cutting the county into four by straight diagonal lines, the proportion in the central area remains fairly constant, but from the sixteenth to the nineteenth century there is a marked shift out of the northeastern sector into the southwest. In 1599, 29 per cent of all houses in the sample were situated in the 160-odd square miles in the northeast, as opposed to 16 per cent in 1879; in 1599, 13 per cent were situated in the 100-odd square miles in the southwest, as opposed to 26 per cent in 1879. Only 1 new house in the northeast enters the sample after 1700 while no fewer than 19 were added in the southwest. There were probably two reasons for this shift to the southwest, of which the first is the plain fact that the country is so

[57] Hempsteadbury and Rawdon House in the late seventeenth century.

[58] Temple Dinsley, Royston Priory, and Much Hadham Hall in the early eighteenth century, Golden Parsonage in the late eighteenth century, and Cheshunt Great House and Salisbury Hall in the early nineteenth century.

[59] Martocks, St. Julians, and Preston Castle.

much duller and less attractive in the northwest. This did not matter much in the sixteenth and seventeenth centuries, when convenience took precedence over aesthetics, and when in any case the formal garden layout around the house effectively blotted out the natural appearance of the countryside. But after Capability Brown and the Romantics had created an interest in the picturesque landscape in the middle of the eighteenth century, the aesthetic potentialities of the site became an important factor governing the choice of location. The reason for the accelerated shift in the nineteenth century must be the greater accessibility of London from the southwest of the county, particularly after the construction of the North-Western Railway line.

The only other significant feature of the geographical distribution of houses is the way many of them tended to cluster along river valleys, especially after the middle of the eighteenth century. The main reason for this is that the new aesthetic of the Romantic landscape demanded a southward facing prospect over some distance, and therefore a site overlooking a valley, preferably from the north. The more ambitious owners also desired a park with a lake, which involved the damming up of a suitable stream. These were the two considerations used by Repton in 1801 to persuade Earl Cowper to pull down Cole Green House, which lay a mile from the river Mimram but on the south side, and to build instead at Panshanger near the river to the north, overlooking a newly constructed lake.[60] The result was a line of four houses clustered along a two-mile stretch of the north bank of the Mimram (Panshanger, Marsden, Tewin Water, and Tewin House).

If the preferred siting of houses changed over time, the one thing that was almost unalterable once the site was settled was the location of the offices, probably mainly because of the cost of rebuilding the ovens and vats of breweries, bakeries, and laundries. Houses were altered, added to, remodeled, refaced, turned back to front, converted, and contracted with extraordinary disrespect for the past. But even in houses which underwent the most frequent and drastic changes, the one thing that remained constant was the location of the offices, which in turn determined the possible orientations of the house. A remarkable example of this is the location of the offices in the much rebuilt house of Markyate Cell.

House Size

The median size of houses with known scale rises to about 1570, fluctuates about a mean for a century, rises again sharply from 1670 to 1710,

[60] Herts. R. O., Cowper MSS 520 (Repton's Red Book for Panshanger).

levels off completely to 1770, rises sharply to 1810, levels off again, and then rises slowly once more after 1840 (see Fig. 12). These changes in the median demonstrate an upward drift in the size of a house considered suitable for a member of the landed elite, a drift that occurred in steps rather than as a continuous process. But changes in the median are a product of the addition of both large and small houses, and they conceal the most significant development of all. This was a

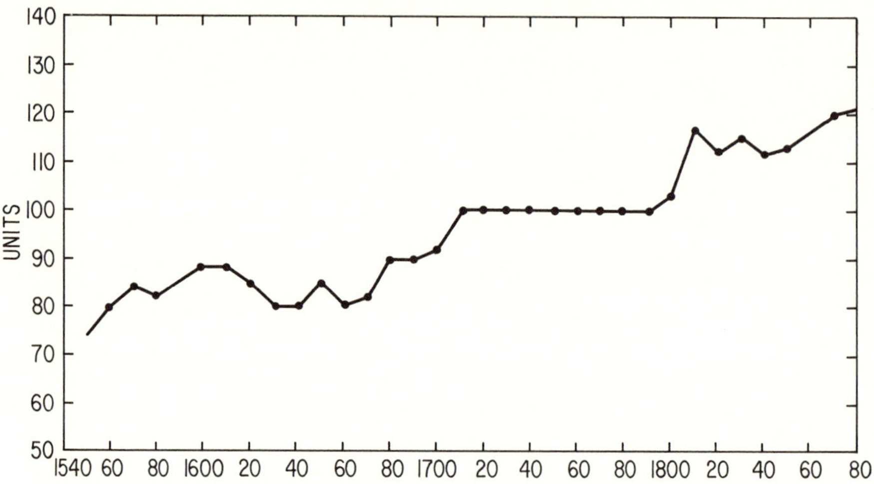

Fig. 12. Median Size of Houses with Known Scale in the Sample

numerical increase in the largest type of house (over 120 units) throughout the whole period, although at a significantly slower pace from 1680 to 1850 than before or after (see Fig. 13). The two periods in which large numbers of the elite were demanding and getting bigger houses were the sixteenth and the nineteenth centuries. The number of really enormous houses (over 160 units) rose as a percentage of the sample up to 1580, but did not change again until 1800. These monsters grew from 1 in 1540 to a total of 12 in 1670, remained unchanged until 1800, and then increased again in the nineteenth century to reach 24 in 1879. Throughout the whole period 7 houses exceeded 250 units at one time or another, of which 3 were more like palaces than houses. Theobalds rose from 350 to 450 units after 1563, until it was taken over by the Crown from the Cecils in 1608. Its replacement, Hatfield, was as large as 520 units from the first building in 1608, a size exceeded only by the 548 units of Ashridge, constructed in the early nineteenth century.[61] Because these giants are so enormous and so utterly untypical, they tend to throw the figures for average house size off balance at certain periods.

Among the lessons we can draw from the examination of house size is that there were three periods in which the local elite sharply in-

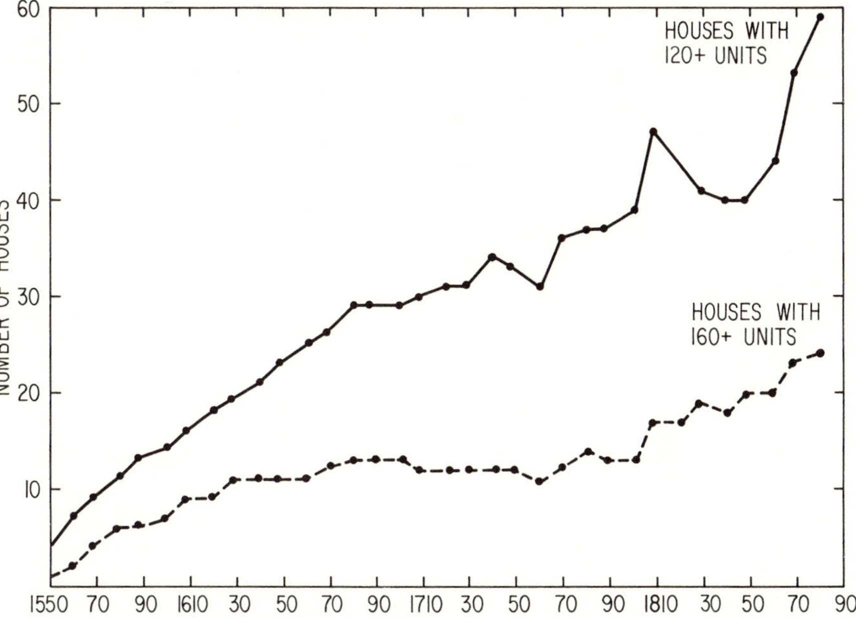

FIG. 13. Count of Large Houses in the Sample

creased their conspicuous consumption in terms of living space, namely 1540 to 1600, 1670 to 1710 and 1790 to 1820. It is no coincidence that these are periods of rapidly rising rental income and/or rapid infiltration of successful businessmen or government officials. But it would be

[61] The 7 giants are:

Dates in Sample	*House*	*Units*
1560-	Cassiobury	260
1563-1608	Theobalds	350-450
1608-	Hatfield	520
1673-	Moor Park	312
1710-1756	Gorhambury	250
1780-	Brocket Hall	270
1820-	Ashridge	548

wrong to assume that the relative lull between 1710 and 1790 meant a proportionate lull in conspicuous consumption. There is reason to think that during this period a very great deal of money was poured into landscaping the grounds and into more and more elaborate interior decoration and furnishings. Once a house reached a certain size (and 120 units seems to be about that size), competition took the form of internal and external aesthetic improvements rather than any further increase in living space. An extreme example of this development is Moor Park. Built on a most lavish scale in the 1670s, it had wings added in the 1720s. But also in the 1720s the original brick exterior was entirely encased in stone, the interior was extensively remodeled by Thornhill and Leoni, and a hill which obstructed the view was physically removed. The total cost is said to have been as high as £150,000, although this seems hardly credible.[62] Twenty years later, more work was done on the interior, and the grounds were redesigned in the new Romantic style with mounds, trees, a lake, and a temple. Twenty years later still, in the 1760s, still more interior decoration work was done, and the most expensive furniture was bought. The net result of all this activity was minimal in terms of building units, but enormous in terms of cost and aesthetic appearance.

What is surprising is the renewed expansion in the volume of living space which began in 1790, which was accompanied by perhaps an even greater expansion of the service area for the accommodation of the servants—a gigantism that became wholly disfunctional after the economic ice age set in with the First World War. Not architecturally interesting enough or old enough to be worth preserving for their own sake, nor modest enough to be habitable in an age of servant shortage, depressed rents, and high taxes, the Victorian houses and house expansions have been the first victims of the social upheavals of the twentieth century.

If we turn to the motives which led to the increase in house size, the principal ones seem to have been desire to provide physical evidence of an increase of wealth, or an increase of status (for example accession to a title), and a desire to play an active political role in the county. Among those making for destruction or abandonment were impoverishment or the acquisition by inheritance or marriage of another house in the county, which was thought to be preferable to live in.

Building Activities

To investigate the amount of building activity and to compare the scale of activity over time, it is necessary to convert into building units

[62] *The Beauties of England and Wales* (London, 1806), VII, 312.

recorded or observed building events, either new buildings or the expansion or remodeling of old buildings. Since so much of the dating, especially of alterations and additions, is conjectural and based on stylistic criteria, a 30-year moving average has been used, partly since most activity can be pinned down within a time span of that length, and partly in order to smooth the curves so that long time trends can be seen more clearly.

The best way to test the reliability of the evidence is to look, not at individual events, but at complete building programs, which may include a number of both additive and non-additive events. It could, for example, be a 5-year phase of activity which included the refacing of the main front, the redecoration of the interior, the addition of a wing, the remodeling of the grounds, and some new stables. Of the 491 building programs, as here defined, 63 per cent are definitely dated, and the other 14 per cent are known to be the work of a given builder, and so dated within fairly narrow limits. Only 23 per cent have been ascribed by circumstantial evidence, based on the events of the life of the owner and the style of the building. Of the 491 building programs, only 20 are ascribed purely on the basis of style and only 12 purely on the basis of biographical data. The quality of the evidence varies a little over time, about one-half being certain before 1700 and about two-thirds thereafter, but building programs dated purely by ascription rarely exceed one-quarter in any 20-year period. Consequently, although dating to individual decades is liable to serious error, 30-year moving averages are pretty secure.

The question which must first be answered is whether or not the resulting trends are skewed by the lack of uniformity in the quality of the data on alterations to houses, which is very good for the late seventeenth century and particularly good from about 1785 to 1835. If the figures for building units rose and fell in conformity with the quality of the data, one would be forced seriously to question the validity of any conclusions which might be drawn. Fortunately, however, there was progressive decline of building activity before, during, and after the first phase of good records, and the second phase covers both a rise and a decline of activity. There is thus no correlation between the quantity of the evidence and the quantity of building activity.

The resultant graph of building activity over three and a half centuries displays a surprisingly jagged profile, with soaring Alpine peaks and deep valleys (see Fig. 14). The prolonged boom of the sixteenth century—the longest in modern times—is a consequence of the very great increase in the numbers of wealthy gentry in the county, and of new demands for more opulent housing. The Jacobean slump is less easily explicable, unless it is that there were now sufficient houses of a sufficient size available in the county to accommodate the elite, who therefore turned their attention to embellishment rather than further expansion. The burst of activity in the 1650s and 1660s is probably peculiar to Hertfordshire, a product of immunity from the ravages of civil war and of proximity to London, which led to the erection of houses like Balls and Tyttenhanger. The long depression

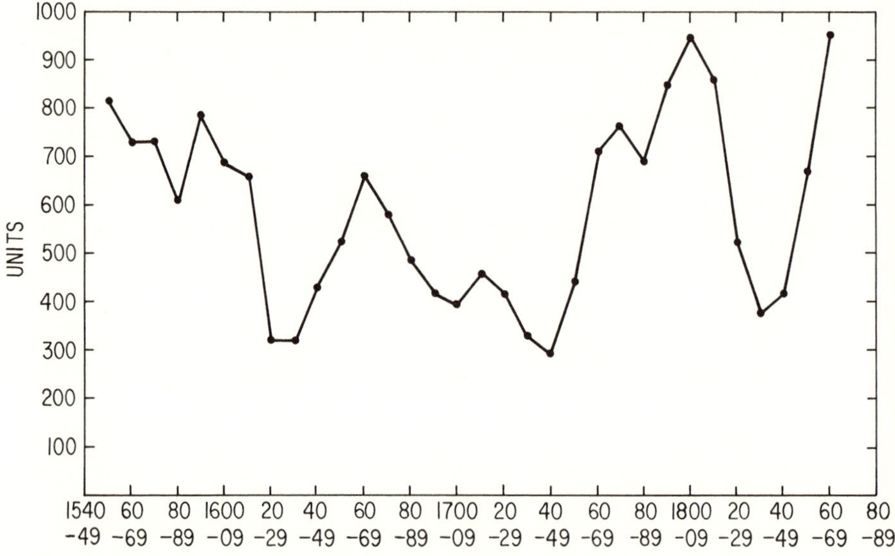

Fig. 14. Total Building Activity (30-Year Moving Average)

of the late seventeenth and first half of the eighteenth century, however, is likely to be closer to the national pattern. The elite remained stable in numbers, and the combined pressures of stagnant rents and a heavy land tax pressed hardly on the established gentry during this period. The revival of activity after 1750 right through the Napoleonic Wars to 1820 may have been more dramatic in Hertfordshire than elsewhere, due to the influx of wealthy London merchants, but it is unlikely to differ generally from the national pattern. The combination of a demand for classical architecture and surplus wealth derived from rising rents and commercial profits created both the incentive and the means for much new building. The collapse of this boom in the 1820s and 1830s coincides with the economic difficulties of postwar England and is reflected in the shift of interest of the leading architects of the day away from country houses and into churches and public buildings. The revival of activity after 1840 reflects the renewed rise of rental incomes, the influx of new business wealth into the mid-Victorian countryside, and the shift of fashion to Gothic architecture.

It is surprising how relatively small a proportion of total additive building consisted of wholly new houses or houses totally rebuilt on old sites, as compared with additions and alterations to existing houses, to make them bigger or more fashionable. Only two-thirds of the total units added between 1540 and 1879 represented new construction or total reconstruction; all the rest were additions and alterations.

Only at the very beginning, between 1540 and 1579, did new building or rebuilding represent as much as one-third of the total number of houses in the sample. Thereafter it never amounted to more than 15 per cent. Since the number of houses in the sample increased so rapidly in the early years, the graph of building activity proportionate to the number of houses in the sample shows by far the highest peak of activity in the sixteenth century (see Fig. 15). Thereafter the graph follows the general lines of that for total activity and calls for no further comment.

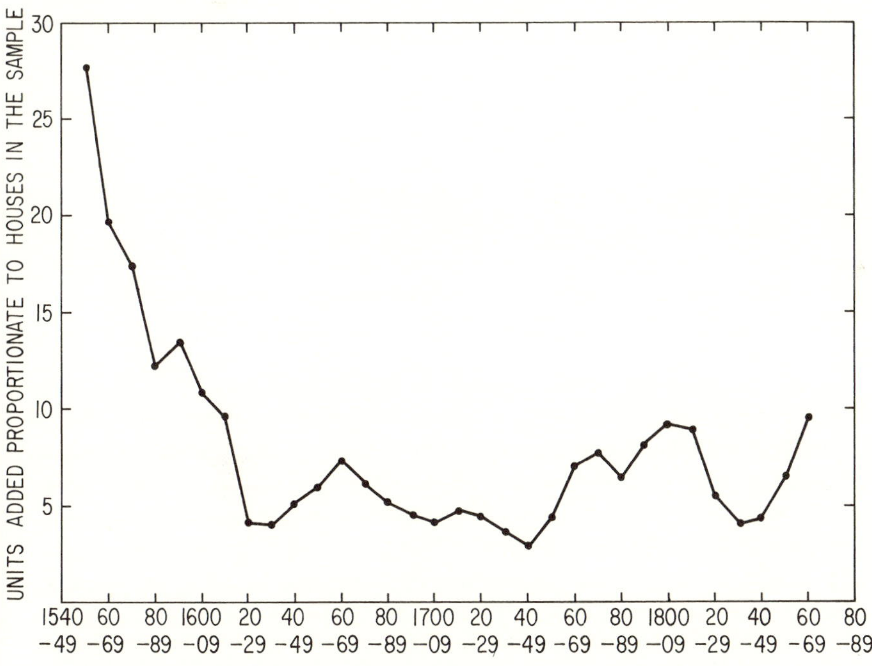

Fig. 15. Total Building Activity Proportionate to the Number of Houses in the Sample (30-Year Moving Average)

A further consideration which must be borne in mind when considering the changing quantity of building in terms of units is that a much larger proportion of alterations to houses in the eighteenth and nineteenth centuries than in the sixteenth and seventeenth centuries did not add to the number of units. That is to say, they took the form of interior decoration, refacing, extensions to offices, new stables, or remodeling of grounds. This can be shown by an inspection of the number of additive events (i.e. events that created units) as the ratio of houses in the sample compared with all positive events (both those which created units and those which did not) (see Fig. 16).

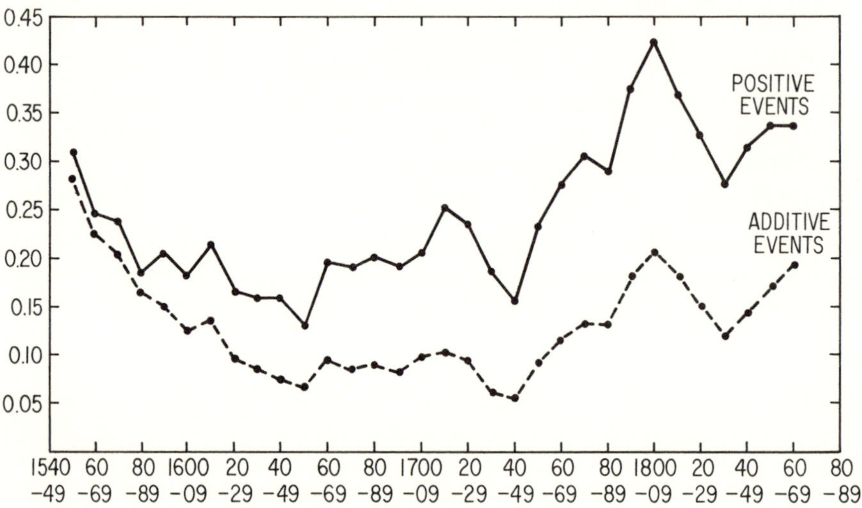

FIG. 16. Positive and Additive Events Proportionate to the Number of Houses in the Sample (30-Year Moving Average)

When compared with the graph of building activity (Fig. 15), that of all positive events shows a rising instead of a falling level of activity in the late seventeenth century, while the late eighteenth-century rise is greatly increased, the peak of the 1800s towering far above all others between 1540 and 1879. This suggests that "non-additive events," which mainly took the form of alterations and improvements to the grounds, interior decoration, and the addition of new stables and offices (see Fig. 17), were particularly numerous between 1680 and 1720, and again between 1790 and 1820. At all times before 1850 the greatest attention was paid to work on the grounds, the two peaks of which were 1680 to 1730 and 1760 to 1800. The first peak represents the development of the formal French garden of the seventeenth century, with its geometrical parterres, walks, and canals, while the second represents the wave of Romantic gardening which began with William Kent in the 1740s, and which in the last half of the century swept away almost all traces of the formal gardens of the earlier period. For reasons which are not at all clear, the building of stables

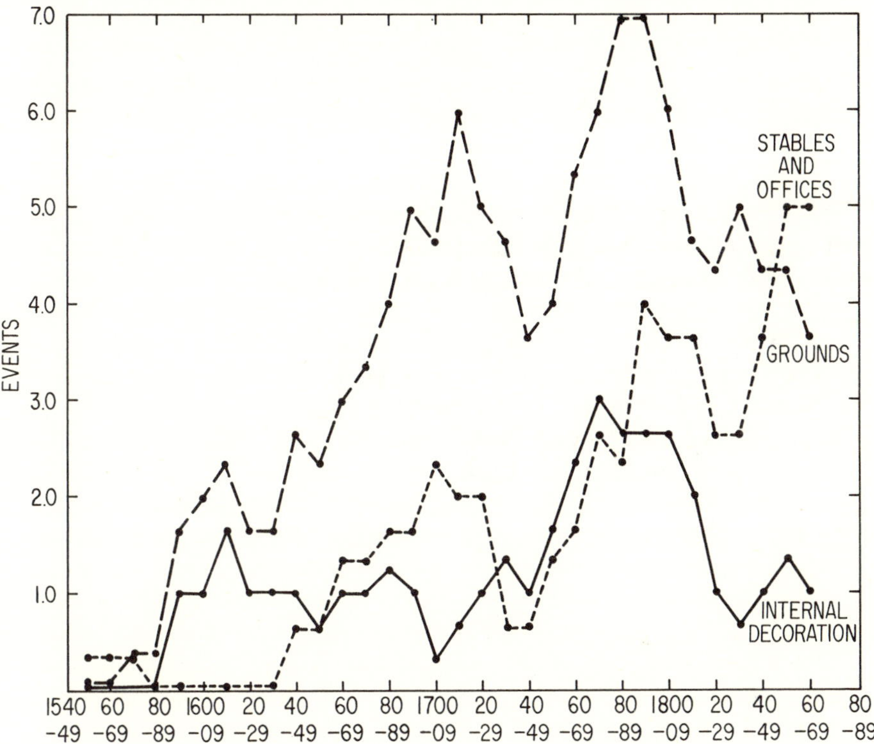

FIG. 17. Types of Non-Additive Events (30-Year Moving Average)

and offices appears to reach a peak around 1710 to 1740, only to fall away again in the mid-eighteenth century. This peak may reflect fluctuations in the survival of evidence rather than in scale of building, but from 1760 to 1810, there was a steady growth of activity. There followed the general early nineteenth-century slump, but from 1850 to 1879 there was an unprecedented burst of activity, the main thrust being not so much stabling as accommodation for the horde of servants so necessary for upper-class Victorian life style. Much less is known about interior decoration, since each succeeding wave destroys much of the evidence for what went before it, but for what it is worth there seems to have been a lot of activity in the early seventeenth century, when many Tudor houses were given Jacobean paneling and plaster work, a lot more in the latter half of the eighteenth century, when Adam decoration was sweeping all before it, and surprisingly little after 1820.

Everything points to the fact that the whole history of house-building in Hertfordshire was dominated by the gigantic burst of activity in the middle and late Tudor period, itself a function of the wealth of the gentry, plus the advent of a new and cheaper building material, namely brick, which revolutionized construction in a county that possessed no local supply of building stones. No fewer than 78 of the 151 houses in the sample were originally built in the sixteenth century. Subsequent generations thus found themselves saddled with a plethora of houses which they could leave alone, add to, reface, or demolish altogether, but which in any case dominated their lives as a none-too-welcome incubus from the past. This explains why so much of the building of subsequent periods consisted of alterations and additions to preexisting houses. The peak of the building boom was the 1540s and 1550s when 13 newly built houses entered the sample, more than in any other 20-year period, including the 1860s and '70s. Another 9 were added in the 1560s and '70s and another 7 in the 1580s and '90s. Moreover, a great deal of smaller house-building was also going on at the same time, proof of which is that many of the houses which entered the sample in the early seventeenth century did so as enlargements of existing smaller Tudor houses, rather than as totally new buildings. Thus in the 1620 to 1639 period 10 of the 15 houses which entered the sample did so by reason of their enlargement. This stock of houses continued to dominate the situation far into the nineteenth century (see Fig. 18), and as a result many owners who wanted something new were obliged to destroy before they could create. For reasons that are not at all clear, substantial demolition prior to construction was quite a common phenomenon between 1640 and 1659, but was extremely rare for a century thereafter (with the exception of 3 out of the 5 reconstructions between 1680 and 1699, all by recent merchant purchasers determined to erect new houses in the height of fashion). Thus between 1700 and 1759 there are only 3 examples of demolition before reconstruction out of 31 houses newly built in that period. By the late eighteenth century, however, many Tudor houses were evidently getting old and in poor condition, there was plenty of money about for total rebuilding, and there was no antiquarian desire to preserve so outdated a style of architecture. So they came tumbling down, 23 of the 42 houses newly constructed between 1760 and 1839 being built on their foundations. There was another lull in the 1840s and '50s, when activity was generally slack, followed by a new destructive outburst in the boom period after 1860, during which 6 of the 14 new houses were built on the foundations of Tudor houses pulled down for this purpose.

In 1740, nearly a third of the houses in the sample still preserved their pre-1600 appearance, and over half their pre-1660 appearance.

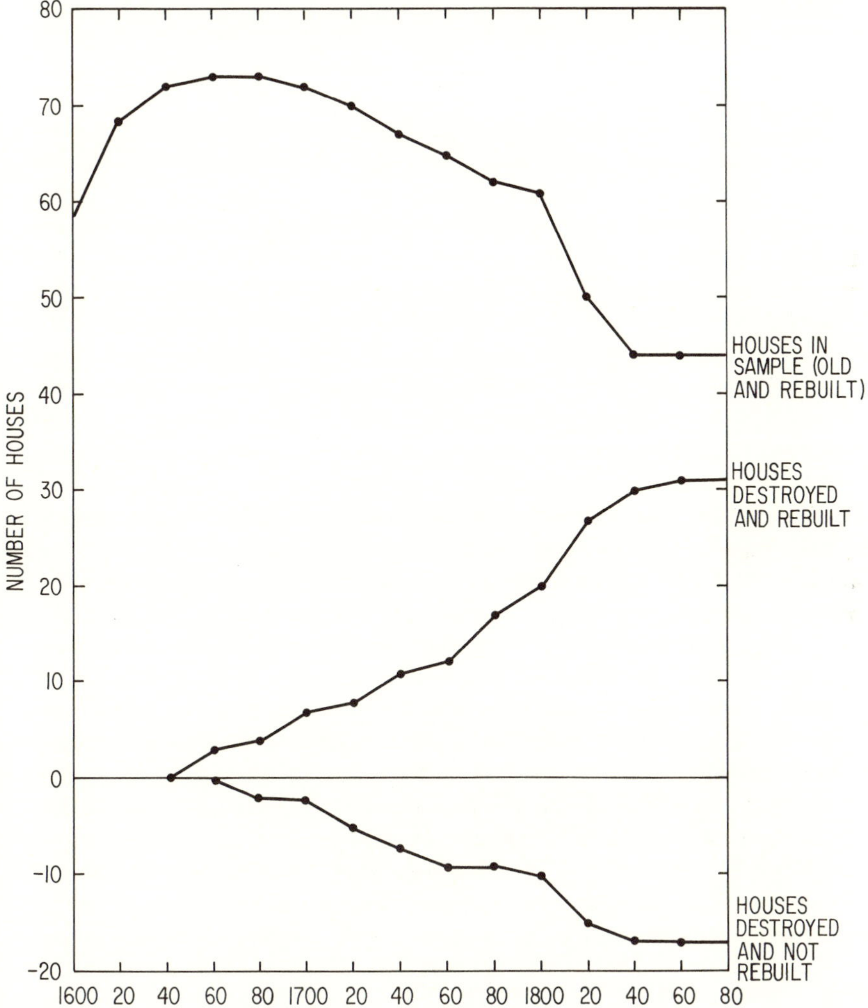

Fig. 18. Count of Pre-1600 Houses in the Sample

On the other hand by 1820 the proportions had been reduced to 3 per cent and 11 per cent respectively. This is proof of the fact that the 80 years between 1740 and 1820 saw an enormous effort to classicize, either by destruction or remodeling, the existing stock of older houses. If we compare the dates of the building of the stock of houses in 1820 with the dates of their external appearance, we find additional evidence of this transformation.

Date	*Date of Original Building*	*Date of External Appearance*
Pre-1599	20%	3%
1600-59	13%	8%
1660-1739	23%	32%
1740-1820	35%	57%

We may conclude that the stock of relatively modern looking houses was at its peak in England in 1600 and again in 1820.

It is interesting to observe the different ways in which the old Tudor houses were adapted and altered to fit changing fashions. In the early seventeenth century there was no new style of architecture to aim at, and enlargement of the standard E-shaped Tudor house was easily accomplished with an addition or extension of the wings. All that was necessary in the way of external refurbishing was the provision of new-shaped gables. In the 1640s and '50s, however, 12 houses were either newly built, rebuilt, or significantly enlarged on a new model, 7 of them by merchants or financiers, and 1 by a lawyer. These "new men" built tall, compact houses of ultimately classical derivation, in a style known as "Artisan Mannerism." The popularity of the new style meant a change in the remodeling of the older houses. If symmetrical, they could still be brought up to date by minor alterations in the fenestration, the addition of another story, and a face lifting of the façade, complete with a Baroque main doorway. If asymmetrical, the only thing to do was to add a completely new block. In the eighteenth century face lifting became more of a problem, since Tudor fenestration was different from classical, with the windows more closely set together, and as a result the only thing to do was often to turn the house back to front and add a completely new front onto the old back quarters. Face lifting of a Tudor house only became easy again with the advent of Gothic and Regency styles in the early nineteenth century.

Conclusion

The dominant feature of the study of houses in Hertfordshire is the overwhelming influence of the proximity of London, whose magnetic attraction diverted the elite from its local responsibilities, but which on the other hand provided a perpetual source of recruitment of new personnel and a perpetual fountain of wealth for new building. In terms of the number of houses which qualify for the sample, the number of new houses added, the number of large houses, and the total amount of building activity, the period 1539 to 1870 divides into three very broad phases: over a century of unsurpassed growth, nearly a century of stability or decline, and a century of renewed activity, broken by a long post-Napoleonic War slump. Throughout the whole period, there was a steady drift from the more inhospitable northeastern sector towards the southwest. Mainly because they were superfluous, many houses dropped out of the sample, especially during the 40 years between 1790 and 1830. The explanations for these shifts of expenditure on houses are clearly related partly to changing profits of agricultural leasing and of business, partly to changing social demands, and partly to changing aesthetic fashions. To elucidate more precisely the complex interrelationships will demand analysis of the social composition of the owners, particularly in their role as builders, and further study of the evidence for fashion, style, and plan of the houses. The purpose of this paper has been to develop a methodology for using quantification to solve problems for which it might superficially seem inappropriate or impossible, and to establish the broad outlines of changes in house construction which these methods have revealed.

II

Religion and Occupational Mobility in Boston, 1880-1963*

STEPHAN THERNSTROM

THAT RELIGION is an element in social stratification has been plain since the seminal work of Max Weber early in this century.[1] Weber's work generated a substantial literature dealing with the relationship between religious affiliation and social status in various societies, and with religious differences in rates and patterns of social mobility. Weber's chief aim, of course, was to establish the connection between religious ideology and the emerging "spirit of capitalism" in precapitalist society, but a corollary of his analysis was the proposition that exposure to "the Protestant ethic" would continue to predispose Protestants to success in the market place in later historical periods, and that Catholicism would continue to inhibit the worldly aspirations of its adherents.

It is this corollary, not Weber's cosmic effort to explain the origins of capitalism, which is the point of departure for this paper.[2] The Weberian corollary about Protestant-Catholic differences in achievement has come under heavy but not entirely persuasive attack of late. Thus Lipset and Bendix found no differences in the occupational mobility of Catholics and Protestants in a 1952 national sample of the U.S. population, but as Gerhard Lenski points out, they ignored the fact that a much larger fraction of the Catholics in the sample had been reared in big cities and should for that reason have fared better occupationally than Protestants, more of whom were of rural or

* I have benefited from the criticism of many scholars. I am especially indebted to Donald J. Bogue, Clyde Griffen, Arthur Mann, Leo Schnore, Gilbert Shapiro, and Charles Tilly.

[1] Max Weber, *The Protestant Ethic and the Spirit of Capitalism*, trans. by Talcott Parsons (New York: Charles Scribner's Sons, 1958).

[2] On this issue the most thorough critique of Weber is Kurt Samuelson, *Religion and Economic Action*, trans. by E. G. French (New York: Harper & Row, Inc., 1964). For a fascinating neo-Weberian analysis of Puritanism as a modernizing influence, see Michael Walzer, "Puritanism as a Revolutionary Ideology," *History and Theory*, 3 (1963), pp. 59-90, and *The Revolution of the Saints: A Study in the Origin of Radical Politics* (Cambridge: Harvard Univ. Press, 1965).

small-town origins.[3] In an analysis of career patterns in Detroit in the mid-1950s Lenski found substantial differences of the kind predicted by Weber, and subsequent research in Detroit points in the same direction.[4] It has been argued, however, that Lenski confounded religion and ethnicity, that Detroit Catholics happen to have come from such low-ranking ethnic groups as the Poles more often than American Catholics in general.[5] Two major studies by Andrew M. Greeley and Peter Rossi, based upon national samples rather than upon data gathered in a single community, portray Catholic occupational achievement in a far more favorable light.[6] About the worldly success of the Jews there is little disagreement: they outperform both Protestants and Catholics according to every recent study which has been conducted.[7]

Whatever the facts of the matter today, however, it would be foolish to extrapolate the findings of current studies back into the past and to assume that the same patterns must necessarily have prevailed then. Catholic doctrine and ritual may have changed relatively little in the past century, but it does not follow that the social and cultural traits of the Church's communicants have changed equally little. It is quite possible that there were substantial Protestant-Catholic differences in

[3] S. M. Lipset and Reinhard Bendix, *Social Mobility in Industrial Society* (Berkeley: Univ. of California Press, 1959), pp. 48-56; Gerhard Lenski, *The Religious Factor: A Sociologist's Inquiry* (paperback edition, Garden City, N.Y.: Doubleday & Co., Inc., 1963), hereinafter referred to as *Religious Factor.*

[4] *Ibid.*, Chap. 3; Albert J. Mayer and Harry Sharp, "Religious Preference and Worldly Success," *American Journal of Sociology*, 27 (1962), pp. 218-27. Mayer and Sharp's conclusions about the low level of Catholic achievement in Detroit, however, rest upon a highly doubtful scheme designed to measure the importance of various background advantages, a scheme which astonishingly ranked Detroit Catholics as high as Episcopalians and Jews in background characteristics. The indexes employed and the weights attached to them are open to serious question, and there was a highly curious failure to control for a manifestly significant background characteristic—father's occupation. My belief that the patterns Lenski found in Detroit in the 1950s continued to operate there rests not upon the Mayer and Sharp paper but upon scrutiny of unpublished intergenerational mobility tables from the 1966 Detroit Area Study, which were generously provided me by Professor Edward Laumann of the University of Michigan.

[5] Bernard C. Rosen, review of *The Religious Factor* by Lenski, in the *American Sociological Review*, 27 (February 1962).

[6] Andrew M. Greeley and Peter H. Rossi, *The Education of Catholic Americans* (Chicago: Aldine Publishing Company, 1966); Andrew M. Greeley, *Religion and Careers* (New York: Sheed and Ward, 1963), hereinafter referred to as *Religion.*

[7] See, for example, Mariam K. Slater, "My Son the Doctor: Aspects of Mobility Among American Jews," *American Sociological Review*, 34 (1969), pp. 359-73; Nathan Glazer, "The American Jew and the Attainment of Middle-Class Rank: Some Trends and Explanations," in *The Jews: Social Patterns of an American Group*, ed. by Marshall Sklare (Glencoe, Ill.: Free Press, 1958), pp. 138-46.

social mobility patterns, political preferences, and other matters a generation or two ago, and that these have only recently been eroded as the Church has become more fully "Americanized." It is even conceivable that Jews were notably less successful at the turn of the century than they have been in recent years. Detroit as portrayed by Lenski, that is to say, may by now be somewhat unrepresentative of the situation of Catholics in contemporary American society as a whole, as Lenski's critics forcefully argue, but it may possibly be unrepresentative only in that it is a city in which the dominant pattern of an earlier era has survived longer than in the society in general.

This, of course, is a hypothesis which cannot be tested by contemporary survey research, however sophisticated. It is a proposition about the past, about a time when religion may have had a quite different social meaning for its followers, and must be tested against evidence drawn from the historical record. The present essay, drawn from a larger study of social mobility in Boston since 1880, seeks to assess the influence of religion upon career patterns in one major city over a period of more than eighty years, and thus to place the current debate over this issue in broader perspective.

Boston, of course, is but a single city, and some critics would argue that it is a far from representative one. I certainly would not claim that Boston is America writ small and that all the findings of this essay may be generalized to the society as a whole without qualification. But it is an inescapable if cruel fact that the task of piecing together the evidence necessary for a systematic analysis of social mobility in the American past is so formidable that the investigator customarily must confine himself to a single city. Given that necessity, and acknowledging the need for similar research in other communities in the future, there are grounds for believing that Boston is a quite satisfactory choice for inquiry into the question at hand. It was—and is—one of the greatest centers of Catholic strength in the United States. If it could be shown that even there Catholics suffered from distinctive career disabilities, as was in fact the case, it would be reasonable to assume that they confronted similar, if not greater, disabilities in places where the Church's position was more precarious. Furthermore, the larger study from which this paper is drawn reveals that, contrary to popular legend, Boston was not an unusually stagnant, caste-ridden community.[8] Overall rates of social mobility in Boston closely

[8] Typical statements of the clichés about the Boston social structure are to be found in Cleveland Amory's *The Proper Bostonians* (New York: E. P. Dutton & Co., Inc., 1947) and William Shannon's *The American Irish* (New York: Macmillan Co., 1963), intelligent journalistic accounts which make claims that are badly in need of critical scrutiny.

resembled those in such cities as Indianapolis, San Jose, and Norristown, Pennsylvania, so that there is no reason to believe that the poor occupational showing of Boston Catholics may be attributed to an unusually constricted and rigid opportunity structure in the community as a whole. It is possible that future studies in other cities will modify or overturn the conclusions of this paper, but in the absence of such studies the burden of proof would seem to lie upon those who would argue the unrepresentativeness of Boston on *a priori* grounds.

Some Preliminary Difficulties

The analysis which follows examines patterns of social mobility in a number of samples of the Boston male population at various points between 1880 and 1963, and there are some technical difficulties which require brief mention. First of all, the information available about the religious affiliation of the men studied is scanty and incomplete. One reason for the paucity of historical research dealing with the issue at hand is that the United States Census and most other American public records suitable for analysis of this contain no information about individual religious preferences; unlike ethnic background and other social characteristics, religion in America is assumed to be a private matter. Six samples of the Boston population were utilized in the present study: 1) a sample from the manuscript schedules of the U.S. Census of 1880 of men aged twenty to thirty-nine; 2) a sample from the same source of youths under twenty in 1880; 3) a sample from marriage license applications of men married in Boston in 1910; 4) a sample from birth records of fathers of male infants born in the city in 1930; 5) a sample of adult male residents of Cambridge and Belmont interviewed in 1963 in the course of a survey conducted by another investigator; and 6) a sample of males born in Boston in 1930, the sons of the fathers who comprised the fourth sample. In only two of these six samples was the religion of each respondent specified.

But in the third sample, of men married in the city in 1910, the sources indicated the type of wedding ceremony which was performed. It was thus possible to distinguish men married by Protestant ministers, Roman Catholic priests, and Jewish rabbis. There was, in addition, a fourth group, those joined in marriage by a Justice of the Peace. But these were only a modest fraction of the total—17 per cent of the marriages, and only 11 per cent of the marriages by those men about whom there was enough information for mobility analysis. The overwhelming majority of Boston's young men at this time were sufficiently religious to marry under church auspices, so that we may analyze group differences in mobility patterns without worrying that large numbers of individuals were part of a religious subcommunity in some sense but could not be identified because they were married by civil ceremony. The religion of sample members was known with some accuracy in the case of the 1910 sample, and it was known in the case of Edward Laumann's survey of Belmont and Cambridge residents in 1963, which included a question concerning religious affiliation. Laumann did not gather any information about career mobility, one of the principal concerns of the present paper, but he did examine intergenerational mobility and kindly made special tabulations of religious differences in mobility patterns for my use, so that his data provides a secure foundation for part of the analysis here.

With two secure points of reference—accurate information about the religious affiliations of members of two of the samples—it seemed appropriate to take an otherwise indefensible liberty with the other samples. It was decided to guess the religious affiliation of individuals on the basis of such data as nationality and name, and to see if the patterns revealed in the samples in which religion was definitely known resembled those in which religion was merely assumed. If not, if the differences were glaring, then obviously the guessing procedure was of doubtful accuracy. But happily the guessing game seems to have been reasonably accurate, for the same patterns do recur in both types of samples.

This is not surprising, for the guessing was not as difficult and arbitrary as might be thought. Men of Irish or Italian birth or parentage were assumed to be Roman Catholics. Likewise for those with Irish names, though actually born in England or Canada. Men from Catholic South German states like Bavaria were also classified Catholic, as were French and Portuguese immigrants. Those of Russian, or Polish origins, and those from Germany with common Jewish names were taken to be Jewish. (In this instance attention was paid to the first names of all members of the family; many German surnames could be either Jewish or non-Jewish, but the presence of a wife or children named after Christian saints resolved the difficulty in many instances.) There was often a further clue in the two 1930 birth record samples, for it was known what hospitals the sons had been born in, and patronage of a Catholic or Jewish hospital was regarded as one indication of possible Catholic or Jewish affiliation.

Some check upon the accuracy of this guessing game was made by examining the 1910 data cards, on which religion was known, and assigning individuals to religious categories on the basis of these other clues without looking at the column indicating type of religious ceremony. This check indicated that proper judgments were made in roughly nine out of ten cases.

It should be noted, however, that in the cohorts where religion is merely inferred, the category "Protestant" is a residual one, including all those who could not reasonably be placed in the Catholic or Jewish pigeonholes. To the extent that errors were made, Catholics and Jews were more often classified Protestant than vice versa. This would mean that Catholic-Protestant and Jewish-Protestant differences are, if anything, understated here, since the Protestant group is to some extent diluted by misclassified Catholics and Jews.

A second difficulty with what follows is that the samples are quite small, and some of the key findings thus attain only a very weak level of statistical significance. The samples together total nearly 8,000 men, but the information necessary for analysis of their mobility patterns was missing for a large fraction of them. Mobility analysis requires knowledge about an individual's status at at least two points in time (career or intragenerational mobility), or about his status relative to his father's (intergenerational mobility). Both types of mobility are important, and it would be ideal to have both types of information for all persons studied. But many of the fathers of men in the samples did not live in Boston, and local sources thus did not specify their occupations. Nor was information about career mobility available in all cases, for large numbers of these men lived in Boston for only a short time, and then moved away. The study assumes that ten years is the minimum interval suitable for the measurement of career mobility, but only 60 per cent of the males in the samples remained in Boston for as much as a decade. As a result of these circumstances, the number of cases upon which the subsequent analysis of career mobility is based is 1,651, while the corresponding figure for intergenerational mobility is 1,658.

In some cases, therefore, the cell numbers on which the percentages in the tables below are based are dismayingly small. This means that some of the findings are significant at only the .90 level, with as much as one chance in ten that chance variation might have accounted for the observed pattern, and some do not even pass that weak test of significance. This is not too troubling, however, for the argument of the paper does not rest upon the pattern observed in any one sample, but rather upon the recurrence of patterns through several separate and independent samples. A finding based on such small numbers that it might be due to mere chance in one of five instances could be attributable to chance less than 1 per cent of the time if it recurred in three separate samples (1/5 x 1/5 x 1/5).[9] It is the consistency of findings between samples, not the high level of statistical significance of any one finding, that gives me confidence in the analysis which follows.

Patterns of Career Mobility

Catholics, Protestants, and Jews in late nineteenth- and twentieth-century Boston characteristically began their careers at different occupational levels and had different prospects of moving up or down the occupational ladder between their first jobs and their last jobs.[10] The measure of status employed here is a rough and ready one. It is assumed that the central divide in the occupational hierarchy of the community was that between non-manual or white-collar and manual or blue-collar jobs, and that movement across this divide was the most important form of occupational mobility.[11] Both of these broad classes

[9] Lenski develops this point well in his appendix on "Sampling Error and Statistical Significance" in *Religious Factor.*

[10] The terms "first job" and "last job" are not strictly accurate. It would require a questionnaire administered to men at retirement to identify these with precision. Those who attempt to reconstruct career patterns of individuals by tracing them through historical records must settle for far less satisfactory data, data pertaining to the date at which the census-taker or some other record-keeper happened to gather information. In this study "first job" was arbitrarily defined as the first job known to have been held by a sample member, so long as he held it prior to age thirty. In many instances an individual was caught at what probably was his first actual job, at the age of sixteen or seventeen perhaps. But in some cases men were already in their twenties before they could be located occupationally, so the concept really pertains to some job held while still a relatively young man. Likewise, "last job" means the last job held in Boston as revealed by the tracing method, so long as it was held at the age of thirty or older. The "last job" of some sample members was held when the individuals in question were in their fifties or sixties, but some died or migrated out of Boston at an earlier point. If there was information to rank them occupationally after they had reached the point of settling down that usually takes place around the age thirty, it was deemed sufficient. The choice of thirty as the watershed was dictated not by the assumptions of today's rebels in the war between the generations but rather by the data of the study itself, which disclosed a marked slowing of occupational mobility for men thirty and above.

[11] Evidence that this occupational classification scheme, with two basic classes and four strata, accurately reflected the distribution of income, security, power, and prestige in the community will have to be deferred to the full report of the study, but an illustrative piece of evidence on the matter of job security may be offered here. The 1900 Census revealed that 17 per cent of the adult males of Boston had been unemployed for a month or more in the preceding 12 months. The rate for lawyers and physicians, however, was a mere 1 per cent, for merchants and bankers 3 per cent, for white-collar workers as a group only 6 per cent. The rate for all blue-collar workers, by contrast, was a striking 24 per cent, and for unskilled blue-collar workers an appalling 41 per cent; calculated from detailed data on 129 occupations in U.S. Bureau of the Census, *U.S. Census of 1900, Special Reports—Occupations* (Washington: U.S. Govt. Printing Office, 1901), pp. 495-98. For evidence of similar class differences in income, see Robert

had important subdivisions, to be sure, and where relevant I will distinguish four occupational strata, dividing the white-collar class into an upper stratum comprising professionals and proprietors or officials of large enterprises and a lower stratum of clerks, salesmen, and petty proprietors, and similarly dividing the blue-collar group into skilled and low manual (semi-skilled or unskilled) employees. But the proper starting point, at least, is to ask about the distribution of the religious groups of the city into the manual and non-manual classes.

There were striking religious differences in the career patterns of Boston residents (see Table 1). At the time they first entered the

TABLE 1. RELIGIOUS DIFFERENCES IN CAREER MOBILITY FROM FIRST TO LAST JOB

	Per Cent of Group				
Birth Cohort and Religion	*Starting in White Collar*	*Ending in White Collar*	*Blue-Collar Climbers*[c]	*White-Collar Skidders*[d]	*Number*
1840-59					
"Catholic"[a]	14*	33*	28	33*	105
"Protestant"	59	65	26	9	196
1860-79					
"Catholic"	41*	43*	20	24*	297
"Protestant"	65	64	25	14	340
"Jewish"	73	85*	57	5	26
1880-89					
Catholic	32*	44	29	23*	203
Protestant	41	50	23	10	151
Jewish	43	60	43*	19	37
Unknown[b]	33	53	33	6	49
1900-09					
"Catholic"	6*	22*	18	20	76
"Protestant"	38	39	13	20	133
"Jewish"	71*	82*	55*	7	38

[a] The quotation marks surrounding the religious group labels except in the case of the 1880-89 cohort are to remind the reader that these are *assumed* religious affiliations and are doubtless erroneous in some cases. As explained in the text, any errors of classification that were made most likely blurred, rather than sharpened, Catholic-Protestant and Jewish-Protestant differences. Quotation marks are similarly used as a caution in subsequent tables.

[b] These 49 men were married by a Justice of the Peace.

[c] This is the proportion of men who began their careers as manual workers but were in white-collar occupations at the time of their last job.

[d] This is the proportion of those who began work in white-collar jobs who fell into a blue-collar post by the end of their careers.

* An asterisk in this and subsequent tables indicates that the figure is significantly different from the Protestant figure at the .90 level of probability, using a one-tail test because the differences were predicted.

K. Burn, "The Comparative Economic Position of Manual and White Collar Employees," *Journal of Business*, 27 (1954), pp. 257-67.

labor market, Jewish youths were disproportionately concentrated in white-collar callings (though the number of cases on which the percentages were computed was too small to make the results more than suggestive). Boston Catholics, by contrast, typically gravitated toward jobs in the lower reaches of the occupational structure. In three of the four cohorts they were far more heavily concentrated in blue-collar callings than Protestants at the start of their careers, and in the fourth somewhat more so. Young Jews, it seems, quickly found jobs working with their heads; Catholics tended to start out working with their hands; Protestants were more evenly distributed between blue-collar and white-collar occupations.

A cautionary note is in order, however, for these generalizations do not apply so clearly to the 1880-1889 cohort, which is the one in which religious information is most reliable. Men married by a priest wore a white collar at the outset somewhat less often than men married by a Protestant minister or by a rabbi, but the disparity was not striking, and the Jewish-Protestant difference visible in the other cohorts does not show at all in this one, which suggests the possibility that the patterns displayed by the other cohorts are perhaps due to errors in religious classification. In the case of the Jews this seems unlikely, for another explanation is readily available. The Jews in the early cohorts were largely of German origins, while those born in the 1880s and married in 1910 were much poorer, recently arrived newcomers from Poland and Russia. By 1930, when the 1900-1909 cohort first worked, the East European Jews were sufficiently established to give their sons as large a head start as the German Jews had in the late nineteenth century—compare the 73 per cent and 71 per cent rate of initial white-collar job-holding for the second and fourth cohorts—but in the 1880-1889 cohort young Jews, like young Protestants and young Catholics, started their careers working with their hands in a majority of cases. And it is likely that Catholic-Protestant differences in first jobs were smaller in the 1880-1889 group than earlier because this sample, unlike the earlier ones, was composed entirely of married men aged 21 to 30 in 1910; quite possibly disproportionate numbers of Protestant white-collar workers in this age bracket were unmarried still and were thus unrepresented in the sample. A similar argument, however, would apply to the group of men born 1900-1909, all of whom were married too. Since the religious differences observed in the first two cohorts reappeared there too, there remains some puzzle about the 1880-1889 group. In any event, even in that somewhat distinctive cohort Catholics differed from Protestants and Jews in the same way as in the other cohorts—that is, they gravitated toward proletarian callings. The point is only that this tendency was not as marked.

With respect to religious differences in rates of movement up and down the occupational ladder between first and last job, there was a clear and uniform pattern, so uniform as to assuage any doubts that may be occasioned by the smallness of the samples and the uncertain accuracy of the information about religious affiliations. Three points stand out clearly.

It is evident, first, that Catholic youths who began their careers as blue-collar workers were just as likely as their Protestant counterparts to move upward later into a white-collar position. At the end of their careers, Boston Catholics were more often working with their hands than Boston Protestants, but the difference was due chiefly to the fact that they were more prone to enter the labor market initially at the manual level. There is no indication, in other words, that Catholic manual workers were less eager for upward mobility into the white-collar world than Protestants, or less successful at realizing their ambitions. Approximately one in four made this move in the course of their careers; in three of the four cohorts the Catholic rate of upward career mobility was actually a shade higher than the Protestant. It was not insufficient upward mobility after their first job that held Boston Catholics back, but the circumstance that destined them to so often take laboring jobs when they first left school and began to work.

A second conclusion suggested by this evidence is that popular folklore concerning the mobility achievements of the Jews is indeed well founded. Not only did an unusually high proportion of Jewish youths in Boston start their careers in the upper reaches of the occupational structure; those who were forced to work in blue-collar callings at the outset were extraordinarily successful at moving into the white-collar world later. Only about half of the Jews who began their careers as laborers—43, 57, and 45 per cent respectively—were still employed in manual work at the time of the last job. The Jewish rate of upward mobility was double that of other groups!

Perhaps the most important pattern visible in these tables, however, is the dramatic tendency of Catholic youths who had begun their careers in non-manual jobs to lose those jobs and to end their lives wearing a blue rather than a white collar, with all that this shift implied for wage levels, employment security, and social prestige. In the 1880-1889 cohort, where religious affiliation is reliably known, Catholics who began their careers in the white-collar world were more than twice as likely as Protestants to fall into a laboring job later on. The differential was a little smaller but still clear for one of the two earlier cohorts, and even larger for the other. Only in the last cohort, men born in the first decade of the twentieth century and at a critical point in their careers during the Great Depression of the 1930s, did the Catholic propensity for high downward mobility fail to manifest itself. Whether this indicates a basic long-term improvement in the position of Boston Catholics, or merely a temporary blurring of religious differences in the face of dismally hard times cannot be answered definitively with the data available, but something more will be said about this issue at a later point.

That there was a distinctive Catholic mobility pattern, a skidding syndrome in which youths who started with a foothold in the white-collar occupational world were unable to maintain it for long, is further evident from an inspection of detailed data on the occupational shifts made by sample members from decade to decade (see Table 2).

TABLE 2. RELIGIOUS DIFFERENCES IN CAREER MOBILITY FROM DECADE TO DECADE

Birth Cohort and Decade	*Per Cent of* Blue-Collar Workers Climbing to White Collar During the Decade: Catholic	Blue-Collar Workers Climbing to White Collar During the Decade: Protestant	White-Collar Workers Skidding to Blue Collar During the Decade: Catholic	White-Collar Workers Skidding to Blue Collar During the Decade: Protestant
1840-59[a]				
1880-90	12 (169)	12 (155)	19* (37)	10 (161)
1890-1900	9 (102)	11 (95)	11* (35)	2 (121)
1900-10	7 (62)	9 (47)	3 (29)	0 (85)
1860-79				
1880-90	13 (40)	17 (36)	50 (24)	35 (34)
1890-1900	17 (83)	21 (57)	22* (37)	12 (113)
1900-10	12 (137)	14 (93)	14* (94)	6 (161)
1870-89				
1910-20	24 (119)	20 (81)	12 (66)	10 (72)
1920-30	9 (65)	11 (45)	10 (62)	9 (54)
1930-40	6 (53)	5 (40)	12 (42)	5 (38)
1890-1909				
1930-40	10 (126)	10 (146)	22 (23)	20 (94)
1940-54	9 (69)	12 (85)	7 (15)	2 (52)
1954-63	4 (28)	10 (31)	15 (13)	6 (34)

[a] The age limits of some of these cohorts have been broadened beyond those given in the preceding table, so as to include men whose "first" jobs—those held prior to age thirty—were unknown because they were already thirty or more at the time the sample was taken. It seemed worth sacrificing the more precise age controls employed earlier to obtain a larger number of cases for analysis. Number of cases in parentheses.

(Sample attrition made it necessary to leave Jews out of consideration here.) There was little difference between the two groups with respect to upward mobility from manual to non-manual jobs over the span of a decade. The Protestant rate of upward movement was a shade higher than the Catholic in eight of the twelve decades observed, but not one of these differences was large enough to be significant at the .90 level, so that the Catholic handicap on this count was slight. With respect to downward mobility, however, the Catholic figure was higher in all twelve instances, and in two-thirds of the cases it was more than 50 per cent higher. Four of these differences were statistically significant.[12]

It could, however, be argued that this apparent skidding syndrome is attributable to the crudeness of the occupational categories employed in the analysis. Suppose that Catholic white-collar workers were heavily concentrated in jobs in the lower reaches of the white-collar class, as minor clerks, salesmen, and petty proprietors, and that white-collar Protestants were typically professionals, prosperous merchants, or managers of large enterprises. That downward mobility from jobs of the former kind would be more common is obvious. If this were the case, the mobility handicap of Boston Catholics would not be that a Catholic white-collar worker was more likely to skid to a manual job than a Protestant who started work in the same occupation; the problem would be the excessive concentration of Catholics in jobs from which downward mobility was common, and their under-representation in more secure non-manual posts.

Inspection of more detailed mobility matrices (not included here), which reveals the career patterns of workers in the upper white-collar stratum and the lower white-collar stratum separately, does not, however, alter the conclusion previously advanced. It is indeed true that the Catholic white-collar class included fewer bankers, physicians, and factory managers than its Protestant counterpart, and more menial white-collar employees. But this fact is not sufficient to explain the prevalence of the skidding syndrome among Catholics, for it appears even when we confine our attention to the experience of men in lower white-collar callings. Protestant clerks, salesmen, and small proprietors were sometimes downwardly mobile; similarly situated Catholics were so far more often.

One could, however, push this line of attack still further, and main-

[12] As is apparent in the table, mobility was strongly related to age. As each of the four cohorts grew older, there was a general tendency toward diminished mobility in either direction, a pattern equally pronounced with both religious groups.

tain that such categories as "low white collar" and "high white collar" are still too crude and heterogeneous. Suppose, for instance, that Catholics in the low white-collar stratum were typically clerks in small groceries, while Protestant white-collar youths were typically bank clerks. Though the job designation is the same—"clerk"—the jobs themselves differ radically in many respects, one obvious one being that the bank clerk is situated on a ladder with higher rungs which are clearly visible and quite possibly within his grasp, whereas the grocery clerk may be in a "way-station" calling which he might abandon (or be forced to abandon) a few years hence, older but no better equipped for other white-collar positions than he was when he started. That a group of grocery clerks should experience more downward mobility in the course of their careers than a group of bank clerks would hardly be surprising.

I cannot explore this issue much further, alas, both because the sources of occupational information did not unfailingly make the necessary distinctions, often supplying no more than the datum that so and so was a "clerk," and because the size of the samples limited the possible breakdowns by precise occupational title even when it was provided. But there was enough evidence on this point to persuade me that the Catholic skidding syndrome cannot be explained away in this manner. The sample taken from the manuscript schedules of the U.S. Census of 1880 permitted some analysis of this issue. It revealed that Catholic youths were somewhat more frequently store clerks and less often office clerks than Protestants; of all low white-collar employees, 53 per cent of the Catholics and 41 per cent of the Protestants clerked in stores rather than offices. Clerking in a store was indeed a less secure white-collar job than clerking in an office; downward mobility from such positions was a little more common. But it was not so much more common, nor was the disproportionate concentration of Catholic youths in these posts so great, as to fully account for the Catholic propensity to skid.

There were, in sum, important religious differences in career mobility patterns, with Jews enjoying a clear advantage over Protestants, and with Catholics bringing up the rear. The Catholic handicap, however, lay not in insufficient upward mobility in the course of a typical career, but in two other weaknesses: an initial heavy concentration on the lower rungs of the occupational ladder and a pronounced tendency for those Catholics who did start out reasonably well situated to lose their white-collar posts and to drop down into a blue-collar calling as they grew older.

Fathers and Sons

However interesting and valuable, analysis of social mobility *within* the span of an individual's career is sorely limited in a crucial respect. The level of a man's first job is a highly imperfect measure of his actual starting point in the occupational race, for there are advantages (or disadvantages) stemming from the position of his family in the social stratification system which do not necessarily have their impact at the time of first job but are felt only later. Thus the legendary factory owner who insists that his son begin at the bottom to learn the business but who later provides him with a cushy executive position. It is for this reason that the scholarly literature on social mobility concentrates on movement from generation to generation, on the extent to which sons "inherit" the occupational level upon which their fathers worked.

It is particularly important to consider the influence of parental status in interpreting measures of the career mobility of different groups whose social origins may have been very different. The preceding analysis, for example, would appear in a very different light if it could be shown that: 1) coming from a working-class rather than a middle-class family exerted a powerful influence on the subsequent careers of young men in Boston in this period; and 2) that Catholic youths came from working-class homes far more often than their Protestant or Jewish rivals. If that were the case, the explanation of the poor showing of Catholic youths would be greatly simplified; the skidding pattern, for instance, would appear as a natural reversion to the social level of their fathers. To explore this possibility we must examine the relationship between the last occupation held by sons in the sample and the occupation of their fathers.

The sources did not indicate the occupations of fathers not living in Boston, so that the number of cases for this analysis is even smaller than in the previous section. This made the number of Jewish cases too few to be of even illustrative value, so that only Catholics and Protestants are treated. It happens that no information was available on the occupations of the fathers of the men in the 1900-1909 cohort, so that this cohort had to be dropped. But by way of compensation the material is richer for the more recent past. Laumann's 1963 survey in Belmont and Cambridge, two communities within the Boston metropolitan area, offers one valuable point of reference. And in addition we may use some data pertaining to a sample of sons born in Boston in 1930. No tabulation of the career mobility of these youths was given earlier because many were not working in Boston in 1954, our first trace year for the cohort, presumably because they were in the armed services. But substantial numbers had reappeared by 1963, making it possible to relate their job level at age thirty-three with that of their fathers' regular occupations.[13] It will be possible, therefore, with these two sources of evidence from the early 1960s to say something more about the issue mentioned at the outset of this paper—the question of religious differences in mobility patterns in contemporary America.

We may control for the influence of having a father who was especially favorably or especially unfavorably situated occupationally by looking at religious differences in the mobility of sons born into working-class homes and sons born into middle-class homes separately, as in Tables 3 and 4.

TABLE 3. RELIGIOUS DIFFERENCES IN OCCUPATIONAL ACHIEVEMENT AT CAREER'S END: WORKING-CLASS SONS

	Per Cent of Group with Last Job in				
Birth Cohort and Religion	*High White Collar*	*Low White Collar*	*Skilled*	*Low Manual*	*Number*
1840-59					
"Catholic"	5	31	21	44	62
"Protestant"	13	35	29	22	48
1860-79					
"Catholic"	4*	33	25*	37*	298
"Protestant"	9	36	30	24	226
1870-89					
Catholic	6	41	17	37	66
Protestant	10	33	30	28	40
c. 1890-1930[a]					
Catholic	16*	16	21	47	170
Protestant	26	15	21	38	62
1930					
"Catholic"	5	32	20*	42	49
"Protestant"	6	22	35	37	69

[a] This is based upon a retabulation of the data from Edward Laumann's previously described sample of Cambridge and Belmont. No breakdown of intergenerational mobility by religion is supplied in the published version, *Prestige and Association in an Urban Community*, but the author very kindly performed the tabulation upon request and furnished the results to me. The relatively high rate of upward mobility into the high white-collar class for both groups is doubtless attributable to the fact that residents of Cambridge and Belmont hold such jobs with somewhat greater frequency than the labor force of Boston proper, a feature that is evident in Table 4 as well.

[13] The matter of determining father's "regular" occupation was not so simple, in fact, because of the high volume of career mobility in the community. In instances

The overall rate of upward mobility for working-class sons in general was quite impressive; neither the Catholic nor the Protestant sectors of the laboring class were a closed caste (see Table 3). But clear religious differences in opportunities for advancement were evident in all but the last of the five samples. In the first four, Protestant youths climbed to the top of the occupational ladder more frequently than Catholics; in each Catholics were more prone to end their careers in unskilled or semi-skilled laboring jobs. It was only in the earliest two cohorts, however, that Catholic working-class sons had less access to jobs at the lower white-collar level—clerical, sales, and petty proprietorships—and then their margin of disadvantage was slight. In the later samples Catholics actually gravitated toward these positions more frequently than Protestants. It was not that they found the middle-class impossible to penetrate, but that they clustered somewhat more than their Protestant rivals in the less rewarding and demanding middle-class positions. And those Catholic youths who were unable to climb out of the working class were less likely to obtain a skilled job and correspondingly more likely to work in the least desirable low manual callings.

In the very last sample, of youths born in Boston in 1930, Catholics seem to have fared a little better than Protestants. It is difficult to know how seriously to take this evidence, because the men in question were still in mid-career, but it is possible that the development Greeley and Rossi discern in their national sample—the apparent thrust of Catholic working-class sons into middle-class callings at about the same pace as Protestants—is apparent in these Boston figures. If so, however, it was a quite recent development, a distinct departure from the historic pattern manifested by previous generations of Catholic residents of the city.

A similar shift of pattern did not take place among Catholics and Protestants of middle-class origins (see Table 4). The number of cases for analysis is dismayingly small in most of the samples, but the consistency of pattern is striking. In every cohort, Protestant middle-class youths ended their careers in the upper white-collar category far more frequently than Catholics of similar class background; in each Catholic men skidded into blue-collar jobs, and especially low-skilled manual jobs, much more often than Protestants. For instance, in the case of the sample of men born in the 1870s and 1880s, in which religious

---

in which a father held jobs at various levels at different points in his own career, the point of comparison for the intergenerational analysis was the father's occupation at the time the son first entered the labor market.

identification is most precise, Catholic middle-class sons obtained only 40 per cent as many high white-collar posts as Protestants, and three and a half times as many ended their careers at the bottom of the occupational heap.

It might be thought that the relative inability of Catholic middle-class youths to penetrate the upper reaches of the occupational structure and their unusual propensity to skid into manual jobs indicate only that the control for social class background employed in the analysis is too crude. If the typical "middle-class" Protestant father was

TABLE 4. RELIGIOUS DIFFERENCES IN OCCUPATIONAL ACHIEVEMENT AT CAREER'S END: MIDDLE-CLASS SONS

	Per Cent of Group with Last Job in				
Birth Cohort and Religion	*High White Collar*	*Low White Collar*	*Skilled*	*Low Manual*	*Number*
1840-59					
"Catholic"	29	18*	35*	18	17
"Protestant"	38	49	5	8	78
1860-79					
"Catholic"	24*	50	13	13*	46
"Protestant"	42	42	9	6	179
1870-89					
Catholic	16*	48	8	28*	25
Protestant	40	48	4	8	25
c. 1890-1930					
Catholic	53*	20*	14	13*	74
Protestant	84	6	9	1	67
1930					
"Catholic"	0*	57	14	28	14
"Protestant"	21	47	16	17	43

a lawyer and his Catholic counterpart the proprietor of a small grocery, we could expect the career trajectories of Protestant and Catholic sons to differ greatly, for we would be comparing a marginal lower-middle-class group with a solidly upper-middle-class group. When the data are tabulated so as to distinguish high white-collar from low white-collar families, Catholic fathers prove to have indeed been more often in the latter category. But this did not explain away the distinctive career patterns of their children. The same tendencies manifest in Table 4 reappear in these more refined tabulations as well (not given here).

Taking into account the social class background of sample members, in sum, does not modify the conclusions ventured earlier concerning the occupational handicaps of Boston Catholics. In one way, indeed, the relative position of Catholics seems worse than had appeared earlier. Though in the course of their careers Catholic youths climbed from blue-collar to white-collar callings about as frequently as their Protestant rivals, Catholics from working-class families experienced less upward intergenerational mobility than Protestants in all the samples except that of men first entering the labor market in the post-World War II period. Catholic working-class sons moved into the lower reaches of the middle class in large numbers, but less often attained top-ranked professional and managerial posts and were more likely to end their careers as mere unskilled or semi-skilled laborers.

What is more, Catholic youths who grew up in relatively privileged circumstances—whose fathers held a middle-class job of some kind—were much less successful than Protestants of comparable class origins. They won their share or more than their share of routine clerical and sales jobs but were heavily underrepresented in upper white-collar and heavily overrepresented in menial low manual jobs in all five cohorts.

Religion or Nationality?

In an earlier paper I demonstrated that neither first nor second generation immigrants in Boston fared as well as native-born men of native-born parentage in the occupational competition.[14] Now it happens, of course, to have been the case that in late nineteenth-century America the Roman Catholic Church was overwhelmingly a church of immigrants and their children; even today Catholics are far more often of recent immigrant stock than the population as a whole. There were indeed sharp differences in the social mobility of Catholics and Protestants, but how can we be sure that these differences are not spurious, the result not of religion per se but of underlying differences in national origins which happen to have been correlated with religion?

At first blush the problem seems relatively simple. Most of Boston's Catholics were immigrants, or at least the descendants of fairly recent immigrants, but by no means all of Boston's immigrants were Catholics. The size of the samples was too small, and the overlapping of religious and nationality categories too great, to permit a thorough multivariate analysis, in which religious differences could be tabulated with nationality held constant, and vice versa. But it is easy enough to show that classifying individuals by religion rather than ethnic generation—

[14] See my paper, "Immigrants and WASPs: Ethnic Differences in Occupational Mobility in Boston, 1880-1940," in *Nineteenth-Century Cities: Essays in the New Urban History*, ed. by Stephan Thernstrom and Richard Sennett (New Haven: Yale Univ. Press, 1969).

thus including Protestant immigrants with old-stock American Protestants—sharpens rather than blurs the differences that can be observed when first or second generation immigrants are compared with old-stock Americans. In the sample of men born between 1870 and 1889, for instance, 15 per cent of the foreign-born middle-class males had skidded into a working-class occupation by the end of their career, but almost four in ten Catholic middle-class youths. In this sense religion exerted a more powerful influence than ethnic generation.

There is a more complicated issue, here, however, for it happens that Boston's Catholics in the period of the study were largely drawn from a few ethnic groups. A clear majority were of Irish descent, and many of the rest were Italian-Americans. It is clear that what we have isolated as the Catholic mobility syndrome was not simply a first or second generation immigrant syndrome, but what of the possibility that it was an Irish-American and Italian-American syndrome? The relative smallness of the non-Irish and non-Italian Catholic population of the city until fairly recently and the limited size of our samples yield too few cases of this kind for an analysis which might illuminate the influence of religion per se, purified of its association with nationality. If religion and nationality were so closely entwined historically that they cannot be disentangled analytically there is little to be done, except to note the possibility that study of another city in which the Catholic population was largely of other national backgrounds—Milwaukee, for example, with its German and Polish Catholics—might lead to different conclusions. The German Catholics of Poughkeepsie, New York, did not display the Boston Catholic pattern.[15] Thus "Catholic" here must be taken as shorthand for "Irish and Italian Catholic." Since those two nationalities have been the backbone of American Catholic strength historically, this is perhaps not too grave a limitation.

Toward an Explanation of Group Differences in Achievement

Differences in ethnic origins and religious affiliations were clearly associated with differences in occupational achievement. Some groups fared notably better than others in levels of initial occupational placement and in subsequent mobility up and down the social scale. To explain *why* this was the case is extraordinarily difficult with the sketchy evidence at hand. Adequate data about a number of variables of possible relevance—information, for instance, on the educational background of sample members—were simply not available. A rough

[15] Clyde Griffen, "Making It in America: Social Mobility in Mid-Nineteenth Century Poughkeepsie," *New York History*, 51 (October 1970), pp. 479-99.

estimate, however, may be made of the relative importance of a few of the factors most likely to be significant.

DISCRIMINATION

One invitingly straightforward explanation of the difficulties experienced by Boston's Catholic immigrants and their children is that they were treated unfairly in the market place—that prejudiced Protestant employers were unwilling to give Catholics jobs for which they were duly qualified, and that Protestant bankers unfairly refused needed credit to aspiring Catholic businessmen.

It certainly is true that in late nineteenth-century Boston the overwhelming majority of those who were in a position to hire, promote, fire, or lend money to others were Protestant Yankees, and even today this element of the population is overrepresented in management and banking. That many such persons were very unfavorably disposed toward Catholics is well known. Back in the 1880s Boston upper-class circles warmly applauded the anti-Catholic tirades of Edward A. Freeman, whose ingenious solution to America's social problems was to hope that every Irishman would kill a Negro and then be hanged for it![16] As late as the 1920s the word "Protestant" frequently appeared as a necessary qualification in want ads published in the Boston *Transcript.*[17] Joseph P. Kennedy left Boston for New York in those years because of his conviction that certain doors in the local business world would always remain closed to him because of his religion. It is undoubtedly true that until fairly recently religious and ethnic prejudice restricted the opportunities open to Boston Catholics to some degree, especially at the top of the economic structure in such areas as finance.

Sheer prejudice, however, cannot be more than part of the explanation of the difficulties experienced by Catholic newcomers, because other groups that fared much better seem to have encountered similar hostility, most notably the Jews. Prejudice against immigrants in general, and especially against the so-called "new immigrants" from Southern and Eastern Europe, was rising sharply in the late nineteenth and early twentieth centuries. Freeman directed his attack against not only the Irish but against all "non-Anglo-Saxon" immigrants, and the animus of groups like the Immigration Restriction League was felt chiefly

[16] Barbara M. Solomon, *Ancestors and Immigrants, A Changing New England Tradition* (Cambridge: Harvard Univ. Press, 1956), p. 235, hereinafter referred to as *Ancestors.*

[17] J. J. Huthmacher, *Massachusetts People and Politics, 1919-1932* (Cambridge: Belknap Press of Harvard Univ. Press, 1959), p. 235. The Irish themselves frequently complained about what they took to be discriminatory treatment by employers; see, for example, the *Boston Pilot,* January 3, 1880.

by more recent newcomers, many of them non-Catholic.[18] By the turn of the century, Boston School Committee members of Irish descent had arrived at a certain modus vivendi with their Yankee colleagues, both groups deploring the "new immigrants" and calling for more strenuous efforts to "Americanize" them via the public school system.[19] Whatever the importance of discrimination in holding back newcomers in general, therefore, it is doubtful that it suffices to explain the sharply different experiences of Catholic and non-Catholic immigrants and their children.

BACKGROUND HANDICAPS

A second circumstance that affected the economic adjustment of particular groups was that some arrived with background handicaps that impaired their ability to compete: illiteracy, inability to speak English, lack of vocational skills, unfamiliarity with the rhythms of urban life.

Such factors inevitably influenced the adjustment of newcomers to American life. Ireland and Italy (at least Southern Italy, from which most immigrants came) had experienced little industrialization and urbanization when the flow of migrants across the ocean was at its height. Thus it was that approximately half of the English, Scotch, and Welsh immigrants to the United States between 1875 and 1910 had worked in skilled jobs before migrating, but barely a tenth of the Irish and not many more of the Italians.[20] Of the Irish immigrants living in Boston in 1909 who had been employed before their departure to America, 64 per cent had done agricultural work, and 42 per cent of the Italians, as opposed to a mere 2 per cent of the Jews.[21] The latter had been city dwellers in the Old World. Although not as many Jews as legend would have it were merchants and professionals, about two-thirds had been in skilled trades, and this clearly gave them an important initial advantage over some of their rivals.[22]

It is impossible, however, to account for the differential occupational adjustment of the various immigrant groups in these terms alone. If

[18] Solomon, *Ancestors, passim.*

[19] Rina Davis, "The Immigrant and the Boston Public Schools, 1870-1920" (unpublished seminar paper, Brandeis University, 1969).

[20] Brinley Thomas, *Migration and Economic Growth: A Study of Great Britain and the Atlantic Economy* (Cambridge, England: Cambridge Univ. Press, 1954), Tables 80-84.

[21] U.S. Immigration Commission, *Report*, Vol. 26 (Washington: U.S. Govt. Printing Office, 1911), 473, hereinafter referred to as *Report.*

[22] S. Joseph, *Jewish Immigration to the United States from 1881 to 1910* (New York: Columbia Univ. Press, 1914); J. Lestschinsky, "Jewish Migrations, 1840-1946," in *The Jews: Their History, Culture and Religion*, Vol. 2, ed. by L. Finkelstein (Philadelphia: Jewish Publication Society of America, 1949).

ability to speak English was a significant asset—a plausible assumption—the Irish obviously had it. If literacy was of consequence, the kinds of Irish newcomers arriving in the late nineteenth century, unlike their predecessors, were again better equipped for the competitive struggle than many other groups. Only a tenth of the first generation Irish male heads of household in Boston in 1909 were unable to read and write, but twice as many Jews (22 per cent) and four times as many Italians (41 per cent) could neither read nor write.[23] Nor was it the case, as has sometimes been thought, that Jews typically brought substantial amounts of capital with them to the New World and enjoyed a head start for that reason. This was true to some extent of the German Jews, but the predominantly East European Jewish group arriving in the late nineteenth and early twentieth centuries entered the country with no more money in their pockets than the Italians and less than the Irish, who had about the same mean wealth as Scandinavian immigrants.[24] There are, in short, a good many discrepancies between the ranking of immigrant groups in terms of various background handicaps and their ranking in terms of occupational performance after their arrival.

Even if the background handicap argument could be developed so as to explain virtually all of the variation in the performance of the different first generation groups, it would leave the problem of the differential achievements of members of the succeeding generation. There were group differences that remained visible after the immigrating generation had passed from the scene and that do not disappear when the occupational achievements of the first generation are held constant analytically. Thus the skidding syndrome exhibited by the children of Irish and Italian Catholic newcomers who had already gained a foothold in the white-collar world. Old World background handicaps per se can hardly explain this. Something about the organization and culture of ethnic groups in the New World must have been involved.

THE GHETTO AS A MOBILITY BARRIER

One feature of ethnic group life in American cities that has often been identified as an obstacle to assimilation and mobility is residential segregation. The tendency of groups to cluster together, it has been

[23] Immigration Commission, *Report*, p. 496. Similar patterns appear in the national data from the 1900-1901 report of U.S. Commissioner-General of Immigration, as compiled by Frederick A. Bushee in "Ethnic Factors in the Population of Boston," *Publications of the American Economic Association*, 3rd series, 4 (May 1903), p. 19, hereinafter referred to as "Ethnic Factors."

[24] *Ibid.*, p. 14.

argued, "maintains visibility and awareness of the status of the ethnic group both for its own members and for other segments of a city's population," and blocks access to opportunity in a variety of ways.[25] Children growing up in the ghetto, it is thought, are confined to an environment that limits their aspirations and impedes their development as productive citizens.

Certain of Boston's immigrants have been heavily concentrated in particular neighborhoods. The Index of Dissimilarity between Italian immigrants and native-born Americans living in the city in 1880 was 74, which means that 74 per cent of the Italians would have had to move to other areas of the city for the group to be distributed in the same residential pattern as natives, and the figure for Russian-born newcomers was 55. In 1910, similarly, 66 per cent of the Italian and 48 per cent of the Russian immigrants were ghettoized by this measure.[26]

There are, however, two crucial weaknesses of the ghetto hypothesis as an explanation for the differential occupational achievement of Boston's immigrants and their children. First, as shown elsewhere in the larger study from which this paper is drawn, the population of the city was amazingly fluid during the entire period, and the turnover rate was especially high at the lower rungs of the class ladder upon which immigrants were characteristically located.[27] Though there were distinct clusterings of particular groups at different points in time, not very many of the *same individuals* comprised the group over time. If the presumably pathological effects of ghetto living depended upon being trapped there for long periods of life, rapid population turnover was an important solvent.

It could, of course, be that some ethnic groups were much less mobile spatially than others, and that the Irish and Italians of Boston were slow to move up the occupational scale because they were strongly rooted in their respective ethnic subcommunities and unaware of or uninterested in the opportunities that might have been available to them in other cities. In fact, however, Catholics in the samples

[25] Stanley Lieberson, *Ethnic Patterns in American Cities* (New York: Free Press of Glencoe, 1963), p. 6, hereinafter referred to as *Ethnic Patterns.*

[26] *Ibid.*, p. 209.

[27] Details on the extraordinarily high population turnover rates that prevailed in nineteenth-century Boston are provided in Stephan Thernstrom and Peter R. Knights, "Men in Motion: Some Data and Speculations on Urban Population Mobility in Nineteenth-Century America," *Journal of Interdisciplinary History*, 1 (Autumn 1970), pp. 7-35; also available in Tamara K. Hareven, *Anonymous Americans: Explorations in Nineteenth-Century Social History* (Englewood Cliffs, N.J.: Prentice-Hall, Inc., 1971).

displayed higher but not dramatically higher persistence rates, on the average, than Protestants in comparable occupations, and it was the highly successful Jews who were the least migratory of all groups (see Table 5).

TABLE 5. RELIGION, OCCUPATION, AND PERSISTENCE OF SAMPLE MEMBERS IN THE CITY OVER TEN YEARS

	Decade and Per Cent of Group Persisting		
	1880-90	*1910-20*	*1930-40*
Religion			
Catholic	61	43	59
Protestant	66	42	56
Jewish	74	44	75
Religion and Occupation[a]			
High white collar			
Catholic	83	75	b
Protestant	74	50	55
Low white collar			
Catholic	69	56	84
Protestant	68	51	58
Skilled			
Catholic	63	39	67
Protestant	60	36	62
Low manual			
Catholic	58	37	50
Protestant	50	38	51

[a] There were too few Jews in the sample to permit cross-tabulation of persistence rates by occupational level.
[b] Too few cases for percentaging.

A second objection to the ghetto hypothesis as an explanation of differential occupational achievement is that there was no consistent relationship between the extent to which the city's ethnic groups were concentrated in ghettos and their occupational ranking. The least segregated of Boston's immigrants (as measured by an Index of Dissimilarity for 1880 and 1950) included the highly successful English and the relatively unsuccessful Irish. The most segregated groups included the highly successful Russian Jews and the unsuccessful Italians. When the city's immigrants are arrayed in two lists, according to their degree of residential segregation and to their proportion of members in laboring jobs, the ordering of the two lists is almost completely unrelated. The rank correlation (Spearman's r) between the two is a mere .10 for 1880 and an even lower .08 for 1950.[28] Important though it may have been in affecting other realms of behavior, residential segregation was apparently not an important source of differential group mobility.

DIFFERENTIAL FERTILITY

A simple demographic explanation of the relatively poor occupational performance of Boston's Irish and Italian Catholics is that they tended to have larger families than members of other groups and consequently found it more difficult to provide career assistance to their sons. The more children there are in need of aid, presumably, the less a father can do to encourage and finance their education and to provide capital backing for business ventures. The historical data available to test this explanation are very sketchy, but they do not seem to sustain it. In the late nineteenth century, the birth rate of Irish immigrants living in Boston was only a shade higher than that of Scotch and English newcomers and was lower than the German and Swedish rate.[29] What is more, the Irish death rate, much of it due to infant mortality, was the highest of any group, and this further limited the number of second generation youths who lived long enough to avail themselves of career backing from their families. The Italian birth rate, it is true, was extraordinarily high then, but so too was the birth rate of Russian Jews. In 1909 when the U.S. Immigration Commission conducted its survey in Boston, Jewish immigrant families in the city were distinctly larger on the average than Irish immigrant households and nearly as large as Italian families; the respective figures for mean family size for Jews, Irish, and Italians were 5.28, 4.80, and 5.52.[30] The second generation Irish household, what is more, contained

[28] The rank correlation was performed for the groups for which data were available: English, German, Irish, and Swedish immigrants in 1880, and these four plus Polish, Russian, and Italian newcomers in 1950. Occupational distribution data were taken from published censuses; indexes of residential dissimilarity from the native-born white population from Lieberson, *Ethnic Patterns*, p. 209.

[29] Birth and death rates by group from reports of Boston City Registrar, as compiled in Bushee, "Ethnic Factors," pp. 44-51.

[30] Immigration Commission, *Report*, p. 448. Though this refers to a Canadian rather than an American city, and at a somewhat earlier time—the middle of the nineteenth century—it is pertinent to note that research in progress by Michael B. Katz and a team of investigators at the Ontario Institute for Studies in Education reveals that Irish Catholics in Hamilton, Ontario, tended to have unusually *small* families and that family size was positively rather than inversely related to social class rank; see Working Papers #6-10, 12, and 20 of The Hamilton Project, available from the Institute.

4.30 persons, not much larger than the typical Yankee household (3.49) of the day (no figures are available for other second generation groups). There were more Jewish than Irish sons and nearly as many Jewish as Italian sons to draw upon family resources. The differential fertility hypothesis thus cannot explain the group differences in career patterns that were manifest in the late nineteenth and early twentieth centuries.

This may have become a more significant consideration in the years since World War I. Solid evidence on religious or ethnic differentials in family size in Boston during this period cannot be obtained, but a number of studies in other communities suggests that Catholics tended to have larger families than Protestants of similar class status, and Jews smaller families.[31] This religious differential, furthermore, was relatively small at the lower socio-economic levels and sharpest at the highest levels. This may indeed have had some bearing upon the distinctive skidding syndrome of middle-class Catholic youths in the later samples. But since the pattern was evident long before the differential in family size first appeared, the latter obviously cannot be a sufficient explanation for the former. Nor is it likely that family size was an important cause of the limited upward intergenerational mobility of Catholics of working-class origins, for religious differences in family size seem to have been slight within the working class.

INSTITUTIONAL COMPLETENESS

It may seem paradoxical, but it is possible that the very strength and cohesiveness of the Boston Irish and Italian Catholic communities negatively affected the mobility prospects of many of the children growing up within them. A sociologist, Raymond Breton, has suggested that there may be an inverse relationship between the "institutional completeness" of an ethnic community—the degree to which ethnic organizations can perform all of the services its members require, whether religious, educational, political, recreational, or eco-

[31] Samuel A. Stouffer, "Trends in the Fertility of Catholics and Non-Catholics," *American Journal of Sociology*, 41 (September 1935), pp. 143-66; Frank W. Notestein, "Class Differences in Fertility," *Annals of the American Academy of Political and Social Science*, 188 (November 1936), p. 33; P. K. Whelpton and C. V. Kiser, "Social and Psychological Factors Affecting Fertility," *Milbank Memorial Fund Quarterly*, 21 (July 1943), pp. 221-80. Some post-World War II studies fail to find clear Protestant-Catholic differences in fertility; R. Freedman, P. K. Whelpton, and A. A. Campbell, *Family Planning, Sterility and Population Growth* (New York: McGraw-Hill, 1959); *Statistical Abstract of the United States: 1958* (Washington: U.S. Govt. Printing Office, 1959), Table 40. Cf. Lenski, *Religious Factor*, pp. 235-43 for a dissenting view.

nomic—and the likelihood that members of the group will be upwardly mobile in the larger society.[32] To the degree to which a group is inward-looking and insulated from contact with "outsiders," its members may develop values which are deviant by the standards of the larger society, or even if they hold the same values they may not learn socially accepted methods of pursuing them. It is, of course, true that a cohesive, disciplined group can act in concert to attain certain objectives—a classic example often mentioned in contemporary discussions of the racial crisis is the Irish takeover of the big city political machines in the late nineteenth century. But what is too often overlooked is that such a victory—winning control of 3,000 jobs in the Public Works Department, let us say—may involve seizing one kind of opportunity *at the expense of other opportunities.* The success of the Irish in the political sphere was not matched by comparable gains in the private economy.

The solidarity of the Boston Irish, and the completeness with which the community was organized, was certainly notable. In his study of nineteenth-century Boston, Oscar Handlin noted that the Irish were the only group with a full, independent, institutional life, the only group which "felt obliged to erect a society within a society."[33] Among more recent comers to the community, the Italians would also rank very high in this regard. But then so too would the Jews, or to take another highly successful group not present in significant numbers in Boston, the Japanese-Americans. Institutional completeness, it would seem, can be associated with worldly success or with a lack of worldly success, depending upon the values of the ethnic group in question.

CULTURAL VALUES

It is with some reluctance that I turn to group values as a possible explanation of differences in occupational achievement. Reluctance because explanations of this type tend to be tautological and difficult

[32] Raymond Breton, "Institutional Completeness of Ethnic Communities and the Personal Relations of Immigrants," *American Journal of Sociology*, 52 (1964), pp. 193-205. For a similar view, see Leo Grebler, Joan W. Moore, and Ralph Guzman, *The Mexican-American People: The Nation's Second Largest Minority* (New York: Free Press of Glencoe, 1970): "Interaction and involvement with institutions of the Host Society are important steps towards assimilation and acculturation. To the extent that the receiving ethnic community provides new members with a prepared institutional structure, furnishing both protection and isolation, a significant opportunity for assimilation becomes relatively weak or ineffective" (p. 48).

[33] Oscar Handlin, *Boston's Immigrants, 1790-1880: A Study in Acculturation* (rev. ed.; Cambridge: Belknap Press of Harvard Univ. Press, 1959), pp. 158-63.

to verify independently. "Why did the Irish move up the occupational scale less rapidly than other groups? Because the Irish placed less value on worldly success, or defined success in a different way. How do we know that Irish values were truly different from those of other groups? Because the Irish moved less rapidly up the occupational scale." Even when such interpretations are buttressed by evidence which makes them more than merely tautological, there is always a question as to whether the subculture of the group is truly a cause or only a *consequence* of the group's status. Nevertheless, it does appear that there was something distinctive about the cultural patterns of the Boston Irish and Italians that did exert an influence upon the career patterns of their children that may be distinguished from the general influence of parental social status.

The point about the Irish is not that they held fatalistic, hierarchical, peasant values that discouraged worldly activity. It is possible, though by no means altogether clear, that this characterization might apply to the famine Irish who flocked into the city around the middle of the nineteenth century, but these were certainly not the values that were expressed by spokesmen of the group in the late nineteenth and twentieth centuries.[34] *The Pilot*, for example, consistently spoke the language of Horatio Alger in these years.

If the Irish, however, were eager to succeed, perhaps quite as eager as other groups, their conception of success was parochial. The emphasis was upon winning secure positions within bureaucratic structures rather than upon entrepreneurial activity. Politics, from one point of view, was the salvation of the Irish, supplying them with secure jobs of a blue-collar or menial white-collar sort, but it may have been their curse as well, directing the attention of their most talented youngsters away from the business and professional callings that offered greater gains and limiting their horizons to the secure and the familiar.

As for the Italians, a number of perceptive observers of the Boston Italian community have perceived a distinctive subculture which di-

[34] For the debate about the culture of the famine Irish in Boston, cf. *ibid.*, which stresses fatalism and pessimism, with Francis R. Walsh, "The Boston *Pilot* and the Boston Irish, 1835-1865," unpublished paper for the 1969 annual meeting of the American Historical Association. From my reading of *The Pilot* in the late 1870s and 1880s, I am convinced that, by then at least, the themes emphasized by Walsh—optimism and mobility—were clearly dominant. Faith in the ability of man to improve himself and his world was the watchword, and there were repeated injunctions to develop the traits that were thought conducive to upward mobility; see, e.g. issues for 6/23/77, 5/8/80, 9/28/80, 2/5/81, 3/5/81, 10/8/87. The shift, however, may indicate that *The Pilot*'s views had become less representative of the Irish community as a whole.

rected energies away from the world of work, or at least from those callings which are most highly valued and rewarded in the larger society.[35] The most recent of these accounts describes the Italians as "urban villagers" and finds that even among the second generation "the idea that work can be a central purpose of life, and that it should be organized into a series of related jobs that make up a career is virtually nonexistent. . . ."[36] These studies, it is true, have focused on two particular and quite special Italian neighborhoods, the North End and the West End. These are the most heavily Italian districts of the city, and the great majority of their inhabitants are manual laborers. Middle-class Italians and those aspiring to become middle class are least likely to be found there, and one suspects that similar studies of Italians in the more mixed and higher status neighborhoods of such communities as Medford, Malden, or Arlington would yield a different impression of the values of the group as a whole, but it is certainly significant that large numbers of Boston Italians have been exposed at some point in their lives to the subculture of the North and West Ends.[37]

Though a sizeable Irish-Catholic lower middle class emerged fairly early, and later a comparable Italian group, they did not provide a solid launching pad for greater gains in the next generation, perhaps because their members neither hungered for further advancement for their sons nor feared loss of face if they became policemen or plumbers, so long as the work was steady. It is this, we may surmise, which accounts for one of the intriguing findings in Laumann's recent study of social stratification in Cambridge and Belmont. Laumann asked his respondents a series of questions designed to reveal the extent to which they made sharp distinctions between the status levels of various occupations. "High status discriminators" were those who conceived the occupational structure as a ladder with many rungs; "low status discriminators" made fewer distinctions and were less inclined to believe that a clerk was socially superior to a carpenter and an accountant to a bus driver. It turned out, interestingly, that Catholics scored lower on the index of status discrimination than Protestants,

[35] William F. Whyte, *Streetcorner Society: The Social Structure of an Italian Slum* (Chicago: Univ. of Chicago Press, 1943); Walter Firey, *Land Use in Central Boston* (Cambridge: Harvard Univ. Press, 1947), Chap. 5; Herbert J. Gans, *The Urban Villagers: Group and Class in the Life of Italian Americans* (New York: Free Press of Glencoe, 1962).

[36] *Ibid.*, p. 124.

[37] Humbert S. Nelli's *Italians in Chicago, 1880-1930: A Study in Ethnic Mobility* (New York: Oxford Univ. Press, 1970) makes little attempt to measure mobility systematically, but it provides valuable detail on Italian movement outside the areas of initial settlement.

and men of Irish descent notably lower than those of any other ethnic background.[38]

Another possibly distinctive aspect of the culture of the American Irish and Italians concerned attitudes toward property ownership and investment in education. In an earlier study of the Irish laborers of Newburyport, Massachusetts, in the nineteenth century, I suggested that the relative lack of upward occupational mobility by the sons of these men was part of a cultural pattern which placed a very high value upon home ownership, which in that setting was attainable only by placing children to work at an early age and consequently depriving them of an education which might have furthered their own careers.[39] However, the sketchy evidence available on property ownership in Boston did not reveal a similar inverse relationship between family property accumulation and intergenerational occupational mobility for members of the 1880 sample, the only sample for which suitable property data was available. Nor, it should be added, was there any indication from an analysis of ethnic differences in property-holding that the Boston Irish displayed the same hunger for real estate as the Newburyport Irish. (There were not enough Italians in the 1880 sample to discuss their behavior on this count.) Possibly this was because of a special characteristic of the Boston housing market—that it contained a very low proportion of single-family dwellings which could be purchased inexpensively. Possibly, too, the failure of the study to gather data on property ownership for the large numbers of sample members fleeing to the suburbs obscured a pattern that was in fact present. Perhaps the Irish and Italians who moved from Boston proper to Cambridge, Somerville, Watertown, and similar communities in such large numbers were more like their Newburyport brethren and made the trade-off that they did.[40] At present, however, it cannot be established that the distinctive occupational mobility patterns of the Boston Irish and Italians were linked to distinctive attitudes to-

[38] Edward Laumann, *Prestige and Association in an Urban Community: An Analysis of an Urban Stratification System* (Indianapolis: Bobbs-Merrill, 1966), p. 110. Unlike other Catholics, however, men of Italian descent tended to rank high on the index of status discrimination, a finding which does not square with my argument. One's impression from the works cited in note 35 above is that the Italians of the North and West Ends would score very low on this measure; possibly those Italians who escaped to Cambridge and Belmont were reacting strongly against that cultural pattern.

[39] Stephan Thernstrom, *Poverty and Progress: Social Mobility in a Nineteenth-Century City* (Cambridge: Harvard Univ. Press, 1964), pp. 155-57.

[40] A projected study of "Intrametropolitan Migration, Public Finance, and Property Values: A Socioeconometric Study," by Matthew Edel, Department of Economics, M.I.T., and Elliot D. Sclar of the Florence Heller School, Brandeis University should clarify this issue.

ward the relative importance of property ownership and the education of their young.

Although there is no support at present for the claim that the desire to accumulate property led Irish and Italian parents to underinvest in their children's education, there is direct evidence that their children did obtain less schooling than those from other groups, and that Jewish youths were unusually well educated. The U.S. Census of 1950 reported the educational and occupational attainments of first and second generation immigrants in the Boston area in some detail (see Table 6). From 27 to 31 per cent of the members of the three predominantly Protestant second generation groups in the twenty-five to

TABLE 6. EDUCATION, OCCUPATION, AND INCOME OF SECOND GENERATION IMMIGRANTS (AGES 25-44) BY FATHER'S EDUCATION AND OCCUPATION, 1950[a]

Ethnic Background and	*Per Cent of Second Generation Men*			*Family Background (Estimated)*[e]	
Dominant Religious Affiliation[b]	*With 1 or More Years of College*	*High White-Collar Occupation*[c]	*High Income*[d]	*Median School Years of Father*	*Per Cent Fathe White Collar*
Catholic					
Irish	21	19	13	8.3	18
Italian	11	17	9	5.2	19
Protestant					
English	27	29	19	10.3	51
Swedish	28	27	23	8.7	17
German	31	31	23	10.3	40
Jewish					
Russian	44	46	27	8.1	53

[a] Calculated from published U.S. Census data.

[b] The religious classification is, of course, quite imperfect. Some of the Germans were Jev in fact, and some were Catholics. There were English Catholics, and even Irish Protestant The Census does not, alas, supply similar tabulations for religious groups, so this is the be approximation that can be made.

[c] This is the proportion employed in the two census categories "professional, technical an kindred workers" and "managers, officials and proprietors, except farm," and thus is not precise comparable to the high white-collar category used for the sample data elsewhere in the prese study. Petty proprietors cannot be separated out from the census tabulations. If that had bee possible, some of the group differences visible here would doubtless be accentuated. In pa ticular, it is highly likely that many of the Italians in "high white-collar occupations" by th classification were in fact proprietors of small fruitstands, newsstands, and the like.

[d] Per cent earning more than $4,000 the previous year, which placed them in the top sixt of the income distribution for all second generation persons earning income in the city. Th income figures unfortunately include females, which tends to lower them in general.

[e] In the absence of direct evidence about the education and occupation of the fathers c second generation men, figures for first generation males aged forty-five or more were taken a a rough baseline.

forty-four age bracket had attended college for a year or more, and a striking 44 per cent of the largely Jewish second generation Russians. The figures for Irish and Italian Catholics were much lower—21 per cent and 11 per cent respectively. This was doubtless a major reason why second generation Catholics held a much smaller share of jobs at the upper white-collar level—only two-thirds as many as the Protestants and less than half as many as the Jews—and were similarly underrepresented in the top sixth of the income distribution pyramid.

One cannot, of course, draw the immediate inference that Catholic immigrants tended to value education less highly than their Protestant or Jewish counterparts, for the explanation may lie in the differing social characteristics of the immigrating generation. Some groups had much less education in the Old World than others; some, as a result of the background handicaps they brought with them and other circumstances, were more heavily clustered on the lowest rungs of the occupational ladder. It is well known that the children of relatively uneducated and unskilled fathers tend to obtain less education than those from better educated and more prosperous families. A study of students who graduated from Boston high schools between 1916 and 1934 disclosed that almost two-thirds of those from well-to-do homes but less than a third from families in the lower occupational brackets continued their education further.[41] It is possible, then, that the educational and consequent occupational handicaps of second generation Catholics revealed in Table 6 were due entirely to the fact that their fathers were more frequently uneducated workingmen.

The Census did not report this information in a manner that permits a direct test of that hypothesis, but some gauge of its validity may be gained by assuming that the educational and occupational rank of the fathers of these second generation men was roughly equivalent to that of the city's first generation immigrants aged forty-five or more in 1950. (The correspondence is obviously imperfect, for some of the foreign-born males forty-five or older had no sons who lived in Boston, and many of the second generation men aged twenty-five to forty-four did not have a father residing in Boston as of 1950, but it is hard to see why these flaws would appreciably impair the validity of the measure for the purposes to which it is put here.)

Applying this rough control for parental attainments reveals that part of the educational underachievement and consequent occupational handicap of second generation Catholics did stem from their father's lack of education. Italian fathers ranked far below all others

[41] Robert K. Merton and Bryce Ryan, "Paternal Status and the Economic Adjustment of High School Graduates," *Social Forces*, 22 (1944), pp. 302-06.

in median school years completed, and the Irish fell well behind two of the three Protestant groups. But there are two important anomalies. Russian immigrants had even less education than the Irish, and yet their children attended college much more frequently than those from any other group. A second important anomaly is that Swedish fathers had only a shade more schooling on the average than Irish fathers (a difference of less than half a year), and yet substantially more of their children were educated beyond the high school level.

That the children of Jewish immigrants were more than twice as likely to attend college as their Irish counterparts with equally uneducated fathers appears less surprising when the occupational achievements of Jewish fathers are taken into account. More than half of them held middle-class jobs, but less than a fifth of Irish fathers. Despite their lack of education, Jewish immigrants moved very rapidly into white-collar callings, particularly as proprietors of small shops and manufacturing concerns, and this, of course, put them in a far better position to educate their sons than any of their Catholic rivals.

The special Jewish commitment to education, however, stands out as remarkable when they are compared not with the Irish but with a Protestant group with an equally large and better educated first generation middle class—namely the English. Almost the same fraction of both immigrating groups attained middle-class jobs, and the English immigrants had attended school an average of two years more than the Russians. But 44 per cent of the second generation Russian Jews and only 27 per cent of their counterparts of English stock attended college, and a correspondingly higher proportion of the former found employment in the upper reaches of the middle class and were in the top income bracket.[42] This seems to be a clear example of the way in which the cultural values of a group can shape the career patterns of its children in a distinctive manner.

The other anomaly in the rankings—the relatively high educational,

[42] The data are not presented in a form to permit definite conclusions, but there are strong indications of the Jewish commitment to education in the U.S. Immigration Commission's report on the children of immigrants in Boston schools in 1909; *Report*, Vol. 30, pp. 175-292. This may have been related to the high proportion of Jewish fathers reported as being in business for themselves—45 per cent, as opposed to 5 per cent for the Irish—but it must be noted that most of those businessmen were peddlers with very, very low incomes. The average annual earnings of Jewish male immigrants in Boston were only $396, well below the Irish figure of $510 and not far above the Italian figure of $338; Immigration Commission, *Report*, Vol. 26, p. 481. The Jews were far more frequently entrepreneurs than the Irish, but they were not as yet nearly as successful financially as the latter.

occupational, and income position of second generation men of Swedish stock whose fathers had little more schooling than Irish immigrants—is suggestive of a cultural difference too. The comparison between the Irish and the other two Protestant groups—English and German—is perhaps unfair, because the first generation English and Germans had more schooling and better jobs than their Catholic rivals. But immigrants from Sweden closely resembled those from Ireland both in their low educational level and in their overwhelming concentration in blue-collar jobs, and yet the second generation Swedish outperformed the Irish by all three measures of achievement.

The educational and occupational achievement of second generation Jews and the relative lack of achievement of Catholics thus cannot be explained away by holding the educational and occupational attainments of their parents roughly constant. There were very large group differences in the characteristics of the immigrating generation, to be sure, and these left a clear imprint upon the record of their children in school and at work. But a residue of unexplained variation remains when this is taken into account, a residue which suggests that the Jews placed an especially high value on higher education and the careers which it opened the door to, while Catholics were somewhat less dedicated to educational and occupational achievement for their sons than Protestants with comparable schooling and similar jobs.

This evidence pertains to second generation men born between 1906 and 1925, observed in 1950, and it is, of course, possible that things have changed since then. Although Catholic adults still were sharply underrepresented in the ranks of college graduates in 1961, younger Catholics were completing college in about the same proportion as Protestants.[43] Had the Boston sample data been more extensive in their coverage of the past two decades, permitting a closer analysis of recent trends, they might have disclosed the same improvements in the Catholic achievement level that have shown up in the two national studies by Greeley and Greeley and Rossi.

If there was such a change in Boston, however, it was indeed a change, a sharp departure from a well-established historical pattern. Whatever the relationship between religion and social mobility in present-day America, there were distinct ethnic and religious subcultures in the American city of the past. Although a wide range of circumstances influenced the ability of different groups to make their way in the workaday world, differences in group culture played a significant role. Whether these cultures are best described with religious

[43] Greeley, *Religion*, pp. 29-30.

labels, as Weber presumably would argue, or with labels based upon country of origin cannot be determined from a study of a community with Boston's particular ethnic and religious mix. But the fact that nationality and religion were correlated in the particular way that they were in one major city in the late nineteenth and twentieth centuries is certainly consistent with Weber's emphasis. In any event, we are reminded that current survey research dealing with religion and economic behavior reveals not timeless patterns but new, and possibly temporary, circumstances.

III

Social Mobility and Political Radicalism: The Case of the French Revolution of 1789

GILBERT SHAPIRO AND PHILIP DAWSON

THE CONCEPT of social mobility has long been an overworked and mistreated servant of both ideology and theory.* Recently, careful definition of the concept and measurement of the phenomenon have begun to be achieved. Little progress has as yet been made, however, in analyzing the influences of different sorts and degrees of mobility upon the other variables that characterize social systems, even though it was these influences that originally drew attention to social mobility itself. Prominent among them, in a wide range of social theories, has been the supposed relationship between social mobility and political behavior, especially behavior directed toward drastic change in the social system.[1]

As students of a historical situation in which a revolution actually occurred, we have attempted to discover how the perceptible opportunities for upward movement from an important class affected its political orientation, and whether or not most of its members reacted

* This paper is based in part upon data collected for "Quantitative Studies of the French Revolution," a long-term research project carried on by Shapiro with the collaboration of Sasha Weitman and John Markoff. In particular, the content analysis of the *cahiers de doléances* used here was prepared jointly by Shapiro, Weitman, and Markoff. The project has been funded in part by the National Science Foundation Division of Social Sciences, grant number GS 845, which is gratefully acknowledged. Preparation of this paper has been very much facilitated by Jean-Paul Bertaud, who examined for us fourteen provincial almanacs, in the Bibliothèque Nationale, in order to provide enumerations reported in column 3 of the Appendix. Earlier versions of the paper have received thoughtful and very helpful comments from George V. Taylor, John Markoff, and several participants, notably Alan B. Spitzer, in the conference on applications of quantitative methods to political, social, and economic history, held at Chicago in June 1969.

[1] Seymour M. Lipset and Reinhard Bendix, *Social Mobility in Industrial Society* (Berkeley: Univ. of California Press, 1959), hereinafter referred to as *Social Mobility*, provided an excellent analysis of measurement problems for different types of mobility, and results of important studies up to 1960 comparing nations and time periods. They say (p. 6): "Most studies of social mobility have almost completely ignored the question of social consequences."

collectively as frustrated, would-be beneficiaries of upward movement. This is a collaborative study crossing disciplinary boundaries: Dawson is a historian, Shapiro a sociologist. Since the two professions are generally being drawn into closer relations, we offer a few preliminary remarks about our experience of collaboration.

A master historian a generation ago, Georges Lefebvre, criticized an abstract comparison of revolutionary exaltation with religious fanaticism and remarked: "It is not enough to say that the pure historian finds no reward in this; sociology, whose future I cherish, finds none either, for what it asks of history is a supply of concrete observations."[2] While agreeing with Lefebvre's criticism, we should like to have replied that concrete observations do not present themselves, properly selected and interpreted to test hypotheses, any more readily in historical study than in an investigation of contemporary society or in the physics laboratory. That the facts speak for themselves appears to us an elementary misconception; it is, however, implied by a division of labor between the historian who collects facts and the sociologist who deploys them for or against theories. Our experience indicates that in order to collaborate a sociologist and a historian must communicate effectively in planning their work, not simply after the concrete observations have been supplied. To put the point another way, it is necessary to join two systems without destroying the special nature of either. This requires the historian to develop greater ability to analyze data in the light of various hypotheses, and therefore some familiarity with the ways in which data can be analyzed, including the uses of computers, statistics, and the theoretical ideas that generate hypotheses. It requires the sociologist to become acculturated in a historical context different from his own, and to develop greater capacity to keep in mind the details which define that context. If historical data are to be regarded as relevant to a problem having some general theoretical interest and are to be susceptible to analysis by available techniques, the historian must become part sociologist. If data are to be used to test or to develop theories, the sociologist must grasp their meaning within a particular matrix of institutions, culture, and available evidence, and hence become part historian. Finally, collaboration between the two disciplines can be undertaken only with the state of each in view. We turn, then, to a cursory examination of sociological writing about social mobility and of historical writing about its significance at the outset of the French Revolution.

[2] *Revue Historique*, 176 (1935), p. 79.

I

RENEWED theoretical discussion of the political consequences of social mobility and immobility would be salutary even without new data on an especially interesting example. The theoretical and empirical literature of sociology is highly contradictory on the matter. For example, Ranulf has attempted to show how lower middle-class populations, highly restricted in their mobility opportunities, have regularly been attracted to extremely repressive political movements, from the ancient Greeks to the Nazis.[3] More recently, Bettelheim and Janowitz have found evidence that anti-Semitism, which can be interpreted as a similar political movement, is related to downward mobility on the part of those who hold such attitudes.[4] In their assumptions and in the implications of their data, these two studies apparently contradict both the dominant ideologies of recent decades: Marxism and liberalism. A Marxist perspective on capitalism anticipates a hardening of class lines which will help to generate a revolution freeing the oppressed. A liberal perspective typically depicts various kinds of frontiers providing access to enhanced life-chances for deprived groups, thereby legitimizing the stratification system and hence stabilizing the political order. Marxism and liberalism hold contrasting expectations as to the future of social mobility under capitalism; they are in agreement that restrictions on mobility would provoke radical, insurrectionary responses, and that widespread upward mobility would assist the formation of a conservative attachment to the current system.

In their initial study of the American right wing, Bell and his associates bravely took this dilemma by both horns. They claimed that individuals attracted to extreme reactionary movements, in the United States recently, have been recruited mainly from two categories in the population: on the one hand, those frustrated in their desire for upward mobility or experiencing downward mobility, and, on the other hand, those moving upward "too fast." Some critics saw this as a self-contradictory position. In a later version, bringing their analysis of the 1950s up to date and trying to explain the attractiveness of the

[3] Svend Ranulf, *Moral Indignation and Middle Class Psychology* (Copenhagen: Munksgaard, Ltd., 1938; repr., New York: Schocken Books, 1964).

[4] Bruno Bettelheim and Morris Janowitz, *Dynamics of Prejudice* (New York: Harper & Row, Inc., 1950), pp. 57-61. It is noteworthy that in this study anti-Semitism was related to mobility far more strongly than to static measures of "background variables." The authors say that anti-Negro intolerance revealed a similar pattern. Their interpretation concentrates on the frustration of groups in their mobility aspirations, rather than the fate of an individual struggling for advancement in a static structure.

John Birch Society, the authors answered by pointing out, accurately, that there is no necessary contradiction in attributing a political movement to instabilities in the status of its adherents, whether upward or downward movements.[5] Still, we are surprised by the suggestion that stability of status, and not opportunity, is the cement that binds any American consensus that may exist. Whatever the fact, the theory proposed by Bell and his associates emphasizes instabilities of status and thus converges with Lenski's concentration on the presence or absence of consistency among an individual's status positions, when these are indicated by more than one criterion.[6]

Finally, a currently popular line of thought sees political instability and revolutions originating in the rapidly rising expectations, the disorganization of personal life, and the inability to meet new demands and conform to new social norms, all phenomena supposedly generated when large numbers of a group advance to a new level of prosperity or social acceptance.[7]

In short, some authors explain reactionary attitudes by referring to downward mobility or intolerable restrictions on upward mobility; others explain radical or revolutionary attitudes as results of these experiences; still others explain extreme political attitudes of either type by referring to rapid mobility regardless of its direction. These theories have important, differing implications for social policy, most obviously now in the contexts of race relations in the United States and the political consequences of economic development in Asia, Africa, and South America. Careful, systematic analysis is needed to

[5] Daniel Bell, ed., *The New American Right* (New York: Criterion Books, 1955), and *The Radical Right* (Garden City, N.Y.: Doubleday & Co., Inc., 1963).

[6] Gerhard E. Lenski, "Status Crystallization: a Non-Vertical Dimension of Social Status," *American Sociological Review*, 19 (1954), pp. 405-13. This article generated much interesting research, reviewed by Lipset and Bendix in *Social Mobility*, esp. pp. 255-69.

[7] Alexis de Tocqueville, *L'Ancien régime et la Révolution*, ed. J. P. Mayer and André Jardin (2 vols.; Paris: Librairie Gallimard, 1952-53), I, 222, hereinafter referred to as *Revolution*: "To the extent that there developed in France the prosperity which I have just described, people's minds appeared more disturbed and uneasy; public discontent sharpened; hatred of all the old institutions grew. The nation was moving visibly towards a revolution. Moreover, the parts of France which were to be the principal starting point of that revolution are precisely those where [economic] progress is most readily to be seen" (our translation).

Emile Durkheim, *Suicide: A Study in Sociology*, trans. by John A. Spaulding and George Simpson (Glencoe, Ill.: Free Press, 1951), in Book 2, Chap. 5, struggled over the significance of his finding that the suicide rate tends upward in periods of prosperity and came to closely related conclusions which have been very influential. Much is made of the same notion by Eric Hoffer, *The True Believer: Thoughts on the Nature of Mass Movements* (New York: Harper & Row, Inc., 1951), in a discussion concentrated on political radicalism rather than the more abstract concept of anomie.

alleviate the confusion of theories. We can undertake no more than a minimal effort to clarify the matter in order to make our findings intelligible.

In part, the confusion stems from the fact that persons or families may be "mobile" in as many ways as the surrounding society is stratified. Theorists of status crystallization observe discrepancies on the three stratifying criteria isolated by Weber, power, prestige, and life-chances. Lipset and Bendix, for example, say that low prestige combined with high economic position is likely to predispose people toward radicalism; and they cite as an example the French bourgeoisie in the late eighteenth century.

Further confusion arises from the fact that an entire stratum of society, such as a Hindu caste, may shift in its power, prestige, or life-chances, in relation to other strata. This probably ought to be described as a structural change in the stratification system, rather than mobility within the system. The political consequences of two such different kinds of occurrences could hardly be expected to have much in common. In the 1780s, the French stratification system was a political issue, and thereafter, in 1789 and 1790, it was legally restructured.

Life-chances can be enhanced by successful enterprise in an unchanged location within a system of classes. A black American can be occupationally successful, but he remains black. Under the Old Regime in France, a commoner could gain great wealth and come to be regarded as a "notable," without attaining the ceremonial honor and fiscal advantage of being a "noble." Increased economic security, or adoption of the life style of a nobleman, may have political consequences different from those that would follow an actual transition into a higher class or juridical estate.

One important meaning of "mobility," then, is actual movement of persons from a particular conventionally defined group to another, the mark of membership in such groups being participation in intimacy of access to other members and in their recognized privileges. In modern society, the lines between such groups are indistinct and almost illicit. Sociologists like Warner have to "discover" them; their existence is debated; and we develop elaborate methodological devices to locate individuals in the system. In eighteenth-century France, such groups were defined in law and jurisprudence, and everyone was presumed to know where he and others stood. Crossing the line between commoner and noble status was clearly only one type of upward social movement, but is the type with which we are concerned here. Enrichment and a change of occupation within a class were important for many individuals, both commoners and nobles; there was also downward mobility, which likewise affected both commoners and nobles and which has not been investigated or even much discussed with reference to the origins of the French Revolution: these two topics do not form part of our investigation, and we are aware that findings as to them may in the future modify the framework within which it is intended to fit. These omitted topics would involve relatively refined problems of evidence and measurement. Movement from the commoner to the noble class, on the other hand, was a gross change: not merely increased prosperity, enhanced power, or elevated prestige, but the resultant of all three, the attainment of a new, legally certified social identity and, therewith, a collection of privileges and prerogatives which included important fiscal advantages, bearing significantly on future wealth, and enforced patterns of symbolic deference, guaranteeing the individual's public honor. It seems to us sound, as well as convenient, to consider this kind of gross upward movement in relation to political consequences, before any attempt is made at a more delicate analysis.

Two further clarifications are needed for our purpose. First, in examining the social system, we distinguish the incidence of actual movement from the perceptible structure of opportunities for movement. Second, in considering the effects on individuals, we distinguish the participant, recently or prospectively engaged in social movement, from the spectator, perceiving the movement of others and drawing from it, perhaps, conclusions as to the character of the social system. Each of these distinctions requires a few words of comment.

Opportunities for upward mobility may be indicated in several ways that affect a man's political orientation. Among the indications, certainly, are the actual movements of other individuals, who enter or leave his own group. Other indications may be myths thoroughly inculcated, legal rules, or (the matter on which we concentrate) the number and nature of clearly institutionalized routes of visible social advancement.[8] In modern American society, were it not for the widespread habit of modifying one's acceptance of official myths in the light of perceptible realities, it might be said that the ideological construct, "equality of opportunity," renders actual opportunity unimportant. In eighteenth-century France, where the official and dominant

[8] A major conclusion of Lipset and Bendix is that great discrepancies exist between measurable mobility and prevailing beliefs about mobility in Western societies. As they say, "Clearly, further research is needed to discover what combinations of mobility rates and subjective evaluations have actually occurred, and to examine the consequences which different combinations have had," *Social Mobility*, p. 260.

ideologies placed positive value on stability of status, we should suppose that a contradictory reality was important and that exceptional institutionalized routes for upward mobility had a strong effect on the perception of existing opportunities. Hence the aspect of social mobility that we measure is an array of institutions which was an important determinant of the perceptible opportunity for a bourgeois to become legally a nobleman.

The participant and the spectator may perceive social movement differently. When it is institutionalized as a recurrent event, involving elements of ritual, with relatively few, very noticeable participants, then its principal systematic effect may be upon the spectators and their collective political behavior rather than upon the would-be or actual participants. Especially might this be true in a society where the legitimacy of an institution did not necessarily depend, in general, on its accessibility to would-be participants. Not everyone could be king in eighteenth-century France, but the functioning of the institution of kingship could nevertheless be, and in fact was, until 1792, very diversely judged by different subjects. So it was, we suggest, with the institutions that until 1790 provided ennoblement for commoners.

II

In historical and other writings intended to explain the revolution of 1789, the opponents of the revolution first suggested the idea that envy and frustrated aspirations among the bourgeoisie eventuated in a radical determination to level social distinctions. Edmund Burke said that commoners who had become wealthy were not, as they ought to have been, accorded rank and esteem by the nobility. "The two kinds of aristocracy were too punctiliously kept asunder; . . . This separation . . . I conceive to be one principal cause of the destruction of the old nobility," even though the destruction could be approved only by men with a "sour, malignant, envious disposition. . . ."[9] Similarly, Taine included in his system of explanation a growing rancor and hostility of the bourgeois against the nobles who blocked every path to individual success. Taine attributed the growth of these feelings simply to the development of a bourgeois sense of identity, resulting from the growth of bourgeois wealth and intellectual cultivation.[10] It was not he, however, who said that the important change consisted of increasingly effective efforts to exclude commoners from high positions

[9] *Reflections on the Revolution in France*, ed. by William B. Todd (New York: Holt, Rinehart and Winston, 1959), pp. 70-71, hereinafter referred to as *Reflections.*

[10] *Les origines de la France contemporaine*, 1e partie, *l'ancien régime* (Paris: Hachette, 1876), p. 412.

in the army, the judiciary, the administration, and the church hierarchy. As far as we can discover, such an assertion was first made much later in a thin dissertation by a law student, Louis Dollot,[11] without any facts which could constitute evidence that career opportunities were actually closed any more than they had been a generation or a century before.

A much different analysis is to be found in the work of Tocqueville. He recognized that a bourgeois could obtain ennoblement by acquiring one of the several thousand offices which conferred it, and that thus the French nobility was in a sense open, as the English aristocracy, in a different way, was claimed to be. But he thought such an analogy valueless.

> If the middle classes of England, far from carrying on a war against the aristocracy, remained intimately united with it, this was not primarily because the aristocracy was open but rather, as I have said, because its form was unclear and its boundary unknown; not so much because one could enter it as because one never knew when one was in it; with the result that everyone who approached [membership in the aristocracy] could believe himself to be part of it, associate himself with its government, and derive some prestige or some profit from its power.
>
> But the barrier that separated the nobility of France from the other classes, although it could very easily be crossed, was always fixed and visible, always recognizable by striking and odious signs to those who remained outside it. Once one had crossed the barrier, one was separated from all whom one had just left by privileges which were burdensome and humiliating to them.
>
> The system of ennoblement, therefore, far from diminishing the hatred of the commoner against the *gentilhomme*, on the contrary increased it immeasurably; it was embittered with all the envy that the new noble inspired in his former equals. This is what caused the Third Estate, in their grievance lists, to show more irritation against the ennobled than against the nobles, and, far from asking that the way from the commonry [into the nobility] be opened wider, they asked that it be narrowed.[12]

[11] *La question des privilèges dans la seconde moitié du XVIIIe siècle* (Paris: Pedone, 1941), p. 51.

[12] Tocqueville, *Révolution*, I, 152-53 (our translation). In this passage, Tocqueville attributes to Burke the analogy between the French nobility and the English aristocracy as to openness; but we cannot find any such statement in Todd's scrupulous edition of the *Reflections*.

Tocqueville's suggestion was that the commoners' indignation was occasioned, not by obstacles in the way of individual success, still less by any supposed enhancement of such obstacles, but rather by a detour around the obstacles, a detour available—unequally—by way of ennoblement. This suggestion can readily be linked with Tocqueville's emphasis on equality as an objective of revolutionary change.

On the whole, the ideas of Taine and Dollot rather than those of Tocqueville on this matter have been adopted by recent writers. In a sociological essay, Elinor G. Barber sought to clarify the position of the bourgeoisie in the French class structure and to exemplify the usefulness of theories of stratification drawn from the writings of Talcott Parsons and Robert K. Merton. Her conclusion set forth two main points.[13] First, many bourgeois experienced inner conflict as to social mobility: they shared the attitude, predominant in the society as a whole, which disapproved rapid change in social status; and yet they possessed certain qualifications and attitudes appropriate for upwardly mobile individuals, notably rational self-reliance and emphasis on personal achievement. (This conflict of values, Mrs. Barber said, was mitigated, not intensified, by the practices leading to ennoblement.) Secondly, the growing exclusiveness of the noble class precipitated the alienation of many bourgeois from the existing class system, especially among those who desired legal, military, or ecclesiastical careers.

The theme of frustrated bourgeois career aspirations and growing noble exclusiveness has been absorbed into general historical writing intended to present syntheses of existing knowledge. Ernest Labrousse wrote that the eighteenth-century bourgeoisie was developing a class consciousness based on wealth, intellectual cultivation, and collective experience in town life; at the same time, the obstacles placed by the nobility in the way of bourgeois career success were hardening, as the army, the judiciary, and the church hierarchy came to be dominated at the top by a closed noble caste.[14] More recently, Robert R. Palmer has written that "the appearance beside them of persons like them except in birth seems to have made the upper classes more self-consciously aristocratic. Many evidences suggest a growing exclusive-

[13] *The Bourgeoisie in Eighteenth-Century France* (Princeton: Princeton Univ. Press, 1955), pp. 141-44. The first point is more acceptable than the second, which explicitly relies on Dollot's unsupported assertion that noble exclusiveness became more extreme; indeed, on page 11, Mrs. Barber referred to "the destruction . . . of the adaptive mechanism, of the possibility of ennoblement. . . ."

[14] *Le XVIIIe siècle. Révolution intellectuelle, technique et politique (1715-1815)* (Paris: Presses Universitaires de France, 1953), p. 348. A mild objection to this was registered by Henri Calvet in the *Revue d'Histoire Moderne et Contemporaine*, 1 (1954), p. 303.

ness."[15] This statement was meant to apply to Europe as a whole, but the evidence cited concerning France emphasizes the self-consciousness, not any new and effective closure, of aristocratic circles.

Neither the Taine-Dollot hypothesis nor the Tocqueville hypothesis has ever been subjected to any kind of quantitative test. The former has been preferred, apparently, because it seems to provide a credible explanation. It is indeed possible to envisage a prerevolutionary situation in which the upward movement of ambitious individuals was obstructed, followed by a revolutionary situation in which the obstruction was perceived as part of the existing regime. Such a perception could then have been transformed into an ideological antipathy to the whole system by which the channels of mobility were defined, an antipathy that spread—impelled by powerful emotions and guided by the logical interconnections in the social fabric—developing into an attack on the social and political system as a whole. This line of thought is attractive because it helps to explain the identification of bourgeois class interest and revolutionary political objectives. And it makes this explanation possible without resort to any anachronism of economic history: an important advantage, for George V. Taylor has recently shown the very limited and politically non-revolutionary character of capitalism in eighteenth-century France.[16]

Biographical evidence seems to provide some support for the theme of frustrated bourgeois aspirations. Sieyès's father was a small-town legal practitioner, and his own career certainly seemed destined to carry him no higher than his position in 1789: vicar-general of the bishopric of Chartres, a position little better than that of a canon of the cathedral and clearly subordinate to the episcopacy which was filled with noblemen. Thus it appears easy to account for the sweeping condemnation of the nobility written by Sieyès in the pamphlet *Qu'est-ce que le Tiers État?* Similarly, in the National Assembly, a number of revolutionaries stood just below the horizontal fissure that divided nobles from commoners. Such was Jacques Cottin, of Nantes, who held the office of king's secretary (in actuality, an ennobling sinecure) in the chancellery of Brittany. As early as May 1789, he manifested "an

[15] "Social and Psychological Foundations of the Revolutionary Era," *New Cambridge Modern History* (Cambridge, England: Cambridge Univ. Press), VIII, 421-47, on p. 434.

[16] "Types of Capitalism in Eighteenth-Century France," *English Historical Review*, 79 (1964), pp. 478-97, supplemented by important observations on the similarities between bourgeois and noble landowners in "Noncapitalist Wealth and the Origins of the French Revolution," *American Historical Review*, 72 (1967), pp. 469-96.

unimaginable fury against the nobility,"[17] and on the night of 4 August it was he who called for the complete elimination of seigneurial lawcourts.[18] Standing just below the line between commoners and nobles, he was eager to see it erased. On the other side of the same line, the most intemperate spokesman for noble prerogatives was a newcomer to the noble class, Duval d'Esprémesnil, a judge in the Parlement of Paris whose father, a commoner, had served as a royal official in India. In the National Assembly, a commoner noted that the ennoblement of the Duval family was so recent as to render preposterous his references to "our ancestors,"[19] and a nobleman who hoped for conciliation with the Third Estate regretted Duval's leading role.[20] We can thus find political sentiments at both extremes manifested by upwardly mobile individuals: Cottin, a revolutionary who was still legally a commoner, and Duval d'Esprémesnil, a reactionary who had become legally a noble. Further research would perhaps reveal that men fearful of mobility downward, or striving even more intensely yet unsuccessfully for mobility upward, engaged in especially violent language and unconventional political behavior. Such evidence would remain anecdotal until a mass of biographies was systematically examined.

Our interest here, in any event, is not in the psychological traits of individual revolutionaries but rather in the political functioning of the social system during the winter and spring of 1789 before the great revolutionary outbreaks. In investigating this, we measure, as the independent variable, local differences in the opportunities for ennoblement provided by the institutional structure. We measure, as the dependent variable, local differences in radicalism in the grievance lists drawn up at the electoral meetings to choose deputies for the Estates-General of 1789. We seek to discover whether, in places where ennoblement opportunities were plentiful, the bourgeoisie was more or less radical than where ennoblement opportunities were scarce.

III

The transition from the commoner to the noble class involved both social and legal criteria and was usually gradual. Among commoners,

[17] Adrien Duquesnoy, *Journal*, ed. by Robert de Crèvecoeur (2 vols.; Paris: Picard et Fils, 1894), I, 21.

[18] Jacques-Athanase Lombard de Taradeau, "Lettres (1789-1791)," ed. by Louis Honoré in *Var Historique et Géographique*, 2 (1925-28), p. 236.

[19] Duquesnoy, *Journal*, I, 108.

[20] Charles-Élie, marquis de Ferrières, *Correspondance inédite, 1789, 1790, 1791*, ed. by Henri Carré (Paris: A. Colin, 1932), p. 63.

a *bourgeois vivant noblement* (who obtained his livelihood from proprietary income and refrained from any occupation incompatible with noble class membership) had already taken a recognized step toward becoming a noble. Among nobles, there was an important distinction between the *anobli*, whose status was recently attained, and the *gentilhomme*, whose paternal ancestors would ordinarily have been noble for at least a century or four generations. The degree to which the *bourgeois vivant noblement* remained socially a commoner, and the degree to which the *anobli* was accepted by other nobles as a social equal, is difficult to clarify and was doubtless variable in accordance with times and places.

Legally, the status of noble could be attained in three ways. It could simply be conferred by royal letters patent. It could be obtained through military service at or above the rank of captain, if certain other conditions were fulfilled. It could be acquired through incumbency in an ennobling office in the royal administration or judiciary.

In the late eighteenth century, ennoblement by letters patent was not frequent. Having examined a mass of source material on this point, Marcel Reinhard concluded that in the four decades ending in 1789 the king ennobled about 400 individuals (and with them, their male and female descendants) in the whole kingdom.[21] Even for the study of the actual rate, the ennoblement of 10 men per year would have little impact on the analysis. Since we are considering the perceptible opportunity for ennoblement, we observe also that the conferral of letters patent was not readily predictable, and we disregard it.

Ennoblement through military service was very difficult except for those who attained the ranks of general officers, ranks which were in fact held mostly by men already noble. Research by David D. Bien has revealed that, of 1,738 officers eligible for ennoblement through holding the ranks of *maréchal de camp* or *lieutenant-général*, in 1750 or later, only 92 thereby became nobles.[22] The rate of this type of ennoblement is even lower, fewer than 3 men per year. In addition, this means of ennoblement was not confined to local institutions but was available to very small numbers through a national institution, sub-

[21] "Élite et noblesse dans la seconde moitié du XVIIIe siècle," *Revue d'Histoire Moderne et Contemporaine*, 3 (1956), pp. 5-37, based on a systematic examination of the archives of the *chambre des comptes* of Paris, the *cour des aides* of Paris, the *Dictionnaire des ennoblissements* by Godet de Soudé, and other sources. The total of 400 is given on p. 29.

[22] "Social Mobility in Eighteenth-Century France," a mimeographed paper written in 1966 and communicated to us by Professor Bien, to whom we are very grateful. The proportion of generals born in the bourgeoisie was about the same (5 per cent) a century earlier: André Corvisier, "Les généraux de Louis XIV et leur origine sociale," *XVIIe Siècle*, Nos. 42-43 (1959), pp. 23-53.

ject to the chances of war. Ennoblement through military service, therefore, is likewise omitted from our description of local differences in opportunity.

The usual way of attaining the legal status of noble was through holding civilian office. In the only full study of the nobility of a province, Jean Meyer found that 303 families of Brittany were ennobled from 1700 to 1788. Of these, 60 per cent attained noble status through offices in Brittany, and 19 per cent through offices in Paris.[23] The opportunities to attain noble status in this way varied geographically, since they depended on the institutional structure.

Regional variations have caused some historians of the French Revolution to point out the futility of attempting to determine a national average or a typical situation. We agree that it is futile—because it would be useless. Whether ennoblement was frequent or infrequent, as a national average, would in itself tell us nothing about the genesis of the revolution. On the contrary, we view geographic variation as an advantage, since it permits us to study differences in political responses between regions with high and low rates.

In all, there were 40 cities and towns where, in 1789, ennobling offices existed. Since the royal administration and the royal judiciary had established officials in about 400 towns, it is evident that the opportunity for ennoblement through office-holding was a species of privilege enjoyed by a small minority of localities in the kingdom.

The number of ennobling offices ranged from 2, in Angers, to about 1,000, in Paris.[24]

The duration of the incumbency required to achieve ennoblement varied from two years to two generations. (A generation of service ordinarily consisted of 20 years' service by one office-holder or his death while in office.) In only 4 localities was it possible to achieve ennoblement in fewer than 5 years. In 20 localities it was possible to achieve ennoblement in one generation. In 16 localities it was possible to achieve ennoblement through office-holding only in two generations. (In theory, father and son might both enter office on one day and both die on the next day; but in practice, two generations usually meant an elapsed time of about 40 years.)

Offices were not simply mechanisms for crossing the legal barrier between the commoner and noble classes. Each office conferred a particular degree of professional and political prestige, together with specific legal privileges and exemptions. Some offices brought very

[23] *La noblesse bretonne au XVIIIe siècle* (2 vols.; Paris: S.E.V.P.E.N., 1966), p. 427.

[24] See Appendix below.

large pecuniary rewards, others little or none. Each office entailed duties, which ranged from the emptiest of formalities to onerous tasks for which specialized knowledge and conscientious effort were expected.

Ennobling offices were not equally available to all prospective purchasers in a locality. In some institutions, many offices were preempted by noblemen and were inaccessible to commoners. Especially was this true in the parlements, where most newly vacant offices of *conseiller*, in the years between 1774 and 1789, were filled by men already noble: this number ranged from 62 per cent of the vacancies, in the Parlement of Metz, to 100 per cent at Aix, Nancy, and Rennes; it averaged 82 per cent.[25] Thus in some localities there was an apparent opportunity for ennoblement, indicated by the total number of offices in existence, and a smaller real opportunity defined by the number of offices which might be acquired by commoners.

These variable characteristics of offices, relative scarcity, long or short periods of incumbency required for ennoblement, different degrees of prestige and power, trivial or burdensome duties, small or large profits, and the extent of actual preemption by noblemen, all affected the prices of offices. In one locality, the prices of ennobling offices did not all move upward or downward over a period of time. In Bordeaux, there were four types of ennobling offices, and each type showed a different price trend. The offices of king's secretary in the two chancelleries were already among the most expensive in the city during the 1730s; they required no training, entailed no work, yet conferred nobility in one generation; their prices rose dramatically from the middle of the century onward, almost doubling from about 1760 to 1789. Offices in the parlement, on the other hand, fluctuated in price during the middle years of the century and from 1775 onward fell steadily, reaching a lower average price than the offices in the court of tax appeals. Having discovered and analyzed these trends, William Doyle concluded that ennoblement through office-holding continued to be very attractive just before the revolution but that the other reasons for acquiring such offices seemed to decline in importance.[26] His findings emphasize the complexity and the local character of the factors determining the prices of offices.

[25] The data are in the footnotes of an article by Jean Égret, "L'aristocratie parlementaire française à la fin de l'ancien régime," *Revue Historique*, 208 (1952), pp. 1-14. An erroneous average, 58 per cent, was calculated as a result of a misreading of this article by Franklin L. Ford, *Robe and Sword. The Regrouping of the French Aristocracy after Louis XIV* (Cambridge: Harvard Univ. Press, 1953), pp. 145-46, and has been repeated by several other writers.

[26] "Le prix des charges anoblissantes à Bordeaux au XVIIIe siècle," *Annales du Midi*, 80 (1968), pp. 65-77.

The market for offices in eighteenth-century France can fairly be compared to a real estate market in the mid-twentieth century. The determination of economic value was complicated by a discrepancy between current prices and tax assessments. The official capital values, prepared in 1771 for tax purposes, were lower than the market prices for many offices in the 1780s. For other offices, especially those owned by nobles and sold by them to other nobles, however, the official capital values were higher than the current market prices.[27] We have been unable to discover enough market prices to justify using them in our analysis. We have found official valuations for about three-fourths of the offices,[28] but at a later point we shall indicate why we do not use these data directly, either.

The market for offices resembled a real estate market in another respect also. The information by which a prospective purchaser might discover an impending vacancy was available in gossip, letters from friends, and advertisements in the rudimentary newspapers usually entitled *Affiches*. The sporadic media of information help to account for the degree to which local and regional demand dominated each of the markets for offices. The weakness of the national component in the demand for offices is important for our analysis, concentrated as it is upon geographic differences in ennoblement opportunities and political sentiments.

The dominance of local and regional demand for offices is indicated by the geographic origins of office-holders. The single institution which was most important nationally for ennobling offices was the great chancellery in Paris, with its 317 king's secretaries. During the 1760s, 150 men entered such offices: 36 per cent had been born in Paris; 23 per cent had been born within a circular region bounded by Amiens, Reims, Orléans, and Évreux; and 41 per cent had been born outside that region.[29] These figures, based on baptismal records, under-

[27] Fréteau, a nobleman who entered office as a councillor in the Parlement of Paris in 1764 and was elected to the Estates-General in 1789, revealed that the Treasury reimbursed a larger sum for his office than it would have brought if sold. *Moniteur*, 19 March 1791.

[28] The capital values of many offices are stated in the reports by the liquidation commissioner in 1791, preserved in the Archives Nationales, D XVII 9, Nos. 123-27. These include figures for 8 of the 13 parlements, 17 of the 19 chancelleries, 5 of the 8 *chambres* or *cours des comptes*, 1 of the 4 *cours des aides*, and 14 of the 29 *bureaux des finances*. Summary data are given in the Appendix below.

[29] "Nobiliaire armorial des secrétaires du roi au grand collège," *Annuaire de la noblesse de France* (1923-30, in installments) indicates the locality of baptism for men entering office. This list stops with the new entrants of May 1769. Earlier installments, from 1904 through 1921, covered the king's secretaries entering office from 1705 to 1759; the list carries forward the work of Abraham Tessereau, *Histoire chronologique de la grande chancellerie de France* (2 vols.; Paris, 1710).

state the degree to which demand for these offices was concentrated in Paris. Biographical information shows that actually about half the new king's secretaries had been residents of Paris for years before entering office. The geographic distribution of birthplaces was very similar for the new office-holders in the court of coinage, which has been well characterized by François Bluche as a "veritable ennobling machine."[30] In the years between 1760 and 1790, a total of 74 men entered ennobling offices in the court: 36 per cent were natives of Paris; 22 per cent were natives of the region bounded by Amiens, Reims, Orléans, and Évreux; and 42 per cent were natives of places outside the region.

In provincial capitals, the geographic origins of the holders of ennobling offices display a roughly analogous pattern. In the chancellery in the Parlement of Dijon, in the years between 1760 and 1790, the new king's secretaries numbered 62 men, of whom 20 per cent were born in Dijon, 18 per cent came from elsewhere in northern Burgundy (from Auxerre to Beaune), 16 per cent from southern Burgundy (from Autun to Mâcon), 10 per cent from Lyon or its neighborhood, and 36 per cent from more distant places.[31] The *bureau des finances* in Poitiers, unlike the institutions we have just mentioned, required two generations' office-holding to achieve ennoblement. There, half the office-holders came from Poitiers itself, and the range of geographic origins was narrow, scarcely extending outside Poitou.[32]

Thus there was a widely diffused interest, extending all over the kingdom, in the acquisition of ennobling offices. But men resident in the localities where ennobling offices existed clearly enjoyed a disproportionately good opportunity to obtain them. It is, we believe, indubitable that in these localities the well-to-do, educated commoners

[30] François Bluche, *Les magistrats de la cour des monnaies de Paris au XVIIIe siècle, 1715-1790* (Paris: Les Belles Lettres, 1966) indicates the locality of baptism for every new office-holder. The quoted phrase appears in another of Bluche's works, *Les magistrats du Grand Conseil au XVIIIe siècle, 1690-1791* (Paris: Les Belles Lettres, 1966), p. 32.

[31] André Bourée, *La chancellerie près le Parlement de Bourgogne de 1476 à 1790* (Dijon: A. Bellais, 1927).

[32] Adrien Bonvallet, "Le bureau des finances de la généralité de Poitiers," *Mémoires de la Société des Antiquaires de l'Ouest*, 2nd ser., 6 (1883), pp. 137-424, lists the office-holders on pp. 340-74. In the 1760-90 period, 46 men entered ennobling offices. The names of 32 fall in the part of the alphabet presently covered in the monumental work of Henri, Paul, and Joseph Beauchet-Filleau, *Dictionnaire historique et généalogique des familles du Poitou* (2nd ed.; Poitiers: Oudin, 1891-1915, and Fontenay-le-Comte: Lussaud frères, 1963—), I, 111, 237, 394, 609; II, 41, 61, 162, 303, 618, 740; III, 26, 59, 65, 118, 254, 268, 298, 373, 412, 541, 787; IV, 338, 587; V, 122, 172.

generally had a comparatively keen awareness of the whole process of ennoblement through office-holding.

IV

RADICAL sentiment was expressed in varying degrees in the *cahiers de doléances* drawn up in the process of convoking, and electing deputies to, the Estates-General of 1789. These documents have been used and abused ever since then as indicators of the state of public opinion. But used with proper caution they reveal regional variations in the sentiments of the groups represented in the assemblies which adopted them. We have devised five methods of measuring radicalism in such documents and have applied them to a selected category of the documents.

There are as many different categories of *cahiers de doléances* as there were kinds of groups privileged to assemble for the purpose of choosing delegates in the indirect electoral process of 1789. We restrict ourselves to the general *cahiers* of the Third Estate and the Nobility. A brief explanation is needed to make clear the meaning of this choice.[33]

In the Third Estate, the eligible voters were all French subjects at least twenty-five years old, included in the tax roll of their locality, and neither noblemen nor clergymen. In the countryside and the small towns, each parish or community having a separate tax roll held a primary assembly, in order to draw up its list of complaints and grievances and to choose delegates to an assembly for the whole electoral circumscription. (This was, in most parts of the kingdom, a judicial district called a *bailliage* or a *sénéchaussée.*) In 290 large towns, there were 2 stages, rather than 1, within the locality. First, each occupational corporate group would assemble, draw up its list of complaints and grievances, and choose delegates; then, these delegates would constitute an assembly for the town, to draw up a list of complaints and grievances and choose delegates to the assembly for the whole electoral circumscription.

Some electoral circumscriptions elected deputies who went directly to Versailles. Others, however, sent delegates to still another assembly, that of the *bailliage principal*, where the deputies to the Estates-General were elected and a list of grievances was adopted. It is the *cahiers*

[33] The authoritative description of the complex details and local variations in the convocation procedures is provided by Armand Brette, *Recueil de documents relatifs à la convocation des Etats Généraux de 1789* (4 vols.; Paris: Imprimerie Nationale, 1894-1915). More accessible is Beatrice F. Hyslop, *A Guide to the General Cahiers of 1789* (New York: Columbia Univ. Press, 1936, reprinted 1967). Our description here is extremely simplified.

de doléances intended to be taken to Versailles, known to historians as the "general" *cahiers*, that we study here, regardless of the number of preliminary assemblies involved.

In the Second Estate, each noble was permitted to appear, or to send another noble with power of attorney, wherever he possessed a fief or, if without a fief, in the assembly of nobles for the *bailliage* of his residence. There were no preliminary assemblies, and all the *cahiers* adopted were "general" *cahiers*.

Among historians, there has been a long debate over whose views are presented in the *cahiers de doléances*. As to the grievances of country parishes, particularly, much discussion has centered on the existence of "model" *cahiers* drafted elsewhere and circulating in the villages. For our investigation, this debate is irrelevant for two reasons. First, nearly every general *cahier* in the Third Estate was preceded by a number of village *cahiers* and one or more town *cahiers*, any of which could have served as a "model" to be adopted or rejected in whole or in part. The process of adoption, in the *bailliage* assemblies, was usually regarded with sufficient seriousness to permit our reliance on the adopted *cahier* as an authentic expression of the views of the final electors. Second, the electors in the final *bailliage* assemblies of the Third Estate, having been chosen by preliminary assemblies, were mostly notable personages in their villages and towns and were therefore precisely the group of commoners for whom ennoblement was a conceivable possibility or even an ambition.

Our content analysis of these *cahiers* is borrowed from a larger study of the origins of the French Revolution which encompasses the *cahiers* of other groups and many measures of regional variations in the social structure of the Old Regime and in political behavior during the revolution.[34] The method of content analysis used in the larger study, and applied here, must be described briefly.

The procedure attempts to break new ground in content analysis in a number of ways. It joins the human coder to a computer (figuratively) so as to establish an appropriate division of labor between the coder and the scientists who utilize the coded material. In this two-step process, the human coder is used to isolate a semantic unit, the "grievance," and to translate it into a standard, mnemonic, analytically organized language comprehensible both to humans and to computers. We have attempted to avoid including among the coder's responsibilities a task which properly belongs to the scientist himself: the attri-

[34] The results of the larger study will be reported in a volume, *Quantitative Studies of the French Revolution*, now in preparation. Pending that publication, copies of mimeographed progress reports can be obtained by writing to Shapiro.

bution of historical and theoretical significance to observations. By the use of computer programs, the analyst defines Boolean conditions for retrieval and scoring, using his historical and sociological judgment as to what kinds of concrete grievances are relevant to his various purposes. The coder is supposed to function on the model of a common translator between natural languages, such as English and French, only his translation is from French to a limited vocabulary, with a syntax and grammar standardized and simplified for convenience in programming. Some loss of meaning is involved, as in any act of translation. The amount of loss can only be judged after much analysis of the results, and by critics after their publication. We are thus far satisfied with our preliminary observations of reliabilities (in the conventional sense) obtained by these methods, but the serious study of reliability with such a code is a major task which we have only begun.

We instructed the computer to measure radicalism in different ways producing five scores for each document. (In the list which follows we indicate parenthetically the rationale for each score.)

Demands for equality. The computer was instructed to count any grievances included in a very long list of specific items such as: a generalized demand for equality; abolition of the nobility; abolition of various kinds of seigneurial dues; abolition of tax privileges; establishment of a single tax to be paid by every property owner; organization of elected assemblies of any kind upon a one-man-one-vote basis; open access to holding public office; equality before the civil and criminal law in any of its manifestations. (In the ideological situation of 1789, as is made clear by many pamphlets before and after the adoption of the *cahiers*, equality was a central and mobilizing idea in radical attitudes.)

Demands for change. The computer was instructed to count the number of grievances explicitly calling for the *abolition* of existing laws or institutions, the *replacement* of them by others, or the *establishment* of new ones, regardless of the laws or institutions mentioned. (Thorough or drastic change indicated by such verbs is, in our minds, a constant meaning of the term "radicalism.")

Similarity to the decree of 4 August 1789.

Similarity to the Declaration of the Rights of Man adopted from 19 to 26 August 1789. This document, and the decree of 4 August, were coded in the same coding language used for the *cahiers*, and the computer was instructed to provide a score representing the degree to which each *cahier* contains demands having the same effect as the provisions of these two enactments. (This procedure is based on the historical fact that the National Assembly was carried forward in

August 1789 by cataclysmic national and Parisian upheavals and reached a point of radical action which neither its members nor their constituencies could have envisioned, or demanded in the *cahiers*, during the spring. Extremely few of the *cahiers* in effect anticipated in a substantial degree either of these enactments; to the degree that they did so, they were, in the political context of March and April 1789, radical.)

Total number of grievances. The computer was instructed simply to count the number of distinct grievances or demands in each *cahier*. (In the Third Estate *cahiers*, with their predominant tone favoring change, this number should be highly correlated with our dependent variable.)

Brief explanations are needed for two methodological decisions which are to some degree controversial but which seemed to us necessary. First, we departed from the custom of attempting to remove the effect of sheer scale of a document before analyzing the content analysis scores. The logic underlying this custom is identical with that which dictates that raw data in demographic and economic research are converted into appropriate rates, by dividing the raw data by some population figure. The difficulty in mechanically following conventional procedure here would be that the scale of the document, that is, the number of grievances stated, is itself a measure of our dependent theoretical variable, and removing its effect upon another measure (by standardization or partialling) would remove precisely the variance we wish to measure. The use of the raw scores under these circumstances is perhaps unconventional, but is not without precedent.[35] Second, no significance levels are reported for the statistics presented below. Our argument against them is the most powerful classical argument, that we are studying (with some few missing cases) an entire population and not a sample. Nevertheless, a number of rather small correlations are presented, and their theoretical meanings discussed, and this makes some statisticians uncomfortable, probably for good reasons having to do with the reliability of observations and perhaps not at all with sampling. It might be alleged that our low cor-

[35] "Yet there is an important sense in which total unreduced product is a much safer single measure for comparisons of economic growth—safer in that it precludes the danger of omitting, for consideration of both causes and results of economic growth, a basic element—human population itself." Simon Kuznets, Wilbert E. Moore, and Joseph J. Spengler, *Economic Growth: Brazil, India, Japan* (Durham, N.C.: Duke Univ. Press, 1955), p. 12. Further, "a *per capita* . . . measure . . . carries with it the danger of neglecting the denominator of the ratio . . ." *ibid.*, pp. 12-13. See also Samuel A. Stouffer, *Social Research to Test Ideas* (New York: Free Press of Glencoe, 1962), p. 267.

relations may reflect highly unreliable data rather than small historical effects. In reply, we would point to the consistency of the small correlations found for the Third Estate, the absence of even small consistent correlations for the Nobility, and the high correlations with our urbanization measure, all of which will be set forth in our results.

Finally, a word is required on the units measuring the populations of documents observed. The data reported result from examination of all the extant general *cahiers* of the Third Estate and of the Nobility. Differences between the number of Third Estate *cahiers* and the number of Nobility *cahiers* reported are due to differences in the Convocation regulations for the two Estates and to differential survival of documents. For the 40 towns having ennobling offices, *cahiers* of each Estate are missing in 5 towns and we report data on the other 35 (or, when we exclude Paris, 34).

Analysis of the relation between the radicalism scores and the ennoblement opportunities was carried out in two stages. This was done because four-fifths of the electoral circumscriptions contained no ennobling offices at all, while in the electoral circumscriptions that contained ennobling offices there was a wide range in the number of such offices. First, then, we compared all the electoral circumscriptions having no ennobling offices with all those having some ennobling offices, by reference to the average score on each measure of radicalism in the *cahiers*.

The results of this first stage in the analysis are set forth in Table 1. They are highly consistent with what we have called the Tocqueville hypothesis, to the effect that where there were opportunities for ennoblement the *cahiers* of the Third Estate were more radical. By every measure of radicalism examined, the Third Estate *cahiers* were more radical where there were some ennobling offices than where there were none. According to the Tocqueville hypothesis, ennoblement opportunities could generate radicalism only in the Third Estate and there would be no reason to believe that the Nobility was more radical where there were opportunities for ennoblement than where there were not. These measures show the *cahiers* of the Nobility, in contrast to those of the Third Estate, exhibiting small and inconsistent differences in radicalism as between circumscriptions with and those without opportunities for ennoblement. By themselves, the radicalism scores for the Third Estate tell us only that there is a difference between two sets of regions, a difference which can be attributed to factors other than the presence or absence of ennoblement opportunities. The radicalism scores for the Nobility tell us that whatever produced the systematic difference observed in the Third Estate must be some factor that operates differently on the Nobility. The opportunity for ennoblement is one such factor.

The second stage in the analysis was limited to those electoral circumscriptions containing one or more towns with some ennobling offices. This stage consisted of the computation of correlation coefficients to measure the relationship between the radicalism scores and the number of ennobling offices. The results of this computation are

TABLE 1. MEAN SCORES ON FIVE MEASURES OF RADICALISM IN *CAHIERS* OF THE THIRD ESTATE AND THE NOBILITY IN LOCALITIES WITH AND WITHOUT ENNOBLING OFFICES

	Third Estate			*Nobility*		
	Mean Scores for the Localities:			*Mean Scores for the Localities:*		
Radicalism Measured By:	*With Some Ennobling Offices*	*With Some Ennobling Offices (Paris Excluded)**	*With No Ennobling Offices*	*With Some Ennobling Offices*	*With Some Ennobling Offices (Paris Excluded)**	*With No Ennobling Offices*
Demands for Equality	18.7	18.6	16.1	2.4	2.4	3.2
Demands for Change	115.3	112.9	90.6	58.5	58.0	51.1
Similarity to Decree of 4 August	20.0	19.9	17.8	5.5	5.5	6.2
Similarity to Declaration of Rights	7.7	7.2	5.8	6.9	6.7	6.2
Total Number of Grievances	316.3	305.1	228.2	193.5	191.3	159.8
NUMBER OF LOCALITIES	35	34	147	35	34	119

* Paris has been excluded from the analysis in this column in order to determine whether th relationships observed continue to exist in the absence of its unique contribution.

presented in Table 2. They likewise are consistent with the Tocqueville hypothesis, although less decisively so. In the Third Estate, small but consistently positive correlations are found between the number of ennobling offices in the electoral circumscriptions and the five scores measuring radicalism in the *cahiers*. In the Nobility, generally, negative correlations are found between the number of ennobling offices and the scores on radicalism. It is worth pausing to note the effects of excluding Paris from the analysis. In the Third Estate, exclusion of Paris diminishes the correlation for the radicalism score measuring similarity between the *cahiers* and the Declaration of the Rights of Man, but *increases* the correlation for the radicalism score measuring similarity between the *cahiers* and the decree of 4 August. In the Nobility, exclusion of Paris shifts all the correlations in a negative direction, and this reflects the liberalism of the Paris nobility. Excluding Paris from the analysis does not, however, alter the essential findings.

TABLE 2. CORRELATIONS BETWEEN FIVE MEASURES OF RADICALISM AND NUMBER OF ENNOBLING OFFICES, IN CIRCUMSCRIPTIONS HAVING SOME ENNOBLING OFFICES

	Third Estate		*Nobility*	
Radicalism Measured By:	*Paris Included*	*Paris Excluded*	*Paris Included*	*Paris Excluded*
Demands for Equality	.10	.11	.02	—.08
Demands for Change	.31	.19	—.04	—.39
Similarity to Decree of 4 August	.13	.23	—.08	—.15
Similarity to Declaration of Rights	.52	.13	.29	.01
Total Number of Grievances	.42	.19	.06	—.28
NUMBER OF LOCALITIES	35	34	35	34

The number of ennobling offices serves as one indicator of opportunity for upward movement, in that their very existence symbolized an aspect of social realities. But where ennobling offices were held by incumbents who were already noble, the number of such offices might be an inadequate measure of opportunity. Here we recall the distinction between apparent and real opportunity. The former might have an ideological effect, through perception of institutions which, in principle, provided channels for upward movement. The latter would refer to opportunity in the literal sense, the possibility for a family to move from one social group to another. In order to differentiate the effects of apparent and real opportunity on political attitudes, we subtract from the number of ennobling offices the number occupied by men already noble. If real opportunities for ennoblement were the operative ones, we should find a greater correlation between the "corrected" number of ennobling offices and the radicalism scores than between the raw number of such offices and the radicalism scores. The correlations between the "corrected" number of ennobling offices and the radicalism scores are set forth in Table 3. Comparing it with Table 2, we find the correlations generally somewhat lower. We conclude that any influence of opportunities for ennoblement upon radicalism that is reflected in Tables 1 and 2 is probably due to the presence of the ennobling institutions and their privileged incumbents, rather than to the existence of real opportunities for ennoblement. This finding constitutes a modification of the Tocqueville hypothesis, since we are now obliged to give greater weight to the symbolic meaning of apparent opportunity for ennoblement and to the collective effect on the spectators of ennobling institutions, rather than to the real opportunity for ennoblement and the effect on frustrated upwardly mobile individuals.

TABLE 3. CORRELATIONS BETWEEN FIVE MEASURES OF RADICALISM AND NUMBER OF ENNOBLING OFFICES, AFTER SUBTRACTION OF ESTIMATED NUMBER OF OFFICES OF CONSEILLER OCCUPIED IN EACH LOCALITY BY NOBLEMEN

Radicalism Measured By:	*Third Estate Paris Excluded*
Demands for Equality	.04
Demands for Change	.15
Similarity to Decree of 4 August	.15
Similarity to Declaration of Rights	.18
Total Number of Grievances	.16

An ennobling office that costs a large sum, or that requires two generations' service to achieve ennoblement, presents a slighter opportunity than an office that is inexpensive in terms of either money or years. Our data on the economic values of offices are incomplete and consist of official taxable values rather than current prices. But our data on the length of service required to achieve ennoblement are complete and accurate. For the offices whose capital values we know, the correlation between those values and the number of years' service required to achieve ennoblement is strong: —0.69. In view of these facts, we chose to use the required number of years of service as an indicator of the sacrifice needed to achieve ennoblement by holding an office. For each locality with some ennobling offices, other than

Paris, we calculated the average "cost" of ennoblement through office-holding, measuring cost in years. The greater the cost, the slighter the real opportunity for ennoblement. The correlation between this measure of cost and the radicalism scores is set forth in Table 4. The correlations are all close to zero. This is another indication that obstacles to real opportunities for ennoblement were, in general, unimportant in generating radicalism in the Third Estate *cahiers*.

TABLE 4. CORRELATIONS BETWEEN FIVE MEASURES OF RADICALISM AND LOCAL MEAN NUMBER OF YEARS IN OFFICE REQUIRED FOR ENNOBLEMENT BY THE OFFICES IN EACH LOCALITY

Radicalism Measured By:	*Third Estate Paris Excluded*
Demands for Equality	−.13
Demands for Change	.02
Similarity to Decree of 4 August	.00
Similarity to Declaration of Rights	−.01
Total Number of Grievances	−.09

Apparent opportunities for ennoblement are consistently correlated positively with radicalism scores in the *cahiers* of the Third Estate. This does not mean that radicalism can be explained merely by reference to the number of ennobling offices. Other independent variables might be far more important. Several such variables can be represented, for example, by the size of the population in the principal town of an electoral circumscription. The presence of administrative and judicial institutions with ennobling offices surely contributed to urban growth in some localities. In 35 *bailliages* where ennobling offices existed, indeed, the correlation between the number of such offices and the population of the principal town is 0.91, so that to a considerable degree the two variables reflect the same more fundamental social reality. But when we exclude Paris, this correlation declines to 0.30. It therefore appears useful to consider partial correlations between the number of ennobling offices and the scores for radicalism in the Third Estate *cahiers*, controlling for the population of the principal town in each electoral circumscription. The results appear in Table 5. The small correlations between the number of ennobling offices and the radicalism scores become even smaller when the statistical effect of town size is removed, although they do not completely disappear. This suggests that opportunities for ennoblement, and other mobility phenomena, are relatively weak historical forces, which should not be studied in isolation as they have been in the sociological and historical writing that provided our point of departure.

TABLE 5. PARTIAL CORRELATIONS BETWEEN FIVE MEASURES OF RADICALISM AND NUMBER OF ENNOBLING OFFICES, WITH EFFECT OF POPULATION OF PRINCIPAL CITY IN THE CIRCUMSCRIPTION REMOVED

Radicalism Measured By:	*Third Estate Paris Excluded*
Demands for Equality	.03
Demands for Change	.07
Similarity to Decree of 4 August	.17
Similarity to Declaration of Rights	—.08
Total Number of Grievances	.09

We turn, then, from apparent opportunities for ennoblement, as an independent variable helping to account for radicalism in the bourgeoisie, and consider instead the population of the principal town in the electoral circumscription. The correlation between that population figure and the radicalism scores is consistently positive, as is shown in Table 6. Indeed, on four of our five measures of radicalism, the relationship is stronger than that between ennobling offices and radicalism which we set forth in Table 2. Only when radicalism is measured by similarity of the *cahier* to the decree of 4 August is the correlation about the same for the one independent variable, the population of the principal town, as for the other, the number of ennobling offices.

TABLE 6. CORRELATIONS BETWEEN FIVE MEASURES OF RADICALISM AND POPULATION OF PRINCIPAL TOWN IN THE CIRCUMSCRIPTION, IN CIRCUMSCRIPTIONS HAVING SOME ENNOBLING OFFICES

Radicalism Measured By:	*Third Estate*	
	Paris Included	*Paris Excluded*
Demands for Equality	.14	.27
Demands for Change	.37	.43
Similarity to Decree of 4 August	.11	.25
Similarity to Declaration of Rights	.65	.63
Total Number of Grievances	.47	.36
NUMBER OF LOCALITIES	35	34

Up to this point, we have avoided using the term "urbanization," but clearly some such concept is measured by the population of the principal town in an area. The difficulty with the concept, in the present context, is that it includes all kinds of mobility, social as well as geographic, together with an array of economic and psychological variables. This suggests to us that further quantitative study of the immediate origins of revolutionary change might usefully concentrate on refinement of the concept of urbanization, with particular reference to eighteenth-century France, and on analysis of the separable variables making up that larger system of forces which included social mobility.

V

On the relationships between social mobility and political behavior, sociological writing is in a confused and confusing state. Historical writing that relates social mobility to the origins of the French Revolution of 1789 relies on supposition more than on evidence, but offers two discernible hypotheses. One, presented by Taine and elaborated by Dollot, explains the alienation of many bourgeois from their hierarchical society by referring to blocked aspirations and frustrated strivings for upward social movement. The other, presented by Tocqueville, explains bourgeois antipathy to the nobility by referring to the visible possibility of deserting the bourgeois class to enter a noble class distinguished, with an intolerable clarity, from the rest of the populace.

Frustrated strivings for upward mobility may have had important effects on individual revolutionaries. But it should be axiomatic, as sociologists, historians, and politicians continue to rediscover, that a revolution is not made only by its forerunners and leaders. In the developing political environment of 1789, the winter and spring were not dominated by a bourgeois desire to destroy the nobility. Yet there were consistent geographic correlations between the existence and number of opportunities for ennoblement and the degree of radicalism manifested in the *cahiers de doléances* of the Third Estate. These correlations permit us to conclude that the social system was affected politically by the ennoblement process, that the effects operated through the spectators of this process more than through frustrated, would-be beneficiaries of it, and that, as between the Taine-Dollot hypothesis and the Tocqueville hypothesis, we should choose the latter because of its superior value in explaining the politics of the social system as a whole. The obscurity surrounding the matter of social mobility and revolutionary change in 1789 has thus been diminished by quantitative study of the *cahiers de doléances* and the geographically varying number of ennobling offices.

The opportunities for ennoblement, and the problematic character of social mobility represented by these opportunities, were however comparatively unimportant in generating within the bourgeoisie a desire for revolutionary change. The several variables resulting in the existence of a large town in an electoral circumscription had a combined effect that was more important. One of these variables was the presence of institutions in which there were ennobling offices. The other components in urbanization ought to be examined together and systematically distinguished from one another in future quantitative research on the genesis of the revolution of 1789.

APPENDIX

ENNOBLING OFFICES IN 1789, BY LOCALITIES

1 Institution	2 Rapidity of Ennoblement	3 Number of Ennobling Offices	4 Percentage of Conseillers Already Noble	5 Capital Value in 1791, in Livres
		PARIS		
Grande chancellerie	1 gn.	317		122,000
Requêtes de l'hôtel	1 gn.	80	100	108,000
Grand Conseil	1 gn.	56	22	
Parlement	1 gn.	165	89	57,000
Chancellerie, parlement	1 gn.	8		
Chambre des comptes	1 gn.	211	54	80,000
Cour des aides	1 gn.	67	53	57,000
Cour des monnaies	1 gn.	42	5	
Bureau des finances	1 gn.	29		85,000
Châtelet	1 gn.	5	100	
Châtelet	40 yrs. or death in office after 20 yrs.	68	12	21,000
Municipalité	2 yrs.	4		
Municipalité	1 gn.	3		
		AIX		
Parlement	2 gn.	69	100	45,000
Chancellerie, parlement	1 gn.	21		85,000
Cour des comptes & aides	2 gn.	46	56	32,000
Chancellerie, comptes	1 gn.	22		75,000
Bureau des finances	2 gn.	27		40,000
		ALENÇON		
Bureau des finances	2 gn.	24		47,000
		AMIENS		
Bureau des finances	2 gn.	27		
		ANGERS		
Municipalité	4 yrs.	2		
		ANGOULÊME		
Municipalité	20 yrs.	2		
		ARRAS		
Conseil provincial	2 gn.	23		29,000
Chancellerie, conseil	1 gn.	22		84,000
		AUCH		
Bureau des finances	2 gn.	11		31,000

Continued

ENNOBLING OFFICES IN 1789, BY LOCALITIES (*Continued*)

1 *Institution*	2 *Rapidity of Ennoblement*	3 *Number of Ennobling Offices*	4 *Percentage of Conseillers Already Noble*	5 *Capital Value in 1791, in Livres*
		BAR-LE-DUC		
Chambre des comptes	2 gn.	14	93	
		BESANÇON		
Parlement	1 gn.	67	87	
Chancellerie, parlement	1 gn.	49		85,000
Bureau des finances	2 gn.	13		
		BORDEAUX		
Parlement	2 gn.	100	65	
Chancellerie, parlement	1 gn.	26		85,000
Cour des aides	2 gn.	45		
Chancellerie, aides	1 gn.	13		
Bureau des finances	2 gn.	30		51,000
		BOURGES		
Bureau des finances	2 gn.	26		
Municipalité	20 yrs.	1		
		CAEN		
Bureau des finances	2 gn.	24		60,000
		CHÂLONS-SUR-MARNE		
Bureau des finances	2 gn.	29		
		CLERMONT-FERRAND		
Cour des aides	2 gn.	29		
Chancellerie, aides	1 gn.			
		COLMAR		
Conseil souverain	2 gn.	27	20	
Chancellerie, conseil	1 gn.	22		85,000
		DIJON		
Parlement	2 gn.	81	79	35,000
Chancellerie, parlement	1 gn.	26		85,000
Chambre des comptes	2 gn.	53		
Bureau des finances	2 gn.	27		50,000
		DOUAI		
Parlement	1 gn.	32	64	62,000
Chancellerie, parlement	1 gn.	30		85,000
		GRENOBLE		
Parlement	1 gn.	61	84	33,000
Chancellerie, parlement	1 gn.	31		85,000
Chambre des comptes	1 gn.	45		31,000
Bureau des finances	1 gn.	31		

Continued

Ennobling Offices in 1789, by Localities (*Continued*)

1 *Institution*	2 *Rapidity of Ennoblement*	3 *Number of Ennobling Offices*	4 *Percentage of Conseillers Already Noble*	5 *Capital Value in 1791, in Livres*
		La Rochelle		
Bureau des finances	2 gn.	12		
		Lille		
Bureau des finances	2 gn.	17		40,000
		Limoges		
Bureau des finances	2 gn.	28		56,000
		Lyon		
Bureau des finances	2 gn.	30		41,000
Municipalité	2 yrs.	4		
		Marseille		
Sénéchaussée	1 gn.	9		
		Metz		
Parlement	2 gn.	54	62	33,000
Chancellerie, parlement	1 gn.	24		85,000
Bureau des finances	2 gn.	23		
		Montauban		
Cour des aides	2 gn.	31		
Chancellerie, aides	1 gn.	18		51,000
Bureau des finances	2 gn.	30		45,000
		Montpellier		
Cour des comptes & aides	2 gn.	125	17	
Chancellerie, comptes	1 gn.	20		85,000
Bureau des finances	2 gn.	30		
		Moulins		
Bureau des finances	2 gn.	27		
		Nancy		
Parlement	2 gn.	42	100	
Chancellerie, parlement	1 gn.	27		85,000
Chambre des comptes	2 gn.	25	29	
		Nantes		
Chambre des comptes	2 gn.	94		45,000
Municipalité	2 yrs.	1		

Continued

ENNOBLING OFFICES IN 1789, BY LOCALITIES (*Continued*)

1 *Institution*	2 *Rapidity of Ennoblement*	3 *Number of Ennobling Offices*	4 *Percentage of Conseillers Already Noble*	5 *Capital Value in 1791, in Livres*
		ORLÉANS		
Bureau des finances	2 gn.	30		
		PAU		
Parlement	2 gn.	57	64	33,000
Chancellerie, parlement	1 gn.	19		85,000
		PERPIGNAN		
Conseil souverain	2 gn.	18	71	
Chancellerie, conseil	1 gn.	19		84,000
		POITIERS		
Bureau des finances	2 gn.	27		
Municipalité	20 yrs.	2		
		RENNES		
Parlement	2 gn.	84	100	34,000
Chancellerie, parlement	1 gn.	21		85,000
		RIOM		
Bureau des finances	2 gn.	29		44,000
		ROUEN		
Parlement	2 gn.	96	76	
Chancellerie, parlement	1 gn.	38		85,000
Cour des comptes & aides	2 gn.	132	9	33,000
Chancellerie, comptes	1 gn.	4		
Bureau des finances	2 gn.	29		
		SOISSONS		
Bureau des finances	2 gn.	27		52,000
		TOULOUSE		
Parlement	2 gn.	112	82	
Chancellerie, parlement	1 gn.	22		
Bureau des finances	2 gn.	32		
Municipalité	4 yrs.	6		
		TOURS		
Bureau des finances	2 gn.	29		43,000

SOURCES:

Column 1: François Bluche and Pierre Durye, *L'anoblissement par charges avant 1789* (2 fascicules, Paris, 1962).

Column 2: *ibid.* (Note: "1 gn." = one generation, i.e. 20 years' service or death while in office.)

Continued

ENNOBLING OFFICES IN 1789, BY LOCALITIES (*Continued*)

Column 3: For the *bureaux des finances*, Jean-Paul Charmeil, *Les Trésoriers de France à l'époque de la Fronde* (Paris, 1964), p. 18, tabulates the numbers of offices in 1788. For other institutions, our data on the number of offices are more or less approximate, and come from the following sources (by localities):

Paris: *Almanach royal*, 1789, and François Bluche's works on the Parlement, the Grand Conseil, and the Cour des monnaies.

Aix: Louis Wolff, *Le Parlement de Provence au XVIIIe siècle* (Aix, 1920); Charles Carrière, "Le recrutement de la Cour des comptes, aides et finances d'Aix-en-Provence à la fin de l'ancien régime," 81e Congrès National des Sociétés Savantes, Rouen-Caen, 1956, *Actes*, pp. 141-59; Capitation, offices de judicature, généralité d'Aix, 1789 (MS, A. D. Bouches-du-Rhône, C 3317).

Arras: *Almanach historique et géographique d'Artois*, 1789.

Bar-le-Duc: Charles-Pierre de Longeaux, *La chambre des comptes du duché de Bar*, ed. Dumast (Bar-le-Duc, 1907).

Besançon: *Almanach historique de Besançon et de la Franche-Comté*, 1786.

Bordeaux: *Étrennes bordelaises*, 1789.

Clermont-Ferrand: *Calendrier d'Auvergne*, 1777.

Colmar: *Almanach d'Alsace*, 1789.

Dijon: *Almanach du Parlement de Bourgogne*, 1789.

Douai: *Calendrier général du gouvernement de la Flandre, du Hainaut et du Cambrésis*, 1789.

Grenoble: *Almanach général de la province de Dauphiné*, 1789.

Marseille: *Almanach de Marseille*, 1789.

Metz: *Almanach des Trois Évêchés*, 1789.

Montauban: Daniel Ligou, "Étude fonctionnelle de la population de Montauban à la fin de l'ancien régime," 86e Congrès National des Sociétés Savantes, Montpellier, 1961, *Actes*, pp. 579-602.

Montpellier: Pierre Viallès, *Études historiques sur la Cour des comptes, aides et finances de Montpellier* (Montpellier, 1921), p. 75; Charles d'Aigrefeuille, *Histoire de la ville de Montpellier*, ed. La Pijardière (4 vols.; 1875-82), II, 440.

Nancy: *Almanach de Lorraine et Barrois*, 1789; Hubert de Mahuet, *La Cour souveraine de Lorraine et Barrois* (Nancy, 1959).

Nantes: Meyer, *La noblesse bretonne au XVIIIe siècle*, p. 186.

Pau: *Tableau annuel, historique et géographique du Béarn*, 1784; Pierre Delmas, *Du Parlement de Navarre et de ses origines* (Pau, 1898), p. 113.

Rennes: Meyer, *La noblesse bretonne au XVIIIe siècle*, p. 235; Frédéric Saulnier, *Le Parlement de Bretagne* (2 vols.; Rennes, 1909), I, 20-21.

Rouen: *Almanach de Normandie*, 1787.

Toulouse: *Almanach historique de Languedoc*, 1789; Axel Duboul, *La fin du Parlement de Toulouse* (Toulouse, 1890), pp. 71-75.

Column 4: For the parlements and *conseils souverains*, Jean Égret, "L'aristocratie parlementaire française à la fin de l'ancien régime," *Revue Historique*, 208 (1952), pp. 1-14, provides (in footnotes) the numbers of new *conseillers laïcs* in 1774-89 and the numbers of these known to have been exempted from a tax on ennoblement, the *marc d'or de noblesse*, after having presented documentary proof of preexisting noble status. For some of the other institutions, we were able to derive comparable figures, as Égret did, from the pertinent lists of office-holders and the work of Robert de Roton, *Les arrêts du Grand Conseil [sic, for conseil du roi] portant dispense du marc d'or de noblesse* (Paris, 1951).

Column 5: Rapports de liquidation d'offices remis au comité de judicature par le directeur-général de la liquidation, 1791 (MSS, Archives Nationales, D XVII 9, Nos. 123-27). We report average or typical sums for the least expensive ennobling offices in each institution.

IV

How Protest Modernized in France, 1845-1855

CHARLES TILLY

ONE FAMILIAR argument says that the early stages of industrialization shatter the stability of traditional societies and therefore incite the rapid swelling of violent protest.* Another familiar argument tells us that mature industrialism brings a gradual dwindling of violent protest. Combined, the two arguments produce the expectation that over the course of industrialization violent protest will first increase quickly and then decline slowly, the peak coming early in the process:

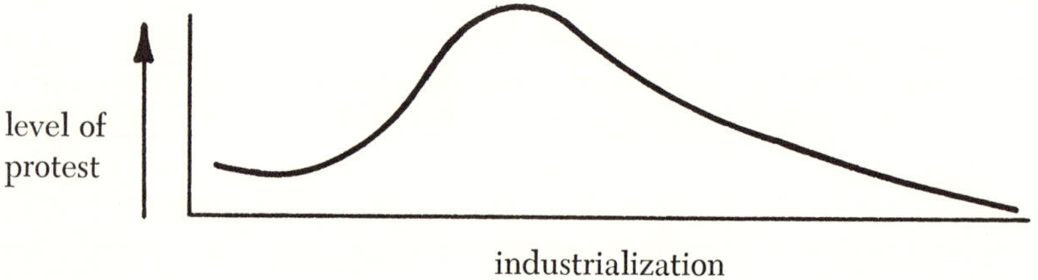

The arguments which lead to this expectation are quite diverse in detail. They range from examinations of the organizational logic of protest movements to analyses of the changing gap between expectation and achievement to treatments of the efficiency of repression and control under changing technical conditions. They have in common the vision of an equilibrium, balance, or order upset by industrialization and only painfully restored or replaced.[1]

Such data as we have from contemporary international comparisons

* The Mathematical Social Science Board, the National Science Foundation, and the Canada Council all supported portions of the research reported here; thanks be to them. I am especially grateful to Muhammad Fiaz, Abdul Qaiyum Lodhi, Sue Richardson, and Freddi Greenberg for assistance, and to Leo Loubere and Peter Amann for criticism.

[1] An indispensable inventory of such views appears in Henry Bienen, *Violence and Social Change* (Chicago: Univ. of Chicago Press, 1968). A convenient quintessence is S. N. Eisenstadt, *Modernization: Protest and Change* (Englewood Cliffs, N.J.: Prentice-Hall, Inc., 1966).

appear to support these expectations. When the authors of the *World Handbook of Political and Social Indicators*, for example, graph their estimates of violent deaths against per capita GNP, they produce a curve strikingly like the ideal one above.[2] When the Feierabends relate a composite scale of political instability for 84 countries over the years 1955 to 1961 to another composite representing modernity between 1948 and 1955, they find the greatest instability in their middle group, the least in their modern one.[3] And Ted Gurr's curve representing a compound civil violence score over the years 1961 to 1965 shifts somewhat to the right, but still describes the same pattern of curvilinearity.[4]

Except for Sorokin's classic yet inconclusive treatment of the problem, and except for studies of war, the available quantitative cross-national studies of instability, disorder, and violence treat the recent experience of contemporary nations, and treat it cross sectionally.[5] Any conclusions they offer concerning the eventual stabilization wrought by mature industrialism depend on the comparison of nations *now* maturely industrial with others not *now* so blessed. The weaknesses of projections of population growth or urban concentration as a function of industrial activity from the base of cross sections of the 1930s and 1940s should make us think thrice before trying to project violent protests in the same way. We need some evidence dealing directly with change over time.

What happened in history? Western historians have often joined the sociologists in treating industrialization as a process of quick disruption followed by slow stabilization. Peter Stearns's sweeping survey of European society concludes:

> Industrialization and associated changes began to reduce the older structures rather quickly. New forms of transportation and communications facilitated new and larger organizational structures. People and goods were concentrated in unprecedented numbers. New or-

[2] Bruce M. Russett and others, *World Handbook of Political and Social Indicators* (New Haven: Yale Univ. Press, 1964), p. 307.

[3] Ivo K. Feierabend and Rosalind L. Feierabend, "Aggressive Behaviors within Polities, 1948-1962: A Cross-National Study," *Journal of Conflict Resolution*, 10 (September 1966), pp. 249-71.

[4] Ted Gurr and Charles Ruttenberg, *The Conditions of Civil Violence: First Tests of a Causal Model* (Princeton: Center of International Studies, Princeton Univ. Press, 1967), p. 67, and, more generally, Ted Gurr, *Why Men Rebel* (Princeton: Princeton Univ. Press, 1970).

[5] Pitirim A. Sorokin, *Social and Cultural Dynamics*, Vol. III: *Fluctuation of Social Relationships, War and Revolutions* (New York: American Book Co., 1937); Lewis F. Richardson, *Statistics of Deadly Quarrels* (Pittsburgh: Boxwood Press, 1960); Quincy Wright, *A Study of War* (Chicago: Univ. of Chicago Press, 1942). See also the bibliographies of Gurr and Bienen.

> ganizations were required in this situation. Factories grouped workers, capital, and materials on an unprecedented scale. Almost immediately they reduced the importance of the family for the working class. Concomitant legal and economic changes attacked the guild and the village. Soon even the family firm was threatened as business units developed radically new methods of finance and management. . . . The traditional institutions did not give way easily. Much of the history of the industrial period can be understood in terms of resistance to new organizations in the name of old. . . . Elements of these protests continued into the twentieth century.[6]

Stearns goes on to posit a second crisis of transition from production-orientation to consumption-orientation. The main drift, in his view, nevertheless consisted of the gradual adjustment of once-traditional societies to the shock of industrialization. The adjustment included the eventual decline of protest.

What does the record show? By now twenty or thirty countries have passed through extended periods of industrial growth. Around 1960 something like forty countries had majorities of their labor forces in non-agricultural employment. On the whole, these countries do suffer fewer deaths from group violence than other countries. Their governments are generally less vulnerable to coups and revolutions. All things considered, they are more stable politically and less inclined to death-dealing disturbances than they used to be.

Even those cautious statements, however, call for qualification: the more industrialized countries probably make up in war the deaths they save in domestic quarrels, continuity of government by no means proves that the governed are content, deaths may well decline while protest swells into new shapes, strong governments like that of Nazi Germany sometimes take over the business of death and destruction with enthusiasm. The qualifications tatter the picture of the process as one of balance/shock/imbalance/slow restoration of balance. They underline the desirability of close, systematic analysis of the historical experience of those nations as they industrialized.

As a small contribution to that enterprise, I want to raise questions about nineteenth-century France. The France of 1357, 1572, 1648, or even 1789 surely deserves to be called traditional; we could hardly call it stable, orderly, or nonviolent. Surely the France of 1948, 1958, or 1968 had arrived at modernity of a kind; it had not achieved calm. From the first glance, the history of violent protest in France con-

[6] Peter N. Stearns, *European Society in Upheaval* (New York: Macmillan Co., 1967), p. 401.

founds our conventional view of the relationship between industrialization and protest.

In an intelligent essay, J.-W. Lapierre lays out some thoughtful distinctions:

> At the beginning of industrialization in Europe the violence of workers' insurrections was essentially a violence of protest. Workers, especially the most highly skilled, those who were still half artisans, revolted against mechanization for fear of unemployment, and broke machines or demonstrated for their removal. . . . Then, as union organization grew stronger, as the labor movement gained the power to oppose the oppressive violence it was enduring, workers' violence became a violence of *contest* instead of protest. Later, with the Paris Commune and, especially, the Russian revolutions of 1905 and 1917 . . . violence began to serve a political program; it was not just a violence of contest, it was a violence of transformation, of innovation, in a word, of *revolution*. One still finds that form of violence, weakened and abortive, in Spain in 1935 or in the French sitdown strikes of 1936. But it is a fact that in the economically and technically most advanced societies violence appears mainly in wildcat strikes or in regions where it is more or less traditional, as in the regions of Nantes or Saint-Nazaire in France. That violence is hardly more than a violence of *bargaining* which often overwhelms union leaders and hinders them in their negotiations with employers. However, the diminution of violence and the change in its significance obviously do not mean that tension and and conflict have disappeared.[7]

Later, Lapierre adds that "If it is true that violence is diminishing in management-worker conflicts, it must be said that it may be increasing in other sorts of conflicts," and then cites farmer-government, racial, male-female, and generational conflicts. These distinctions do not have a great deal of analytic power. But they catch some of the changing reality of collective violence in France and suggest the utility of decomposing the big, ominous word "violence" into its multiple meanings, settings, and forms.

Lapierre also tells us that sometime around the middle of the nineteenth century an important shift in the character of labor violence occurred. He calls it the shift from protest to contest. He has set his finger down, it seems to me, on a set of changes far wider than the labor movement. As late as the 1840s, the predominant forms of col-

[7] J.-W. Lapierre, "La violence dans les conflits sociaux," in Michel Amiot *et al.*, *La Violence dans le monde actuel* (Paris: Desclée de Brouwer, 1968), pp. 147-48.

lective violence in France were rather old-fashioned: the tax revolt, the food riot, the anti-conscription rebellion, and the forcible invasion of fields or forests very much so, the attack on machines and urban rebellion less evidently so. By the 1860s, these forms of collective violence had almost totally disappeared. They were replaced by violent strikes, demonstrations, and similar complex, organized actions. How that happened is the subject of this paper.

These pages will offer some reflections and some evidence concerning the changing character of collective violence in France during the critical years from 1845 to 1855. Protest and collective violence are not, let me admit at once, the same thing. There are many nonviolent protests, and some violent incidents involve no substantial grievances. Nor does the frequency of violence accurately gauge a society's level of discontent; repression too often prevents violence-inducing activities from occurring, and police or armies perform too large a share of the violence which actually occurs, for that to be the case. Collective violence deserves particular attention because:

1. almost all important movements of protest sooner or later produce some violence;
2. the presence of violence ordinarily indicates that some participants in a collective action are strongly committed, concerned, or agitated;
3. collective violence above a certain scale (when not entirely at the hands of agents of the state) almost inevitably involves a threat to the political authorities' control over means of coercion, and therefore takes on political significance *ipso facto*;
4. events involving collective violence (as compared with "protest" or "conflict" or "coercion" in general) are relatively easy to identify and bound.

As a practical matter, we have some hope of working out from violent protest to other movements of discontent. We have almost no hope of moving far in the opposite direction.

Let us also restrict our attention to collective violence within national states. The argument to follow has some implications for struggles among states and for struggles in the absence of national states, but it would be difficult and useless to work them out here. The argument will be ponderous enough without that burden.

Here is a simple model of the political process producing collective violence. Imagine three entities within a defined population:

First, the principal formal structure exerting control over the legitimate means of coercion: the *government*.

> SECOND, a number of groups sometimes engaging in collective action and contending for influence over the operation of the government, but varying in coherence and strength: the *contenders.*
>
> THIRD, a smaller set of the contenders actually sharing power (albeit unequally) over the government, having routine means of influencing each other and exerting some collective control over which groups belong to their number: the *members of the polity*; for short: the *polity.*

Making this work as a general model of politics would take all sorts of explanations, qualifications, and elaborations. Sometimes, for example, more than one government is operating in a population, and other times there is none at all, in this sense of the word. Again, the groups in question often overlap: a given individual may belong simultaneously to two different contenders, say, a tribe and a guild. The simple model nevertheless seems like a reasonable start for an analysis of collective violence.[8]

Here is the path of argument I propose to explore: large structural changes in a society like urbanization and industrialization do not in themselves generate collective violence, but they strongly affect the number, identity, and organization of the contenders, which in turn determine the predominant forms and loci of collective violence. In the short run, the magnitude of collective violence depends on an interaction of the tactics of contenders and the coercive practices of the government. In the longer run, the magnitude of collective violence depends on the established means by which contenders can enter and leave the polity, and the frequency with which entries and exits actually occur. These rather elliptical statements obviously need some elucidation. Figure 1 presents the argument schematically.

Let us consider a few variable characteristics of these entities and attempt to anticipate their effects on collective violence. In dealing with contenders, governments vary from weak to repressive. All other things being equal, the level of collective violence is probably curvilinear with respect to repressiveness. It is low for very weak govern-

[8] The model belongs to a growing stream of "organizational" interpretations of conflict and social movements, within which these are some of the outstanding recent writings: F. G. Bailey, *Stratagems and Spoils* (Oxford: Basil Blackwell, 1969); Amitai Etzioni, *The Active Society* (New York: Free Press of Glencoe, 1968); William Gamson, *Power and Discontent* (Homewood, Ill.: Dorsey, 1968); Anthony Oberschall, "The Theory of Mobilization for Social Movements" (unpublished paper, Yale University, 1969); Arthur Stinchcombe, "Social Structure and Organizations" in *Handbook of Organizations*, ed. by James G. March (Chicago: Rand McNally, 1965); Eric Wolf, *Peasant Wars of the Twentieth Century* (New York: Harper & Row, Inc., 1969).

ments because other organizations have seized the resources worth fighting for and because the government lacks its own means of violence. It is low for very repressive governments because contenders are cowed and lack the means of violence. It is higher in between.

Contenders vary in organization from simple, small, local groups recruiting largely through inheritance (which we may lump together as *communal*) to complex, large, wide-ranging specialized groups recruiting through voluntary adherence and/or personal qualifications

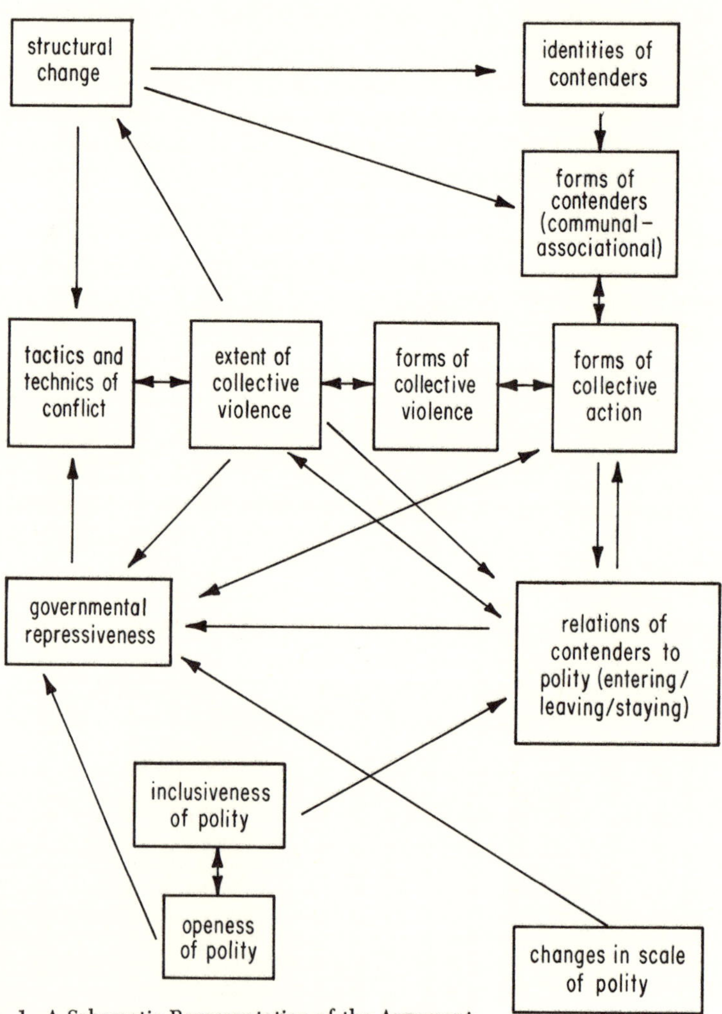

Fig. 1. A Schematic Representation of the Argument

(which we may lump together as *associational*). In the European experience, lineages, religious congregations, villages, and members of local markets have been typical communal contenders, while political parties, secret societies, industrial firms, and trade unions have been typical associational contenders. To the extent that contenders are communal, their collective actions—and hence the collective violence in which they engage—will tend to be localized, uncoordinated, dependent on normal rhythms of congregation like those of marketing, churchgoing, or harvesting, hard for the participants themselves to keep within bounds. To the extent that contenders are associational, their collective actions will tend to be disciplined, large in scale, deliberately scheduled, and organized in advance. The very form of collective violence will therefore differ substantially from one to the other. The food riot exemplifies the violence of communal groups, the turbulent demonstration the violence of associational ones. In an essay attacking Parson Malthus, written in the time of the Luddites, the poet Southey made this worried observation:

> If at any former time the mob were inflamed with sedition, they were a headless multitude, bound together only by the momentary union of blind passion; they are now an organized association, with their sections, their secret commissions, and their treasury.[9]

He was watching the emergence of collective violence based on associations.

Contenders also vary in their current relationship to the polity. Some are so weak and incoherent as to be practically irrelevant to its operation. Some are actively bidding for membership, some are members pursuing their own interests, and some are in the process of losing their memberships. I suggest that:

1. the complete outsiders rarely take part in collective violence of any kind;
2. the members engage in it mainly through the proxy of police, troops, and other specialists in coercion, mainly in the attempt to exclude others from power, and secondarily as an outgrowth of shows of strength which are not intrinsically violent;
3. contenders losing their memberships fight that loss to the extent of their organizational ability, and therefore frequently get involved in collective violence;
4. contenders actively bidding for membership engage in collective

[9] Robert Southey, *Essays, Moral and Political* (London: John Murray, 1832), pp. 125-26. This particular essay, titled "On the State of the Poor," was written in 1812.

> violence with great frequency, both because the show of force is a means of claiming membership and because the members of the polity resist their claims with force.

I also suggest that those losing membership (indignantly) define their problem as the deprivation of specific long-established rights, those bidding for membership (just as indignantly) define their problem as the fulfillment of rights long due them on general grounds, while the members pay more attention to commitments and perquisites than to rights and duties.

Polities vary in inclusiveness, openness, and scale. Some include a very low proportion of all contenders, a situation which probably promotes attention-getting violence at the same time as it encourages the establishment of relations of patronage and corruption. A polity is open to the extent that all contenders meeting known general tests have access to membership through legitimate nonviolent means; on the whole, the level of violence probably declines as the openness of the polity increases. Inclusiveness and openness depend on each other to some extent, since exclusive polities normally remain exclusive through rigorous, uneven, or even impossible, tests of membership.

The easiest conception of scale is no doubt the number of people under the control of the polity. I have no hypotheses to offer relating the character of violence to scale as such. I want instead to call attention to the possibility that its character changes significantly when major leaps in scale occur. This can happen through the quick acquisition or loss of population in war and conquest. It can happen through the weakening of large polities in favor of the smaller polities contained within them, as was the frequent experience of early empires at the deaths of their rulers, and the recurrent problem of some European areas like Sicily and Spain in more recent times. It can happen, finally, through the winning out of a larger polity over smaller ones.

Modern Europe has seen two major movements of this last kind. The first was the long struggle of national governments to tame all their rivals—communes, provinces, estates. The second was, and is, the supplanting of national governments by supranational blocs, alliances, and administrative units. The victory of the national government over local and regional governments meant that membership in the smaller polities lost much of its value; for those members at the smaller scale which did not become members at the larger scale, it was like being forced out of the polity altogether; it was a loss of political identity.

People resisted that nationalization of politics throughout Europe. Kings imposed their tax power, their conscription power, their judicial power with only the bloodiest difficulty on populations which were already quite used to being taxed, drafted, and judged by the agents of smaller governments. It is fascinating to see how regularly the resistance returned when the central government weakened temporarily in war or revolution. France, for example, produced great waves of resistance to the tax collector *after* the revolutions of 1789, 1830, and 1848.

As a first approximation, it helps to sort the major varieties of collective violence occurring in Western Europe during the last few centuries into three categories: primitive, reactionary, and modern. Let me avoid discussing the distinctions lengthily here, since I have rehearsed them *ad nauseam* elsewhere.[10] The primitive forms (which include the brawl among rival groups of artisans, the feud, the fights of youths from neighboring villages, and so on) are the typical collective violence of established communal members of small polities. The reactionary forms (which include the invasion of fields, the tax revolt, the food riot, the anti-conscription rebellion, and perhaps machine-breaking) all expressed the resistance of communal members of small polities to the claims of national governments and national economies. The modern forms (the violent versions of strikes, demonstrations, revolutionary movements, and the like) typically involve associational contenders for power, accepting rather than resisting the priority of the national government over its rivals. The typology rests on two distinctions: 1) between contenders for power organized communally and those organized associationally, 2) among contenders unrelated to the national polity, those resisting its claims, and those bidding for power within it.

In Europe as a whole it appears that the primitive forms of collective violence prevailed before the rise of national states, the reactionary forms predominated during their struggles for sovereignty, and the modern forms did not become the standard varieties of collective violence until the national state had won without question. In general, that means during the nineteenth century. The timing of these shifts differed significantly, to be sure, from country to country. Furthermore, the three types do not represent *stages* in any strict sense; the modern forms of collective violence, for example, emerged in those urban areas already heavily involved in the national polity centuries before they became preeminent in France as a whole, and the primitive forms reappeared from time to time long after then. Here is the point: the relative frequencies of the three basic types of

[10] *Ad maximam nauseam* in "The Changing Place of Collective Violence" in *Essays in Social and Political History*, ed. by Melvin Richter (Cambridge: Harvard Univ. Press, 1970) and "Collective Violence in European Perspective" in *Violence in America*, ed. by Hugh Graham and Ted Gurr (Washington: U.S. Govt. Printing Office, 1969).

collective violence changed decisively as the focus of French politics went from local to national and the characteristic form of contenders for power went from communal to associational. In short, the transformation of the character and locus of the struggle for power in France in turn transformed collective violence flow much more directly from the political process than we have customarily said, and that interpretations of violence in terms of undifferentiated tension, aggressive instincts, marginal men, uprooted masses, or adolescent rebellion badly miss the mark. James Payne asks of contemporary Colombia: ". . . is violence inevitable in the Colombian system?"

> The problem, I insist, is basically political. It is related to the status and employment incentives of participants and the contest in which the struggle for these rewards takes place. Any solution to the problem of violence must either alter the incentives of participants or the political framework which shapes their behavior.
>
> This is not the view generally taken by students of comparative politics or American policy-makers. The popular position holds that deprived masses seeking to better their standard of living are the cause of political violence. . . . Although superficially convincing, the privation explanation for political conflict may be highly misleading. It ignores participants, particularly leaders, their motives for participating (incentives), and the strength of these motives. And it fails to recognize the decisive role played by leaders in finding and focusing demands. Movements of political violence seldom occur spontaneously. They grow out of a context defined by leaders, from over demands agitated by leaders, against targets identified by leaders and are often organized and directed by leaders.[11]

Payne's declaration applies much more widely than to Colombia alone. It applies to most collective violence in France.

Yet I concede in advance to a pair of likely objections. First, the argument does not deal adequately with economic grievances, incentives, and conflicts. Most likely the missing element is an analysis of markets parallel to the analysis of politics. Second, the scheme exaggerates the coolness and calculation of collective violence; it neglects the rage, the euphoria, the release, the festival madness felt by many participants in different varieties of collective violence. So be it for now. Both aspects have been overemphasized in the past, and unduly divorced from politics. The argument of this paper takes up the underdeveloped side of the problem.

[11] James L. Payne, *Patterns of Conflict in Colombia* (New Haven: Yale Univ. Press, 1968), pp. 295-96.

What happened to industrialization? I would say that its effects—and those of its close cousin, urbanization—on collective violence are deep but indirect. Contrary to folklore, the immediate impact of early industrialization and urbanization is very likely to reduce the level of violent protest. At least that seems a reasonable statement for Western Europe's historical experience. There the widespread de-industrialization of the countryside and the rush of countrymen to the city removed men from settings in which they had the capacity for angry collective action and placed them in baffling new settings where it took a long time for them to acquire collective identities, awareness of common interests, and sufficient organization to permit joint action. The new organization did eventually emerge. Men massed in large, homogeneous groups—most notably in the mine, the factory, and the working-class neighborhood—open to organization on a much larger scale than before. They rearranged the fundamental divisions of class and interest by giving control over liquid assets and the industrial apparatus far greater importance than control over land. Many features of urban-industrial life promoted the formation of special-interest associations like political parties, clubs, and unions. Thus industrialization and urbanization did not in themselves incite violence, but they did affect who was contending for power, and how; that, in turn, determined the predominant forms of collective violence.

To understand that this organizational process, rather than a process of disruption leading to explosions of anger, may be the basic link between industrialization or urbanization and collective violence, we have to clear away a number of misconceptions. The first is that there *is* a close correlation between rapid urban growth and rebellion. Let us consider where and how cities were expanding in the France of the 1830s and 1840s.

For the period 1821 to 1836, the departments most emphatically combining mass in-migration and rapid urban increase were Bouches-du-Rhône, Haute-Garonne, and Seine—which means Marseille, Toulouse, and Paris. During that time, Bordeaux, Nantes, Lyon, Saint-Etienne, Toulon, Rennes, the Lille-Roubaix-Tourcoing complex, and their vicinities all had their moments; on the whole, migration to these places seems to have been much more local than in the cases of Paris, Toulouse, and Marseille. Among the other large towns, only Reims was building steadily, while such places as Rouen, Amiens, Nîmes, Orléans, Caen, and Montpellier were close to stagnant.

The correlation between urban growth and political turbulence at this scale is rather weak. While it is true that fast-growing Paris, Nantes, Bordeaux, Lyon and their departments were exceptionally turbulent in the 1830s, so were slow-moving Nîmes, Grenoble, and

Auxerre. Conversely, Marseille, Toulouse, Saint-Etienne, and several of the other leaders experienced rather little violent conflict during the period. Even Paris underwent its greatest growth (especially its growth through migration) just *after* the July Revolution and *after* Louis Napoleon's seizure of power.

The information historians have recently assembled concerning the participants in the Parisian insurrections of the 1830s and 1840s likewise challenges the idea that the uprooting and immiseration attendant on urban growth throw up rebels. David Pinkney's painstaking enumeration of the crowd in the Revolution of 1830 brings out its continuity with the *sans-culottes* of four decades before.[12] Tailors, printers, carpenters, masons, locksmiths, shoemakers, and their like fought in the streets: little people from small workshops and established trades. Only the apparent withdrawal of petty tradesmen from insurrectionary forces strikes a student of the 1789 revolution who turns to Pinkney's account as a significant change.

We get a strong sense of continuity in the shorter run as well. The same categories of artisans led the strike activity of the years surrounding 1830 and reappeared in the streets for the frequent riots of the early 1830s. The same hot spots in the city—Grève, Châtelet, and Palais Royal—continually attracted idle workers, police spies, political discussion, and violent protest. One difference between the later agitation and the days of the 1830 revolution which might deserve attention is the greater role students apparently played in the outbursts after the revolution. Certainly the prefect of police (whose reports at one point recommended the suspension of students who took part in riots) found their comings and goings of the greatest interest. But then he and his agents spent much of their time eying the politically active groups of men who were likely to organize or join demonstrations and *coups de main.* There was enough order in Parisian disorder that accurate word of impending disturbances often appeared in the prefect's daily bulletins. The notes of 3 and 4 June 1832, for example, correctly anticipated real trouble at the funeral of General Lamarque. The rebellion of 1834 was seen so far ahead that some historians have concluded it was deliberately provoked.[13]

Now, the authorities themselves commonly held to the standard theory of "dangerous classes" thrown up by urban growth, uprooting migration and misery, vulnerable to all sorts of political agitation. The

[12] David H. Pinkney, "The Crowd in the French Revolution of 1830," *American Historical Review,* 70 (October 1964), pp. 1-17.

[13] Archives Nationales, F^7 3886, bulletins de Paris, 3 and 4 June 1832; F^7 3887, bulletins, 10-12 April 1834.

prefect of police declared that the many Parisian riots of winter 1830-1831 were:

> organized by madmen and led by badmen . . . whoever knows anything about the seditious movements which have stricken the capital has noticed that the good workers were not only absent from these disorders but bothered by them. The frightful misery which is continuing to grow, the lack of work, which is throwing an idle and hungry population on the street, threaten us with serious disturbances, if that state of suffering does not change. One can see without difficulty how easy it will be for clever agitators to sway the minds of workers dying of hunger and make them believe that a government under which they suffer is worthless. The Republicans will sow disorder and the Carlists will not miss their chance to harvest.[14]

In short, the set speech of a big-city chief of police, then as now.

Unquestionably hungry, idle workers reliably produced political disturbances in Paris. The crowds that in September 1831 formed to drink wine and argue politics at the Place de Grève, Châtelet, and Palais Royal, then streamed out to break machines, demonstrate against the price of bread, stone the National Guard, or protest against the Russian capture of Warsaw included plenty of unemployed shoemakers, weavers, and other artisans. But they were hardly the dregs.

The insurrections of 1834 kept up the continuity. While the months after mid-1832 produced fewer violent disturbances and more strikes than the first two years of the July Monarchy, the essential pattern did not change. Perhaps working-class political associations became more active and influential. In any case, the early months of 1834 produced a staccato of minor disturbances like the one in February which began with the shouting of Republican slogans and of insults to National Guardsmen around the wineshops of the Palais Royal, and ended with the arrest of a cooper, a sadler, and a mechanic—the latter carrying the rulebook of the Société des Droits de l'Homme, a "manual of the duties of a republican," a tricolor cockade, and a packet of drawings depicting Phrygian bonnets and other revolutionary symbols.[15]

The barricades of April 1834 brought out these three workers' fel-

[14] Archives Nationales, F[1C] I 33, report of 22 August 1831.

[15] Archives de la Préfecture de Police, Paris: A[a] 422, report of "attroupement séditieux," 1 February 1834.

lows.[16] Among the persons arrested for taking part in the street fighting, we find a familiar cross section of Parisian craftsmen—shoemakers, tailors, binders, and so on—plus a handful of students, clerks, and others. If we exclude troops sent in to crush the rebellion, the same is true of the killed and wounded. Of one group of 41 arrested participants for whom careful dossiers were established, 11 were native Parisians and all the rest had established residences in the city; the only two without occupations were thirteen and fifteen years old. Except that the famous *accusés d'avril* included more of the bourgeois Republican elite, the collective portrait of those put on trial for taking part in the insurrection is pretty much the same. Rebellion grew out of the solid, established working class.

In their different ways, Duveau, Rudé, Coornaert, and Gossez have all said that the same state of affairs held through the middle of the century.[17] Slowly the workers of big industry came into political action, but only slowly. In 1848 and 1851 their part was still small. Nor did the outcasts, the uprooted, the criminals have much to do with the major mid-century rebellions. Gossez did find a high proportion of migrants among the participants in the June Days, but located the genuine drifters and delinquents in the armed forces. The information available from Paris, in sum, confirms the rebellious character of its population, but negates the notion that the disruptive effects of industrialization, mass migration, and urban growth account for it.

There was, however, one direct way in which the growth of great cities incited rebellion. That was by increasing the demands made on the hinterland. Taxation and conscription are subtle cases, the demand for food a more straightforward one. Although a large mythology says otherwise, the nineteenth-century food riot occurred mainly as a response to the pressure of urban demand on the rural food supply in times of crisis, when normal, highly commercialized suppliers like those of the Beauce could not meet the demand. People rioted against the withholding or withdrawal of grain from the local market to

[16] Archives de la Préfecture de Police, A^a 422, troubles de 1834; Archives de la Seine, $V^8D^6$14, 6e arrondissement, report of dead and wounded; Archives Nationales, BB^{30} 294, tableau synoptique des accusés d'avril; Archives Nationales, F^7 3887, bulletins de Paris, 10-18 avril 1834; Archives Nationales, F^9 1162, victimes d'avril 1834.

[17] Georges Duveau, "L'Ouvrier de 1848," *Revue Socialiste*, n.s. Nos. 17-18 (January-February 1948), pp. 73-79; George Rudé, *The Crowd in History, 1730-1848* (New York: John Wiley & Sons, Inc., 1964); Emile Coornaert, "La Pensée ouvrière et la conscience de classe en France de 1830 à 1848" in *Studi in onore di Gino Luzzato* (Milan: Giuffrè, 1950), III, 12-33; Rémi Gossez, "Diversité des antagonismes sociaux vers le milieu du XIXe siècle," *Revue Économique* (May 1956), pp. 439-57; Gossez, "Organization ouvrière à Paris sous la Seconde République," *1848. Revue des Révolutions Contemporaines*, 41 (1949), pp. 31-45.

serve the national market. Sometimes it served the international market. In 1839 and 1840, the shipment of grains to England from La Rochelle, and the consequent pressure on the grain-producers of La Rochelle's hinterland, placed the greatest cluster of food riots along the supply lines of the port.[18]

In fact, the alternation between demand direct from Paris and demand filtering through the ports produced two substantially different geographic patterns for the food riot. The first was an arc to the south and west of Paris, beyond the intensely farmed areas which supplied it in normal years. The second was a series of smaller arcs around the Atlantic ports. The bursts of riots in 1816-1817, 1829-1830 and 1846-1847 followed the Parisian pattern. Those of 1839-1840 and 1853-1854 hugged the ports. Paul Gonnet's catalog of troubled rural areas from 1829 to 1832—"a great semicircular band going from the Nivernais to the Vendée, and then from the estuary of the Loire to that of the Seine" recalls what we know of the early 1790s. The mysterious, abundant cases of arson during the same years followed much the same path.[19] During the smaller subsistence troubles of 1853, on the other hand, a handy review of "troubles à l'occasion de la cherté des subsistances" gives the places of honor to Vendée, Haute-Vienne, Charente-Inférieure, Gironde, Deux-Sèvres, Morbihan, and Tarn; except for the Tarn, they were departments strongly affected by the demands of the Atlantic ports.[20]

In the short run, then, the growth of industrial cities did incite rebellion—not by unmooring urban men, but by placing new, intolerable pressures on their brethren anchored in the countryside. In the medium run it probably damped rebellion by displacing men from social settings in which they had the capacity for collective anger and action. In the long run urbanization and industrialization caused the shift from communal to associational bases for collective action, and thus deeply affected the form, locus, and personnel of collective violence.

They also probably reshaped repression, both because they placed

[18] Maurice Lévy-Leboyer, *Les banques europées et l'industrialisation internationale dans la première moitié du XIXe siècle* (Paris: Presses Universitaires de France, 1964), p. 533, citing Archives Nationales, BB[18] 1375-83.

[19] Paul Gonnet, "Esquisse de la crise économique en France de 1827 à 1832," *Revue d'Histoire Économique et Sociale*, 33 (1955), p. 251. Archives Nationales, CC 550, "Etat de tous les incendies qui ont éclaté depuis 8 août 1829"; BB[18] 1183 *et seq.*, multiple reports of fires.

[20] Archives Nationales, BB[30] 432, "Tableau comparatif indiquant par mois le nombre et la gravité des faits portés jusqu'à ce jour dans les tableaux mensuels," "troubles à l'occasion de la cherté des subsistances 1853-1854," "jugements et arrêts rendus sur les poursuites relatives à la cherté des subsistances, 1853-54."

unprecedentedly large concentrations of potentially rebellious men close to the centers of government, and because technical innovations closely associated with urban-industrial growth (the railroad, for example, and the telegraph) gave governments new, rapid, efficient means of control over dissidence.

Where was France by 1845? By then Frenchmen had accumulated a long experience with a centralized state. They had also taken part in at least three violent changes of regime, and many more attempts, in sixty years. The July Monarchy, itself the product of a revolution, was fifteen years old. France was then one of the world's two or three most prosperous nations, relatively advanced in her industry, relatively well-endowed with cities. Just about half her labor force was already in non-agricultural employment, although many workers were scattered through small towns and villages. About a quarter of the population lived in urban places (which means, by French standards, communes with at least 2,000 people in the central settlement), although well under 10 per cent were in true cities of 50,000 or more. There was a fledgling railroad system (400-odd kilometers of track in 1840, about 1,500 in 1845, compared with 4,000 or 5,000 kilometers each in Great Britain and Germany), and factory production was beginning to take over the textile industry. France differed from her industrializing neighbors in having a slow-growing population. The French birth rate had been declining steadily since late in the previous century, generally faster than the death rate.

The pace of these changes was moderate during the 1830s and 1840s, then accelerated during the 1850s and 1860s. After 1850 the rural population (although not the agricultural population) finally began to shrink permanently after centuries of irregular growth. Extra hands (especially, I think, hands left idle by the withering of cottage industry) migrated from the countryside in unprecedented numbers. During the years after 1850, the railroad network expanded quickly, the metal-working industries came into their own, and the factory-based portion of the textile industry led the growth of the economy.

Figure 2 gives some indications of the changing pace of the French economy over the nineteenth century's middle years. It presents Maurice Lévy-Leboyer's recent estimates of production in a) industry, construction, and agriculture combined, b) industry alone, c) the "leading sectors" of the textile industry: manufacturing from cotton and imported wool.[21] Lévy-Leboyer calculates the following annual rates of growth of industrial production for the period under study:

[21] Maurice Lévy-Leboyer, "La croissance économique en France au XIXe siècle, résultats preliminaires," *Annales; Economies, Sociétés, Civilisations*, 23 (July-August 1968), pp. 788-807.

	Manufacturing	*Manufacturing Plus Construction*
1825-35	2.4%	1.4%
1835-45	3.2	3.6
1845-55	2.8	2.6
1855-65	2.3	3.2

Fig. 2. Lévy-Leboyer's Production Estimates, 1828-1862

We are dealing, then, with a period of persistent but moderate growth in the economy as a whole. There was some acceleration in the most advanced segments of French industry after 1850, after a considerable break in 1847 and, especially, 1848. Our period from 1845 to 1855 was, on the whole, a time of economic expansion and modernization. But no economic catastrophe, no major shift in the pace of growth, and no fundamental change in the direction of structural transformation accounts for the large difference in the character and frequency of violent protest between the 1840s and the 1850s.[22]

A good deal of my own work on this problem is going into the study of 674 disturbances which occurred in France from 1830 to 1860. A *disturbance*, in this case, is an interaction between at least two formations (or one formation attacking the property of another one), in the course of which some person or property is damaged or seized over resistance, and in which at least one formation has 50 or more members. All of these criteria obviously require further definitions and conventions. The sample consists of every event meeting these criteria trained readers encountered in a systematic day-by-day scanning of two French national newspapers over the entire period. The descriptions of the events actually coded once they entered the sample, however, also included a great deal of information from court reporters like the *Gazette des Tribunaux*, from historical works, and from French national archives.

The main body of data under analysis consists of machine-readable descriptions of these events and their settings, stored on punched cards and tape, combining detailed numerical codes with textual material and supplementary comments from coders. A typical record for an event includes 20 or more punched cards. From the evidence so far at hand, I judge that the sample includes every event occurring in France from 1830 to 1860 and otherwise meeting our criteria which absorbed a thousand man-days or more—1,000 men for 1 day, 250 men for 4 days, or some similar combination. Below 200 man-days, it becomes noticeably incomplete, and significantly overrepresents Paris and other big cities.

The year-by-year graph of the number of disturbances (see Fig. 3) displays three peaks: 1832, 1848, and 1851. Although we do not con-

[22] For arguments which attribute extensive political effects to what appears to be a relatively mild dip in the economy as a whole, see C. E. Labrousse, ed., *Aspects de la crise et de la dépression de l'économie française au milieu du XIXe siècle* (La Roche-sur-Yon: Imprimerie Centrale de l'Ouest, 1958), Bibliothèque de la Révolution de 1848, tome XIX; Labrousse, "1848-1830-1789: Comment naissent les révolutions," *Actes du Congrès historique du centenaire de la Révolution de 1848* (Paris: Presses Universitaires de France, 1948), pp. 1-20.

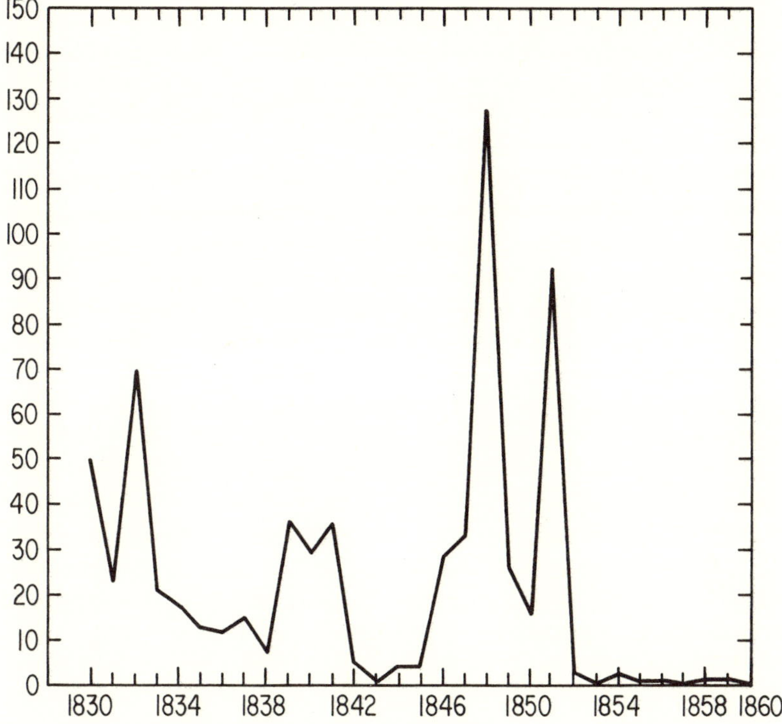

FIG. 3. Number of Disturbances by Year, 1830-1860

ventionally treat 1832 as a major time of troubles, it produced collective violence running from an abortive insurrection in Paris to tax and food riots in the provinces to widespread guerrilla in the counter-revolutionary west. We already recognize 1848 as a revolutionary year. Yet many of the year's disturbances were food riots, tax revolts, and similar events coming well after the February revolution and not belonging in any obvious way to the same action. The disturbances of 1851 occurred mainly in the course of the resistance to Louis Napoleon's December *coup d'état*; 76 of the year's 92 disturbances came in December. The major blocks of turbulent years ran from 1830 to 1843, 1839 to 1841, and 1848 to 1851. The time from 1842 through 1845 brought little collective violence. The really impressive period of calm, however, came after Louis Napoleon put down the resistance to his coup.

There is certainly no clear connection between the pacing of economic activity and the cadence of collective violence over the 30 years. The product-moment correlation coefficient between the number of disturbances in a given year and the change in Lévy-Leboyer's industrial production index from the previous year, for example, comes out to —.002. Nor would it be easy to link the major series of disturbances to large swings in the economy. Whatever the relationship, it is more complicated than that.

Yet the transformation of the French economy did transform collective violence. The line of argument developed earlier suggests that the strongest and most immediate effect of industrialization on collective violence touches its form rather than its frequency. In particular, we ought to find a decline in communal bases for collective violence, a rise in associational bases, an increase in the organization and scale of the collective actions resulting in violence, an eventual urbanization and industrialization of the groups and the places most actively involved.

All of these changes were proceeding over the middle years of the nineteenth century. There was, however, nothing gradual about it. The reactionary forms like field invasions, tax rebellions, food riots, and machine-breaking did fade away, but only after a last tremendous outburst around 1848. The modern forms of collective violence based on associations did take over, but only after long cumulation in the most advanced sectors of French society, and with a sudden expansion into the rest of the society, likewise around 1848. Collective violence did urbanize and industrialize, but at a different pace from French society.

Let us examine some long-run changes in the character of French collective violence before bearing down on the period immediately after 1845. Table 1 presents evidence of the changing magnitude of disturbances over the three decades from 1830 to 1860, and three much later decades from 1930 to 1960.[23] The figures display a general rise in the scale of the typical disturbance over the 130-year period. To be sure, the total number of participants estimated to have taken part in all disturbances fluctuated greatly from decade to decade. Our estimate for the 1850s is only 107,000, after 434,000 for the revolutionary 1840s. Again, the 1940s (although permeated with the violence of World War II, most of which our criteria ignore) threw up an estimated 224,000 participants, which swelled to over 350,000 in the following decade. But the size of the *average* disturbance rose from the nineteenth century to the twentieth. There are some signs that the growth was already going on from 1830 to 1860.

[23] Totals vary slightly from table to table because of missing data, but not enough to affect the conclusions offered in this paper.

TABLE 1. INDICATORS OF MAGNITUDE OF DISTURBANCES BY DECADE 1830-1860 AND 1930-1960

Item	*1830-39*	*1840-49*	*1850-60*	*1930-39*	*1940-49*	*1950-60*
Number of Disturbances	258	293	116	336	93	169
Number of Formations	563	733	263	802	221	431
Formations per Disturbance	2.2	2.5	2.3	2.4	2.4	2.6
Total participants (1,000s)	282	434	107	740	224	371
Mean Participants	1,093	1,482	923	2,202	2,410	2,197
Median Participants	350	350	500	500	838	625
Mean Man-Days*	1,895	2,584	1,518	2,223	2,386	2,184
Median Man-Days*	400	400	600	500	838	650
Mean Killed and Wounded	28.2	17.6	33.0	19.4	185.2	23.0
Median Wounded	10	2	23.0	10	24	10
Mean Arrested	30	30	139	23	23	84
Median Arrested	30	19	58	1	23	7
Per Cent Lasting Over One Day	16	18	24	4	4	5
Man-Days Per Man	1.7	1.7	1.6	1.0	1.0	1.0

* These figures represent the number of days *on which* men took part in collective violence and thus greatly overestimate the time actually spent in collective violence.

The contrasts between means and medians for participants and man-days reflect the tendency of disturbances in the nineteenth century, and especially the 1840s, to include a very small number of big and bloody outbreaks like the June Days of 1848, and a large number of small events. The twentieth century brought a somewhat more even distribution. Likewise the average duration of disturbances (as measured by the number of successive days on which there was violence) declined. At the beginning the typical disturbance was the running local battle with the tax collector, which occasionally spilled over into a rebellion of all the villages in a whole valley; at the end it was the massive one-day demonstration in Lyon or Paris, which sometimes turned into a battle with counterdemonstrators or riot police. Behind that transformation lay the rise of associational contenders for power.

Graphing the magnitudes of disturbances, as in Figure 4, brings out the transformation clearly. The three dimensions represent the mean number of participants in a disturbance, the man-days per participant, and the number of disturbances in each decade. The volume of the solid therefore represents the total man-days in disturbances during the decade. The graph shows at a glance that the 1840s produced the largest volume of participation in disturbances. The shapes of the solids changed in an interesting way. The surface of the solid seen from the left represents the man-days in the average disturbance. In the nineteenth-century decades it was broad and short; in the twentieth, narrow and tall. As duration declined, participation rose. The quantitative shape of collective violence changed.

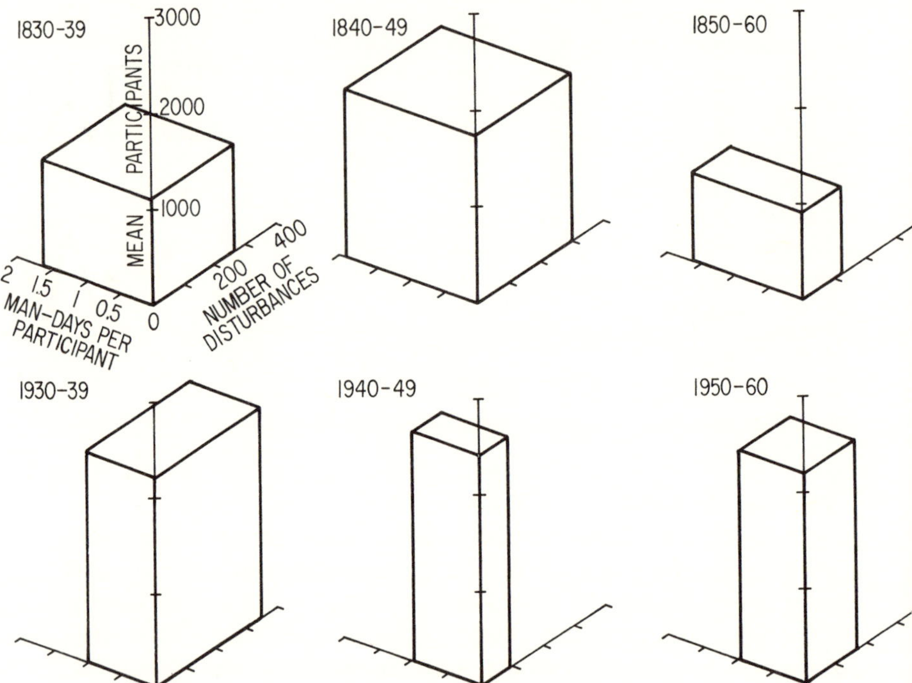

FIG. 4. Magnitudes of Collective Violence, 1830-1960

As it happens, strikes followed the same course.[24] From the 1880s (when the first really comprehensive data on strikes became available) to the Second World War, the mean strikers per strike rose irregularly from 200 to around 700. After remaining around 5 or 6 days for decades, on the other hand, the median duration fell precipitously to a single day some time during or after the massive unionization of the Popular Front. Strikes also became tall and thin. The timing is different from the transformations of collective violence, but the processes are surely related. In both cases, complex organizations not only capable of mobilizing many men for protest, but also fairly effective

[24] Data on strikes from Edward Shorter and Charles Tilly, "The Shape of Strikes in France, 1830-1960," *Comparative Studies in Society and History*, 13 (January 1971), pp. 60-86.

in *de*mobilizing them once the issue was decided or the point was made, assumed a larger and larger role in the preparation of the confrontations between contenders and authorities.

Some related things happened to repression. From the nineteenth century to the twentieth, casualties in disturbances went up as arrests went down. The rise in casualties actually resulted from a decrease in killing and a great increase in wounding. The repressive forces did all the arresting and most of the killing and wounding. I believe that the shifts in arrests and casualties came largely as a result of the transfer of the work of repression from armies to police forces, and the concomitant development of crowd control tactics involving light wounding and selective arrest. That remains to be proven. There is no doubt that new police forces came into being and expanded over the period, that what the authorities saw as a threat from the urban mob provided one of the main incentives to the organization of the new forces, that the police took over repression, or that crowd control procedures altered considerably. So much else was going on at the same time, however, that singling out the effects of tactical rearrangements is very tricky.

The rise of the police shows up with a number of other changes worthy of interest in a tabulation of formations taking part in disturbances (see Table 2). A "formation" is a group of people acting collectively and (at least in some significant regard) distinctly from other participants. Formations including military or police units comprised a fairly constant third of all formations taking part throughout the six decades. Formations including police, however, went from about 10 per cent in the 1830s to over 30 per cent in the 1950s. Troops disappeared from all but the most serious occasions.

At something like the same pace, the simple crowd not obviously united by common creed or organization gave way: a sixth of all formations from 1830 to 1849, under a tenth in the 1850s, a fiftieth after 1930. The "ideological" crowd clearly identified as Legitimist, Republican, Communist, Action française, or something else of the sort became much more prominent. As we might expect, people united by their attachment to the same market, water, land, or forest virtually disappeared from collective violence. As we might not expect, the proportion of groups distinguished by common occupation remained about the same, except for the repressive 1850s. (Hidden behind those constant proportions, however, is the displacement of peasants, shopkeepers, and government employees by workers in modern industry.) After 1940, groups identified by outside origin—for example, Germans, Americans, Algerians—played a larger part than before. Almost all

TABLE 2. PERCENTAGE DISTRIBUTION OF FORMATIONS TAKING PART IN DISTURBANCES, 1830-1960

Type of Formation	*1830-39*	*1840-49*	*1850-60*	*1930-39*	*1940-49*	*1950-6*
Simple Crowd	16.4	17.1	8.9	1.5	3.3	1.5
Crowd with Distinct Ideological Identification	13.6	9.4	12.0	47.6	17.9	33.3
Guerrillas, Bandits, Private Armies	3.1	0.4	10.1	0.1	1.2	0.2
Other Organized Activists	0.7	0.5	10.1	0.5	2.4	1.7
Public Officials	3.5	6.0	4.3	1.0	3.7	1.5
Officials Plus Troops or Police	4.2	5.7	13.2	0.5	0.0	0.2
Regular Troops	5.9	3.0	5.8	0.1	6.1	0.8
Other Military	11.2	10.5	4.3	0.1	2.0	0.4
Police and Military	5.0	4.9	6.2	6.8	7.7	3.6
Police	5.1	9.0	10.1	20.0	19.1	28.6
Occupational Group From Same Locality	2.1	3.4	0.0	1.6	2.4	1.1
Occupational Group From Same Factory/Industry	5.8	5.4	3.9	5.7	11.8	8.6
Other Occupational Group	9.1	8.4	0.8	7.3	10.2	8.0
Group Identified by Outside Origin	1.9	1.6	0.4	3.5	10.6	6.9
Users of Same Market, Water, Land, or Forest	2.4	4.4	1.9	0.7	0.0	0.0
Others and Unclassifiable	10.1	10.2	8.1	2.8	1.6	3.6
TOTAL PER CENT	100.1	99.9	100.1	99.8	100.0	100.0
Number of Formations	573	735	258	808	246	475

these changes involved a shift away from casual congregation, communal organization, and uncoordinated protest toward the deliberate collective action typified by the demonstration or the strike.

The information available so far does not permit a genuine examination of the occupational characteristics of participants in disturbances. Most of the people we identify as activists or as members of ideological crowds, for example, also have occupations. Sometimes (as in the case of a few major conflicts to be discussed later on) mass arrests, multiple casualties or eyewitness reports left enough of a record to make possible an occupational analysis of a population which appeared in a non-occupational guise. For the great bulk of disturbances, however, the closest approach we can make is to examine the changing distribution of those formations which are clearly identified by occupation or industry.

Table 3 employs a set of categories adapted from French censuses to classify formations taking part in disturbances from 1830 through 1860. Over the three decades, we had too little information to make any decision about the occupational composition of a fifth of the formations; in another seventh of the cases, the group was clearly quite heterogeneous with respect to industry; a small number of formations (about 3 per cent over the three decades) combined 2 or 3 well-identified industrial groups. The big, growing categories were police, military, and public service—which includes mayors, tax collectors, and game wardens, among others. Together they comprised 34 per cent of the formations in 1830-1839, 40 per cent in 1840-1849 and 47 per cent in 1850-1860. The state, or at least its employees, was becoming more heavily involved in collective violence.

TABLE 3. INDUSTRIAL CATEGORY OF FORMATIONS IN DISTURBANCES, 1830-1860

Industrial Category	*1830-39*	*1840-49*	*1850-60*
Insufficient Information	33.9	15.6	34.8
No Distinct Category	10.9	19.8	5.2
Combination of Distinct Categories	2.4	2.6	5.2
Agriculture, Forests, Fish	4.3	4.6	2.2
Extractive Industries	1.6	0.4	1.5
Metal and Metalworking	0.3	0.4	0.0
Food	0.3	0.4	0.4
Chemicals	0.0	0.0	0.0
Paper, Printing	0.0	0.4	0.0
Leather	0.2	0.1	0.4
Textiles	2.1	2.0	0.7
Wood	1.0	0.0	0.4
Stonework	0.5	0.8	0.0
Construction	0.7	0.7	0.0
Commerce	4.7	5.9	0.0
Liberal Professions	1.6	1.1	0.4
Police/Military	17.3	20.2	18.0
Other Public Service	16.3	20.3	29.2
Other Industries	1.9	4.5	1.5
TOTAL PER CENT	100.0	99.8	99.9
Number of Formations	578	732	267

The subtraction of those large categories leaves little for the other segments of French industry. Yet it is intriguing to see some suggestions of change after the 1840s: an apparent decline in the participation of peasants, merchants, professionals, and textile workers, compensated by a rise in coalitions of several distinct occupational groups. Some segments of those categories—notably shopkeepers, weavers, small-holders and petty lawyers—had figured importantly in major disturbances from the revolution on; historians like George Rudé have suggested that by 1848 the old reliable rebels were starting to give way to workers in modern industry. The estimates we have of the labor force of the time (see Appendix Table A-1) indicate that the shift, if shift it was, did not simply reflect the declining bulk of these categories in the population. Although the agricultural population was increasing more slowly than the rest of the labor force throughout the nineteenth century, it did not actually reach its numerical peak until the 1920s. Agricultural workers, however, disappeared rapidly from disturbances after 1850. They did not reappear in sizeable numbers until they had adopted new and complex forms of organization decades later. Textile workers were a somewhat different case, since their absolute numbers began a slow decline somewhere around the middle of the nineteenth century; they had 12 per cent of the labor force before 1845, 11 per cent in 1856, 9 per cent in 1886. But they seem to have dropped out of collective violence faster than that, probably because in the first half of the century the protestors came disproportionately from the dispersed, small-scale, dying sectors of the industry.

So far as the fragmentary data on strikes before 1890 can instruct us, there was no strong connection between the industrial distribution of strikes (see Appendix Table A-2) and that of formations taking part in collective violence. The textile industry produced close to half the strikes recorded up to that point. Textile workers did not constitute anything like half the violent formations. The rising strike-proneness of miners in the 1840s did not bring miners as such into disturbances more often. And so on. Yet I expect that when the matter is examined more closely, a connection between propensity to strike and propensity to join in collective violence will appear. Peter Stearns has pointed out how much the strikes of the July Monarchy centered in the established crafts and older centers of manufacturing rather than the big new industries and the fast-growing cities in which they were located.[25] The strikes described in Aguet's compilation and in the Ministry of Labor's *Associations professionnelles ouvrières* bear him out.[26] Up to the 1848 revolution not only did textiles, construction,

[25] Peter N. Stearns, "Patterns of Industrial Strike Activity in France During the July Monarchy," *American Historical Review*, 70 (January 1965), pp. 371-94.

[26] Jean-Pierre Aguet, *Les grèves sous la Monarchie de Juillet (1830-1847)*

woodworking crafts, and printing dominate the strike statistics, but the textile plants involved were especially the smaller, older ones.

Furthermore, the centers of strike activity were largely the same places that produced frequent political disturbances. In Aguet's list, the departments contributing five or more strikes in the years 1830 to 1834 were Bouches-du-Rhône, Rhône, Seine, and Seine-Inférieure; from 1835 to 1839 they were Nord, Seine, and Seine-Inférieure; from 1840 to 1844, Gard, Hérault, and Seine. Paris easily tops the list, with Rouen a distant second; these comparisons exaggerate the preeminence of Paris, but not so much as to give it the wrong rank.

By the 1880s textiles still produced the most strikes, but the mining, leather, and metal industries had become reliable sources of conflict, while woodworking and printing had faded. The departments of Nord and Rhône had toppled the Seine from its supremacy, Aisne, Ardennes, Marne, and Vosges were now in its range, and the region of Rouen had all but disappeared from view. By that time, the areas of large-scale, modern production dominated the strike scene. During the July Monarchy, even though the relatively modern agglomerations of Saint-Etienne and Lille were already producing strikes, most of the industrial conflicts broke out in the areas where the workers had accumulated a longer political history.

Unlike the situation late in the century, almost none of the nineteenth-century political disturbances we are considering here began as peaceful strikes, and none at all as strikes with explicitly political objectives. The only years in which Aguet mentions more than three strikes breaking into violence are 1833, 1840, and 1846. The general correspondence between the maps of strikes and of disturbances does not come from counting the same things twice.

On the other hand, the word "strike" singles out the successfully concerted work stoppage from a much wider range of industrial conflicts carried on by the same workers in the same period—the many so-called *coalitions* nipped by the police before they had a chance to act, the demonstrations, slowdowns, damaging of goods, and breaking up of machines which filled the *Gazette des Tribunaux* of the 1830s. The many strikes of 1833 in Paris, Rouen, Le Havre, and the surrounding area, for instance, appeared in the midst of many more incidents involving the same categories of tailors, shoemakers, carpenters, and other craftsmen—incidents including active Republican agitation. The strikes grew out of a much larger matrix of collective action.

(Geneva: Droz, 1954); Direction du Travail, *Les associations professionnelles ouvrières* (4 vols.; Paris: Imprimerie Nationale, 1899-1904).

Nor were these primarily strikes of despair. For the period of Aguet's compilation, a constant 70 to 75 per cent of all the strikes he reports made bids to raise wages, improve working conditions, or reduce working hours, rather than reacting to cuts or new restrictions. To be sure, wages, working conditions, and hours gave French workers of the 1830s and 1840s ample cause for complaint. And most of these bids failed. The point is that the strikes grew out of a conscious effort, not a last gasp of pain. The most miserable did not shout the loudest. "In the midst of conditions of such misery that extreme and frequent protest might be expected," Mr. Stearns has written, "the French industrial worker was almost totally quiescent."[27] At the same time, the artisans of the older centers were pursuing their collective interests energetically.

The wind bears all these straws in the same general direction. First, urban artisans in old crafts like typography and cabinet-making probably took part in the disturbances of the 1830s and 1840s more frequently than the distribution of formations suggests. They took part in mixed groups of workers united by local contacts as well as in formations confined to a single craft. Second, there probably was some connection between the capacity to strike and the capacity to carry on the sorts of collective action which led to violence, even if they occurred at different phases of an occupational group's existence. Both required organization and shared goals. Third, over the nineteenth century the center of gravity for both strikes and collective violence involving workers as such shifted from the old artisanal industries to the new factory-based ones, but with a considerable lag behind the growth of new industries. The lag, I think, represents the time required for establishing contacts, developing consciousness of a common fate, and organizing for collective action.

As the process went on, the groups appearing in collective violence acquired increasingly definite political orientations. The table below shows the proportions of formations assigned some particular political identification by the sources from which we drew our accounts. (Qualification: this tabulation assigns troops and police to the regime unless there is definite information to the contrary; later tables will clear up the distinction.) The data establish the dwindling of formations without any clear political identification, and the rise of formations definitely opposed to the current holders of power. This does not necessarily mean that Frenchmen were becoming more disaffected. It does mean that various disaffections clustered increasingly around national political labels and programs.

[27] Stearns, "Patterns of Industrial Strike Activity," p. 372.

Apparent Political Identification	*1830-39*	*1840-49*	*1850-60*	*1930-39*	*1940-49*	*1950-60*
None noted	33.3	30.5	24.7	5.6	18.9	8.4
Regime	46.5	57.3	44.8	40.5	32.2	41.5
Other	20.2	12.2	30.5	53.9	48.9	50.1
TOTAL	100.0	100.0	100.0	100.0	100.0	100.0

What was going on from 1830 to 1860 comes out more clearly in Table 4, which separates the major political labels from each other. During the first decade Orleanists (who, of course, came to power in July of 1830), Republicans, and, especially, Legitimists appeared in violent encounters with the regime. After 1839 various shades of Republicans were practically alone in violent opposition. Their place in disturbances grew after 1849; Bonapartists joined them briefly before their hero seized power at the end of 1851. And over the entire period the proportion of formations lacking any clear political identification shrank from a third to a quarter. Considering how often we consider the nineteenth century to be a time of diffuse "working-class" protest, this is news in itself. Workmen were often involved, but in their political guise rather than their economic one.

TABLE 4. POLITICAL IDENTIFICATION OF FORMATIONS IN DISTURBANCES, 1830-1860

Apparent Political Identification	*1830-39*	*1840-49*	*1850-60*
None Noted*	79.8	87.8	69.5
Orleanist	4.2	0.5	0.0
Legitimist	8.3	0.9	0.8
Republican	4.6	4.1	18.9
"Radical"	0.2	4.7	4.2
Bonapartist	0.7	0.8	3.1
Other	2.3	1.1	3.5
TOTAL PER CENT	100.1	99.9	100.0
Number of Formations	568	737	259

* Includes repressive forces and government functionaries, except where positive evidence of political identification appears.

An analysis of the immediate background of disturbances amplifies these conclusions. "Immediate background" means the collective action, if any, in which a formation was engaged just before starting to interact with other formations taking part in the disturbance. This time there are three important qualifications: 1) "strike" means the workers involved were actually picketing or otherwise acting together as part of the strike, and not just on strike; 2) in the absence of contrary information, the classification assigns troops and police to "collective action not clearly connected with the disturbance"; 3) "preparation for violence" not only rests on a certain amount of retroactive inference from the nature of the collective violence in some cases, but also covers a number of events like demonstrations to which demonstrators came armed. Table 5 displays the data.

TABLE 5. IMMEDIATE BACKGROUND OF FORMATIONS' PARTICIPATION IN DISTURBANCES, 1830-1960

Immediate Background	*1830-39*	*1840-49*	*1850-60*	*1930-39*	*1940-49*	*1950-60*
Insufficient Information	5.8	5.1	5.3	0.5	0.6	2.2
Not Acting Collectively Before Disturbance	4.4	4.1	2.1	1.6	0.3	0.1
Collective Action Not Clearly Connected with Disturbance*	27.0	29.0	20.9	18.7	15.6	18.6
Peaceful Meeting	19.5	15.9	7.8	13.0	11.1	8.7
Organizational Activity	3.0	3.0	8.8	3.7	1.6	2.9
Community Activity: Parade, Ceremony, Election, Market	4.1	4.2	1.6	3.5	1.6	0.5
Demonstration	11.7	6.0	12.0	19.1	18.1	24.6
Other Presentation of Demands	2.7	4.2	2.9	3.2	2.2	3.5
Preparations for Violence: Arming, Positioning	15.1	19.4	31.6	22.9	32.4	28.6
Closing or Blocking Public Places	3.3	4.6	5.6	3.5	3.8	3.5
Strike	0.4	0.9	0.5	5.9	9.8	4.6
Other	3.0	3.7	0.8	5.3	2.9	1.3
TOTAL PER CENT	100.0	100.1	99.9	100.9	100.0	99.1
Number of Formations	564	734	263	806	221	433

* Includes repressive forces, except where positive evidence of inaction or of other action appears.

On the whole, our twentieth-century accounts give clearer indications of the immediate background. This has less to do with any improvement in the quality of reporting than with a change in the nature of the action itself. The ties of collective violence to complex, planned, coordinated group actions increased. The statement does not apply to routine organizational activities—meetings, ceremonies, elections, and the like—which fluctuated without obvious pattern from decade to decade. It does apply to the growing prominence of strikes, although strike activity never accounted for as much as the fifth of the formations.[28] Demonstrations were more common contexts for collective violence than strikes were. About 10 per cent of the nineteenth-century disturbances, and about 20 per cent of the twentieth-century disturbances, grew directly from demonstrations. (In fact, the figures for both periods should be higher, since a certain number of demonstrations are hiding in the heading "preparations for violence.") In the later period the government more often deployed its repressive forces in anticipation of a disturbance, and protestors often prepared deliberately for a violent showdown. Each learned to anticipate—and, in a curious sense, coordinate itself with—the other's action.

All this implies a shift in the objectives of participants in disturbances—perhaps the riskiest matter on which we have had to make judgments in the course of this research. Appendix 2 to this paper contains the portion of our codebook dealing with objectives. The coder assessed the major objectives of each of the formations to the extent that those objectives appeared openly, through word or deed, *in the course of the disturbance itself.* We were willing to attribute the objective of "self-defense" to a formation which actually defended itself; we did not, however, assume that Republicans in 1831, or Communists in 1931, or any political group no matter when, were attempting revolution unless they either said so or attempted to seize the major instruments of power.

Table 6 classifies the objectives. Since the coder could classify up to three objectives per formation, there are many more objectives than formations. The small increase in the average number of objectives assigned to a formation may well result from the increasing explicitness of those objectives. Throughout the entire period, the proportion of "random, unfocused" action (true free-for-alls, simple merrymaking, wanton destruction) remains trivial. Peacekeeping and repression occupied a predictably high proportion of the formations through the years under study, although they gave way to interpersonal attacks and self-defense in the 1830s (when many food riots, tax rebellions, and the like ran their course before the troops got to the scene) and the 1930s (when an important part of the action consisted of Com-

[28] Most of the massive sit-down strikes of 1936 to 1938, however, meet our criteria for disturbances. We are analyzing all of them separately. The only ones included in these tabulations are those involving some violence beyond the occupation of the premises.

TABLE 6. DISTRIBUTION OF MANIFEST OBJECTIVES OF FORMATIONS TAKING PAR[T] IN DISTURBANCES, 1830-1960

Manifest Objectives	*1830-39*	*1840-49*	*1850-60*	*1930-39*	*1940-49*	*1950-6[0]*
Random, Unfocused	1.2	0.5	0.3	0.4	0.2	0.6
Damage of another Formation	8.0	4.0	4.6	12.8	8.1	8.9
Other Damage	2.4	3.0	0.8	0.5	1.6	1.0
Seizure or Control of Persons	0.4	2.3	0.7	0.5	0.9	0.4
Seizure or Control of Places	1.4	3.0	7.9	4.7	12.8	2.7
Seizure or Control of Commodities	4.2	3.8	0.3	0.3	0.7	0.1
Seizure or Control of Other Objects	5.9	5.5	6.1	3.8	2.4	12.1
Protesting Actions of Others	13.2	11.3	9.7	15.6	11.7	9.9
Other Protests: Prices, Working Conditions, Etc.	5.0	7.6	6.8	6.9	5.2	11.2
Demands for Specific Local Changes	6.9	9.0	4.1	3.8	4.8	2.7
Demands for Specific National Changes	5.1	2.0	1.8	1.8	3.1	6.9
Demands for General Political, Social or Economic Change	2.3	3.3	12.7	10.5	9.0	2.1
Defense of Self or Own Property	28.0	25.2	24.9	25.2	23.3	26.3
Peacekeeping, Repression	15.2	17.4	18.6	11.3	15.4	14.5
Other	0.8	2.1	.5	1.8	.9	.6
TOTAL PER CENT	100.0	100.0	99.8	99.9	100.1	100.0
Number of Objectives Classified	1,247	1,619	606	2,055	579	1,094
Objectives Per Formation	2.2	2.2	2.3	2.5	2.6	2.5

munist demonstrators battling counterdemonstrators from the Right, and vice versa).

In general, the largest breaks appear, unsurprisingly, between 1860 and 1930 and, more surprisingly, between the 1840s and the 1850s.[29] There are only two well-defined long trends. The first is for attempts to seize commodities (of which the food riot is the quintessential example) to disappear. The other is for demands for national and general political, social, and economic change to expand. The emergence of

[29] An Index of Dissimilarity computed for adjacent columns of the table comes out as follows:

1830-39 vs. 1840-49	1840-49 vs. 1850-60	1850-60 vs. 1930-39	1930-39 vs. 1940-49	1940-49 vs. 1950-60
21.8	25.2	29.8	18.9	21.5

North African nationalism as a fundamental political issue and incitement to collective violence in the 1950s diverted even that trend to some extent. The fact is that the long-run shifts in manifest objectives are smaller and less decisive than I expected them to be, or that our standard treatments of the rise and reintegration of the working class suggest they ought to be.

Maybe that is the point. Over the full six decades a solid majority of the objectives classified have an obvious political component; if the formations are not doing the repressive work of the government, they tend to be complaining about the way it does its work, or demanding changes in the distribution and use of power. Which objectives prevail in a given period, however, depends on who is joining in collective violence, who the contenders for power are, what relations they have with the government. Once said, it is obvious. The facts behind the statistical increase of "other protests" concerning prices, working conditions, etc. in the 1950s, for example, are the springing up of a highly organized Poujadist movement adept at dramatizing its opposition to government fiscal policy, and the expansion of farmers' organizations skilled at staging spectacular protests—blocking roads with tractors, or dumping potatoes in mid-city. In short, the fluctuation of objectives manifested in collective violence follows the fluctuation of political issues outside of violent encounters.

What, then, of the contrast between the 1840s and the 1850s? The 1850s saw a decline of property damage, of struggles for control of particular commodities or persons, of protests against particular actions of others, of demands for specific local changes; struggles to control places, protests against conditions like prices, and demands for general social changes assumed larger places than before. Concretely, the attack on machines, the tax rebellion, the invasion of land, and the food riot virtually disappeared; France passed through a brief but widespread civil war in 1851 (hence the struggles over public buildings, symbols of office, and whole communes); then came a regime under which any protest at all was difficult and dangerous.

The largest part of the transformation occurred during the short life of the Second Republic. Two fundamental processes shaped the collective violence of those years from 1848 through 1851. First, France mobilized. I mean that with great rapidity Frenchmen who had been little involved in national affairs formed, joined, or aligned themselves with groups contending for power on a national scale, became aware of the connections between their own fates and those of the nation, acquired information about the structure of power and ideas about what it should be, and exchanged commitments with men working in national politics. The same process had occurred before, most notably in 1789, and then reversed itself. This time it began from a higher base, went much farther, and receded little. Despite the compromises and constraints of the new Napoleon's regime (for example, his whittling away of manhood suffrage without quite repealing it), the flourishing of the press, the formation of clubs, the electoral campaigning, the widespread suffrage, and the very revolutionary activity of 1848 drew ordinary men firmly and irreversibly into national politics.

That does not mean the Common Man came to power, any more than the tremendous mobilization of consciousness and commitments engineered by thoroughgoing fascism guarantees an effective voice to the masses. It does mean that men found it much harder to ignore the national scene, and much harder to accomplish anything requiring collective effort or common resources without working through men operating on a national scale. Another way to put it, indeed, is that the national state won a durable victory over local power-holders and traditional particularisms. Louis Napoleon simply captured and consolidated.

That suggests the second large process: a cycle in which a disparate coalition made a revolution, some members of it gained control of the mechanisms of government, only to face widespread resistance when they sought to stabilize their control and to reimpose old demands of the state on its citizens, and were finally displaced by stronger, more ruthless men. Similar cycles had run themselves out from 1789 to 1795 and from 1830 to 1834, and are probably quite common in major transfers of power. The cycle divided the collective violence of the period into three phases: 1) the initial revolutionary struggle, consisting mainly of the insurrections in Paris, Marseille, Rouen, Lyon, and other big cities and the immediate repercussions of those insurrections; 2) the simultaneous concentration of power and formation of resistance from both retired members of the revolutionary coalition (as in the June Days) and others opposed to the reestablishment of governmental controls (as in the Forty-Five Centime Revolt); 3) the consolidation of the new regime and its leveling of its opposition, quintessentially in the insurrection of 1851.

The scheme oversimplifies; the revolutionary combats, for example, spilled over into acts of vengeance like the attacks on railroads near Paris and on Jews in Alsace. Yet the shift from revolutionary *élan* to struggle between consolidators and resisters clearly occurred. In the decade following 1845, the peak months for disturbances were:

Month	*Number of Disturbances*
January 1847	21
February 1848	14
March 1848	19
April 1848	35
June 1848	19
September 1848	14
December 1851	76

January 1847 culminated the last great wave of food riots France ever experienced. After the beginning of the revolution in February 1848, we could put the beginning of the second phase of concentration and resistance somewhere around the elections of April 1848, and the beginning of the phase of consolidation around the end of the same year—perhaps with Louis Napoleon's election as president, in December. No matter if the dates are dubious or the phases overlapping. Here is the conclusion that counts: the character of the fundamental political conflicts going on in France changed significantly, appeared clearly in the nature and timing of collective violence, and set the pattern for subsequent political life and protest.

Two of the principal moments of the transition came with the June Days of 1848 and the insurrection against Louis Napoleon's *coup d'état* in 1851.[30] Although historians are only beginning to wring the necessary evidence on the matter from the abundant archives, there are accumulating signs that both events rested on organization of an unprecedented scale. Not that a single conspiracy caused one or the other. Quite the opposite: new structures formed for other types of collective action provided the frameworks of rebellions few people anticipated and no one planned. The June Days grew from the working-class political organizations which bourgeoned after the February revolution and from the unparalleled opportunity for political education, agitation, and organization provided by the establishment of National Workshops to contain the Parisian unemployed. The 1851 insurrection gained much of its great scope from the rapid penetration of Republican organizations, both public and secret, from their bases in major cities into receptive sections of the countryside.

[30] I owe, and gladly give, thanks to Lynn Hollen Lees for supervising the early part of our work on the June Days, to Abdul Qaiyum Lodhi for doing much of the analysis of 1851 plus several of the comparisons presented here, and to Ted Margadant for correcting a number of my mistaken ideas about the insurrection of 1851. Mr. Margadant's forthcoming Ph.D. dissertation in History at Harvard goes much farther into the political structure of the rebellion than this paper can.

The Parisian rebellion of June 1848 holds a place in Western historiography as the first great proletarian insurrection. By contrast with its predecessors, it deserves the label. Up to that point the old crafts organized in small shops had staffed the rebellions of Paris. In June both semi-skilled workers from construction and employees of the newer factory-based industries appeared in unprecedented numbers. Perhaps 25,000 Parisians joined the rebellion at one point or another. At least 60,000 men took part in putting it down. Of the 2 groups—but mainly of the rebels—some 800 met death.

The action left a tremendous archival residue. One of the insurrection's by-products makes it possible to get a remarkably clear picture of the rebels themselves. It is a huge register containing brief, standardized descriptions of close to 12,000 persons arrested for taking part in the insurrection.[31] Of the 11,744 persons listed, about 5,000 were convicted by the courts; of them about 4,300 were sentenced to the penal colonies of Cayenne or Algeria. Like statistics of crime or illegitimacy or suicide, the numbers derivable from such a source depend to an unknown degree on the efficiency and selectivity of the police activity which produced it. Undoubtedly many people who took part in the June Days escaped arrest, and some innocent bystanders found themselves in jail. I am unable so far to rule out the possibility that changes in the French state's repressive tactics produced the apparent changes in the characteristics of rebels we are about to review. It will take careful internal criticism of the sources plus close comparison with well-documented localities and segments of the Parisian population to set reasonable limits on the reliability of these data as descriptions of the insurgents. At least the numbers are large enough, and the repression was thorough enough, to permit historians to go beyond the loose characterizations of the rebels (even those of Georges Duveau, who almost certainly drew some of his impressions from the very same source) they have had to rely on until now.

Table 7 sums up a few characteristics of the persons arrested, grouped according to the industrial categories employed in the Paris Chamber of Commerce's 1848 survey of the labor force.[32] True to the

[31] Archives Nationales, F^7 2586. Rémi Gossez has made a detailed study of the abundant individual dossiers which lie behind the register, as well as the other records of the June Days, but so far has published no more than extremely summary results of his research. Lynn Hollen Lees and I are preparing to publish elsewhere the findings of extensive analyses of this and other sources on the Revolution of 1848 in France.

[32] Chambre de Commerce de Paris, *Statistique de l'industrie à Paris résultant de l'enquête faite par la Chambre de Commerce pour les années 1847-8* (Paris: Chambre de Commerce, 1851). The survey dealt with firms rather than individuals; it therefore neglected such activities as retail trade or public service and

Table 7. Characteristics of Persons Arrested for Participation in the June Days of 1848 by Industry

Industrial Category	*Number of Persons*	*Per Cent Male*	*Per Cent Married**	*Median Age*
Textiles	346	95.6	75.0	36
Clothing	1,045	94.6	56.5	33
Luxury Trades	214	95.3	84.2	32
Printing, Paper	447	99.1	55.6	31
Ordinary Metals	1,334	99.8	57.3	31
Fine Metals	239	99.6	72.7	29
Food	464	97.4	51.3	32
Furniture, Wood	680	99.0	62.7	31
Leather	169	98.8	56.8	32
Carriage-Making	195	100.0	58.0	32
Chemicals	148	98.6	54.5	34
Basketry	135	98.5	67.6	31
Construction	2,077	99.9	58.7	32
Transportation	534	99.4	58.2	34
Retail Trade	791	95.9	67.8	34
Professions, Finance	328	98.8	57.3	34
Services	461	92.6	63.5	34
Military	501	99.4	60.3	31
Other	1,190	95.3	54.8	35
Not Reported	446	93.0	66.7	33
Total	11,744	97.6	59.6	33

* Information available for 2,892 persons only.

reputation of the June Days, the largest single group—over 2,000 men—came from the construction industry. The metalworking industries and the clothing trades came next; every major category supplied a number of recruits. What sets off June 1848 from the insurrections of 1830, 1834, 1839, or even February 1848, however, is the diminished role of shopkeepers and skilled artisans like goldsmiths or printers as compared with factory-based mechanics and semi-skilled workers like those in the construction industry. (Of the 2,077 construction workers, 216 were *terrassiers*, or ditch-diggers, but 575 were masons, and another 631 were carpenters or cabinet-makers.) All categories were overwhelmingly male; women only appeared in more than trivial numbers in the services and the clothing trades, where they were, of course, more numerous to begin with. About three-fifths of the arrestees

understated the labor force in industries including many single self-employed persons and with many unemployed.

were married; other data not reported here show that, contrary to widespread beliefs of the time, almost all had lived in Paris for some time and had established domiciles in the city. Finally, they were surprisingly old, considering the life expectancy of the time and the vigor required for street fighting; the median age was thirty-three for the entire group; only among "fine metals"—goldsmiths, silversmiths, and so on—did it dip below thirty. While new industries were showing up in rebellion, rebellion was still drawing on the established members of the working class.

The insurrection was put down, and bloodily. Ledru-Rollin's attempt at a coup in June 1849 lost out even more quickly. We have the custom of talking as though only a hopeless handful of fanatics were left to join the rebellion which followed the 1851 coup. One standard account goes as follows:

> The coup was brilliantly executed and possibly forestalled an Orleanist plan to put the Prince de Joinville in power. But it was not, like Brumaire, to be bloodless. The reaction of the city as a whole was as yet uncertain. Morny was prepared, if resistance were shown, to let it develop and then to crush it once and for all. So, when a few barricades did go up on the 3rd in one or two quarters, the troops dealt roughly with those who opposed them and unhappily on the 4th incidents on the Boulevard de la Poissonnière provoked them to fire indiscriminately, causing some two or three hundred casualties, including many bystanders. Paris was effectively cowed, but at a price which cost the Prince-President dear. In the provinces, too, in certain regions of the Centre and South, where the Republicans had succeeded in extending their hold, there was resistance which was enough to provide the authors of the coup with the pretext for draconian repression, harsher still than that which had followed the June Days.[33]

And Marx himself asked: "Why did the Paris proletariat not rise in revolt after December 2?"

Now, it is true that in 1851 the workers of Paris did not turn out in anything like the numbers or the proportions of 1848; the Napoleonic government had done its work of neutralization during the previous two years very effectively, and no National Workshops were there to serve as staging areas for rebellion. But the failure of the resistance in December 1851 should not lead us to imagine it did not exist. In France as a whole, close to 100,000 men joined in open insur-

[33] J.P.T. Bury, *Napoleon III and the Second Empire* (London: English Universities Press, 1964), p. 34.

rection, and more than 500 of them met death—most of them in Paris. Thousands of men went to the streets of Paris on the third and fourth of December, but Napoleon's troops frightened many of them away without a struggle. When it came to the genuine street fighting across the barricades of the old city, Ténot concluded that "One would not be far below the true figure in estimating the republicans who dug in for a fight at twelve hundred armed men."[34] Our own estimate puts the total number ever taking part in violent encounters with troops or police at about 2,000 persons. In any case, the mass of men took up arms, built barricades, and held the eastern sections of Paris for a day. Almost 400 of them died in its defense. Somehow "a few barricades," "one or two quarters," and "pretext for draconian repression" understate the scope of the rebellion in Paris, and, even more so, in the provinces.

But who rebelled? The repression of 1851 left a documentary residue like that of the June Days. The residue poses some of the same problems of interpretation, and permits a roughly comparable analysis. The problems of interpretation stand out even more clearly, since our principal source identifies almost 3,000 arrestees, more than the number of persons we can be sure took part in the street fighting. As with the June Days, what we have is an enumeration of the participants in the rebellion *as defined by the government.* Again the comparison of that enumeration with microscopic reconstructions of the insurrection in one neighborhood will eventually be essential.

Furthermore, the sources used here consist of detailed tables dealing with a limited number of characteristics, rather than person-by-person descriptions.[35] That reduces their flexibility. Nevertheless, we have been able to force the data into categories resembling those of 1848.

Table 8 offers a comparison of the June Days and the insurrection of 1851 in the Seine. This time we have estimated rates of participation by industry, using as bases the 1847-1848 Chamber of Commerce survey and the 1851 census. The 1851 insurrection comes out as substantially more bourgeois in character than the June Days, yet far from devoid of workers. Whereas only 2 or 3 per cent of the arrestees of

[34] Eugene Ténot, *Paris en décembre 1851* (Paris: Le Chevalier, 1868), p. 228.

[35] The source is Archives Nationales, BB^{30} 424, "Insurrection de décembre 1851, Statistique." Individual files on suspects and arrestees are stacked up in the Archives Historiques de l'Armée (e.g. AA G^8 190, "Insurrection de 1851, détenus et transportés") as well as elsewhere in Paris and the departments. I have examined some of the relevant materials in the Archives Nationales and the Archives Historiques de l'Armée, but have not used them systematically in the present analysis. The work deserves doing.

1848 came from the professions or finance, they provided almost a fifth of the 1851 contingent. The shares of textiles and clothing, metals, transportation, and construction—especially, that is, those industries which were new to insurrection in 1848—shrank significantly. Food production and the shoe industry, however, contributed larger shares than before. Calculated as rates based on the current labor force, participation ran about a quarter of its previous level. Among those industries for which we have labor force data, construction, food, and metals poured disproportionate numbers into the June Days, while in 1851 retail trade and leather contributed exceptional proportions. Anomalies like that of the food industries—whose estimated labor force grew so much faster than their share of the arrests that the calculated rate of participation dropped to near the bottom—are com-

TABLE 8. INDUSTRIAL DISTRIBUTIONS AND RATES OF ARREST, JUNE DAYS AND 1851 INSURRECTION IN THE SEINE

	1848			*1851*	
Industrial Category	*Per Cent of All Arrests*	*Per Cent of All Transported*	*Arrests Per 10,000*	*Per Cent of All Arrests*	*Arrests Per 10,000*
Textiles	2.9	3.1	94	3.1 (Textiles and Clothing)	21 (Textiles and Clothing)
Clothing	8.9	8.6	116		
Luxury Trades	1.8	1.8	61	2.8	20
Printing, Paper	3.8	4.2	267	5.0	50
Metals	13.4	15.0	377	3.1	47
Construction	17.7	17.1	499	13.1	43
Food	4.0	3.9	444	7.5	30
Chemicals, Ceramics	1.3	1.3	151	0.9	231 (Chemicals, Ceramics; Furniture; Leather)
Furniture	5.8	6.6	187	4.7	
Leather	1.4	1.5	369	14.9	
Transportation	4.5	4.3	177	2.8 (Transportation and Carriage-Making)	27 (Transportation and Carriage-Making)
Carriage-Making	1.7	1.6	141		
Retail Trade	6.7	6.4		5.0	271
Professions, Finance	2.8	2.3		19.4	28
Basketry	1.1	1.3	249	17.7 (Basketry through Not Reported)	102 (Basketry through Not Reported)
Services	3.9	4.1			
Military	4.3	4.0			
Other	10.1	10.3			
Not Reported	3.8	2.7			
TOTAL PER CENT	99.9	100.1		100.0	
Number of Persons	11,744	4,292		2,962	

mon enough in these comparisons to raise serious doubts about the validity of the rates. Let us take that part of the analysis as no more than a suggestion.

In the first hint of what his major thesis on the subject will eventually contain, Jacques Rougerie has published a quick summary of similar data concerning the Commune of 1871.[36] We have used his figures to calculate rates of participation similar to those for 1848 and 1851, basing the calculations on the 1866 census. Rougerie's figures (slightly reworked to fit census categories and cleansed of a few computational errors) appear along with the rates in Table 9.

TABLE 9. DISTRIBUTION OF ARRESTS AND DEPORTATIONS BY INDUSTRY, COMMUNE OF 1871

Industrial Category	*Per Cent Arrests*	*Per Cent Deportations*	*Arrests/ 10,000 Workers*	*Deportations/ 10,000 Workers*
Textiles, Clothing	9.0	9.3	81	7
Luxury Trades	7.6	7.9	368	33
Printing, Paper	2.9	3.0	171	15
Metals	13.0	12.4	527	44
Construction	17.2	17.6	248	22
Furniture, Woodworking	8.8	8.3	1,143	95
Leather	1.2	1.7	191	24
Retail Trade	4.8	3.7	293	31
Employes	8.8	10.5	167	3
Domestic Service	5.4	1.9	134	23
Professions and Finance	3.7	2.7	61	4
Day Labor	16.4	19.6	?	?
Agriculture	1.2	1.5	256	26
TOTAL PER CENT	100.0	100.1		
Number of Persons	31,717	2,807		

Rougerie says of his findings:

The Commune was certainly a workers' insurrection. That working-class character was much more marked in 1871 than it had been in 1851, when the professions, *rentiers*, wholesale and retail merchants, and office workers comprised 27.4% of the total as compared with 15.6% during the Commune. Nonetheless one notices the substantial place of the office workers among the insurgents, and even

36 Jacques Rougerie, *Procès des Communards* (Paris: Julliard, 1964; Collection "Archives"), esp. pp. 126-34.

> more so among the deportees. That is an important fact: it was the first time those that were not quite white-collar workers joined a workers' insurrection. In June, 1848, the office workers fought on the side of the establishment.
>
> Insurrection of which workers? The categories most strongly represented are the ones we have called Metal, Construction and Day-Labor. They are represented in greater proportion than in 1851. . . . That growth came to a large extent from the rapid development these new industries underwent in Paris during the Second Empire. . . . Around 1850 the preeminence of the traditional Parisian industries—clothing trades, shoes, hand crafts, the making of *articles de Paris*—had been seriously shaken, and had probably disappeared.[37]

Most of this is correct, but the comparison with 1851 is misleading in some respects. Where the categories are comparable, the proportions for 1871 actually resemble those of 1848 much more closely than those of 1851. Rougerie is correct in stressing the increasing participation of office workers; only 100 of them appear in the list for 1848. What he has to say about day-laborers carries a little less weight, since the 1848 enumeration contained 216 *terrassiers* and 699 *journaliers*. Furthermore, the rates suggest that the dwindling luxury trades were actually overrepresented in the Commune, along with metals, furniture-making and—even then—retail trade. Although the proportions shifted toward the industries employing numerous semi-skilled workers, then, the shift among rebels probably lagged behind that in the labor force as a whole.

In Table 10 I have laid out provisional calculations of rates for the three insurrections. The figures support the major conclusions which appear to follow from the previous discussion: 1) while all three insurrections drew from a wide range of the Parisian labor force, the insurrection of 1851 had a considerably less proletarian tone than the other two; that is due especially to the inactivity of construction workers in 1851; 2) considering Rougerie's placing of day-laborers, most of whom probably worked in construction, in a separate category from construction, the Commune did draw more heavily on the semi-skilled labor force of Paris than had the previous rebellions; 3) the shopkeepers stuck with the forces of revolution while their old companions, the printers and shoemakers, began to drift away; 4) yet even in 1871 the epicenters of revolutionary activity were the industries staffed by

[37] *Ibid.*, p. 128.

skilled workers. The data need more scrutiny. I offer these only as promising hypotheses.

TABLE 10. RATES OF ARREST FOR SELECTED INDUSTRIAL CATEGORIES IN THE SEINE: JUNE DAYS, 1851 INSURRECTION, AND COMMUNE OF 1871

	Arrests/10,000 Workers		
Industrial Category	*June Days*	*1851*	*Commune*
Textiles and Clothing	109	21	81
Luxury Trades	61	20	368
Printing, Paper	267	50	171
Metals	377	47	527
Construction	499	43	248
Furniture, Woodworking	187		1,143
Leather	369		191
Retail Trade		271	293
Professions, Finance		28	61
Domestic Service		4	134
Agriculture		10	256
Employes			167

All three insurrections were national in impact, but only the insurrection of 1851 was national in scope. Figures 5 through 7 summarize the geographic pattern of the insurrection in three different ways. The first (Fig. 5) expresses the number of man-days expended in disturbances which entered our sample for December 1851. The second distributes the nearly 27,000 arrests over the map of France. And the third (Fig. 7) converts those arrests to rates based on the male labor force reported in the 1851 census.

The three maps resemble each other greatly. Yet it is clear that the repression swept a much larger area than had produced outright violence. The maps show that the major centers of rebellion in 1851 were Paris, the Nièvre (especially Clamécy), the hinterland of Marseille, and a broken ring of departments around Toulouse. My guess is that Republican, Radical, and Socialist organizations, both open and clandestine, spread like vines through the hinterlands of Paris, Toulouse, Béziers, Marseille, and Lyon with the great political mobilization of 1848, that from 1849 on the Napoleonic government was fairly successful at choking or chopping the more visible branches of those organizations, and that the geographic pattern represents the areas in which they and their adepts had survived the thinning out—because they were tough, or because they were invisible. In any case, the effects of

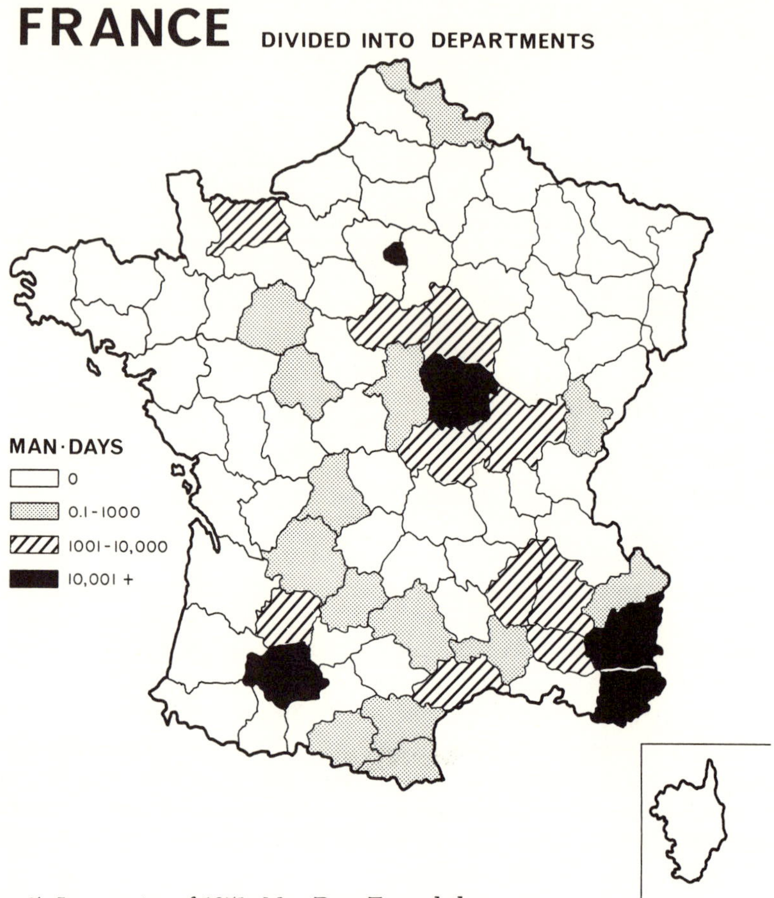

Fig. 5. Insurrection of 1851: Man-Days Expended

those years were deep and durable; the three maps for 1851 bear a considerable resemblance to the maps of Far Left voting during the early Third Republic.

For France as a whole, whom did the government define as insurgents? Table 11 summarizes several characteristics of the persons it arrested. The largest single groups came from agriculture (over 7,000) and from the professions and finance (over 4,000). Construction (close to 3,000) and clothing manufacturing (about 2,500) came next. Every major category, however, contributed rebels. Even by comparison with the Parisian totals, the insurgents were overwhelmingly male. They averaged a bit older (especially the middle-class arrestees) and were

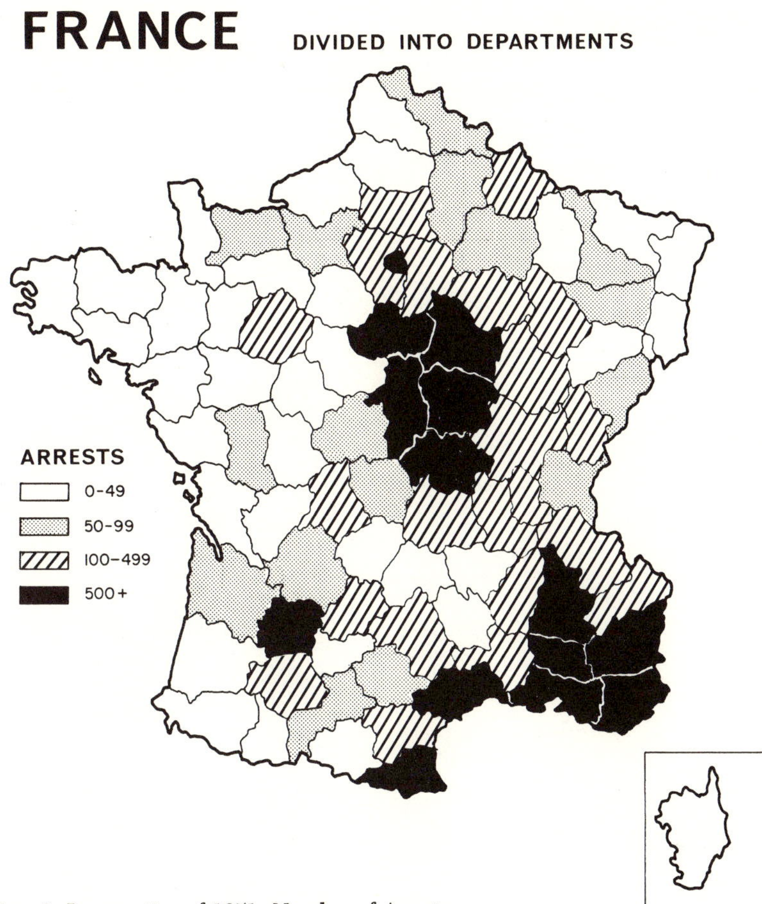

Fig. 6. Insurrection of 1851: Number of Arrests

more likely to be married than their Parisian counterparts of 1848, 1851, or 1871.

What happened to the different groups of arrestees? How harshly the government treated them may or may not tell us how extensively they took part in the insurrection—that remains to be proven—but it does tell us whom the government blamed and feared. I have compared the actual outcomes of the first passes through the courts of the 26,867 persons for whom we have data to the proportions which would have occurred if all industrial categories had shared all fates in proportion to their numbers in the arrested population. Table 12 presents the ratios. On the reasonable assumption that sentencing to

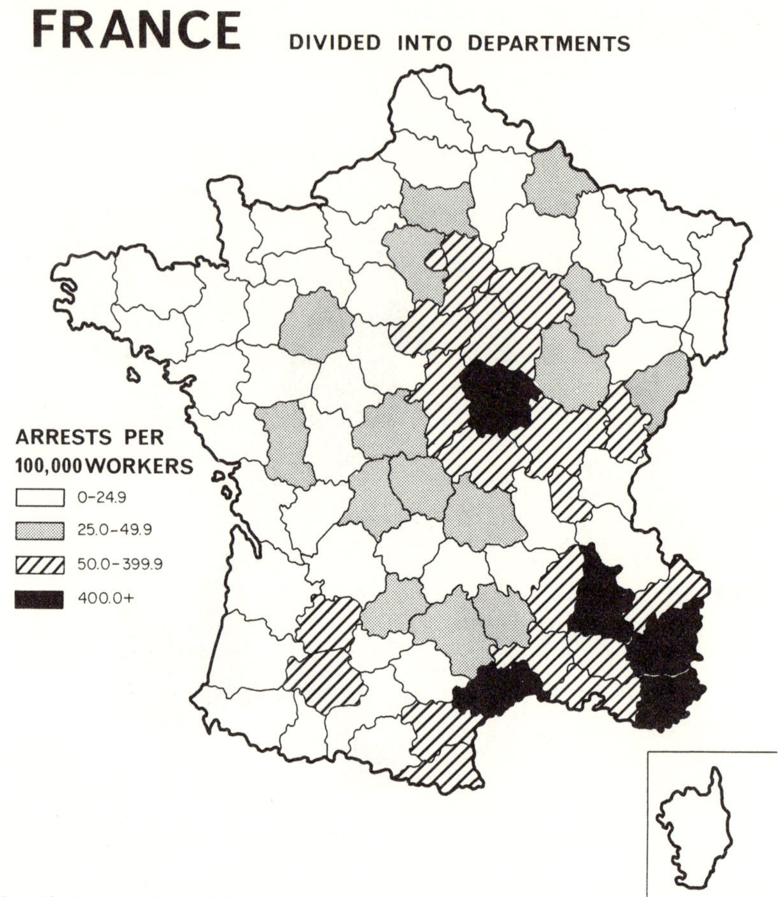

FIG. 7. Insurrection of 1851: Rates of Arrest

Cayenne or Algeria, or transfer to the Conseil de Guerre established to try the major political criminals, marked a man as a serious offender, while release on the first round meant there was nothing to pin on him, one would identify as the hardest hit: metals, food, other manufacturing (leather, chemicals, woodworking, etc.), construction, and retail trade.

Domestics, on the other hand, were apparently likely to be picked on suspicion, then released. The hard-hit industries were those which had been overrepresented in the June Days. The government apparently bore down hardest on people from the industries which previous experience had taught it to fear most.

TABLE 11. CHARACTERISTICS OF PERSONS ARRESTED FOR PARTICIPATION IN THE INSURRECTION OF 1851 BY INDUSTRY

Industrial Category	*Number of Persons*	*Per Cent Male*	*Per Cent Married*	*Median Age*
Textiles	1,062	99.9	61.7	35
Clothing	2,460	99.1	63.2	33
Luxury Trades	209	100.0	61.2	35
Printing, Paper	285	99.6	53.3	33
Metals	783	100.0	68.3	35
Food	1,836	98.8	73.2	37
Other Manufacturing	1,454	99.9	62.0	33
Construction	2,951	100.0	64.9	34
Transportation	683	100.0	68.5	34
Retail Trade	839	99.4	69.4	38
Mining, Etc.	180	100.0	72.8	35
Agriculture	7,411	99.6	65.9	34
Professions and Finance	4,144	99.4	63.7	38
Domestic Service	222	95.9	29.3	28
Other	2,362	96.9	61.3	35
TOTAL	26,881	99.3	64.7	35

The sorting of the dangerous men from the others, however, began before the courts did their work. It began with the initial arrests. We have already seen that over the whole of France the police plucked their largest contingents of suspected rebels from agriculture, the professions, construction, and the clothing trades. We get a somewhat different sense of the matter if we close in on departments which fostered major insurrections in December, and once again consider the under- and overrepresentation of different categories of workers among the arrestees in those departments alone. I have singled out the eight departments which our independent estimates of man-days expended show to have been most heavily involved:

Basses-Alpes	20,550 man-days
Gers	17,300 man-days
Var	16,200 man-days
Hérault	9,700 man-days
Nièvre	8,000 man-days
Drôme	7,200 man-days
Vaucluse	5,600 man-days
Seine	4,000 man-days

TABLE 12. RATIOS OF OBSERVED TO EXPECTED DISPOSITIONS OF PERSONS ARRESTED FOR PARTICIPATING IN THE INSURRECTION OF 1851, BY INDUSTRIAL CATEGORY (EXPECTED = 100)

Industrial Category	*Conseil De Guerre*	*Cayenne*	*Detention in Algeria*	*Exile in Algeria*	*Expulsion from France*	*Forced Residence in France*	*Internment*	*Police Correction-nelle*	*Maison de Correction*	*Surveillance*	*Returned to Prosecutor*	*Released*	*Number*
Textiles	82	42	97	121	39	67	95	82	174	99	61	110	1,065
Clothing	71	79	99	111	68	72	103	81	75	98	127	101	2,455
Luxury Trades	182	164	99	51	118	101	73	81	0	77	430	140	209
Printing, Paper	38	160	60	66	155	57	73	132	985	48	472	165	284
Metals	14	130	124	102	74	70	103	122	118	104	72	86	784
Food	41	123	121	98	79	94	103	93	50	103	110	87	1,836
Other Manufac-turing	120	117	99	112	81	61	106	141	255	87	145	95	1,453
Construction	122	81	108	103	83	80	94	112	94	98	122	96	2,948
Transportation	111	83	96	102	24	80	114	91	135	99	130	108	684
Retail Trade	104	150	91	92	181	136	96	105	111	105	150	85	835
Mining, Etc.	70	64	115	83	61	23	230	164	0	76	45	82	180
Agriculture	112	101	92	113	24	44	94	120	25	117	24	107	7,409
Professions and Finance	74	109	104	71	319	270	117	56	22	89	64	78	4,143
Domestic Service	148	0	66	101	12	18	43	132	420	91	274	165	222
Other	184	101	97	90	69	100	86	104	275	84	225	119	2,360
Number	247	237	4,549	5,032	979	640	2,822	645	29	5,186	664	5,831	26,867

Some of these departments had more than one center of rebellion; the Basses-Alpes broke out in a rash of small rebellions, some of which coalesced into larger spots. Although in all of them an important part of the impulse to rebellion probably came from the cities, they divided between those in which people of a major city (Béziers, Paris, Clamécy) actually carried out an insurrection which was momentarily successful, and those in which the fundamental pattern was the convergence of men gathered from small towns and countryside on the cities of their regions. It is worth asking whether the personnel of the rebellion varied significantly with these variations in pattern.

Table 13 states the rates by industry for the eight departments, grouped into an "urban" pattern of rebellion (Seine, Hérault, Nièvre), a "small-town" pattern (Drôme, Var, Basses-Alpes), and a "mixed" pattern combining some of each (Gers, Vaucluse). It shows that for their numbers in the labor force workers in agriculture were quite rare in the insurrection. In these departments clothing, the luxury trades, printing and paper, food, construction, transportation, the professions, and domestic service were generally underrepresented. Metals, "other manufacturing," and retail trade generally contributed more than their share, while textiles and mining fluctuated most sharply from department to department.

As for the urban, small-town, and mixed patterns of rebellion, no large patterns of difference emerge from the table. Proportionate to the size of the rebellion, arrests were much more frequent in the Seine than elsewhere. Hérault, which produced urban rebellions in Béziers and Bédarieux, came second in that respect, but the "small-town" departments of Drôme and Var also had relatively high proportions of arrests to man-days. Proportionate to labor force the departments of "small-town" rebellion had the most arrests. Among the industrial categories, the only visible tendency is for metals, construction, and textiles to be more highly represented in the "small-town" departments than in the rest. Even that tendency is uncertain.

The large lesson we have to learn from the examination of the June Days and the 1851 insurrection is a simple one: there are no intrinsically volatile industries, only industries which vary in current problems and in the organization of their workers for collective action. In Paris we have no reason to believe that shopkeepers were worse off or more aggrieved than the rest of the population; yet they joined rebellions in exceptional numbers throughout the first half of the century, so long as their intense local organization lasted. As workers in construction and other industries employing many semi-skilled workers acquired coherent organization—rapidly in 1848, slowly at other times—

TABLE 13. INSURRECTION OF 1851: RATES OF ARREST BY INDUSTRY IN THE EIGHT DEPARTMENTS MOST HEAVILY INVOLVED
(Arrests Per 100,000 Workers in Category)

	"Urban"			"Mixed"		"Small Town"		
Industrial Category	*Seine*	*Hérault*	*Nièvre*	*Gers*	*Vaucluse*	*Drôme*	*Var*	*Basses-Alpe*
Textiles	34	509	*	161	52	92	2,266	798
Clothing	19	102	123	52	40	112	188	314
Luxury Trades	20	68	287	176	229	80	257	*
Printing, Paper	50	222	*	107	0	93	12	*
Metals	47	1,247	278	1,375	331	1,680	2,941	*
Food	30	84	134	88	89	141	115	358
Other Manufacturing	231	787	935	272	121	356	1,316	3,071
Construction	43	271	261	114	105	306	441	785
Transportation	27	60	250	30	32	109	126	460
Retail Trade	271	683	*	2,014	527	571	1,105	*
Mining, Etc.	91	13	589	142	384	186	236	*
Agriculture	30	72	27	4	25	38	98	93
Professions and Finance	28	83	107	58	36	119	39	314
Domestic Service	4	28	23	1	5	69	4	45
Other	102	1,478	2,433	359	341	3,339	419	2,479
TOTAL	205	610	456	151	256	488	875	1,069
Number of Arrests	2,918	2,820	1,491	463	678	1,595	3,131	1,667
Arrests Per 1,000 Man-Days of Insurrection	730	291	186	27	121	222	193	81

* Base smaller than 100 workers in the industry.

they, too, joined in collective action both violent and nonviolent. The change in the composition of the rebels from 1848 to 1851, I believe, came less from a shift in the location of anger than in the stripping down of a once-varied revolutionary coalition to the best-organized, zealous core of the Republicans who had been able to survive three years of strangulation.

We need to examine the conflicts of those years more closely. The next series of tables miniaturizes the whole-decade tabulations presented earlier. It includes exactly the same variables and categories for single years from 1845 through 1851. Since shrinking the analysis to a year at a time brings down the number of disturbances or formations to a point where percentages would often be silly or misleading, I have reported raw numbers in these tables. The numbers display considerable changes in the character of collective violence over the crucial period. They also show how much its form and locus shift from year to year in response to fluctuations in the political situation—how closely collective violence is tied to the central political process.

Except for the surprisingly bulky disturbances of 1846, the magnitudes of disturbances varied in cadence with the major political rearrangements of the time (see Table 14). The years 1848 and 1851 produced the *most* disturbances and the largest *totals* of participants, but their big explosions occurred amid many smaller flareups of violence. As a consequence, the *average* disturbance reached its maximum in different years depending on the criterion: 1848 and 1849 for mean participants and man-days, 1846 and 1851 for the medians, 1851 for extent of repression, and so on. In 1846, only two disturbances (in Elbeuf and Tours) exceeded 1,000 man-days, but a series of labor disputes (mainly in the north and around Paris) and the opening set of

TABLE 14. INDICATORS OF MAGNITUDE OF DISTURBANCES BY YEAR, 1845-1851

Item	*1845*	*1846*	*1847*	*1848*	*1849*	*1850*	*1851*
Number of Disturbances	4	27	33	126	27	15	93
Number of Formations	11	67	91	287	72	35	204
Formations Per Disturbance	2.8	2.5	2.8	2.3	2.7	2.3	2.2
Total Participants (1,000s)	1	41	11	271	49	5	97
Mean Participants	171	1,534	327	2,153	1,815	317	1,045
Median Participants	150	1,000	200	400	375	300	638
Mean Man-Days	171	1,604	384	4,470	1,592	676	1,296
Median Man-Days	150	1,000	250	450	375	300	700
Mean Killed and Wounded	3	17	2	29	13	4	42
Median Wounded	1	17	1	1	1	3	31
Mean Arrested	18	23	22	27	84	9	174
Median Arrested	18	19	21	20	17	9	91
Per Cent Lasting Over One Day	0	19	31	17	11	7	28
Man-Days Per Man	1.0	1.1	1.2	2.1	0.9	2.1	1.2

the winter's food riots (especially around Tours) both assumed an exceptional scale. In 1850, on the other hand, tax rebellions predominated. The year brought the final trickle of the last great wave of tax rebellions in French history, plus a half-dozen violent encounters between the (still nominally republican) government and its Republican and Radical opponents. All these incidents were small.

The findings confirm the emergence of disturbances of unprecedented scale during the 1848 revolution and the Second Republic. The relatively large disturbances of 1846 and the relatively small ones of

1850, however, raise doubts about the immediacy and completeness of the rise in the scale of collective violence which I have suggested occurred around mid-century as a result of the rapid growth of complex organizations as contenders for power. The trivial number and mixed character of disturbances from 1852 through 1860 leave the issue open.

The available information on the kinds of formations taking part in collective violence (see Table 15) shows the activation of almost every

TABLE 15. DISTRIBUTION OF FORMATIONS TAKING PART IN DISTURBANCES, 1845-1851

Type of Formation	*1845*	*1846*	*1847*	*1848*	*1849*	*1850*	*1851*
Simple Crowd	2	8	29	42	4	5	18
Crowd with Distinct Ideological Identification	0	5	0	39	18	5	27
Guerrillas, Bandits, Private Armies	0	0	0	1	0	0	26
Other Organized Activists	0	0	0	3	0	0	26
Public Officials	0	2	1	25	4	2	8
Officials Plus Troops or Police	2	4	4	16	4	5	28
Regular Troops	0	1	0	10	6	1	12
Other Military	0	6	2	46	9	3	6
Police and Military	0	9	3	9	3	2	12
Police	2	2	13	12	8	3	20
Occupational Group From Same Locality	1	4	1	15	0	0	0
Occupational Group From Same Factory/Industry	1	4	2	22	5	5	2
Other Occupational Group	2	3	16	16	5	1	1
Group Identified by Outside Origin	0	0	0	12	0	0	1
Users of Same Market, Water, Land, or Forest	0	12	1	2	0	1	1
Others and Unclassifiable	1	6	19	20	4	3	15
TOTAL	11	66	91	290	70	36	203

kind of group in the Revolution of 1848, and a distinct rise of ideology and political activism at the same point. The simple crowd dwindled, the ideological crowd multiplied. Repressive forces took a larger part as the post-revolutionary reaction set in: 23 per cent in 1845-1847, 32 per cent in 1848, 39 per cent in 1849-1851. There is no doubt a connection between the two trends; the provincial officials of the time used to anxiously survey the reports of new incidents as they came in, to determine whether they were "political" and therefore threatening, or "economic" and therefore easier to shrug off. The distinction does not make much analytic sense, as I have tried to show, but a group's public adoption of a label, belief, or program made it much easier for the prefect or the mayor to perceive the threat and send in troops to eliminate it. The rising participation of groups of workers from the same factory or the same industry in 1848 increased that sense of threat.

The table presenting the industrial categories of formations in disturbances from 1845 to 1851 (see Table 16) amplifies these observa-

TABLE 16. INDUSTRIAL CATEGORY OF FORMATIONS IN DISTURBANCES, 1845-1851

Industrial Category	*1845*	*1846*	*1847*	*1848*	*1849*	*1850*	*1851*
Insufficient Information	1	8	26	46	2	12	82
No Distinct Category	1	18	1	63	18	0	12
Combination of Distinct Categories	0	3	2	9	1	0	13
Agriculture, Forests, Fish	2	0	4	13	3	1	5
Extractive Industries	0	2	0	1	0	2	1
Metals and Metal Working	0	0	0	2	0	0	0
Food	0	2	0	2	2	1	0
Chemicals	0	0	0	0	0	0	0
Paper, Printing	0	0	0	0	0	0	0
Leather	0	0	1	0	0	0	1
Textiles	0	0	1	13	1	2	0
Wood	0	2	0	0	0	0	0
Stonework	2	1	0	3	0	0	0
Construction	0	0	1	7	3	1	0
Commerce	1	3	20	4	0	0	0
Liberal Professions	0	0	0	4	2	0	1
Police/Military	2	12	15	62	19	6	35
Other Public Service	2	13	13	56	17	11	52
Other Industries	0	2	7	4	2	0	2
TOTAL	11	66	91	289	70	36	204

tions a bit. At this scale it is clearer than ever that groups of workers *as such* rarely appeared in collective violence, although workers in general played a large part in the collective violence of the time. Police and soldiers, whose business is to get involved in violence, are the principal exception. The surprising number of "commercial" formations in 1847 consisted entirely of merchants attacked by food rioters. The 1848 revolution did bring out a number of formations representing a single industry—notably peasants and textile workers. Otherwise, the many workers joining in collective violence appeared as Republicans, Socialists, or something else.

The sharp rise in political labeling with the revolution appears in Table 17. Through 1845, 1846 and 1847, the only three formations to

TABLE 17. POLITICAL IDENTIFICATIONS OF FORMATIONS TAKING PART IN DISTURBANCES, 1845-1851

Apparent Political Identification	*1845*	*1846*	*1847*	*1848*	*1849*	*1850*	*1851*
None Noted	11	63	91	246	41	29	136
Orleanist	0	1	0	2	0	0	0
Legitimist, Other Monarchist	0	2	0	4	1	0	3
Republican	0	0	0	20	10	5	44
"Radical"	0	0	0	14	15	1	10
Bonapartist	0	0	0	3	2	0	5
Other	0	0	0	1	1	1	6
TOTAL	11	66	91	290	70	36	204

bear some sort of clear political identification were monarchists of one description or another. (To be sure, it was dangerous to be anything else in those days; that is the point.) In 1848 and, especially, from 1849 to 1851 conflict became much more obviously tied to national politics. Republicans, "reds," and Radicals assumed the central place, although Bonapartists and others showed up from time to time. The tax rioters, by and large, did not display clear signs of political affiliation, but the urban insurgents did. That is part of the difference between the reactionary and the modern forms of collective violence. The modern forms were taking over.

The changes in the immediate backgrounds of disturbances, as presented in Table 18, likewise reveal the outpouring of organizational activity in 1848. A handful of the disturbances before then grew out of demonstrations and the like, and more of them began with peaceful meetings. It was with the revolution, however, that meetings, demonstrations, organized protests, and similar deliberate assemblies of men committed to a particular program or party took on major importance as the contexts of violence. (Let me again answer an imaginary critic: the loosening of restrictions on assembly, the holding of relatively free elections, and the change of regime itself did indeed promote just such collective activities; the fact simply confirms the interdependence between peaceful political action and collective violence.) Further-

TABLE 18. IMMEDIATE BACKGROUND OF FORMATIONS' PARTICIPATION IN DISTURBANCES, 1845-1851

Immediate Background	*1845*	*1846*	*1847*	*1848*	*1849*	*1850*	*1851*
Insufficient Information	0	4	12	5	3	0	17
Not Acting Collectively Before Disturbance	1	5	4	11	1	3	5
Collective Action Not Clearly Connected with Disturbance	4	28	38	99	16	12	58
Peaceful Meeting	1	5	32	64	9	7	21
Organizational Activity	0	0	0	22	2	0	33
Community Activity: Parade, Ceremony, Election, Market	1	2	2	28	2	3	3
Demonstration	0	4	5	31	13	5	37
Other Presentation of Demands	0	2	2	17	8	3	7
Preparations for Violence: Arming, Positioning	4	11	11	86	31	8	100
Closing or Blocking Public Places	0	11	1	15	2	5	14
Strike	0	1	0	3	4	2	0
Other	0	2	2	19	8	0	2
TOTAL	11	75	109	400	99	48	297

more, the parties watched and understood each other well enough that deliberate preparations for violence became increasingly common. Of the basic modern settings for collective violence, the strike alone did not emerge to prominence in 1848.

And objectives? Table 19 summarizes the data. With 1850 once more the interesting exception, the striking feature of the years after 1844 is the rapid dissemination of demands for national reform from 1848 onward. We knew, of course, that something like it had occurred. Otherwise we would not have used the term "revolution" for 1848. Nevertheless the data suggest how rarely such demands appeared openly in the course of violent conflicts before the revolution, and how much they continued after power had changed hands. Likewise, among protests, in the narrow sense, men shifted away from objections to general conditions like prices or poverty toward complaints about the specific actions of others. They stopped seizing commodities (which means, especially, grains) and started seizing places (which means, especially, public buildings and whole towns). And damage of machines, houses, or even persons diminished along with the self-defense which ordinarily accompanied it. The shifts in the manifest objectives of the participants trace the nationalization of collective

TABLE 19. MANIFEST OBJECTIVES OF FORMATIONS TAKING PART IN DISTURBANCES, 1845-1851

Manifest Objectives	*1845*	*1846*	*1847*	*1848*	*1849*	*1850*	*1851*
Random, Unfocused	0	1	0	3	0	0	2
Damage of Another Formation	0	2	2	42	3	4	20
Other Damage	0	3	6	25	7	0	2
Seizure or Control of Persons	0	2	1	29	6	2	2
Seizure or Control of Places	0	0	1	32	7	8	40
Seizure or Control of Commodities	0	7	32	10	1	1	0
Seizure or Control of Other or Several Kinds of Objects	4	13	12	27	4	1	32
Protesting Actions of Others	3	9	0	106	19	11	45
Other Protests: Prices, Working Conditions, Etc.	1	23	34	21	7	4	35
Demands for Specific Local Changes	3	18	31	54	4	13	9
Demands for Specific National Changes	0	1	0	21	9	0	11
Demands for General Political, Social, or Economic Change	0	0	0	25	20	0	75
Defense of Self or Own Property	7	35	64	154	36	20	116
Peacekeeping, Repression	4	26	26	114	29	17	84
Other	0	2	2	10	9	0	1
TOTAL	22	142	211	673	161	81	474
Number of Formations	11	67	91	287	72	35	204

violence and its increasing attachment to organized groups pursuing explicit political programs.

The enormous repression of 1851 and 1852, as Louis Napoleon tightened his grip on the instruments of government, drove those groups out of action for some time. Few disturbances broke through the Napoleonic controls. The few disturbances we have captured in our search of the years from 1852 through 1860 mixed old with new:

> *February 1852.* Beaumont (Puy-de-Dôme). A crowd of 200-odd people resisted the arrest of a cooper for poaching and stoned the police in the process.
>
> *August 1852.* Willer (Haut-Rhin). A group of workers gathered to protest the arrest of 17 strikers. The troops on hand arrested one of them for making an "insulting gesture." The crowd attempted to rescue him, but the troops fought them off.
>
> *January 1854.* Quimperlé (Finistère). A group of "workers, women and children" tried to block the loading of a shipment of grain, broke

windows at the house of the merchant involved, and threw stones at the gendarmes and local authorities.

February 1854. Sainghin-en-Weppes (Nord). When two tax inspectors and a police officer arrived to arrest people suspected of evading the tobacco tax, angry groups formed; the inspectors called the gendarmes, arrested a girl carrying untaxed tobacco, found themselves and the gendarmes in a battle with a crowd. The girl escaped, but they held onto two other prisoners.

August 1855. Angers (Maine-et-Loire). Slateworkers from nearby Trélazé had a run-in with gendarmes at a suburban celebration, seized arms at the local *gendarmerie*, marched on Angers, grew to about 600 (including a number of persons associated with the recently prosecuted revolutionary association "Marianne"), were met by troops of the line and dispersed without bloodshed, but not without a hundred arrests.

September 1856. Moulins (Allier). A crowd of women and children dumped the produce and burned the baskets of merchants who had been buying fruit locally and shipping it by rail to Paris.

March 1858. Chalon-sur-Saône (Saône-et-Loire). Shouting "Vive la République," about 50 armed men captured a sentry post and then went to take another military station, where a National Guard detachment stopped them and arrested 14 on the spot. The population did not heed the insurgents' call for barricades.

May 1859. Tarbes (Hautes-Pyrénées). City officials tried to collect fees from countrymen selling their goods in the city's market, encountered fierce resistance, and called gendarmes. A crowd then broke into the local military installation, seized arms and killed some of the gendarmes sent to rout them out. Cavalry, firemen, and troops of the line came in to restore order, and fired on the crowd. Altogether, nine people were killed.

These substantial conflicts took place in the midst of a larger number of disturbances too small to stay in our net: the last scattering of food riots in 1853 and 1854, continual brawls among the teams of French and Piedmontese workers building the railroads, and minor strikes which turned to violence. If the early Second Empire proceeded more calmly than the Second Republic had, it was not so much that Frenchmen had suddenly become contented or pacific, but that their will or capacity to carry on large conflicts had rapidly diminished. At the most, three of the eight incidents just described followed the modern pattern which had been emerging so fast before the 1851 coup. Furthermore, the great, reliable producers of collective violence up to that time—Paris, Lyon, Rouen, and so on—had no part in them. Until the following decade, the Napoleonic system of control was extraordinarily effective, most effective precisely where experience had taught the government that men would join for protest and common action. It was least effective out at the periphery, but actions out there were less likely to threaten the central government seriously.

Collective violence on the larger scale did not reappear in earnest until 1864; it did not achieve anything like the levels of the Second Republic until 1868. Then the mines and mills of the great industrial region of the Nord and of the Lyon-Saint-Etienne axis fostered the bulk of the violent conflict. The sanguinary strikes of 1869 in Aubin, Rive-de-Giers, le Creusot, and elsewhere demonstrated definitively that the balance had shifted away from communal, small-scale, reactionary forms of conflict. The older forms did reappear from time to time, for example in the winegrowers' rebellions after 1905 and the resistance to disestablishment of the Catholic Church about the same time. Yet from the 1860s onward, collective violence grew mainly from conflicts on the large scale, based on associations, focused on deliberately stated political and economic programs.

All this does not mean that conflict became nonviolent. Far from it. But its form and its location within French life changed fundamentally. The French experience underlines a simple, neglected verity: collective violence depends intimately on the political process, and its very nature changes as political men change their ways of organizing collective action.

APPENDIX 1

TABLE A-1. ESTIMATED INDUSTRIAL COMPOSITION OF THE FRENCH LABOR FORCE, 1840-1886 (IN THOUSANDS)

Industry	*1840-45*	*1856*	*1886*
Agriculture, Forests, Fish	7,000	7,305	7,846
Extractive Industries	105	194	253
Metals and Metalworking	305	337	630
Food	256	277	240
Chemicals	20	21	207 (Chemicals and Paper, Printing combined)
Paper, Printing	47	59	
Leather	235	261	326
Textiles	1,560	1,606	1,462
Wood	502	532	404
Stonework, Construction	474	501	745
Other	3,000	3,025	4,567
TOTAL	13,504	14,118	16,680

SOURCE: J.-C. Toutain, *La population de la France de 1700 à 1959* (Paris: Institut de Science Economique Appliquée, 1963, Cahiers de l'I. S.E.A., Serie AF, No. 3), Tables 57, 71, 115-16, 121.

TABLE A-2. DISTRIBUTION OF STRIKES BY INDUSTRY, 1830-1847 AND 1874-1889

ndustry	*1830-34*	*1835-39*	*1840-44*	*1845-47*	*1874-84*	*1885-89*
griculture, Forests, Fish	0.0	0.0	1.1	0.0	0.0	1.2
xtractive Industries	3.7	6.1	8.4	4.8	17.8 (Extractive and Metals combined)	4.7
etals and Metalworking	9.9	4.1	6.3	7.2		10.6
ood	3.7	2.0	3.2	1.2	*	2.6
hemicals	1.2	0.0	1.1	1.2	*	0.3
aper, Printing	11.1	4.1	12.6	3.6	*	2.5
eather	2.5	6.1	3.2	0.0	5.3	7.6
extiles	39.5	53.1	31.6	22.9	41.5	56.2
Vood	12.3	12.2	8.4	25.3		2.2
tone and Construction Materials	13.6	4.1	0.0	6.0	18.2	6.0
onstruction	2.5	8.2	22.1	26.5		4.6
ther	0.0	0.0	2.1	1.2	17.1*	1.7
OTAL PER CENT	100.0	100.0	100.1	99.9	99.9	100.2
Number of Strikes	81	49	95	83	696	767

* In 1874-84, Food, Chemicals, Paper, and Printing are included in Other.

SOURCES: Jean-Pierre Aguet, *Les grèves sous la Monarchie de Juillet (1830-1847)* (Geneva: Droz, 1954); Statistique Génerale de la France, *Statistique annuelle* for individual years 1885-89. The figures for 1830-47 and 1885-89 come from our classification of individual strikes, but the figures for 1874-84 come from a (probably incomplete) tabulation in *Statistique annuelle.*

APPENDIX 2

Excerpt from the General Sample Codebook

Card 82: Formation

A NOTE ON OBJECTIVES

Here the coder makes one of his riskiest judgments. An "objective" appears when participants in the disturbances act collectively toward some possible outcome (a) which they give direct evidence of seeking, especially by spoken or written statement, (b) which most observers at the time could reasonably infer from their action. Objectives immediately relevant to the action take precedence over ultimate objectives like the abolition of the state, but *among* immediately relevant objectives the broadest take precedence. For example, if a group of insurgents seize the railroad terminal, the post office, and police headquarters with the announced intention of taking over the city, the attempt to control the city takes precedence over the struggle to occupy any particular building. If two or three salient objectives appear, code them in the order of their appearance. If there are more than three and the third, fourth, and later objectives fit under the same first-digit section of the code (for example, all under 30: protest) use the general code for that category in the third set and prepare a Comment. Otherwise, choose that combination of three objectives which come closest to being "common, unified and explicitly formulated," and prepare a Comment.

Character of Objectives, Formation

Cols. 31-36

First Objective: Cols. 31-32; Second Objective: Cols. 33-34; Third and Further Objectives: Cols. 35-36

00 Insufficient information
01 Apparently random, tension-releasing, playful
02 Apparently random, brawls
03 Apparently random, direct release of hostility not classifiable below

09 Other unfocussed action: MANDATORY COMMENT

10 Damage of specific object(s), place(s), or person(s) without attempt to maintain control
- 11 Another formation (especially repressive)
- 12 Public buildings, toll barriers, other public structures
- 13 Places of work (includes offices of management but excludes machines)
- 14 Machines, tools
- 15 Utilities: railroads, telegraph lines, etc.
- 16 Commodities
- 17 Buildings owned by private persons, other than places of work
- 18 Land, standing crops

20 Control of object(s), place(s), or person(s), with or without attempt to damage
- 21 Public official or political figure
- 22 Other individuals, including bosses
- 23 Objects of symbolic significance
- 24 Commodities
- 25 Public buildings and facilities
- 26 Places of work
- 27 Places of public assembly and passage: street parks, squares, etc.
- 28 Entire commune or several communes
- 29 Entire country

30 Protest, unspecified
- 31 Of a policy or law
- 32 Of attempt to enforce policy or law (e.g. tax collection)
- 33 Of repressive actions
- 34 Of employers' actions
- 35 Of actions or presence of other person(s) or of another formation
- 36 Of prices
- 37 Of unemployment
- 38 Of working conditions, including wages
- 39 To express solidarity

40 Demand for specific changes on a local level
- 41 For exemption from a national policy
- 42 For removal of local official(s)

- 43 For price controls
- 44 For more employment (by creating more jobs, excluding competitors)
- 45 For exclusion or removal of a technical innovation
- 46 For better working conditions
- 47 For right to strike, organize, unionize

50 Demand for specific changes on a national level

- 51 For a different foreign policy
- 52 For a different domestic policy or law
- 53 For removal of national officials(s)
- 54 For economic controls
- 55 For removal or absence of economic controls
- 56 For lower taxes
- 57 For right to strike, organize, unionize

60 Demand for general changes

- 61 On local level, political and socio-economic
- 62 On local level, mainly political
- 63 On local level, mainly socio-economic
- 64 On national level, political and socio-economic
- 65 On national level, mainly political
- 66 On national level, mainly socio-economic

70 Execution of peacekeeping duties, suppression, repression

- 71 Conciliate or pacify another formation
- 72 Contain or confine another formation
- 73 Disperse another formation, no arrests
- 74 Disperse another formation, arrests
- 75 Deliberate repression, intimidation
- 76 Defend or retake terrain
- 77 Destroy another formation

80 Defense of persons and/or property

- 81 Self-defense
- 82 Defense against attack on persons in another formation
- 83 Defense of public property and places
- 84 Defense of work places
- 85 Defense of own property
- 86 Defense of other private property

ONLY USE THE 90 SERIES AS A LAST RESORT

90 Uncodable combinations: MANDATORY COMMENT

99 Other uncodable objectives: MANDATORY COMMENT

LEAVE BLANK Cols. 37-55

Cols. 56-80: PUBLIC IDENTITY OF FORMATION: ALPHABETIC

If the formation has no definite identity, leave blank. If it has a name, put it here. If it has more than one name, separate them by three spaces.

V

Congressional Elections

GERALD H. KRAMER AND

SUSAN J. LEPPER

1. Introduction

The outcome of any single election contest is the product of many factors.* Some of these influences—an unfortunate turn of phrase in a campaign speech, the weather on election day, a dramatic encounter or debate between opposing candidates—are quite accidental and specific to the election in question. Their historical importance lies in their role in helping to determine who wields the power of a particular office at a particular time. Other factors, however, are the result of more permanent structural regularities in the behavior of the electorate. To the extent that these behavioral regularities are important, they prevent election outcomes from being purely stochastic events; they "bias" the outcomes in some possibly identifiable ways.

Such structural regularities are of interest to the political scientist since they may help to explain the political dominance of particular groups in society, the electoral benefits to an incumbent of pursuing a particular policy, or the political consequences of proposed or possible changes in political structures and procedures (e.g. changes in the term of office of Congressmen or in the residence requirements for voting). Identification of such structural regularities may also help the political historian to assess the roles of social or economic developments in the evolution of the political parties, policies, or structures in the past.

This paper offers a way of formulating some hypotheses about certain structural regularities in voters' behavior and suggests some statistical models for testing the relevance of these hypotheses to Con-

* The research described in this paper was supported by grants from the National Science Foundation and the Ford Foundation. It represents an application and extension of previous work of Kramer's sponsored by the Cowles Commission for Research in Economics under Contract NONR-3055(01) with the Office of Naval Research. The authors are grateful to Norman Dean and Gary Reback for loyal and diligent research assistance.

gressional elections in the U.S. over the past half-century. The results of some preliminary statistical tests of the model are presented.

Before discussing the statistical models as such, let us briefly enumerate some key aspects of the electoral process. In a representative, partisan democracy, a candidate for Congress is offering, if elected, to serve several political roles. The most important are:

1. To serve as a member of the governing party or of the opposition. Hence, the fate of any individual candidate depends, in part, on the views of his constituents toward his party and its position or performance on issues.
2. To represent his constituents' interests and act as their intermediary with other branches of government. As such, the candidate's own effectiveness (as well as personal views and inclinations) is of interest to his constituents. And in the United States, this effectiveness is determined, in part, by a Congressman's seniority, committee assignments, and the like.

Aside from these factors related directly to the political functions of a representative, other important forces operating in an election include:

3. The socio-economic identification of the constituency with the candidates and with the parties. This in turn will depend on the location of district lines and on longer-run social and demographic trends.
4. Institutional characteristics, such as the advantages enjoyed by an incumbent (the franking privilege and low-cost access to the press, radio, and television) and the strength of party coherence (or the mechanical ease of straight-ticket voting) which confers upon weaker candidates a benefit from the "coattails" of strong candidates running on the same party slate.

The purpose of this paper is to develop some statistical models of these forces that will permit quantitative estimates of their relative importance. Section 2 develops the basic structure of the statistical model. In section 3, a highly aggregative, two-sector version of the model is applied to national election data, while section 4 reports the results of some preliminary investigations at the county level. Our results are not conclusive, but they demonstrate, we hope, the feasibility of employing this model-oriented approach to historical political data, and the utility of collecting better data to obtain more useful results. The focus of attention of the two-sector model is on the short-run response of the electorate to the effectiveness of the governing party in executing economic policy; the pull of the coattails of a strong Presidential candidate is allowed for, and the long-run shift from farm to non-farm employment is taken into consideration. The pilot studies at the local level attempt to include the importance of factors related to the effectiveness of a particular candidate in representing his constituents' special interests.

2. The Basic Model

Our starting point for constructing a model of the electorate's choice process is concern with the first factor, the effectiveness of governing teams in pursuing policies which please the constituency.

To the extent that this factor is important, Congressional elections represent a verdict on the incumbent governing team. The precise interpretation of this verdict depends on the decision rule one assumes voters to follow. One might picture the voter as a rational, information-processing individual who proceeds by collecting information of various kinds—party platforms and policy pronouncements, legislative voting records, and perhaps expert or authoritative opinions on these matters. Such a voter analyzes this information in light of his own self-interest and decides which party presents the package of positions closest to the package the voter prefers. He then votes accordingly. This view of the voting decision appears in classical democratic theory and has received extensive modern treatment by Anthony Downs, among others.[1] It has been subjected to empirical tests in various voting studies (where it generally does not fare very well).

In a more realistic setting, however, a voter—even a rational, self-interested voter—may not find it efficient to proceed in this manner. For example, there may be no relevant party or "team" platforms to compare; platforms may (indeed, usually do) concentrate on desired ends rather than specific policy proposals; voters may not feel qualified to make a confident *a priori* assessment of the relative merit of positions on subtle technical issues, or they may recognize that platforms are in no sense binding commitments. Other information, such as the detailed legislative voting records of individual candidates, may be very costly to acquire and analyze, and of only limited relevance to the issues at stake in a national campaign.

These considerations suggest that a more relevant decision rule for voters would be based on readily available information, such as the record of the incumbent party. The past performance of the incumbent

[1] Anthony Downs, *An Economic Theory of Democracy* (New York: Harper & Row, Inc., 1957).

gives some indication of what it would do if returned to office, and of the effectiveness of its policies and personnel.

With respect to short-term variations in voting behavior, we shall, therefore, assume that a decision rule of the following modified "Downsian" type is operative: if the performance of the incumbent party is "satisfactory" according to some simple standard, the voter votes to retain the incumbent governing party in office to enable it to continue its present policies; if the incumbent's performance is not "satisfactory," the voter votes against the incumbent, to give the opposition party a chance to govern. This means that each voter divides all possible policy packages into two sets, those with which he is "satisfied" and those with which he is "dissatisfied." (He need not be consciously aware of "all possible policy packages"; he need only be able to classify the package presented to him by the incumbent as belonging in one set or the other.) The sets of policies thought satisfactory by individual voters will overlap but will not be identical. The set of policies which, if pursued by the incumbent, would lead to, for example, a 20 per cent vote for the incumbent, will be a much larger set than the set leading to an 80 per cent vote.

Thus, for example, let us focus attention on policies that alter voters' personal income. If we assume (as seems reasonable) that all voters prefer higher to lower personal incomes, *ceteris paribus*, then normally the higher the value of aggregate personal income achieved by the incumbent governing team, the larger the number of "satisfied" voters. This relationship would hold with respect to any policy index about which we could assume that all voters preferred, *ceteris paribus*, a higher to a lower value—e.g. number of "successful" negotiations with foreign governments, the reading scores of children graduating from school, the speed with which snow is removed from city streets. Similarly, it may be reasonable to assume that all voters prefer, *ceteris paribus*, lower to higher values of some policy indexes, e.g. the number of American troops fighting overseas, the rate of increase in the consumer price index, urban crime rates. In these latter cases, the lower the values of the aggregate policy indexes achieved by the governing team, the larger the number of satisfied voters.

On the basis of these considerations, a simple linear statistical model can be specified as follows: consider a sequence of elections, numbered 1, 2 . . . T, which are contested by two political parties, A and B.

For election t, let

y_t be party A's share of the two-party vote;

δ_t be $+1$ if A is incumbent,
-1 if B is incumbent;

Δ_t be a measure of the differences perceived by voters between the actual level of economic prosperity during the incumbent's just-ending term in office and voters' conceptions of a minimally satisfactory "expected" level;

u_t be a random disturbance, distributed in some partially specified fashion;

α, β, V be parameters.

With these definitions, a suitable model is of the form

$$y_t = V + \delta_t [\alpha + \beta\Delta_t] + u_t \tag{1}$$

Here, the random variable u_t is interpreted as the net effect of factors not considered explicitly in the model. These include the personalities and campaign tactics of individual candidates running on the party ticket, as well as policy variables—e.g. the state of foreign affairs—which do not pertain to economic prosperity. The quantity V is the vote A would receive, in the absence of incumbency or random effects, if A's economic policies were thought to yield a minimally satisfactory, "normal" level of economic prosperity. In this sense V is a measure of the underlying basic partisanship of the electorate. The parameter β is a measure of the effect of the discrepancy, Δ_t, between actual economic conditions (which might have been highly satisfactory or unsatisfactory during the incumbent's term in office) and the "norm"; from our basic hypothesis, we should expect β to be positive. Finally, α is a measure of the institutional advantage (or disadvantage) of being incumbent.

For an election in which party A is incumbent, A will receive its base vote V, plus the net incumbency advantage α, plus the quantity $\beta\Delta_t$ which reflects the effect of its performance in office; when B is incumbent, then the vote for A will be $V - \alpha - \beta\Delta_t$, since the latter two terms associated with the incumbent now add to B's vote and detract from A's. The other factors embodied in the random term u_t also affect the vote, so that the observed relationship will actually be a scatter of points around these lines.

If we could observe Δ_t over a series of elections, and if we could make suitable assumptions about the effects of the other factors embodied in the latent variable u_t, it would be possible to fit the model to the data and estimate its parameters. In particular, if u_t satisfied the standard Gauss-Markoff assumptions, we could estimate V, α, and β from an ordinary least-squares regression. The intercept term would be an estimate of V and the coefficients of δ_t and $\delta_t\Delta_t$ would be estimates, respectively, of the advantage of incumbency (α) and of the salience of economic issues (β). However, since voters' satisfaction with any given amount of growth of personal income (or other economic variable, such as the level of unemployment or the change in consumer prices) cannot be measured directly (in the absence of suitable survey data), Δ_t cannot be used directly in regression analysis. Observable measures of the incumbent's performance are used instead but this modifies the interpretation of the regression coefficients. For instance, suppose that the rate of growth in real (price deflated) personal income ($\Delta Y = (Y_t - Y_{t-1})/Y_{t-1}$) is used as an index for economic prosperity. If the electorate expects rapid growth in this index, say 6 per cent, then extra benefit (beyond its base vote V) will accrue to the incumbent party only if it achieves income growth of more than 6 per cent; whereas income increases of 4 per cent might be advantageous to a governing team confronted with a less demanding electorate. Thus, the estimated coefficient of $\delta_t\Delta Y_t$ will, in fact, measure not only the salience of economic issues (β) but also how readily voters are satisfied by income gains. This same entwining occurs with respect to the advantage of incumbency per se (α) and the disadvantage to the incumbent of having a "difficult-to-please" constituency. The harder the electorate is to please, the more the estimated coefficient of δ_t will understate the true advantage of incumbency.[2]

[2] To be more precise, let us make the following simple and convenient hypothesis: expectations about year t are formed on the basis of experience during the preceding year, t — 1. With respect to income, for example, we might assume that income is "expected" by the average member of the electorate to grow at some constant and satisfactory "normal" rate r from year to year, and that the percentage discrepancy between actual and expected income, Y_t and $\hat{Y}_t$, in year t is an appropriate measure of Δ_t in (1). Thus, using the relation $\hat{Y}_t = (1 + r)Y_{t-1}$ to express "normal" income in terms of last year's actual income, the relation becomes

$$y_t = V + \delta_t\,[\alpha + \beta(Y_t - \hat{Y}_t)/\hat{Y}_t] + u_t$$

$$= V + \delta_t \left[\alpha + \frac{\beta}{(1+r)} \left(\frac{Y_t - Y_{t-1}}{Y_{t-1}} - r \right) \right] + u_t$$

This relation, however, contains an extra parameter, r, which is neither observable nor able to be estimated directly (i.e. the three parameters α, β, and r are not identified). If y_t is regressed simply on δ_t and $\delta_t(Y_t - Y_{t-1})/Y_{t-1}$, the coefficients of these terms will be estimates of $[\alpha - \beta r/(1 + r)]$ and $\beta/(1 + r)$, respectively. The bias, $-\beta r/(1 + r)$, in the estimate of the advantage of incumbency is unfortunate. It could well be on the order of —.01 to —.02 (if r is in the plausible range of .03 to .04 and β is in the estimated range of .4 to .6) which is large relative to the likely size of α.

Another complication which influences the choice of estimation procedures arises from the possibility of a coattails effect from higher-level races. In particular, if a candidate in a more prominent and higher-level race (e.g. for President) runs well ahead of his ticket because of his personal attractiveness and campaigning ability, some of the extra votes he wins may carry over to lower-level races, as suggested in the introduction. It is necessary to separate this effect from the portion of the vote which reflects the strength of the "team" as a whole if we wish to interpret the vote for the incumbent "team" as a verdict on its policies. Furthermore, unless the coattails effect is allowed for, the disturbances will not satisfy the standard Gauss-Markoff assumptions; the regression estimates would not be efficient nor the estimated standard errors accurate.

Because of their variety, it would be difficult to consider separately the possible effects of various statewide races on the Congressional vote; furthermore, evidence from other sources indicates that statewide factors in general (including coattail effects from statewide races) have little effect on Congressional races, compared to national or local factors.[3] In any event, we will ignore statewide races and consider only the possible influence of Presidential coattails on the Congressional vote.

The modified model then has the following form. In a midterm election, where there is no Presidential contest, the regression equation is

$$y_t^C = \beta_1 X_{1t} + \beta_2 X_{2t} + \ldots + \beta_k X_{kt} + u_t \tag{2a}$$

where y^C is the Republican share of the national Congressional vote (vote being treated as described below), and where for example $X_{1t} = 1$, to give the intercept term (V in equation (1)), X_{2t} is $+1$ if a Republican is President and -1 if a Democrat is, X_{3t} is X_{2t} times the per cent increase in per capita income, and so forth. For elections in Presidential years, we have two relations,

$$y_t^P = \beta_1 X_{1t} + \ldots + \beta_k X_{kt} + u_t + v_t\,, \tag{2b}$$

$$y_t^C = \beta_1 X_{1t} + \ldots + \beta_k X_{kt} + u_t + \gamma v_t\,, \tag{2c}$$

where y_t^P and y_t^C are the Republican shares of the vote for President and Congress, respectively. The same exogenous variables X_{it} appear in both relations, with the same coefficients β_i. The random disturbance u_t, which appears in both equations also, represents the net effect of

[3] Donald E. Stokes and Warren E. Miller, "A Variance Components Model of Political Effects" in *Mathematical Applications in Political Science*, ed. by J. L. Bernd (Dallas: Southern Methodist Univ. Press, 1965).

other unmeasured factors, such as foreign events, which affect the popularity of the party "team" as a whole. The Presidential equation (2b), however, contains a second disturbance v_t, which represents the effect of the specific candidates and campaign tactics in the Presidential race. In the Congressional equation (2c), it is assumed that a certain portion γ (where $0 \leqq \gamma \leqq 1$) of this Presidential effect is also carried over into the Congressional vote. Thus γv_t is the size of the coattail effect in election t. In order to estimate this model, the variable to be explained is defined simply as y^C in midterm election years but, for Presidential-year observations, it is defined as $(y^C - \gamma y^P)/(1 - \gamma)$. An iterative maximum likelihood procedure is then used to estimate values of γ and the other parameters.[4]

Final specification of the statistical model now requires only precise definition of the dependent variable. Difficulties arise in defining the "incumbent team" because, in the United States, party discipline is weak, different offices (President, Senator, and Congressman) are contested at different times, and the Presidency and the two Houses of Congress need not all be under the control of the same party. Individual candidates often do not behave or campaign as loyal members of a party team, and indeed some candidates campaign on the basis of their past or intended future independence of their party's leadership. However, there is considerable evidence, at least for recent times, to suggest that such factors count for very little. For example, Stokes and Miller conclude that in the 1958 midterm election, straight party loyalty was by far the major factor in the vote for Congressmen; they also found that well over half the voters did not know either House candidate in their district, and that of those who knew something about either candidate, only a negligible per cent mentioned legislative or

[4] Briefly, the disturbances are assumed to be normally (and independently) distributed, and the likelihood function is maximized in a stepwise fashion, by assuming a value for the coattails parameter γ, then obtaining conditional estimates of the other parameters and a conditional value of the likelihood function $L(\gamma)$, and then repeating with alternative values of γ until the likelihood is near its maximum. By trying enough values of γ (and spacing them closely enough), the maximizing value $\hat{\gamma}$ can be approximated as closely as desired. In obtaining the results reported below, a relatively coarse grid with a spacing of .05 was used, so that the trial γ— values were 0, .05, .10, etc. (except that when $\hat{\gamma} \angle .05$, a finer grid with a .01 spacing was used). For any assumed value of γ the conditional estimates of the remaining parameters are obtained by what is, in effect, a least-squares regression, where the dependent variable is the Congressional vote y^C in midterm observations and, in Presidential-year observations is a weighted sum of y^C and y^P, specifically $(y^C - \gamma y^P)/(1 - \gamma)$. A complete mathematical derivation is available in Gerald H. Kramer, "Short-term Fluctuations in U.S. Voting Behavior 1896-1964," *American Political Science Review*, Vol. 65, No. 1 (March 1971), pp. 131-43, hereinafter referred to as "Voting Behavior."

policy matters.[5] Although individual races may deviate from the overall pattern, in general it seems that most Congressional candidates appear to most voters simply as Democrats or Republicans, and not as clearly defined personalities with their own policy views and records. A "team" will, therefore, be defined solely in terms of formal party affiliation.

The definition of the "incumbent" party is more difficult. In 8 of the 35 national elections from 1896 to 1964, one party controlled either or both Houses of Congress, while the other controlled the Presidency. In three of these elections—1896, 1920, and 1932—the division of control was a transitory phenomenon which arose only because the President's term happened not to coincide with the beginning of the electoral tide against his party; the same party had formerly controlled all three institutions of government, and then progressively lost control of all three in the midterm and following Presidential elections. In these cases it seems quite appropriate to regard the party occupying the Presidency as the incumbent. The election of 1912, in which control was also divided, is not used in the analysis because the Republican-Progressive split in that year renders it impossible to interpret in our framework. The remaining four cases—the elections of 1948, 1956, 1958, and 1960—are more complicated, and no definition of the incumbent party seems fully satisfactory. However, even when control is divided, the President has greater control over the machinery of government, and normally has greater initiative in policy matters than does the majority party of either House of Congress. Furthermore the President is the most prominent elected official, while the identity of the party controlling the legislature is much less well known. (According to Stokes and Miller, even in the 1958 election, when the Democrats had controlled the House for four years, less than half the electorate was aware of that fact.)[6] For these reasons, we will take the party which controls the Presidency as the incumbent party.

Although the rationalization thus far presented for our model has been cast in terms of registering an affirmation verdict on the "incumbent team" by voting for it or registering a negative verdict by voting for the "opposition," various minor parties also compete in U.S. national elections and regularly manage to win a certain fraction of the vote. During the period from 1896 to 1920, minor parties usually received from 4 to 6 per cent of the total Congressional vote, and sub-

[5] Donald E. Stokes and Warren E. Miller, "Party Government and the Salience of Congress," *Public Opinion Quarterly*, 26 (Winter 1962), pp. 531-46, hereinafter referred to as "Party Government."

[6] *Ibid.*

stantially more in some elections (notably in 1912 and 1914, with the Republican-Progressive split); from 1920 to 1942 the minor-party vote was typically from 2 to 4 per cent, and since then it has generally run less than 2 per cent of the total. Although these levels are generally small, variations within the above approximate limits have often been substantial, relative to the interelection variation in the major-party vote. Hence we should try to incorporate the minor-party vote into the analysis, rather than lose information by simply ignoring it. If we interpret the minor-party vote according to our basic hypothesis, it seems appropriate to regard it as part of the anti-incumbent vote, and to count it along with the major opposition party. Hence (except where otherwise stated), when we speak of the "Republican" share of the vote, this quantity will consist of the Republican share of the total Congressional vote when the Republicans are the incumbent party, but will consist of the Republican plus minor-party share of the total vote when the Democrats are incumbent; the "Democratic" vote is treated similarly.

In previous papers, several models of this general type have been applied to aggregate Congressional election data, employing incumbency, and annual changes in the unemployment, the consumer price level, and per capita income as explanatory variables.[7] A representative version of these models and results is presented below. Let t denote time (measured in two-year intervals, beginning in 1896); R, per capita real (price deflated) personal income; P, the consumer price index; U, the per cent unemployment; and the 0, —1 subscripts denote values for the election year and the year preceding. The model and results are

$$\begin{aligned} y^C = \underset{.54}{\beta_0} + \underset{\substack{-.002 \\ (.0006)}}{\beta_1 t} + \delta\Big[\underset{\substack{-.007 \\ (.007)}}{\beta_2} + \underset{\substack{.47 \\ (.14)}}{\beta_3} \left(\frac{R_0 - R_{-1}}{R_{-1}}\right) \\ + \underset{\substack{.14 \\ (.17)}}{\beta_4} \left(\frac{P_0 - P_{-1}}{P_{-1}}\right) + \underset{\substack{.002 \\ (.003)}}{\beta_5}(U_0 - U_{-1})\Big] + u + \underset{.15}{\gamma} v \qquad (3) \end{aligned}$$

Below each coefficient in the equation is its estimated value, and below that, the estimated standard error (where available). The variance explained by this model was 64 per cent of the total (others ranged

[7] Kramer, "Voting Behavior"; Susan J. Lepper, "Voting Behavior and Aggregate Policy Targets" (paper presented at the 1968 meeting of the American Political Science Association; mimeographed).

down to 48 per cent, depending primarily on whether the trend term was included), and most of this is accounted for by the t and R terms. The t term, significant and negative in every case, indicates a pronounced trend in partisanship away from the Republicans over the period considered. The income term is significant and positive, and its magnitude indicates that a rise in income of 10 per cent would increase the incumbent party's vote share by almost 5 per cent, other things being equal. Results for the income term were very similar in the other models, irrespective of whether income was entered in current or deflated dollars. None of the other coefficients in (3) are significant. In models where income was entered in current (undeflated) dollars the P term became important, but otherwise the price and unemployment terms had no significant effects. The coattails term was insignificant (using a likelihood ratio test) so long as the minor-party vote was included in the dependent variable in the manner described previously. However, with the dependent variable defined as the Republican share of the two-party vote, which is more appropriate for estimating coattails effects, this parameter becomes significant and substantial, on the order of .3.

To summarize briefly, these simple models were surprisingly successful; they typically explained from half to two-thirds of the variance in the vote series, and did so in the manner that theory would lead one to expect: that is, price rises typically hurt the incumbent, while rises in per capita income helped. Examination of residuals and of auxiliary statistics—such as the Durbin-Watson d—reinforce the impression that the models were behaving satisfactorily.

This is not intended to imply that we believe that economic conditions alone provide a satisfactory explanation of voters' behavior. It does seem to suggest that a modified rational-choice model is helpful in explaining short-term fluctuations in the aggregate Congressional vote—fluctuations that are superimposed on long-run dynamics in party allegiance which are undoubtedly influenced by social and demographic factors. Furthermore, it does suggest that economic conditions tend to be a salient issue.

3. A Two-Sector Model

It is encouraging that even a highly aggregative model can account satisfactorily for a substantial portion of the short-term variation in national election results. However, for many purposes a more detailed disaggregated model would be more useful (provided, of course, that adequate data are available). In a given election, different sectors of the electorate may respond differently to overall economic conditions for either of two reasons. First, different sectors may be experiencing somewhat different external conditions, since national economic fluctuations do not affect all parts of the economy identically; the twenties, for example, were times of general economic prosperity, but this prosperity was not shared by farmers. Secondly, even in the face of identical economic conditions, various sectors may still react differently because of differences in their political habits, economic interests and expectations, attitudes toward uncertainty, and so on; in a disaggregated model, these differences would be reflected in separate behaviorial relations for each sector. A disaggregated model could obviously also take account of long-term changes in the composition of the electorate more readily.

Here we consider a simple two-sector disaggregation, into farm and non-farm sectors, for which some data (although not optimal) are readily available. The variables for this two-sector model, focused on the response of the electorate in Congressional elections to policies affecting economic prosperity, are defined as follows:

δ	the incumbency index $= +1$ if the incumbent President is Republican, -1 otherwise.
F	size of farm population = farm population/total population.
YF_0, YF_{-1}	monetary farm income = "Realized Net Income of Farm Operators" (U.S.D.A. definition) in current dollars, divided by total farm population, for current and preceding years.
PF_0, PF_{-1}	farm price index = index of consumer prices paid by families living on farms, for current and preceding years.
RF_0, RF_{1-}	real per capita farm income $= YF_0/PF_0, YF_{-1}/PF_{-1}$.
YNF_0, YNF_{-1}	monetary non-farm income = Personal Income less "Realized Net Income of Farm Operators," in current dollars, divided by total non-farm population, for current and preceding years.
PNF_0, PNF_{-1}	non-farm price index = consumer price index, for current and preceding years.
RNF_0, RNF_{-1}	real per capita non-farm income $= YNF_0/PNF_0, YNF_{-1}/PNF_{-1}$.

The farm data are not optimal for our purposes. The "Realized Net Income of Farm Operators" series is essentially an estimate of total income from farming (value of marketings of farm products, government payments, home consumption of farm products, plus an imputed rental value of dwellings), less total costs of production (payments to hired labor, purchases of intermediate products, rent and interest, etc.). Income to farmers from non-farm sources, and wages paid to hired farm laborers, are thus not included in the series. This income series is available as far back as 1910. (See Appendix for more complete definitions and sources.) The data used in the following analyses were for the election years from 1914 through 1964; 1912 was omitted (for reasons previously discussed) as were the war years 1918, 1942, and 1944 when rationing and price controls would distort the economic variables.

With respect to the farm sector, let y_F^C be the Republican share of the Congressional vote. Let us ignore the random disturbances for the moment and suppose the Republican farm vote could be directly observed. Then a model for the farm vote would be, for example

$$y_F^C = \beta_1 + \delta[\beta_2 + \beta_3(RF_0 - RF_{-1})/RF_{-1}]$$

A similar relation, involving non-farm income, RNF, would hold for the non-farm vote. Since, in fact, we cannot observe the farm and non-farm vote separately, it is necessary to aggregate these two relations; thus, if we weight each sector by its relative size, the total observed Congressional vote will be $y^C = Fy_F^C + (1-F)y_{NF}^C$, and the relation becomes

$$y^C = F\{\beta_1 + \delta[\beta_2 + \beta_3(RF_0 - RF_{-1})/RF_{-1}]\}$$
$$+ (1-F)\{\beta_4 + \delta[\beta_5 + \beta_6(RNF_0 - RNF_{-1})/RNF_{-1}]\} + u + \gamma v \qquad (4)$$

Provided the disturbances satisfy the same assumptions as before (which requires that unmeasured variables affect both sectors similarly), this equation is of the same form as those previously discussed and can be estimated in the same way (after rearranging some terms to eliminate linear dependencies). We consider first the response of voters to changes in per capita real (price deflated) income, equation (5). We then introduce price fluctuations into the equation and also replace real income by monetary income, thereby obtaining equations (6) and (7). The results are reported in Table 1, in which each column contains the estimated coefficients of the variables listed at the left, and the standard error of each coefficient appears below it in parenthesis.

The overall goodness of fit, as measured by the R^2, is rather good and each equation is significant. The coattails parameter (coefficient of v) while substantial, is not significant. Because the equations had

TABLE 1. REGRESSION COEFFICIENTS, STANDARD ERRORS, AND SUMMARY STATISTICS FOR FARM–NON-FARM MODEL

Variable	*Equation 5*	*Equation 6*	*Equation 7*
$(1-F)$	.436	.434	.435
$\delta(1-F)$	−.040 (.019)	−.036 (.023)	−.039 (.023)
$\delta(1-F)(RNF_0-RNF_{-1})/RNF_{-1}$	.637 (.198)	.636 (.211)	
$\delta(1-F)(YNF_0-YNF_{-1})/YNF_{-1}$			.634 (.204)
$\delta(1-F)(PNF_0-PNF_{-1})/PNF_{-1}$		−.171 (.511)	−.702 (.555)
F	.787	.795	.795
δF	.148	.136	.145
$\delta F(RF_0-RF_{-1})/RF_{-1}$	.036 (.260)	−.012 (.307)	
$\delta F(YF_0-YF_{-1})/YF_{-1}$			.012 (.295)
$\delta F(PF_0-PF_{-1})/PF_{-1}$		.419 (1.230)	.320 (1.390)
v	.25	.25	.25
R^2	.76	.76	.77
d statistic	2.56	2.64	2.58

NOTE. The dependent variable is the total vote for Republican Congressional candidates (if the President is Republican, otherwise the Republican plus minor-party vote) as a per cent of the total vote cast; this percentage is adjusted for coattails effects in Presidential election years. The economic variables, changes in income and prices, are measured in percentage terms. All percentages enter the regressions in decimal form. Thus, an increase of .01 (one percentage point) in real, per capita, non-farm income would raise the Republican share of the vote by .006 (six-tenths of 1 per cent) of the non-farm proportion of the population, compared with no change in non-farm income.

to be rearranged for estimation, the standard errors for the coefficients of the F and (1-F) terms (which measure the basic partisanship of the farm and non-farm sectors respectively) were not obtained; however, the two coefficients are significantly different from each other (the estimated standard error of the difference is .08 or .10 in all cases). The farm sector is considerably more Republican than the non-farm sector, and the progressive decrease in the relative size of the farm sector (from about 32 per cent of the population in 1914, to about 7 per cent in 1964) causes the electorate as a whole to become less Republican over time. Hence, this disaggregation accounts satisfactorily for the long-term Democratic trend in U.S. election statistics. (Indeed, the separate, farm and non-farm, partisanship coefficients and the decline in farm population would imply a coefficient of a single trend variable of .003 compared with the estimated coefficient of .002 in the aggregate relation reported in section 2 of this paper.)

A second interesting difference between the two sectors is in the coefficients of the $\delta(1\text{-}F)$ and δF terms, which are measures of the advantages of incumbency. For the non-farm sector this "advantage" is negative (though significantly so only once) and small; the most likely interpretation is that the economic expectations of non-farm voters are relatively high.[8] For the farm sector, on the other hand, the advantage is substantial, on the order of 14 per cent of the total farm vote. (The difference between the corresponding coefficients for the farm and non-farm sectors is significant at .05 in equation (5) and at .10 in (7).) In view of the great importance of price supports and other federal programs in maintaining agricultural prosperity, it may well be that farmers are indeed reluctant to sever their ties with Congressmen belonging to the party of any incumbent administration.

With respect to the economic variables themselves, the estimates for the non-farm sector are of the proper signs (though the price coefficients are not significant), but the results for the farm sector are poor; neither price nor income fluctuations for that sector have any significant effect on the vote. To some extent, this result may have occurred because of statistical problems. Errors in measurement are probably greater for the farm variables, biasing the corresponding coefficients toward zero. As indicated previously, the "realized net income of farm operators" series is not ideal since it omits wages of hired farm labor and income from non-farm sources. The reliability of the farm price index is also open to question, since it is based on mailed replies from voluntary reporters. Furthermore, the farm series are intercorrelated with the corresponding non-farm series.

In addition, it is quite possible that different behavioral relations may apply to the farm and non-farm sectors, as previously mentioned. More specifically, farmers may not hold the government responsible for short-term fluctuations in income resulting primarily from weather and other exogenous factors influencing crops. Instead, they may respond politically to longer-run trends in farm income which would more appropriately reflect general prosperity and specific agricultural

[8] Cf. p. 261 above.

policies. This behavior might be captured statistically by the introduction of lagged values, or moving averages of past values, of economic variables in the regressions. Introduction of lagged values, or moving averages, of economic variables in the one-sector aggregate relation previously described did not contribute to the explanatory power of the regression. For much of the time period under consideration, however, the non-farm sector was large enough for its responses to short-run economic fluctuations to dominate the statistical relation. Similarities between the results, in Table 1, for the non-farm sector and some of Kramer's results for the aggregate one-sector model suggest that this is the case. Without experimenting directly with different specifications for the farm and non-farm sectors, it is impossible to infer the nature of the differences in the voting responses of the two sectors to economic conditions.

Other studies have also considered the effect of farm prosperity on election returns. The study by Rees *et al.* investigated the relationship between net income per farm and the Republican vote, by states, for 1946-1958; they found no relation whatever, which is certainly compatible with our results.[9] V. O. Key, Jr., on the basis of a visual comparison of movements in per capita farm income and the Republican vote, suggests that a fairly strong relationship does exist;[10] however, farm income is highly correlated with national income, so his evidence does not really establish an independent farm-income effect. Nonetheless, agrarian political revolt has been a recurrent feature of American political history, and it is well known that farmers, today, are highly organized and informed politically. Furthermore, much of the focus of their political activity is on economic matters. This suggests that a more complex model, estimated with better data, should be able to capture the political process at work.

4. Experimental County-Level Studies

The earlier work mentioned above and the preceding section of this paper point to definite linkages between economic prosperity and the response of the electorate (at least, the non-farm electorate) toward the governing team. However, further questions about the influence of economic prosperity upon voters can be best explored at a still more disaggregative level. For example, does the electorate, in fact, attribute prosperity to the governing team led by the President or does it at-

[9] Albert Rees *et al.*, "The Effect of Economic Conditions on Congressional Elections 1946-58," *Review of Economics and Statistics*, 44 (November 1962), pp. 458-65.

[10] V. O. Key, Jr., *Politics, Parties and Pressure Groups* (3rd ed.; New York: Crowell, 1952), pp. 211, 591.

tribute these benefits to its own Congressman? Apart from the apparent differences between farm and non-farm areas, are there discernible differences in the influences of economic conditions among regions differing in industrial base (heavy industrial, light industrial, commercial, and raw material producing areas)? These considerations invite the application to local data of the model which seemed to be fruitful at the national level.

In addition to these questions, other possible influences on voters can be considered only at the local level. These influences include the characteristics of particular Congressional candidates in individual races (influences which are assumed to cancel each other out in the national aggregate). Among such interesting, and measurable, characteristics are the incumbency, seniority, and leadership status of a candidate. The incumbent candidate with accumulated seniority and holding a leadership position in Congress could be expected to have an advantage in an election. As suggested in the introduction, his status could be viewed as an asset by voters with favors to gain in Washington. His prestige might also command greater loyalty from his party and would almost certainly gain him greater publicity during his campaign. And, to the extent that his incumbency was associated with recent success by his party, he might enjoy a more favorable position on the ballot. On the other hand, visibility is not always an asset for a candidate. If a committee chairmanship had forced the candidate to take a position on a controversial issue, or led to increased remoteness from his constituency, alleged assets could readily become liabilities. Thus, the influence of such measurable characteristics of candidates on the electorate is likely to be more variable across time and locality than would be expected of economic conditions or other potentially salient issues.

The extent to which incumbency, seniority, and leadership status have systematic positive influences on voters, of course, has significant implications for the operation of the political mechanism. If these factors are important, the system will have some degree of inherent inertia. The average length of service of members of Congress will be longer (as it has been in this century when seniority rules have been in force in Congress), and the composition of Congress will change more slowly. Congressmen will acquire more expertise in the subjects within the jurisdiction of their committees; successful policies may be built upon more systematically, but policy errors may be acknowledged more slowly since the personal prestige of still incumbent Congressmen will be at stake. The possibility of split control between the Congress and the White House is increased. These considerations provide additional reasons for pursuing statistical analysis of voting patterns at the local level.

When focusing on characteristics of Congressional candidates in particular elections, the Congressional district would be a natural unit to use for data collection and analysis. It is the largest area that could be used if one is to avoid the possibility of serious measurement error in constructing indexes of seniority and the like. Because boundaries of Congressional districts are redrawn as population shifts, however, time series analysis cannot be done using the Congressional district as the basic unit, and we have chosen to work instead with county data. County lines are rarely redrawn, and both Presidential and Congressional election results are available on a county basis in many states' archives.

In this pilot study only four counties are considered, and there is no reason to believe that they are particularly representative. An effort was made to select both rural and urban counties, but it was also necessary to choose counties in states where adequate data were available, and which were never (during the sample period, 1896-1964) split between two or more Congressional districts. Counties in densely populated urban areas (e.g. New York City) or in rapidly growing metropolitan areas in the north-central region and on the West Coast have been the most frequently redistricted and are the most likely to contain, or be split among, more than one district. Hence, counties from such areas were not included. The frequency of uncontested elections in some parts of the South also excluded that region.

The counties used in this study are listed in Table 2 which indicates certain of their characteristics in 1960 in comparison with correspond-

TABLE 2. DEMOGRAPHIC CHARACTERISTICS OF REGIONS

rea	*Per Cent Urban Popula-tion*	*Per Cent Negro Popula-tion*	*Per Cent Foreign Stock*	*Per Cent White-Collar Employ-ment*	*Median Income (in $)*	*Per Cent Under $3,000*	*Per Cent Over $10,000*
llegheny, N.Y.	20	0.2	9	38	4,828	26	8
nondaga, N.Y. (contains Syracuse)	81	2.8	27	49	6,691	11	20
niata, Pa.	0	0.1	1	31	4,062	32	4
orthampton, Pa. (contains part of Bethlehem industrial complex)	69	1.1	25	32	5,709	14	11
nited States	70	10.5	19	41	5,660	21	15

ing statistics for the United States as a whole. The table shows that, by omitting major metropolitan areas, we are not only omitting consideration of the possible peculiarities of metropolitan politics as such but are also underrepresenting Negroes, the urban poor, the white-collar professional or office worker, and the urban rich.

A second limitation of this study arises from the difficulty of finding accurate indexes of economic prosperity, for small regions, for the entire 1896-1964 time span under consideration. (As before, the elections of 1912, 1918, 1942, and 1944 were omitted.) Some tentative efforts to use local economic data are discussed below.

New variables were introduced into our basic, modified-rational-choice model to take into account the potential effectiveness of candidates in representing their constituents and possible local institutional effects. These were:

I, Congressional incumbency
= +1 if a Republican incumbent is standing for reelection,
= −1 if a Democrat incumbent is standing, and
= 0 if no incumbent is running;

S, seniority,
= 0 if no incumbent is running, or if the incumbent has served only only one term or less,
= the number of consecutive terms of service beyond the first, if the incumbent has served more than one term;

L, a "leadership" variable,
= 1 if the incumbent has a major leadership position in the House (Speaker, Whip, or a committee chairmanship), or if he is a member of Rules, Ways and Means, or Appropriations Committees,
= 0 otherwise.

In order to take into account, in a simple way, the possible effect of demographic shifts on the partisanship of the county, a linear time trend was also added. Thus, elections were numbered sequentially with the variable t equaling 1 in 1896, 2 in 1900, . . . and 35 in 1964.

A simple model to estimate the effects of incumbency, seniority, and leadership is

$$y^C = \beta_0 + \delta[\beta_1 + \beta_2 \Delta R] + I[\beta_3 + \beta_4 S + \beta_5 L] + \beta_6 t$$

where y^C is the Republican share of the Congressional vote for the county in question, δ and $\Delta R = \left(\frac{R_0 - R_{-1}}{R_{-1}}\right)$ are defined as before, and I, S, and L are the incumbency, seniority, and leadership variables.

β_3 is the advantage arising from being incumbent, β_4 is the additional effect (per term of service) of seniority, and β_5 is the additional advantage resulting from holding a leadership position. The coefficients of the other terms are interpreted as in the preceding sections.

Economic conditions and the Presidential incumbency variable affect the Congressman primarily in his role as a member of, or opponent of, the incumbent Presidential "team." In estimating the effects of these variables, the dependent variable used previously—in which the minor-party vote is interpreted as part of the vote against the incumbent "team"—is probably still the most appropriate. However, for estimating institutional advantages to the individual Congressman, from his personal incumbency, this definition of the dependent variable is no longer appropriate; probably the best that can be done for these purposes is to ignore the minor-party candidates and analyze only the major-party vote. Since we are interested in both "team" and individual variables, the regressions reported below have been run using both definitions of the Republican vote share. y_1 is the definition used previously: the Republican share of the total Congressional vote in the county when a Republican is President, the Republican plus minor-party shares otherwise; y_2 is the Republican share of the major-party Congressional vote in the county.

The possibility of a Presidential "coattails effect" (as discussed above) must also be considered. In the national aggregate regressions initially estimated by Kramer, the value of the coattail parameter, γ, was found to be significant only when y_2 was the dependent variable.[11] Adjustment for the coattail effect is therefore omitted in the county regressions using y_1, but is included in the y_2 regressions.[12]

[11] Kramer, "Voting Behavior."

[12] In Presidential-year elections, the Congressional and Presidential relations are

$$y^C = \beta_0 + \beta_1\,\delta\Delta R + \beta_2 IS + u + \gamma v, \text{ and}$$

$$y^P = \beta_0 + \beta_1\,\delta\Delta R \qquad\quad + u + \;v$$

Multiplying the Presidential relation by γ, subtracting it from the Congressional relation, and dividing the result by $(1 - \gamma)$ yields

$$\frac{y^C - \gamma y^P}{(1-\gamma)} = \beta_0 + \beta_1\,\delta\Delta R + \beta_2 \frac{IS}{(1-\gamma)} + u$$

To correct for the coattails effect, γ is assumed to be a known parameter, whose value in each county is .3, the value estimated for the nation as a whole; thus the dependent variable for each Presidential-year observation is $(y^C - .3y^P)/.7$, and the "local" independent variables (e.g., IS) are also transformed by dividing by .7. No correction is needed in midterm years; the dependent variable is y^C, and the independent variables those appearing in the Congressional relation above, untransformed. Estimates of the β's are obtained by least-squares regressions over all observations.

Representative results for individual counties are reported in Tables 3 and 4. One purpose of these regressions is to check the consistency of results at a lower level of aggregation with the national results. For this reason, the same key economic variables (changes in national per capita personal income, in current dollars, and in the national consumer price index) were used in these regressions as had been used earlier. The presence of "local" variables included in these regressions should not distort comparisons between the implications of the local and national regressions for the response of the electorate to national economic conditions.

TABLE 3. REGRESSION COEFFICIENTS, STANDARD ERRORS, AND SUMMARY STATISTICS WITH DEPENDENT VARIABLE y_1

Regression Variable	*Allegheny*	*Onondaga*	*Juniata*	*Northampton*
V	.621	.592	.499	.404
T	.004 (.002)	.000 (.001)	.002 (.001)	.002 (.003)
δ	—.013 (.016)	—.023 (.014)	.013 (.015)	.048 (.020)
I	.023 (.065)	.003 (.036)	.015 (.044)	—.032 (.030)
I·L	.097 (.042)	—.047 (.033)	.006 (.036)	.013 (.046)
I·S	—.007 (.004)	—.006 (.007)	.000 (.007)	.006 (.006)
$\delta(\Delta Y)$	.580 (.217)	.037 (.204)	.191 (.233)	.264 (.269)
$\delta(\Delta P)$	—1.185 (.446)	—.208 (.410)	—.560 (.440)	—1.012 (.561)
R^2	.440	.300	.163	.249
d	1.833	1.282	1.213	1.730

The percentages of the variance in the vote "explained" by these regressions are substantially lower than in the case of the aggregate regressions, despite the inclusion of the local incumbency, seniority, and leadership terms. This is not surprising, since many idiosyncrasies of individual races (the personalities of the particular candidates involved, local issues and events, local party structure, and so forth), will be relatively more important at the county level and are still not taken into account explicitly in these models. Moreover, deviations between national and local economic trends may be obscuring part of the voters' response to economic conditions.

Nevertheless, all of the coefficients for the prosperity terms (change in per capita income and in cost of living) in Table 3, and all except one in Table 4, are of the proper sign; some are significant.

In order to test whether responsibility for economic conditions is attributed by voters to their individual Congressman, rather than to the Presidential team, a variation of these regressions was also estimated. For this purpose, the dependent variable y_1 was used, and the terms $I(\Delta Y)$ and $I(\Delta P)$ were substituted for $\delta(\Delta Y)$ and $\delta(\Delta P)$. Multi-

TABLE 4. REGRESSION COEFFICIENTS, STANDARD ERRORS, AND SUMMARY STATISTICS WITH DEPENDENT VARIABLE y_2

Regression Variable	*Allegheny*	*Onondaga*	*Juniata*	*Northampton*
V	.568	.602	.482	.359
T	.005 (.002)	.001 (.001)	.002 (.001)	.004 (.003)
δ	.003 (.017)	.016 (.014)	.013 (.016)	.069 (.024)
I	.099 (.053)	–.014 (.028)	.046 (.033)	–.032 (.030)
I·L	.082 (.036)	–.021 (.028)	–.007 (.029)	.022 (.050)
I·S	–.010 (.003)	–.002 (.006)	–.004 (.006)	.007 (.007)
$\delta(\Delta Y)$	.622 (.233)	–.108 (.209)	.114 (.235)	.171 (.330)
$\delta(\Delta P)$	–.745 (.481)	–.094 (.412)	–.478 (.445)	–.877 (.680)
R^2	.466	.107	.224	.286
d	2.254	1.579	.976	1.651

plying the economic prosperity term by the *local* incumbency index means that a good economic performance aids an incumbent Republican Congressman (or hurts the Republican Congressional candidate if he is running against a Democratic incumbent) regardless of the Presidential incumbency. All of the eight coefficients of the prosperity terms were insignificant and, in three of the four county regressions, at least one of these coefficients was not of the proper sign. These negative results lend further support to the basic framework we have been using, interpreting Congressional elections in terms of rival Presidential "teams" of which the Congressional candidates are nominal members.

Tentative steps were also taken to determine whether voters are markedly more sensitive to local economic developments than to national trends. Several crude indexes of local economic conditions were spliced together for a shorter time span (1930 through 1964, omitting 1942 and 1944). These indexes were based, for the earlier years, on a local (Syracuse) chamber of commerce measure of fluctuations in employment in the case of Onondaga, and on Pennsylvania State Government records of county production in the case of Northampton and Juniata. In these cases, the series were extended by splicing them to the U.S. Department of Commerce measures of personal income in the respective states. For Allegheny County, the Department of Commerce statistics of state (New York) personal income earned on farms (wages of agricultural production workers plus farm profits) were used. Several variations of the basic regression model were estimated in order to consider the explanatory power of these very imperfect indexes of local prosperity in comparison with the national indexes. In all cases, regressions based on the local indexes were markedly inferior. The extreme inadequacy of the local indexes, however, undermines any possible conclusions. In order to achieve a strong test of the responsiveness of local constituencies to local economic developments, better measures of local prosperity, consistent across regions, should be obtained for a much larger number of regions. Techniques could then be devised for applying the same regression model to the pooled cross section of time series.

As far as incumbency effects are concerned, both tables show the advantage of membership in the Presidential team (the coefficient of δ) to be small and insignificant (as it was at the national level) everywhere except Northampton County. The advantages from a Congressman's own incumbency (I) appear to be larger in both Allegheny and Juniata counties, when the preferable dependent variable y_2 is used. With this dependent variable, however, the coefficients of the Congressional incumbency term (I) have unexpected negative signs in the other two counties. The leadership term $(I \cdot L)$ is significant and positive, as expected, in Allegheny County; elsewhere, however, it is often of the wrong sign (though never significant). The effects of seniority (the coefficients of $I \cdot S$) are, surprisingly, not positive (Northampton is again the exception) and the significantly negative coefficient in Allegheny County suggests that seniority is a handicap there for a Congressional candidate.

In interpreting these results, certain statistical problems must be kept in mind. The partisanship of the electorate in these counties was strong; this is most clearly indicated by the relatively high and low values, respectively, of the intercept terms for Allegheny County and Northampton County. In fact, in three cases, the Republican "bias" was strong enough to maintain Republicans in Congress a large proportion of the time and, in the fourth county, Democrats held the Congressional seat continuously during the later half of the sample period. In such circumstances, the incumbency effect is difficult to distinguish from the partisanship of the electorate (the corresponding variables are highly correlated). Intercorrelations among the seniority and leadership terms and the time trend are a further problem.

One way of avoiding the entangling of incumbency with patisanship, and seniority with the time trend in partisanship, is to alter the model so that it is unnecessary to include the intercept and t terms. Let us assume, as we did earlier, that the partisanship of the electorate and the indexes of economic prosperity enter with the same coefficients in the Congressional and Presidential relations. Then, in Presidential years, the Presidential relation,

$$y^P = \beta_0 + \beta_1\delta + \beta_2\delta\,(\Delta R) + \beta_6 t + u + v\,,$$

can be subtracted from the Congressional relation,

$$y^C = \beta_0 + \beta_1\delta + \beta_2(\Delta R) + \beta_3 I + \beta_4 IS + \beta_5 IL + \beta_6 t + u + \gamma v\,,$$

to give $y^C - y^P = y_3 = \beta_3 I + \beta_4 IS + \beta_5 IL + (\gamma - 1)v$. ($y_3$ is defined in terms of the Republican share of the major-party vote. Although minor-party voters might be influenced by the seniority and leadership of a candidate, this influence will be independent of the concept of Presidential incumbent and opposition teams used in the definition of y_1.) Estimation with this model has the disadvantage of losing information from midterm elections, but it does ameliorate part of the collinearity problem. Furthermore, by suppressing the error term, u, which represents the effects of omitted variables that almost certainly affect many counties in similar ways in a single election, it opens the possibility of pooling the observations for all four counties in a cross section of time series. The use of pooled data to estimate the relation

$$y_{3,\,i,\,t} = \beta_3 I_{i,\,t} + \beta_4 I_{i,\,t}\, S_{i,\,t} + \beta_5 I_{i,\,t}\, L_{i,\,t} + (\gamma - 1)v_{i,\,t}$$

(where i indicates the county and t indicates the election) reduces the possible intercorrelation of I, S, and L.[13]

[13] The occasional low values of the Durbin-Watson d statistic in the single-county results (most are in the inconclusive region) suggest possible autocorrelation of residuals and need for improvement of the specification. In view of the

Table 5 presents the results from estimating the relation for y_3 for each county separately and for the pooled data from all four counties. The results from the regressions of form (a) tend to support the tentative suggestion from the preceding tables that incumbency is an advantage for a Congressional candidate but that this advantage does not grow with added terms of seniority. Neither does leadership status appear to be any real advantage to an incumbent. The coefficient of the seniority term, in the regressions where it appears in Table 5, is consistently small and significantly different from zero only in one single-county result where it has a counterintuitive negative value. Similarly, in the regressions of form (b) where the seniority term is omitted, the coefficient of the leadership term is not of the expected sign in three of the four single-county results, nor in the pooled regression; in Juniata and Allegheny counties, leadership status actually

TABLE 5. REGRESSION COEFFICIENTS, STANDARD ERRORS, AND SUMMARY STATISTICS WITH DEPENDENT VARIABLE y_3

Regression Variable	*Allegheny* (a)	(b)	*Onondaga* (a)	(b)	*Juniata* (a)	(b)	*Northampton* (a)	(b)	*Pooled* (a)	(b
I	.128 (.041)	.121 (.046)	−.025 (.030)	.000 (.019)	.063 (.032)	.045 (.026)	.043 (.053)	.043 (.038)	.036 (.018)	.03 (.01
I·L	−.012 (.059)	−.087 (.054)	−.039 (.057)	−.052 (.056)	−.070 (.032)	−.067 (.032)	.038 (.143)	.038 (.085)	−.023 (.026)	−.02 (.02
I·S	−.010 (.005)		.009 (.008)		−.007 (.007)		.000 (.012)		−.001 (.003)	
R^2	.536	.370	.145	.066	.289	.233	.149	.149	.072	.07
d	1.335	1.446	1.575	1.208	2.034	2.066	1.107	1.107	1.784	1.79

appears to be a hindrance to a candidate. The coefficient of the incumbency term, on the other hand, has the expected sign in three of the four single-county regressions and in the pooled regressions. The positive coefficients of the incumbency term are marginally significant[14] in two of the four counties; the incumbency coefficients in the pooled regression have the same significance level while the negative coefficients in the results for Onondaga are not significant.

fact that many important influences on county election outcomes are obviously omitted, leading to the poor fit of our regressions, this is not surprising. The value of the d statistic for the results from pooled data in Table 5, however, implies that correlation of residuals among counties may not be a serious problem for this model despite the obvious possibility of intercorrelation among the $v_{i,\ t}$ terms.

[14] At the .05 level in a one-tail test.

A paper by Kain and Ries provides interesting comparisons and contrasts with the results just described.[15] They also focus on the possible influence of incumbency and seniority on voters' choices and, in an empirical analysis of 1962 data from 38 California Congressional districts, find that incumbency is a marked advantage to a Congressional candidate. Indeed, they find that the incumbent standing for reelection can expect to gain a lead over the opposition amounting to 10 per cent of the partisan vote, which is a rather larger advantage than indicated by most of our results. The conclusions presented in Tables 3, 4, and 5 regarding seniority are also supported in the Kain and Ries study; they found it had essentially no effect.

In contrast to our study which relies heavily on time series data and which includes consideration of the voters' response to short-term fluctuations in economic prosperity (in a modified rational-choice model), Kain and Ries use cross-section data exclusively and also consider the relationship between partisanship and more slowly changing socio-economic characteristics of the electorate. From a historical point of view, analysis of political grouping and regrouping around party labels, of the waxing and waning of a party's dominance and of the policy positions adopted by a party all seem to require a merging of the approaches advanced in the Kain and Reis paper and in ours.

[15] John F. Kain and John C. Ries, "Congressmen, Incumbency and Elections," Cambridge: Harvard Univ., 1967. (Mimeographed.)

APPENDIX

THE PRIMARY data sources used for the national data were *Historical Statistics of the United States* (1957), and *Statistical Abstract of the United States*, various issues. These two sources will be referred to as *HSUS* and *SAUS*, respectively, in this appendix. Sources of county data were the Census Bureau's *City and County Data Book*, Decennial Census of Population reports, *Congressional Directories*, and legislative manuals for the relevant states. The data series were obtained as follows:

National election returns and incumbency. For 1896-1948, from *HSUS*, pp. 686-89, 691-92. For 1950-1964, *SAUS* (1966), p. 368.

County election returns. From legislative manuals, for the appropriate years: for New York, *Manual for the Use of the Legislature of the State of New York*; for Pennsylvania, *Small's Legislative Manual*, prior to 1922 and *The Pennsylvania Manual* subsequent to 1922 (our gratitude is due to Professor Samuel Hays of the University of Pittsburgh for locating election statistics for 1922).

Population. Total population for 1895-1940 from *HSUS*, p. 7 (values prior to 1899 obtained by linear interpolation between 1889 and 1899 figures); for 1941-1964, *SAUS* (1966), p. 616. Farm population for 1910-1940, from *HSUS*, p. 15 for 1941-1964, *SAUS* (1966), p. 616.

Income. Personal income (Department of Commerce concept) for 1929-1964 from Department of Commerce, *Survey of Current Business* (August 1965), pp. 32-33; for 1919-1928, *HSUS*, p. 139. Prior to 1919, based on GNP figures from Kendrick,[16] *Productivity Trends in the United States*, pp. 298-99, proportionately reduced to agree with the 1919 personal income value and converted to current dollars with implicit GNP deflators taken from Friedman and Schwartz,[17] *A Monetary History of the United States*, Chart 62.

The "Realized Net Income of Farm Operators" was computed by treating

> "agriculture as one tremendous enterprise, . . . first computing 'gross income' . . . , and then deducting aggregate expenses of production . . .

[16] John W. Kendrick, *Productivity Trends in the United States* (Princeton: Princeton Univ. Press, 1961), pp. 298-99.

[17] Milton Friedman and A. J. Schwartz, *A Monetary History of the United States, 1897-1960* (Princeton: Princeton Univ. Press, 1963), Chart 62.

realized gross farm income . . . represents total cash farm income [i.e., total cash receipts from all farm marketing, including Government payments to farmers], the values of farm-produced food and fuel consumed in farm households, and an imputed rental value for all farm dwellings. Total farm production expenses comprise the aggregate cost to farm operators [including] . . . wages paid for hired labor . . . purchases of feed, livestock, fertilizer . . . outlays for the operation of tractors, trucks [etc.] . . . interest . . . on farm-mortgage loans . . . net rents paid to landlords not living on farms. . . . The figures for realized net income of farm operators are obtained by subtracting total production expenses from realized gross farm income" (*HSUS*, p. 264).

Figures for 1910-1957 from *HSUS*, p. 283; for 1958-1961, *SAUS* (1962), p. 630; for 1962-1964, *SAUS* (1966), p. 616.

Prices. For 1913-1964, the series is the Bureau of Labor Statistics Consumer Price Index, from *SAUS* (1966), p. 356.

"This index . . . measures the average change in prices of goods and services purchased by city wage-earner and clerical-worker families. . . . The weights used in calculating the index are based on studies of actual expenditures by wage earners and workers" (*SAUS* [1966], pp. 349-50; cf. also *HSUS*, pp. 109-10).

For 1895-1912, the Federal Reserve Bank of New York cost-of-living index was used. This index

"was obtained by splicing together parts of indexes already available to approximate a single series. No adjustments were made to the original series other than those necessary to convert to a common base period. . . . For 1890-1909, Paul Douglas' 'most Probable Index of the Total Cost of Living for Workingmen' . . . was used. Indexes for 1910-1912 were derived from the cost-of-living index for Massachusetts . . ." (*HSUS*, p. 111).

Figures were obtained from *HSUS*, p. 127, and adjusted to the same base period as the BLS series described above.

For the farm sector, the Department of Agriculture's index of prices paid by farmers for family living was used. Conceptually, this index is similar to the BLS consumer price index, except that

"the consumer price index includes rents and other services and the farm index does not, and . . . the list of commodities included in the two indexes and their geographical coverage differ because farm family buying differs considerably from that of city families" (*SAUS* [1966], p. 350).

Moreover the farm index is based largely on mail reports from some 35,000 voluntary reporters, whereas most of the prices used in computing the BLS series are obtained from surveys by BLS field representatives. The farm price index for 1910-1957 was obtained from *HSUS*, p. 283; for 1958-1961, from *SAUS* (1962), p. 632; and for 1962-1964, from *SAUS* (1966), p. 632.

Unemployment. As a per cent of civilian labor force:

> "Prior to 1940, these figures represent estimates of unemployment on as comparable a basis to current labor force concepts as is presently possible. . . . Unemployment is calculated as a residual. That is, estimates are first made of the civilian labor force, then of employment; the difference between the two provides the estimates of unemployment" (*HSUS*, p. 68).

After 1940, the unemployment figures are based on field surveys. The figures for 1900-1939 were taken from *HSUS*, p. 73 (prior to 1900, set equal to the 1900-1903 average); for 1946-1961, from *SAUS* (1962), p. 215; and for 1962-1964, from *SAUS* (1966), p. 218.

VI

Some Dimensions of Power in the Thirty-Seventh Senate

ALLAN G. BOGUE

I

"ON coming on any form of organized activity," wrote John Kenneth Galbraith, "—a church, platoon, government bureau, congressional committee, a house of casual pleasure—our first instinct is to inquire who is in charge."[1] The concept of power both fascinates and frustrates the scholar.[2] Its complex foundations and its varied manifestations, both crude and subtle, provide the social analyst with almost endless opportunities for speculation and theoretical formulation. Deceptively easy to explain in simple terms, it is often extremely difficult to study in practice. Men who wield it sometimes conceal the fact; others who occupy positions adorned with the trappings of power may in the end be revealed as hollow men or puppets. Yet the fact remains that some men have the will and skill and resources to influence men and events to a greater degree than others. The discussion of power is, of course, most useful when it helps us to explain why particular decisions were made and why events took the course that they did. We take an essential step in this direction if we can clarify the power structure of any social or political system which we are studying. This paper is a modest effort to discuss some of the dimensions of personal

[1] John Kenneth Galbraith, *The New Industrial State* (Boston: Houghton Mifflin, 1967), p. 47.

[2] The literature on the subject of power, influence, and leadership is voluminous. Robert A. Dahl provides a short summary and introductory bibliography in his article, "Power," *International Encyclopedia of the Social Sciences* (1968), pp. 405-15. See also James G. March, "The Power of Power," in David Easton, ed., *Varieties of Political Theory* (Englewood Cliffs, N.J.: Prentice-Hall, Inc., 1966), pp. 39-70. During the preparation of this paper, I benefited also from reading Terry N. Clark's unpublished paper, "The Sixteen Faces of Power," and from a series of lectures on "Political Power and Elites," presented by Lee Benson in a graduate proseminar at the University of Wisconsin, which he conducted in association with J. Rogers Hollingsworth and myself during the academic year, 1967-68. A number of useful readers have been published recently, and I particularly regret that *Political Power: A Reader in Theory and Research*, ed. by Roderick Bell, David V. Edwards, and R. Harrison Wagner (New York: Free Press of Glencoe, 1969) did not appear until after my research for this paper was completed.

power in the Senate of the Thirty-Seventh Congress, the first to sit during the American Civil War and one whose members passed a great deal of important legislation.

The member of Congress, as a member of that body, may exercise power by obtaining or blocking legislation, by obtaining honors, positions, or contracts for allies, friends, and constituents, by influencing the behavior of members of the executive branch of the government, and in various other ways. Obviously, activity of one sort may be related to other kinds of effort. If one grand power quotient could be prepared for each legislator, it would subsume the myriad ways in which he influenced the activity of others. In this paper, however, the legislative process is our primary concern, although I will mention some of the other aspects of power when they seem relevant.

Who would the members of the Thirty-Seventh Senate have most frequently mentioned, if asked the identity of their most powerful colleague? We can, I believe, make a strong case for William Pitt Fessenden of Maine.[3] In the first place he was the chairman of the Finance Committee, regarded during the Middle Period of American history as a highly important Senate committee. This was the group which considered the appropriation bills sent to the Senate by the House of Representatives, presenting recommendations for change to the senior chamber and shaping its discussion of appropriations matters generally. During the generation before the outbreak of the Civil War, the tariff had become a focal point of sectional differences, and the chairman of the Finance Committee was in a strategic position to mediate Senate policy on this issue. War of course brought fiscal problems of major magnitude and made the labors of the committee more crucial still.

Individuals may fail to develop the power inherent in their offices or discredit them by laziness, ineptitude, or gaucherie. Neither the *Congressional Globe* nor Fessenden's correspondence suggests that the senator from Maine was of that stripe. The letters to his family tell of unremitting and arduous labor which brought him to the verge of complete exhaustion.[4] In the columns of the *Globe*, Senator James A. Mc-

[3] The standard biographies of Fessenden are Francis Fessenden, *Life and Public Services of William Pitt Fessenden* (2 vols.; Boston: Houghton, Mifflin & Co., 1907) and Charles A. Jellison, *Fessenden of Maine: Civil War Senator* (Syracuse, N.Y.: Syracuse Univ. Press, 1962).

[4] The major collection of William Pitt Fessenden's papers is in the Bowdoin College Library, Brunswick, Maine. I have read the microfilmed copies of these papers in the collections of the Wisconsin Historical Society, through the courtesy of the Hawthorne-Longfellow Library, Bowdoin College, and quotations in this text are made pursuant to the instructions contained in a letter from Arthur Monke, Acting Librarian to Allan G. Bogue, December 15, 1966. All Fessenden

Dougall described him as an intimidating figure while he presided at committee hearings, guarding the treasury suspiciously from the representatives of special interests who laid their selfish demands before him.[5] Disagreeing with Fessenden as to the basic principles of the Internal Revenue bill, Senator James F. Simmons asserted that if he "agrees to anything, almost everybody else will."[6] Defending one of the interest groups in his state, Ira Harris of New York fumed, "I confess I am surprised at the tenacity with which all these little provisions are to be insisted upon by the Senator who represents the Committee on Finance, and the tenacity with which his views are supported by the Senate."[7]

During the last weeks of the second session, Fessenden's position as Finance Chairman gave him a unique opportunity to influence the legislative process. As the session dragged through June and into July, the Democratic senators became increasingly restive, threatening to leave and deprive the Senate of a quorum. In mid-June, Fessenden explained the crucial significance of his role in completing the legislative program of the Republicans:

> The tax bill is in the hands of a Committee of Conference, & will be wound up in a day or two. All my other bills will be wound up, or might be, in two weeks, but there are two or three important measures to be finished, and I must keep one of my bills behind them in order to secure sufficient time for their passage.[8]

We see, therefore, in Fessenden a senator who not only occupied a most important committee chairmanship, but a man who understood how to use that position to further the broader legislative designs of his party. Sometimes Fessenden was willing to admit that he was uniquely qualified to hold his position, writing, during the course of the special summer session of this Congress, ". . . there is much in my hands which cannot be so well done by another."[9]

If power may rest in the hands of men in strategic or prestigious positions, the opinions of contemporaries may also guide us to its locus. Fessenden himself provided some testimony on this score when he told of the Maine man who sought his aid in obtaining a place for his

---

letters cited hereafter in this paper are to be found in that collection unless otherwise noted.

[5] *Congressional Globe*, 37 Cong., 2 sess., p. 2,558.

[6] *Ibid.*

[7] *Ibid.*, p. 2,467.

[8] William Pitt Fessenden to Elizabeth F. Warriner, June 15, June 29, 1862.

[9] *Ibid.*, July 21, 1861.

son in the Naval Academy because a respected friend had told him that the President could refuse Fessenden nothing. "How exceedingly embarrassing it is," he wrote, "to be supposed the possessor of any such power—especially when it does not exist."[10] Yet even in this passage of deprecation he spoke in terms of power, and he had earlier written to one of his sons matter of factly, "I have power enough to see that no substantial injustice is done you and will use it, if need be."[11] But it is to Fessenden's respected colleague, Senator James W. Grimes, that we owe the most flattering evaluation of the Maine senator's power—or at least his potential power. Shortly before the beginning of the second session of the Thirty-Seventh Congress, he wrote:

> If you determine to probe the sore spots to the bottom and that right shall be done, we can inaugurate a new order of things and the Country can be saved. You have followers. You can control the Senate—The wicked fear you and will flee before you.[12]

Fessenden, in other words, could count on others to follow his lead. Insofar as I can discover, the correspondence of the senators of the Thirty-Seventh Congress yields no similar tribute from a fellow lawmaker. And when Fessenden and Charles Sumner clashed during the course of the next Congress, the senator from Maine judged his rival by the criterion that Grimes had used. Sumner "has for followers" wrote Fessenden to his son, "two or three drunken rowdies, and small fry. . . ."[13]

Yet Fessenden did not attract the attention of the newspapers during the Thirty-Seventh Congress as did outspoken Radicals like Benjamin F. Wade and Charles Sumner. Doubtless this reflected the fact that he concentrated his efforts on fiscal and monetary policy—less colorful and contentious matters than confiscation and emancipation, although of key significance to the cause of the Union. Nor did he fancy himself an orator, describing himself during the second session as "leaving all the jabber to others, & being content to work like a dog."[14] As one reads the memorial addresses in which the senators paid their last homage to Fessenden, there emerges from the rhetoric and the encomiums a clear picture of Fessenden's style and perhaps no more clearly than in the rather condescending remarks of Charles Sumner, "As Mr. Fessenden rarely spoke except for business, what he

[10] *Ibid.*, December 15, 1861.

[11] William Pitt Fessenden to Francis Fessenden, October 29, 1861.

[12] James W. Grimes to William Pitt Fessenden, November 13, 1861.

[13] William Pitt Fessenden to William Fessenden, May 7, 1864.

[14] William Pitt Fessenden to Elizabeth F. Warriner, February 8, 1862.

said was restrained in its influence, but it was most effective in this Chamber. Here was his empire and his undisputed throne."[15] Sumner made it clear that this was hardly his conception of the senatorial role, but then as now it was the kind of behavior which won the respect of a majority of the members of the Senate. Yet it is also clear that Fessenden was by no means the complete broker in political affairs, a suave or softspoken political manager who built his political capital by doing favors for his colleagues. Many found him austere and stiff necked, or "cold, reserved, and somewhat aristocratic" as one put it; Senator Justin S. Morrill described him as, "holding the formidable power of sarcasm within his compressed lips, it would sometimes escape in sport—quite as often in bitter earnest. This pungency in debate involved him in conflicts, not infrequently with his dearest friends. . . ."[16] His ability and his integrity were the qualities that most impressed his colleagues apparently, and Grimes called him "the highest-toned man I ever knew; the purest man I ever knew in public life, and the ablest public man of my day."[17]

If position and reputation provide clues to power, the process of decision-making is no less revealing, although even the best-documented decisions may inspire various explanations. We have Fessenden's own account of the confirmation of Edwin Stanton as Secretary of War, replacing the unfortunate Simon Cameron. The senators were astounded when President Lincoln nominated Simon Cameron as Minister to Russia and presented Edwin M. Stanton's name to the Senate. Fessenden explained to his cousin:

> It is usual to confirm Cabinet Ministers at once, but I took the responsibility to have the matter laid over for consideration—as I was determined to know what it meant before I acted. . . . Accordingly, I sought and obtained an interview with [Stanton]. . . . If he is a truthful man . . . he is just the man we want. We agreed on every point—the duties of a Secretary of War—the conduct of the War—the Negro question, and everything else."[18]

[15] 41 Cong., 2 sess., *Memorial Addresses on the Life and Character of William Pitt Fessenden, (A Senator from Maine), Delivered in the Senate and House of Representatives, . . . Dec. 14, 1869* (Washington, 1870), p. 13, hereinafter referred to as *Fessenden.* In earlier work in the Congressional debates, I had assumed that the memorial addresses could be safely ignored as fulsome and uncritical eulogies. I have, however, been surprised at the effort which some speakers made to strike an honest balance. Undoubtedly there is exaggeration in the addresses, but a close reading often reveals interesting information about the dead senator as well as about the legislative process and the speakers.

[16] *Ibid.*, pp. 30, 64.

[17] *Ibid.*, p. 43.

[18] William Pitt Fessenden to Elizabeth F. Warriner, January 19, 1862.

Surely it was a man of no little power who could thus delay a crucial administration appointment, constitute himself a committee of one, and conduct a hearing on the appointee's qualifications while his colleagues awaited his judgment.

Of the Republican senators of the Thirty-Seventh Congress, Charles Sumner and Benjamin F. Wade had enjoyed (the Bay State man might have said "suffered") the longest continuous service in the Senate; having won election to that body in 1851.[19] Sumner had traveled widely in Europe as a young man and spent a considerable period abroad during the convalescence which followed Congressman Preston Brook's assault upon him. He maintained a correspondence with a number of eminent British figures. To his personal knowledge of European governments and people he added the information gained from considerable reading over the years in the classics of international law. His selection as chairman of the Senate Committee on Foreign Affairs was quite appropriate. Although the problems of diplomacy were different in many respects from those confronting the Congressional leaders who worked particularly to mobilize the men and materiel of war, few would argue that they were less significant to the outcome of the struggle. The effort to keep major European powers in a posture of neutrality, despite enfevering incidents and provocative situations, demanded patience and resolution in both the administration and the Senate. Sumner did his share in providing both, particularly during the Trent affair, when his moderate views prevailed despite the sword-rattling of more hot-tempered colleagues. Thus we can say that Sumner also held one of the most important chairmanships in the Senate and that on occasion he used it to provide vital leadership. Moreover, in most matters of foreign affairs he cooperated with the President, if not always with the Secretary of State, thus bringing to his advocacy in the Senate the influence of the administration as well as his own prestige and power.

In general the conduct of foreign affairs did not inspire the intense controversy in this Congress that various domestic issues did. And if proposals concerning relations with Haiti and Liberia roused some disagreement it was their bearing on the status of slavery in the United States that attracted attention much more than the details of

[19] Of all the senators of the Thirty-Seventh Congress, Charles Sumner has most attracted biographers. Edward L. Pierce, *Memoir and Letters of Charles Sumner* (4 vols., Boston: Roberts Brothers, 1893-94) hereinafter referred to as *Memoir and Letters*, is still useful. The Civil War years are covered in Vol. 4. David Donald, *Charles Sumner and the Rights of Man* (New York: Alfred A. Knopf, 1970) will stand for some time as a definitive biographical treatment of Sumner's political career during and after the Civil War.

the diplomacy involved. This fusion of issues, however, illustrates another aspect of Sumner's senatorial career during the Civil War. He had been the tribune of the anti-slavery cause; as no other legislator he was the voice of abolition on the Senate floor. The degree to which the anti-slavery forces in states other than Massachusetts chose to send their petitions for emancipation or confiscation to Sumner rather than to the senators of their own states is truly surprising, particularly when their own senators had distinguished reputations as foes of the peculiar institution. Sumner tried to attack slavery in every possible way, and his legislative activity carried him into areas of discussion in which his committee chairmanship did not give him special status. The specific motions which he made in the Senate during the second session of the Thirty-Seventh Senate revealed a very different pattern than did those of Fessenden. With few exceptions the latter's motions concerned issues within the purview of the chairman of the Finance Committee. Several, relating to taxes on cotton and slaves, did also involve the Southern question. By contrast, almost all of Sumner's motions lay outside his major committee assignment.

Contemporary newspaper reporters almost invariably mentioned Sumner when discussing the Senate Radicals. In their accounts he was often termed a "leading" Radical or linked with Benjamin F. Wade and Zachariah Chandler as "Radical leaders." Yet such descriptions may have carried a rather special meaning. Sumner was undoubtedly a leader in that he was an articulate and lucid exponent of much of the ideology of the Radical Republicans. Just as the Communist Party leadership today includes men who are considered to be uniquely theorists, so in a real sense was Sumner. He marshaled arguments for emancipation with cogency and force and his statement of the relationship of the rebellious states to the government of the Union was one of the major theories advanced on that difficult subject. But Sumner's voluminous correspondence does not contain an authoritative statement comparable to the blunt assurance from Senator Grimes to Fessenden, "You have followers." Nor in his own letters did Sumner articulate the concept of power as did Fessenden on occasion. Unquestionably Sumner was sometimes the despair of more practical legislators. "I do most sincerely hope that Massachusetts will have sense enough to remit him to the vocation for which [he] was designed—a professor of rhetoric & a lyceum lecturer," wrote Fessenden on the first day of June, 1862.[20]

Legislative style determines the degree to which a lawmaker realizes the legislative power inherent in his seniority and committee

[20] William Pitt Fessenden to Elizabeth F. Warriner, June 1, 1862.

assignments. No senator answered more roll calls than did Sumner during the Thirty-Seventh Senate. He spoke frequently and many of his contributions to the *Congressional Globe* were truly orations. He was personally honest and indefatigable in running errands and fostering the interests of his constituents. Emerson could say of him, "I think he has the whitest soul I ever knew."[21] John Sherman remarked in his eulogy of Sumner, "on all the vital issues . . . he has been a prominent, conspicuous and influential advocate of the opinions and principles represented by the republican party, which have either been ingrafted in the Constitution of the United States or have controlled the policy of the Government since 1861."[22] But Sherman also noted, "he would not yield even on minor points, and would often fight for a phrase when he endangered a principle. He would sometimes turn his warfare upon his best friends. . . ."[23] Justin Morrill mentioned "his persistency in pushing his own measures to the front, though to their present hurt or to the hurt of others. . . ."[24] Sumner was "not always a practical statesman" admitted George S. Boutwell of Massachusetts in a phrase that others came close to echoing.[25] He had, said one of his old colleagues in the Senate, "the egotism of genius and the impatience of fanatical conviction."[26]

No doubt Sumner would not have been Sumner had he played the political broker among his colleagues. He had not, after all, won either local fame in Boston or national fame in Washington during the 1850s by plying the arts of conciliation. But, perhaps in rationalization of his own inadequacies, Sumner did have a reasoned conception of his legislative role. During the memorial observances for Fessenden, Sumner maintained, ". . . without neglect of business, the Senate has become a center from which to address the country. A seat here is a lofty pulpit with a mighty sounding-board, and the whole wide-spread people is the congregation."[27] Probably Sumner believed that he did indeed speak to the "whole wide-spread people" when he rose in the Senate and perhaps the victory of the Republicans and the crumbling power of the slavocracy convinced him—he who had been a lonely spokesman of the anti-slavery forces in the early 1850s in the Senate—that this was indeed the way to move a nation. The statesman spoke in the Senate to convert the people and they in turn pressed the laggards

[21] 43 Cong., 1 sess., *Memorial Addresses on the Life and Character of Charles Sumner, (A Senator of Massachusetts), Delivered in the Senate and House of Representatives, . . . Apr. 27, 1874 with other Congressional Tributes of Respect* (Washington, 1874), p. 34, hereinafter referred to as *Sumner.*

[22] *Ibid.*, p. 45. [23] *Ibid.*, p. 46. [24] *Ibid.*, p. 23.

[25] *Ibid.*, p. 14. [26] *Ibid.*, p. 97.

[27] 41 Cong., 2 sess., *Fessenden*, p. 12.

in Congress to accept the new challenge or replaced them. If this was Sumner's interpretation of the rise of Republicanism, such strategy could attract few of his fellow senators, facing, as they did, the terrible immediacy of the war; they must make decisions now. To some of his colleagues, Sumner's rhetoric sounded hollow indeed. But Sumner also believed that discussion could change the minds of colleagues, hard set against his wishes, often recounting, according to Senator Allen G. Thurman, instances in which thorough debate had meant the difference between the success and failure of legislative measures.[28]

Another aspect of Sumner's legislative style is worth mentioning. In a legislative chamber where men ostensibly were equals, although such equality let it be agreed was modified by membership in the minority or majority party, by seniority and committee assignments, and by personal style, the senator who could mobilize the power of the executive to his own ends was clearly in a very favorable position. The extent of Abraham Lincoln's influence in Congress is a subject of dispute, but that he did possess power none can argue. During the sessions of the Thirty-Seventh Congress, Sumner tried diligently to enlist the chief executive in support of his most cherished objectives. He sprinkled his letters to John Bright and to the Duchess of Argyll with allusions to conversations between the President or the cabinet officers and himself. Writing to the Duchess in November of 1862 he rejoiced that emancipation was to be won and exclaimed, "How many dreary conversations I have had with the President on this theme, beginning sixteen months ago!"[29] As was well known, he developed the habit of staying in Washington for some time after the close of each session, thus enabling him to confer with officers of the executive branch after the pressure of Congressional business had subsided.[30]

Other senators of the Thirty-Seventh Congress were obviously very influential men also. As chairman of the Committee on Territories, Benjamin F. Wade of Ohio guided the Senate on subjects that had come particularly to symbolize the sectional divisions within the nation during the 1850s. As chairman of the Joint Committee on the Conduct of the War, he terrorized members of the armed forces and those who thought to assist or serve them as no other senator. Considerable evidence testifies to his power.[31] But in contrast to such men

[28] 43 Cong., 1 sess., *Sumner*, p. 17.

[29] Charles Sumner to the Duchess of Argyll, November 17, 1862. See also Sumner to John Bright, December 23, 30, 1861, August 5, 1862. Pierce, *Memoir and Letters*, IV, 57-59, 83, 108.

[30] *Ibid.*, pp. 64, 83, 92.

[31] The best biography of Wade is Hans L. Trefousse, *Benjamin Franklin Wade, Radical Republican From Ohio* (New York: Twayne Publishers, 1963).

as Wade, Fessenden, and Sumner let us establish another reference point and briefly discuss a senator who was relatively unsuccessful as a member of the majority party despite long service and high status among the founders of the Republican Party.

The election of John P. Hale to the Senate from New Hampshire in 1846 was the most notable political victory of the anti-slavery forces to that time.[32] Although not reelected in 1853, he returned to the Senate in 1855, and he could claim total service in the chamber greater than that of any other Republican member of the Thirty-Seventh Senate. The Republican senators of that body selected him as chairman of the Committee on Naval Affairs. But Hale apparently failed to realize his potential power because of shortcomings in his legislative style. Portraying him with sympathetic objectivity, his most recent biographer describes a man who waged guerilla warfare against the majority with considerable success while he was a member of the opposition. But as a member of the party in control of the government, he found it difficult, even impossible, to assume a more responsible posture. His biographer called him a maverick, as well as a guerillist, and the apelations are perhaps too kind.[33] Extremely conscious of his senatorial prerogatives and sensitive to slights, real or imagined, he was exasperated when some of his requests for patronage at the Navy Department were ignored. When he learned that the Secretary, Gideon Welles, had used his brother-in-law to purchase vessels for the Department in New York, he excoriated that gentleman in terms that made his colleagues wince. Both the chairman of the Senate Committee on Naval Affairs and the Secretary of the Navy convinced themselves of each other's corruption in short order. Hale thereafter expended much of his energy in efforts to expose malfeasance in Welles's department and in bickering with the Secretary concerning appointments. Hale even carried the quarrel to the point of trying to cut the Secretary's request for iron-clads from 20 to 12 vessels and suggesting that the authorization to have them constructed be given to the President rather than to Welles. These were dubious tactics at a time when the Navy was hard pressed to fulfill its obligations.

[32] I have in this account generally followed John P. Hale's latest biographer, Richard H. Sewell. See *John P. Hale and the Politics of Abolition* (Cambridge: Harvard Univ. Press, 1965), pp. 196-207, hereinafter referred to as *John P. Hale.* I have, however, read the John P. Hale Papers in the New Hampshire Historical Society, Concord, New Hampshire, and other relevant sources. My short discussion is probably slightly less sympathetic than that of Professor Sewell, who has portrayed Hale's complex and sometimes puzzling personality with both understanding and objectivity.

[33] Sewell, *John P. Hale*, pp. 199, 205.

Gideon Welles was delighted when the New York *Tribune* published a story in December 1863, suggesting that Hale had sold his influence in obtaining the parole of a man under indictment for defrauding the War Department. In the meantime Welles had come to depend upon other members of the Committee on Naval Affairs, notably Senator Grimes and Senator Solomon Foot, to represent the interests of the Navy in the Senate. Hale's perversity was not restricted to his relations with Gideon Welles. He tried to stampede the Senate into endorsing Captain Charles Wilkes's ill-considered action in removing Confederate envoys from the British vessel, the *Trent*, thereby embarrassing Sumner and more responsible Republicans.[34] He taunted the supporters of the bill to create a department of agriculture by charging that they were more concerned with the votes of farmers than with the welfare of agriculture.[35] Even if true, the comment must have irked the practical politicians in the party who were more intent on party-building than was Hale. But the comment was apparently typical of the strain of flippancy or even irresponsibility which marked his conduct as a senator.

During the Thirty-Eighth Congress, Hale's colleagues placed their evaluation of him on record. Although the Judiciary Committee did not recommend censuring him for unethical practices, it did report a bill which forbade Congressmen to accept fees in return for representing clients in the departments of the government, "other than its judiciary tribunals." More indicative of the dissatisfaction of his colleagues was the suggestion that he might be deprived of his committee chairmanship. The senatorial caucus of Republicans did not take this action in December of 1863, but when New Hampshire legislators rejected Hale's bid for reelection in 1864 the senators preemptorily made Grimes of Iowa chairman of the Naval Affairs Committee despite Hale's piteous pleas to be allowed to hold the post until his term expired in March 1865. If the stature and power of some Republican senators waxed during the war years poor "Jack" Hale was not among the group. His apparently was a story of lost opportunities; for him access to power had come too late.

II

OBVIOUSLY we can estimate the power wielded by senators in a general sort of way by using the kind of evidence that we have considered here. If we wish only to discover outstandingly able or notoriously inept legislators, we can be quite accurate. Few would deny

[34] Pierce, *Memoir and Letters*, IV, 53.
[35] *Congressional Globe*, 37 Cong., 2 sess., p. 2,014.

that Fessenden seemed to wield a great deal of power in the Thirty-Seventh Congress or that John P. Hale's legislative influence was considerably less. But evidence concerning many senators is not so plentiful and is more difficult to interpret. Nor can we safely assume that lack of evidence reflects lack of power. Manuscript collections are at best accidental accretions; newspaper reports of the nineteenth century were just as likely to emphasize the bizarre incident and the flamboyant but unstable character as today. The man who is secure and confident in the realization of his power may be much less inclined to speak at great length in Congressional debate than some ambitious but distrusted colleague. This being so we can understand why some scholars yearn for more objective criteria which they can use to assess the relative power of lawmakers in a particular legislative session. Roll calls provide the most comprehensive and "hardest" data concerning the activities of individual legislators. Can we extract from such artifacts indexes which show the relative power of an individual legislator in a given Congress? It will become clear that we have still some distance to go in developing a trustworthy measure; yet it will be evident also I hope that the scholar who investigates the use of such measures may well be able to clarify his understanding of the legislative behavior in a particular Congress.

In his study of the senators of the United States between 1947 and 1957, Donald R. Matthews presented an index of legislative effectiveness, "obtained by dividing the number of bills and resolutions that a senator sponsored which passed in the Senate by the total number he introduced."[36] Much too cautious to argue that his index of legislative effectiveness reflected legislative influence, Professor Matthews did suggest that it might indeed do so. But he was careful to emphasize that some legislators did not expect some of their bills to attract serious attention from colleagues and that obviously some bills were of greater significance than others. He suggested also that such a measure might inadequately reflect the work of a legislator who made great contributions in committee but was less effective in open debate.[37] Since nineteenth-century sources are somewhat less satisfactory than those of Professor Matthews, an index of legislative efficiency which is more simply constructed may be prepared by compiling the percentage of each senator's motions that passed in committee of the whole or in the Senate proper. This index also has obvious shortcomings. A motion to adjourn during the consideration of unimportant matters is

[36] Donald R. Matthews, *U.S. Senators and Their World* (Chapel Hill: Univ. of North Carolina Press, 1960), pp. 278-79.

[37] *Ibid.*, p. 278.

hardly equivalent to a motion to amend an important clause in major legislation. The senator who offers a small number of innocuous amendments may rank higher in such an index than his real power or influence warrants. But the measure has its attractive features also. The lawmaker who wields power is usually respected by his colleagues; they do not treat his recommendations lightly. Generally, too, such a legislator possesses the wisdom and the sense of timing that prevents him from making ill-advised or irrelevant motions. And in making a motion the senator in a real sense places his prestige on the line; he has called for the approval or disapproval of his colleagues. Men who are consistently overruled in such tests are not likely to stand high in the respect of their colleagues nor to have great influence upon them.

When confronted with a number of measures, none of which inspire complete confidence, we may well learn something by comparison. In such work the mere manipulation of the data may suggest relationships that had not occurred to us. A number of scholars have tried to clarify the concept of power as it is reflected in the working of legislative bodies. But few have actually tried to develop specific measures of power and construct such indexes for particular groups of legislators. The ideal method would allow us to examine the contributions of each legislator to the passage of various types of legislation, scoring each lawmaker's contribution in comparison to the contribution of all other legislators. When we try to think in such terms, conceptual and practical problems of great magnitude immediately appear. How does one measure the contribution of a legislator who introduces an important bill, or adds a saving amendment to it in committee, or orates at length upon the floor, urging passage, or quietly collects old political debts by persuading half a dozen wavering colleagues, for whom he has done favors or supplied crucial votes in the past, that they should support the bill? Historians can sometimes reconstruct in considerable detail the contribution of particular legislators to specific pieces of legislation. But it is impossible to do so for all the members of a legislative chamber when even a small number of bills is involved, let alone considerable numbers. Even were that possible, the task of giving appropriate scores for contributions of different kinds is a most difficult one. But if we can agree that one stage of the legislative process symbolizes the whole and if it is possible to analyze that stage in quantitative fashion we can move forward. The most obvious point for such an attack is the voting process and from it a few scholars have tried to distill a numerical measure that will summarize the individual legislator's contribution to the many hearings, debates, and votes of a legislative session or to particular categories of them. At the most obvious level of analysis two processes are involved in any roll call. The legislator contributes directly to the outcome of a roll call by voting yea, nay, or absenting himself. We can prepare scores which summarize such activity very easily. But there is an additional dimension to the lawmaker's behavior as well—his effort to bring other individuals into a majority.

Some years ago Robert A. Dahl endeavored to refine the concept of legislative power and to illustrate the use of the measure which he developed.[38] How, he asked in effect, can we estimate the probability that the actions of Senator A influenced other senators to vote with him in a particular division? Space is inadequate to summarize the subtleties of his argument or the various stages in the development of the formula which allowed him to score legislators in comparison to each other. He recognized the importance of knowing the initial reaction of legislators to a piece of legislation as well as their eventual responses, but he found that the only uniform evidence available to show that a legislator might have influenced a division beyond his own vote was the vote itself. By making paired comparisons of the voting of legislators in an appropriate set of roll calls, he was able to estimate the probability that a vote on legislation of this type would pass when the two legislators opposed each other. To amend one of Professor Dahl's summary statements slightly, he posited that the power of Senator A was greater than that of Senator B if the probability that the Senate would pass a motion was greater when Senator A favored a bill and Senator B opposed it than when Senator B favored a bill and Senator A opposed it. In his calculations he derived these probabilities from the actual voting performances of the senators. The crucial statistics were of course the actual number of times that A had voted with the majority on a particular type of proposal when B was in the minority and the actual number of times that B had voted with the majority when A was opposed. The most powerful lawmakers were the legislators with the greatest number of favorable power relationships. "On the analogy of the measurement of force in classical mechanics," such a measure may be termed a "Newtonian" index.[39] Professor Dahl warned that it did not distinguish between the real movers and shakers and chameleon or satellite legislators who simply voted with the majority or attached themselves to a powerful legislative figure and followed his lead in voting.

Duncan MacRae, Jr. and Hugh D. Price prepared a critique of

[38] Robert A. Dahl, "The Concept of Power," *Behavioral Science*, 2 (July 1957), pp. 201-15.

[39] Dahl, "Power," p. 414.

Professor Dahl's work in which they criticized his analysis rather severely.[40] If Senator A's vote on a measure revealed the fact that he had worked in its behalf prior to the division, the same assumption must be made, argued MacRae and Price, for all senators. This eliminated any "logical basis" for measuring change in attitude for "if all voting 'yea' are presumed to have favored the measure previously and worked for its passage (and the converse for 'nays'), then there is no opportunity for anyone to exercise any 'power' to change anyone else's stand."[41] The logic of this position is attractive but in practice Professor Dahl used a set of roll calls from which he derived probabilities, and it is doubtful that the criticism fully reached its mark.

MacRae and Price also brought their very considerable knowledge of scalogram analysis to bear on Dahl's argument. Legislators, they maintained, "often cast roll-call votes so as to locate themselves along a one-dimensional continuum in a given subject-matter area." They pointed out that the legislators "nearest the median of the distribution of legislators along this continuum . . . necessarily have the highest indexes of power, in the sense of Dahl's operational definition."[42] Such continua were reflected, they believed, in Guttman scalograms.[43] Legislators whose voting records place them in the center of scalogram rankings do vote with the majority to a greater extent than do those in polar positions and unquestionably the basic determinant of high ranking in Professor Dahl's index was the proportion of times that an individual voted with the majority.

The crucial element in the argument of MacRae and Price lay in their explanation of the relation between the scalogram and the Dahl measure. They wrote, "This [scalogram position] will depend only on . . . [legislators] . . . taking certain positions relative to their colleagues, as a result of their own values or of constituency pressures and not by their exercising influence, nor by their being 'chameleons' or 'satellites.' "[44] Professor Dahl, of course, was not presenting an interpretation of legislative behavior in which leadership or power functioned to the exclusion of personal values or constituency pressures. And if constituency pressure affected the positions which lawmakers took, why not "colleague" pressure? In illustration of a scale, showing

[40] Duncan MacRae, Jr., and Hugh D. Price, "Scale Positions and 'Power' in the Senate," *Behavioral Science*, 4 (July 1959), pp. 212-18, hereinafter referred to as "Scale Positions."

[41] *Ibid.*, p. 212. [42] *Ibid.*, p. 213.

[43] An introduction to the technique and literature of Guttman scaling is found in Lee F. Anderson, Meredith W. Watts, Jr., and Allen R. Wilcox, *Legislative Roll Call Analysis* (Evanston: Northwestern Univ. Press, 1966), pp. 89-121.

[44] MacRae and Price, "Scale Positions," p. 213.

the attitudes of senators concerning foreign aid, MacRae and Price drew a straight line which they labeled "isolationist" at one end and "internationalist" at the other, subdivided by five x's, representing the votes which divided the legislators into six different scale types, ranging from most isolationist in this instance to most internationalist. If the roll calls were scalable "practically any power that is exercised has to operate through the location of . . . [the] . . . cutting point," they wrote.[45] And again, they noted, "in a scalable set of roll calls the senators do not (by definition) shift position appreciably from one segment to another."[46] At the time, the authors apparently believed that scalograms reflected attitudinal continua which were essentially frozen during a single session.

Used originally in psychological testing, Guttman scaling in legislative research is performed in effect by isolating a roll call in which a small group (a) opposes a large majority; then searching the votes for another one in which members of that group are again found in agreement but are joined by additional legislators, group (b); then scanning the roll calls for another in which the first two groups (a and b) voted together but were joined by an additional group (c) and so on. The order in which additional legislators are added to the members of group (a) serves as a ranking of their extremeness (their scale types) on the issues under consideration in the roll calls. The items in a scale matrix are not added in chronological sequence.

The scale that is based on legislative roll calls, is a different artifact than one based on the responses to the questions of a psychological test. The subjects who take such tests answer the questions in one sitting; the items of a legislative scale are accumulated over periods of time, ranging from a few minutes, hours, or days to perhaps as many as nine months. It is hard to believe that some legislators, whose votes scale, do not change their attitude on particular issues somewhat during the time span that the roll calls in some scalograms cover. Indeed, one of the pioneers of scaling analysis in political history, William O. Aydelotte, has reported instances of scales with high reliability coefficients in which some individuals reversed themselves when they were given an opportunity to vote for a second time on a particular measure.[47] Some roll calls might fix the position of legislators at one end of a scale or the other quite early in a session, but centrists might retain considerable freedom of movement for a longer time.

The anchor vote in a scale usually reveals a great disproportion in

[45] *Ibid.*, p. 216. [46] *Ibid.*, p. 217.

[47] In conversations with this writer.

the number of legislators ranged in the minority and majority. This disproportion decreases as more votes are added to the voting matrix until its center is reached and then increases again as the die-hard opponents of the minority in the anchor roll call are revealed. Some alteration in these proportions can occur without destroying a scale, and such changes could spell the success or failure of a proposal in roll calls found near the center of a scale matrix where the votes become close. Indeed the transfer of six votes from the majority to the minority in every roll call of many scales would not affect the quality of the scale appreciably, but it might well change the outcome of a number of roll calls in the center of the scale matrix.

Nor do all roll calls in a legislative policy sector necessarily scale together. From a set of 87 roll calls on Southern issues (see below), there emerged scalograms containing the following number of items: 52, 7, 7, 5, 4, and 3. Most of the smaller scales were quite strongly correlated with the largest one, suggesting that they were variations of this dominant scale. In such circumstances it is possible that personal power relationships may have moved roll calls from one scale to another. Of the 87 roll calls, 9 had no strong scaling relationships with other votes. There are also, of course, in most legislative scales a small number of individual responses, designated as errors, which occur when lawmakers break scaling patterns and vote contrary to the way in which their other responses indicate that they should. Occasionally some legislators are so erratic in their responses that they are better ignored in the construction of scales. Power relationships may underlie these kinds of deviancy.

MacRae and Price showed that there was a considerable correlation (.57) between a ranking of legislators based on the distance from the median scale type and the Dahl power ranking. They suggested that the residual variation in Dahl's list that was not explained by the scale scores "might represent something nearer to influence," or perhaps simply "a discrepancy due to . . . [the differing] . . . methods and assumptions" involved in the construction of the two measures.[48] These critics of Professor Dahl's approach made an extremely interesting contribution in explaining the relationship between his power index and the scaling pattern derived from the same roll calls. But it is possible that they interpreted their findings more rigorously than was justified.

Other scholars, particularly William H. Riker, have investigated an approach to legislative power that initially seems to differ somewhat

48 MacRae and Price, "Scale Positions," p. 217.

from that discussed above.[49] Working from the fundamentals of game theory, they suggest that the legislator who casts the vote that makes a majority in any roll call is the most powerful man in that division. His power to cast the pivotal vote, should, if used to further his own influence, allow the legislator to anticipate reciprocal action or other rewards from those who desired him to join with them in forming a majority. American legislatures do not in general tally votes so as to allow the researcher to identify the legislator who casts the pivotal vote—in most cases American lawmakers would be hard put to identify this individual in any roll call, but the probability that a particular legislator did cast the pivotal vote can indeed be calculated. If a vote tally stands 19 to 18, for instance, the probability that each member of the majority cast the crucial vote is 1/19; that of a member of the minority is zero. Across a range of important roll calls the legislator with the highest average probability score would ostensibly have wielded the most power. Obviously this is a restricted definition of power.

A little thought will convince one that there is a good deal of similarity in the computation of the Dahl index, rankings based on scalogram position, and the simple game theory model. The man who voted with the majority a great deal should score well in all such measures.

III

For various categories of legislation in the senate of the Thirty-Seventh Congress, second session, I prepared a scale rank order listing and the two varieties of power indexes, simplified in the case of the Dahl index to facilitate computer calculations. I constructed the index of this type by calculating the proportion of times that measures of a particular type passed when A voted for them and B opposed them and compared this with the proportion of times that measures of the same type passed when B voted in support and A was in the opposition. In comparing the voting of Senator Orville H. Browning and Senator

[49] The basic model is described in L. S. Shapley and M. Shubik, "A Method of Evaluating the Distribution of Power in a Committee System," *American Political Science Review*, 48 (September 1954), pp. 787-92. William H. Riker's efforts to use the model were in his judgment somewhat unsatisfactory. See William H. Riker, "A Test of the Adequacy of the Power Index," *Behavioral Science*, 4 (April 1959), pp. 120-31, and William H. Riker and Donald Niemi, "The Stability of Coalitions on Roll Calls in the House of Representatives," *American Political Science Review*, 56 (March 1962), pp. 58-65. Also of interest is R. Duncan Luce and Arnold A. Rogow, "A Game Theoretic Analysis of Congressional Power Distributions for a Stable Two-Party System," *Behavioral Science*, 1 (April 1956), pp. 83-95.

Benjamin Stark in a set of roll calls the results were 21/26 and 5/26, and Browning was assumed to be more influential than Stark in the area of legislative concern delimited by this set of roll calls.

In the analysis that follows I have concentrated on the roll calls generated by legislative proposals that dealt with Southerners and their institutions during the second session of the Thirty-Seventh Senate, particularly the status of slaves and bills providing for the confiscation of the property of Southerners. I do not argue that those senators who were most influential in shaping and passing such legislation were the most powerful members of the upper chamber. A definitive study of the problem of power in this session must survey all categories of legislation. But the Southern issues represent a very interesting part of the legislative output of this session, and there is a strong possibility that the most powerful lawmakers in this sector of legislative activity should be considered the most potent members of the Senate. The attitude of the Republicans toward the peculiar institution of the South was the unique feature which distinguished them from their opponents at the time and from the members of the political parties in earlier eras of our political history. Nothing absorbed as much of their interest and time as did the Southern legislation. The man who could exercise power in these proceedings may well have been influential in other areas as well. On the other hand, such a legislator may have given his whole energies to Southern questions and let others control the outcome of less exciting legislative issues. At an early stage of this research, I selected those roll calls on Southern issues that posed substantive questions, along with a number of related procedural roll calls that appeared important—numbering 87 in all.

Rank order indexes of the three types, based upon the 87 roll calls relating to Southern issues, mainly slavery and confiscation, clearly are related. (See Table 1 and Appendix A.) In each case the relation was stronger than .5, using a gamma rank order coefficient. Computational procedures perhaps accounted for some of the variation. In computing the game theory index I scored each member of the Senate on every roll call considered; absences were assumed to reflect zero power, a reasonable position, although unflattering to the man who was confined to his boarding house with a bad cold. This index also weights the scores of members of the majority in a roll call in proportion to the closeness of the vote; the probability of being the pivotal voter was obviously higher for the members of a 19-man majority in a 19-18 vote than in a roll call in which the result was 34 to 3. This too seems an appropriate procedure. In calculating the paired comparison index, I was forced to ignore roll calls in which one member of the pair was absent. The ranking based on the scalograms incorporated still different procedures in the handling of absences since the individual legislator was excluded from a scale if absent in 50 per cent or more of the roll calls included in it. And the scale position ranking was based solely on the distance of the senators from the center of the scales, assigning equal weight to the members of the minority party clustered at one end of the scaling continuum and to the members of the majority party in an extreme position at the other end.

Are there other, more or less independent measures, which we can use to verify the "power" indexes? Two possibilities come to mind. In

TABLE 1. INDEX CORRELATIONS*

	Game Theory Index	*Newtonian Index*	*Scale Rank Index*	*Legislative Efficiency Index (General)*	*Legislative Efficiency Index (Southern Issues)*	*Committee Power Index*
Game Theory Index (Southern Issues)						
Newtonian Index (Southern Issues)	.87					
Scale Rank Index (Southern Issues)	.58	.71				
Legislative Efficiency Index (General)	.59	.50	.31			
Legislative Efficiency Index (Southern Issues)	.54	.59	.23	.77		
Committee Power Index	.67	–.06	.20	.89	.89	

* A rank order gamma coefficient of correlation is used in this table. Much of the data would have supported a coefficient more powerful than a rank order measure but the basic ordinal nature of the Guttman scale ranking and the bi-fold data of the committee power index suggested the use of a coefficient that could be used in all calculations. A sixteen cell contingency table underlies all measurements but those in the last line. Experimentation showed that coefficients based on a 25 cell table were only slightly weaker. Correlations with the committee power index are based on four-celled tables and this variant of gamma is of course Q. Gamma is more generous than some other coefficients; Q is extremely generous when one cell of the table is blank but this was not the case in any calculation here. The phi equivalent of the .67 in the last line is slightly above .4.

the first place, some social scientists suggest that outputs are an adequate reflection of power. If we wish to locate the major sources of power in a political system, we can examine the legislation and ask, "Who got how much?" Power structures and decisional manipulation must in the end produce results; why not therefore let the results identify the holders of power? Perhaps the efficiency index discussed earlier can be accepted as a convenient summary of such results. I prepared, therefore, such an index by analyzing the results of 364 floor motions, all of those bearing on the legislation considered in this study. Some senators made few motions, but 26 offered 5 or more which allowed the preparation of a rank order list (Appendix B). This listing did correlate with both the game theory and paired probability indexes at the .5 level. This legislative efficiency index was based on all the legislation considered, and the power indexes used in Table 1 were based on 87 votes relative to the South. Was legislative efficiency in the gross, so to speak, more or less related to the indexes than would have been a measure based solely on slavery and confiscation issues? I was able to build a shorter legislative efficiency ranking concerned with the Southern issues and the correlations were much the same.

The roster of committee chairmanships provides another more or less independent criterion of influence. Thirteen Republican senators chaired committees with four or more Republicans in the membership. Undoubtedly, these were in general the most important Senate committees, although the numbers criterion did produce one questionable result. The chairman of the Committee on Revolutionary Claims was included in the list; the chairman of the Public Lands Committee was not. Adding the President Pro Tempore to the group provided a list of fourteen Republican senators who held the most prestigious offices open to the lawmakers of the upper house. We have here, of course, a positional index—that some members of the group might discredit themselves or fail to reach their potential goes without saying. By dividing the Republican "power" rankings in two, we can see that membership in the chairman group correlated somewhat interestingly with the game theory ranking and legislative efficiency indexes but not with the paired comparisons or scale rankings.[50]

[50] The committee chairman list was very strongly correlated (.97 in a bi-fold rank order correlation) with a list ranking the Republicans in order of their continuous service in the Senate. The basic relationship involved in the discussion of this paragraph, some would say, therefore, is that between seniority and power. A bi-fold correlation of the game theory index and the seniority list of the Senate as a whole was .48. My efforts to develop a comprehensive ranking of committees in terms of committee prestige and to use this ranking in turn to prepare a status ranking of all senators have thus far produced unsatisfactory results.

The correlations suggest that the game theory index may reflect voting power more clearly than the Newtonian index. But there is no reason to assume that it eliminates the chameleon-satellite problem. Its rank order is, however, reasonable in obvious respects. When based on a representative list of slavery and confiscation roll calls, it tells us that Republicans were more powerful than Democrats and Border Unionists. Fessenden, a highly successful committee chairman by all accounts, appeared quite high in the index, while John P. Hale, so unsuccessful as to lose his chairmanship, ranked far lower. The senator heading the list, Senator Daniel Clark of New Hampshire, has been of little interest to historians of the Civil War, but he did play a crucial role in this session. He served as chairman of the select committee on the confiscation bills, one of the most difficult and important assignments of the session.

Clark was one of two Republican senators with a perfect attendance record in the roll calls underlying the power indexes on slavery and confiscation. This suggests the possibility that attendance may explain the rank order to a considerable extent. I first tested this possibility by dividing a ranking based on the Republican attendance into quartiles and comparing these with the quartiles of the game theory power index, using a sixteen cell contingency table. The gamma coefficient of association was .56. Closer examination, however, showed that most of this strength was attributable to a strong relation between the lowest quartiles of the two indexes. Here were clustered a group of Republicans with poor attendance records. When the fourth quartiles were removed to create a nine-cell table, the association fell to between .22 and .05 depending upon the mechanics of conversion. Obviously, considerations other than attendance were important in the upper levels of the listing. What level of association existed between the committee chairman list and the attendance ranking? This coefficient was .9. The major committee chairmen attended more faithfully than the rank and file Republicans, suggesting perhaps that they were more concerned with the details of legislation, that they had fewer outside involvements, and that they were more willing to participate in debate, all possibly attributes of the man of influence in a legislative assembly.

We should be cautious in trying to interpret Table 1; the total number of senators was small and the data peculiar in various respects. In common sense terms the credibility of the different indexes varies. The scale ranking was inserted for comparative purposes rather than as an effective measure of power. Rank in it varies in proportion to the number of times that individual senators voted with the majority. It is true, of course, that powerful legislators usually do vote with the majority frequently. Scale rank, however, does not distinguish such men from chameleon or satellite lawmakers. In practice the Newtonian index differed from scale ranking by ascribing different degrees of power to members of the majority and minority parties. The game theory measure, although also reflecting the tendency of legislators to vote with the majority, gives additional weight to votes cast with the majority when the margin of victory was small.

The legislative efficiency indexes are somewhat attractive. They reflect specific actions in which lawmakers proposed alternatives to their colleagues and the latter gave clear-cut responses to these acts of leadership. But it is difficult to obtain sufficient data of this kind to evaluate the success of all legislators in any given session. Few would dispute the suggestion that the major committee chairmen of the dominant party must have represented a far greater pool of power than that found among their remaining Republican colleagues. But since the committee power index merely divides the Republicans into two groups, it is a rather blunt instrument for the purposes of analysis.

The table of correlations suggests that we can separate our indexes into two groups: one composed of the game theory, Newtonian, and scale rank indexes and the other including the two legislative efficiency rankings and the committee power index. These affinities probably reflect similarities in the proxies for power that underlie the two groups of rankings. The first three indexes are linked primarily to voting majorities, while the others focus on conscious acts of leadership or formal positions of leadership. Although admonitions about the futility of using high-powered statistical methods on low-powered data are very relevant here, some elementary factor analysis adds somewhat to our understanding of Table 1.

A centroid factor analysis shows that two factors account for most of the variance in the table of correlation. The committee power index loaded more heavily than any other variable on the second of these extracted. Clockwise orthogonal rotation to maximize this loading produced the loadings shown in Table 2. The impression of clustering derived from the correlations is reinforced. Of the majority-oriented indexes, the game theory index clearly is more strongly related to the committee power index than the other two measures of that type. It is certainly of some utility as a success score at least, and it discriminates between legislators to a greater extent than do the efficiency and committee power indexes. For these reasons I shall use it in the following pages to bring out some of the facets of the conflict between

TABLE 2. MAJOR FACTORS IN TABLE 1

Indexes	*Factor Loadings* I	II
1. Game Theory	.82	.43
2. Newtonian	.99	.08
3. Scale Rank	.75	.11
4. Legislative Efficiency (1)	.32	.87
5. Legislative Efficiency (2)	.31	.87
6. Committee	00	1.0

Radical and Moderate Republican senators during the long session of the Thirty-Seventh Congress.

The Guttman scales revealed a clear pattern of voting in the 87 roll calls on Southern issues and cluster blocing suggested a cutting point in the scales that divided the Republican senators into a group of 17 Radicals and 14 Moderates.[51] (I have described these procedures elsewhere.) The association between the Radical-Moderate grouping of the Republicans and the game theory power index was —.43, indicating that Moderate Republicans were most common in the upper reaches of the index. Even so 6 Radicals—Clark, Foot, Sumner, Henry Wilson, Wade, and King—did appear among the top 16 Republicans in the power index.

51 Republican Radicals and Moderates

Radicals

Chandler (Mich.)
Clark (N.H.)
Foot (Vt.)
Grimes (Ia.)
Hale (N.H.)
Harlan (Ia.)
Howard (Mich.)
King (N.Y.)
J. H. Lane (Kan.)
Morrill (Me.)
Pomeroy (Kan.)
Sumner (Mass.)
Trumbull (Ill.)
Wade (O.)
Wilkinson (Minn.)
Wilmot (Penn.)
Wilson (Mass.)

Moderates

Anthony (R.I.)
Browning (Ill.)
Collamer (Vt.)
Cowan (Penn.)
Dixon (Conn.)
Doolittle (Wis.)
Fessenden (Me.)
Foster (Conn.)
Harris (N.Y.)
Howe (Wis.)
H. S. Lane (Ind.)
Sherman (O.)
Simmons (R.I.)
Ten Eyck (N.J.)

After the 87 roll calls on slavery and confiscation had yielded the Radical-Moderate grouping, I searched for the roll calls that showed strong disagreement between the two groups. There were 21 such divisions among the 87 roll calls; the remaining 277 roll calls under study added 37 more, some in the categories of national economic legislation and others produced by procedural roll calls or other measures that did not seem very important in the early stages of this research. These 58 roll calls are particularly interesting to the researcher because they delineate the major matters at issue between the Radicals and the Moderates during this session. I used these roll calls, therefore, to create power indexes of the game theory type. In one index the power quotients of the individual senators were averaged across the set of 58. Then the set was arranged in chronological order, broken in half, and each subset of 29 used to prepare an index. The breaking date was June 7, 1862, when slightly more than a month of the session remained and when the conflict between Radical and Moderate was rising to a climax. This procedure, I hoped, might reveal changing patterns of influence over time.

In general the members of the Moderate group, were high in the new index based on the 58 high-conflict roll calls, their relative positions only slightly altered, either upward or downward. But the correlation coefficient, measuring the association of the Radical-Moderate grouping with the new power index was —.51, as compared to —.43 when the original power index was used. Some Radicals fell in the ranking of all senators in the session by large amounts. Sumner's ranking dropped 25 places, that of King by 34, and Wade fell 30 places. Conversely a number of Democrats and Border Unionists appeared in the upper half of this index, and most senators of these persuasions were in higher positions than in the original game theory ranking. No less than 11 of them ranked above Sumner in this index. The Moderate Republicans were making majorities in the high-conflict roll calls by voting with numbers of Democrats and Border Unionists; the Radicals, losing places in the majority in such votes, are found lower, sometimes much lower in the ranking, whereas in the original slavery and confiscation index the Moderates had voted with the Radicals sufficiently often so that all Republicans appeared above all Democrats and Border Unionists in it. When I separated the items of the high-conflict index into two, the new indexes showed that 10 Republicans changed their positions by 10 places or more during the last 6 weeks of the session. Increased attendance or absences account for much of the change in the rankings of several men (Simmons, James H. Lane, and James Dixon), but other differences may reflect changes in attitude.

TABLE 3. MOBILE SENATORS IN HIGH-CONFLICT INDEXES

Rank Order (High-Conflict Index)	*Senator*	*Rank Order Change After June 7*
4	Doolittle	+13
10	Clark	+11
16	Simmons	+22
8	Browning	−13
32	Lane, J. H.	+23
41	Harlan	+18
23	Wilson, H.	−19
36	Trumbull	+11
25	Dixon	−28
31	Grimes	−12

The Republicans who stood at the top of the game theory power indexes were all Moderates with the exception of Clark, a marginal Radical who softened his attitude on Southern legislation during the last six weeks of the session for the sake of compromise. But were they leaders, satellites, or chameleons? We can suggest perhaps that satellites and chameleons would not score high on the legislative efficiency index. When we eliminate men from consideration who ranked low in either the legislative efficiency index or the game theory power indexes, we are left with a much smaller number of men—Clark, James R. Doolittle, and Fessenden. Did one or more of these men mobilize the Moderates? I have already discussed Fessenden's general contributions and style. There is no evidence in his correspondence that he consciously tried to rally the Moderates on Southern matters, but he did sharply rebuff Radicals like Wade and Trumbull on the floor of the Senate when they tried to whip the Moderates into a more radical posture during the debates on the confiscation bills.[52]

What of Doolittle and Clark? We have only to read the former's correspondence to understand that he had ambitions to lead. He himself believed that his efforts in behalf of the colonization amendment to the District of Columbia emancipation bill made that important piece of legislation acceptable to a majority of the senators.[53] But if he did have a substantial hand in constructing a Moderate bloc in this session, he did not retain the palm for long. In many respects Daniel Clark is more of an enigma than Doolittle. His contributions on the

[52] *Congressional Globe*, 37 Cong., 2 sess., p. 2,203.

[53] James R. Doolittle to Mary Doolittle, April 4, 1862. James Rood Doolittle Papers, Wisconsin State Historical Society, Madison, Wisconsin.

TABLE 4. QUARTILE RANKING OF SELECTED SENATORS IN FIVE INDEXES

Senators	*Legislative Efficiency (General)*	*Game Theory (Southern Issues)*	*Game Theory (High Conflict)*	*Game Theory (High Conflict to June 7)*	*Game Theory (High Conflict after June 7)*
Clark	I	I	I	II	I
Doolittle	I	I	I	II	I
Fessenden	I	I	I	I	I
Hale	III	III	II	II	II
Saulsbury	IV	IV	III	III	II
Sumner	II	I	III	III	III
Wade	II	II	IV	III	IV

floor and in committee suggest a man of real ability and a mere cipher would not have emerged as chairman of a select committee, entrusted with the explosive confiscation issue. But his candidacy did not inspire enthusiasm in New Hampshire when his term expired in 1866, and he retreated to the federal bench. Historians of the Civil War have in general ignored him. Was he perhaps Fessenden's surrogate in the confiscation debates? The *Springfield Republican*'s special correspondent described him during the third session of this Congress:

> . . . tall, easy, elegant in his bearing, with a strong face deeply lined, seems like a Boston lawyer. A man of the deepest convictions, the most uncompromising principles, he never betrays the one, nor is false to the other, and on no one does the burden of our national sorrow seem to lie with a heavier weight.[54]

Certainly he was Fessenden's friend as well as his colleague, and common ties of region and Whiggery joined them as well; ally is probably a more appropriate term than surrogate or lieutenant.

With Tables 3 and 4 before us we can return briefly to Sumner and Hale who were discussed in company with Fessenden in Part I of this paper. Although Sumner scored in the lower part of the upper quartile of the general index based on Southern issues, his radical stance placed him in a lower position in the high-conflict roll calls. Not, however, in so low a position as Senator Wade, who was more extreme in his radicalism than was Sumner. Both Sumner and Wade were more successful in winning approval of their floor motions than was Hale. The senators approved 85 per cent of Clark's motions, 72 per cent of Fessenden's, 64 per cent of Wade's, 51 per cent of Sumner's, and only 29 per cent of the proposals which Hale made. But the senior senator from New Hampshire was hardly so frustrated as the Delaware Demo-

[54] Weekly *Springfield Republican*, March 7, 1863.

crat, Willard Saulsbury, who submitted motions to his colleagues 9 times and was rebuffed in every instance.

IV

IF we place the most conservative possible interpretation upon the "power" indexes, they are merely measures of the voting success of the individual legislator. The lawmaker who votes consistently with the majority will stand high in both the Newtonian and game theory rankings. There is also reason to believe in both cases, that legislators who marshal majorities, as well as contribute their votes to them, would score well. In this respect the game theory index incorporates a weighting factor that is lacking in the other system of measurement. Close votes are one criterion of significant roll calls, and the close vote may identify a division in which the lawmaker of influence made a major contribution to the outcome.[55] The game theory index also uses all of the evidence in the voting records, since absences were scored as illustrations of zero probability, and I discarded votes in which one or the other of the lawmakers under comparison was absent in the Newtonian model used here. The game theory index correlated more strongly with other measures of power that have some claim to independence than did the Newtonian index. The student can also use the game theory index very easily, and with interesting results, to show changes in the voting patterns of individual legislators. But neither the game theory model nor the Newtonian model will clearly distinguish between the leader and the chameleon or satellite lawmaker. I suggest that the use of a legislative efficiency index similar to the one used in this study, or that developed by Professor Matthews, may be helpful in that respect. There are perhaps other indications of influence which should be considered in an analysis of this sort. The size of constituency proved to have little explanatory power here. But other constituency characteristics may have been important in this or other eras. Ingenious scholars, it is hoped, will suggest other relevant correlates of power.

What does this study tell us about Civil War politics? The indexes confirm some of the drift of the subjective evidence discussed in the first section of this paper. They suggest that Fessenden of Maine was indeed one of the most powerful, and probably the most powerful, of the senators during the second session of the Thirty-Seventh Congress,

[55] William H. Riker, "A Method for Determining the Significance of Roll Calls in Voting Bodies," in *Legislative Behavior: A Reader in Theory and Research*, ed. by John C. Walhke and Heinz Eulau (Glencoe, Ill.: Free Press, 1959), pp. 379-80.

insofar as the Southern question was concerned. But was he master in his own house? Of the concerns of the Finance Committee, the Internal Revenue Bill was most important, and Fessenden ranked high in the game theory index based on the 51 votes generated by that measure. The analysis of Southern issues also shows that two senators whom historians largely disregard may also have played important roles during this session—Clark and Doolittle. Scalogram and cluster bloc analysis suggest that Fessenden was a Moderate Republican, positioned toward the Radical side of the group; Doolittle was somewhat more moderate than Fessenden, and Clark was a Radical who occupied a place in that group rather close to the boundary between the Radicals and the Moderates, and who moved somewhat toward the Moderates in close votes during the latter part of the session. By our measures, the famous Radicals—Sumner, Wade, and Chandler—did less well than the leading Moderates in this session. Although the Radicals were greater in number than the Moderates, they were less successful in close votes than were the members of the smaller group, because Democratic legislators and Unionist senators from the Border States cast their votes with the Moderates in crucial roll calls. If the Radicals did come to dominate the Republican Party during the Civil War, they had not consolidated their power to the point of controlling the voting in the Senate during the second session of the Thirty-Seventh Congress. The essence of Fessenden's power on Southern issues, if such he had, lay particularly in his ability to influence the Moderate Republicans.

Indexes of the type that I have used here will almost invariably rank individuals if based on a considerable number of roll calls. Absences and random differences of opinion would produce that result, irrespective of more fundamental factional or ideological disagreement. So we should inquire: "How important were the distinctions among individual legislators that the indexes reveal?" And if they did reveal power relationships, were these strongly structured and stable or were they in flux? Were the men of extraordinary influence acquiring power, consolidating it, or losing it? With such questions in mind we should consider some of the behavioral parameters of this Congress.

For the first time in its short history the Republican Party was in control of the executive branch and both Houses of Congress. Certainly in the Senate the Republicans lacked an effective opposition; the consolidating influence which powerful opponents provide was absent. The Thirty-Seventh Congress could be expected, therefore, to be one in which the abler or more ambitious Republican lawmakers contested with each other for control of the legislative process.

Republicans had various party antecedents—they had been Whig, Know-Nothing, and Democrats. Although they had adopted much of the economic program of the Whigs, they were most clearly united in their opposition to slavery. But there were great differences of opinion among Republicans as to the most appropriate policies which they should follow concerning that institution as well. During the second session the national government was directing a great war against those who maintained the peculiar institution. It would have been surprising indeed had not differences of opinion developed both as to the objectives of the war and the degree to which the Republicans should build a record in other legislative areas. The war effort also made huge amounts of patronage at least potentially available to legislators, tempting them to try to use it for partisan or personal ends or, at the very least, complicating the relations of the lawmakers with both their constituencies and the executive branch of the government. If in theory there was more patronage available than ever before in the nation's history, legislators were more fearful perhaps than ever before that political rivals might use it to their own ends.

The war created an atmosphere of recurrent crisis in which extreme proposals might attract even congenitally moderate men, and at the same time the conflict greatly increased the day-to-day business of Congress. To the inconveniences of boardinghouse or hotel life and the unpleasantness of the Washington climate there was thus added the pressure of greatly increased work. At the same time, constituents, job seekers, and lobbyists besieged them. At night the rumbling of army freight trains, the clatter of artillery caissons, the tramp of marching columns, and the serenades of military bands disturbed their rest. They agonized over the knowledge that the decisions in which they participated and the legislation which they passed might send thousands of men to their deaths. Such worry was all the more poignant in the minds of introspective men like Fessenden who had sons in the armies of the Union.

Former members of the Whig Party were a majority among the Republican legislators and in that party they had cherished the theory of legislative supremacy over the executive. Efforts of the President to exercise strong leadership over Congressional activity might therefore be expected to meet opposition. And finally this Congress was linked by membership and tradition to its predecessors and the patterns of sectional opposition, and the institutional frictions of the past could be expected to continue to some extent at least within it—despite the extraordinary conditions under which its members met.

The behavioral parameters suggest that there may not have been a strong structure of leadership within the second session of the Thirty-Seventh Congress. I cannot elaborate the point here, but the ability of the Moderates to resist the Radical Republicans seems to have weakened in subsequent sessions. In part this may reflect the fact that Fessenden did not, in the end, consolidate his claims to authority. An intense man whose letters suggest that he suffered both from tension headaches and colitis, he may have devoted too much of his energy to the problems of the Finance Committee. In retrospect some of his colleagues expressed reservations about the quality of his leadership. One of the more politically astute senators of the era, Anthony of Rhode Island remarked, ". . . to honest but transient public opinion, founded on limited observations and shallow reasoning, Mr. Fessenden, I have sometimes thought, did not give the consideration that was due. . . ."[56] Senator Williams of Oregon admitted that "he towered in mind among those around him like Saul in form among his countrymen," aside from "the discussion upon the slavery question" in which the Oregonian apparently reserved the palm for Sumner. But he qualified his remarks by adding that "upon any novel and exciting question where the road to success seemed to lie through recklessness and temerity . . . [Fessenden] . . . did not possess the requisite qualifications for a great parliamentary leader. . . . He was so careful not to do wrong that sometimes he seemed afraid to do right."[57] His former colleague Lot Morrill asserted, "He had little ambition for mere power, and less use for it. Patronage he did not covet or employ as a support. . . ."[58] Nor did the voting success of the Moderates during the second session provide substantial foundations for the future. It was achieved because Democrats and Border Unionists voted with the Moderates to scotch the proposals of the Radicals. In legislative politics as in war it is dangerous business to consort with the enemy.

On the other hand, there is little reason to doubt that Fessenden, Clark, and Doolittle were highly influential during this session, or for that matter, that Fessenden continued to be a very important member of his party. Some social scientists have been disappointed in earlier experimentation with power indexes because they proved to have less predictive power than hoped. But this shortcoming does not necessarily mean that the indexes misrepresented reality at a particular time. Leaders may fail to exercise their potential power and the surge of events may distort or destroy earlier relationships if these have not been firmly set. Both processes were apparently at work during later sessions of the Civil War Senate.

[56] 41 Cong., 2 sess., *Fessenden*, p. 19.
[57] *Ibid.*, p. 23. [58] *Ibid.*, p. 9.

APPENDIX A

Senator	State	Party*	Rank Order, Newtonian Index (Southern Issues)	Rank Order, Game Theory Index (Southern Issues)	Rank Order, Game Theory Index (High-Conflict Votes)	Scale Type in Domi- nant Sc (Southe Issues)*
1. Anthony	R.I.	R	7	9	2	11
2. Bayard	Del.	D	48	48	47	
3. Browning	Ill.	R	31	15	8	10
4. Carlile	Va.	U	38	38	27	3
5. Chandler	Mich.	R	23	23	23	22
6. Clark	N.H.	R	6	1	10	19
7. Collamer	Vt.	R	2	14	14	13
8. Cowan	Penn.	R	27	32	13	10
9. Davis	Ky.	U	40	36	9	2
10. Dixon	Conn.	R	1	22	25	16
11. Doolittle	Wis.	R	5	5	4	12
12. Fessenden	Me.	R	10	6	5	15
13. Foster	Conn.	R	3	3	1	14
14. Foot	Vt.	R	19	4	22	18
15. Grimes	Ia.	R	30	19	31	22
16. Hale	N.H.	R	13	28	20	16
17. Harlan	Ia.	R	15	24	41	20
18. Harris	N.Y.	R	11	12	21	14
19. Henderson	Mo.	D	36	35	19	7
20. Howard	Mich.	R	25	21	35	17
21. Howe	Wis.	R	8	7	11	17
22. Johnson	Tenn.	D	33	46	49	
23. Kennedy	Md.	U	49	45	39	1
24. King	N.Y.	R	26	16	40	22
25. Lane, H. S.	Ind.	R	12	18	17	14
26. Lane, J. H.	Kan.	R	18	25	32	21
27. Latham	Cal.	D	39	42	29	5
28. McDougall	Cal.	D	37	39	28	9
29. Morrill	Me.	R	17	27	37	21
30. Nesmith	Ore.	D	43	44	30	
31. Pearce	Md.	D	46	47	48	
32. Pomeroy	Kan.	R	21	17	38	22
33. Powell	Ky.	D	45	40	6	0
34. Rice	Minn.	D	32	41	34	
35. Saulsbury	Del.	D	47	43	26	0
36. Sherman	O.	R	16	11	12	11
37. Simmons	R.I.	R	4	29	16	15

	State	*Party**	*Rank Order, Newtonian Index (Southern Issues)*	*Rank Order, Game Theory Index (Southern Issues)*	*Rank Order, Game Theory Index (High-Conflict Votes)*	*Scale Type in Dominant Scale (Southern Issues)***
8. Stark	Ore.	D	44	34	18	4
9. Sumner	Mass.	R	20	8	33	20
0. Ten Eyck	N.J.	R	9	2	3	14
1. Thomson	N.J.	D	42	49	46	
2. Trumbull	Ill.	R	28	20	36	22
3. Wade	O.	R	22	13	43	22
4. Wilkinson	Minn.	R	24	26	44	22
5. Willey	Va.	U	35	33	7	6
6. Wilmot	Penn.	R	29	30	45	22
7. Wilson, H.	Mass.	R	14	10	23	20
8. Wilson, R.	Mo.	U	41	37	24	2
9. Wright	Ind.	N U	34	31	15	8

* R = Republican U = Unionist (Southern Whig)
D = Democrat N U = Northern Unionist (Wright of Indiana, formerly Democrat)

** The Guttman scale is an ordinal ranking, and one cannot, therefore, average legislator cores across a set of scales to find mean scores. However, it is possible to convert scale type osition into percentiles of a scale; each member can be given the median percentile within hat scale type as a numerical score—for example, 97—and legislator scores can then be averged across a set of scales, weighting individual scale scores in proportion to the number of tems in each scale. A ranking based on the average scale position of the senators in the Southern ssues set of 87 roll calls was used to prepare the ranking (i.e. distance from the center of the cale) underlying the correlations in the third row and third column of Table 1.

APPENDIX B

Legislative Efficiency Index
(Five Or More Motions)

Senator	State	Party	Motions	Per Cent Successful
1. Clark	N.H.	R	13	85
2. Collamer	Vt.	R	6	83
3. Fessenden	Me.	R	25	72
4. Trumbull	Ill.	R	17	71
5. Doolittle	Wis.	R	10	70
6. Sherman	O.	R	21	67
7. Wade	O.	R	14	64
8. Cowan	Penn.	R	5	60
9. Wilson, H.	Mass.	R	17	59
10. Grimes	Ia.	R	20	55
11. Sumner	Mass.	R	33	51
12. Foster	Conn.	R	8	50
13. Harris	N.Y.	R	11	45
14. Powell	Ky.	D	11	45
15. Chandler	Mich.	R	5	40
16. Anthony	R.I.	R	6	33
17. Harlan	Ia.	R	6	33
18. Henderson	Mo.	D	6	33
19. Hale	N.H.	R	17	29
20. Davis	Ky.	U	18	28
21. King	N.Y.	R	11	27
22. Howe	Wis.	R	8	25
23. McDougall	Cal.	D	10	20
24. Rice	Minn.	D	5	20
25. Browning	Ill.	R	8	12
26. Saulsbury	Del.	D	9	00

VII

The Disintegration of the Conservative Party in the 1840s: A Study of Political Attitudes

WILLIAM O. AYDELOTTE

THIS PAPER raises, in a small context, a large question: the relation of parties to issues.* This question, or various aspects of it, has been extensively discussed over the past century, by both scholars and laymen. I have summarized elsewhere some of the arguments that have been advanced[1] and need not repeat myself. It suffices to say here that there is strong testimony, from many who have given attention to the subject, to the effect that parties are not related to issues and are not doctrinal bodies, that major issues of controversy are often not party questions, that parties in any smoothly running parliamentary system must operate on the basis of a consensus on fundamentals and must pursue identical or closely similar objectives and that, only if they do this, will the system function effectively. Various historians have claimed that such a consensus did in fact exist in British politics in the nineteenth century, and this opinion was also expressed by a number of well-informed contemporary observers.

Not all students of political history accept these views, however, and a number of important writers have argued, with appropriate qualifications, that parties do on the whole represent different interests, and have protested against an overemphasis on consensus in political history.[2] I have myself found, in an earlier study of British parties in the 1840s, evidence indicating a close relationship between parties and

* I wish to acknowledge with thanks the help, in the preparation of materials for this paper, of my assistants, Paula Adix, David W. Gebhard, William J. Marland, Don R. Smith, and Phyllis E. Steele.

1 W. O. Aydelotte, "Parties and Issues in Early Victorian England," *Journal of British Studies*, Vol. 5, No. 2 (May 1966), pp. 95-101, hereinafter referred to as "Parties and Issues."

2 See, for example, John Higham, "The Cult of the 'American Consensus': Homogenizing Our History," *Commentary*, Vol. 27, No. 2 (February 1959), pp. 94-95, 99; Seymour M. Lipset, *Political Man: The Social Bases of Politics* (Garden City, N.Y.: Doubleday & Co., Inc., 1960), pp. 220-23, 290-94, 306-09; and David B. Truman, *The Congressional Party: A Case Study* (New York: John Wiley & Sons, Inc., 1959), pp. vi-vii.

issues in that period, a complex but unmistakable pattern of party voting on a large number of subjects. The findings suggested that earlier denials of the ideological orientation of British parties in the mid-nineteenth century needed to be substantially qualified.[3]

I wish now to take up another aspect of this question and to make a comparable inquiry, not for two parties, but for two factions within a single party. These are the two groups into which the Conservative Party split in the famous disruption of 1846 over the repeal of the Corn Laws. The episode raises interesting questions about party cohesiveness in the mid-nineteenth century, and it may be possible to advance the discussion of these questions by a study of the division lists. The emphasis here is rather different from that in my earlier paper, which dealt with the relation of issues to party unity. I am now concerned with the relation of issues to party disruption: how far the breaking up of a party was related to ideological matters.

The "Peelites" and the "Protectionists," the two groups to be considered, will be defined arbitrarily as those members of the Conservative Party who voted, respectively, for or against the bill to repeal the Corn Laws in the famous division on the third reading on 15 May 1846. Tellers and pairs will be counted so as to include the attitudes of as large a number of men as possible. By this criterion there were 114 Peelites and 241 Protectionists. This definition is not wholly satisfactory since a small number of Conservatives voted differently on the second reading on 27 March 1846. There were also other Conservatives who sat in this Parliament but did not vote on the third reading. Many of them were no longer in Parliament by May 1846, and this group included a number of advocates of repeal whose conversion to free trade had necessitated giving up a seat, since the patron of the seat took a different view. Yet the definition has at least the virtue of being unequivocal. It also includes a large number of men, for the division on the third reading of the Corn Law Bill was a big one, 327-229, adding to 556 which, with the 4 tellers and the 20 pairs, brings the total of recorded votes to 600, 92 per cent of those eligible to vote.

These remarks are addressed to two general questions. First, how far can these two groups be distinguished by their votes in other divisions, not only in 1846 but also before and after? This information may give at least some indication of the strength or importance of this line of cleavage within the party. It may also be useful to observe on

[3] Aydelotte, "Parties and Issues," pp. 106-14.

what other subjects, besides the Corn Laws, the two groups disagreed. Scholars have been interested in the relation of the Corn Law question to other issues, the way in which it brought other disagreements and resentments into focus, and its role as a symbol of the struggle between the agricultural and the commercial or industrial interests.[4] It may be interesting to see how far statistical evidence can be found that is consistent with such speculations.

Second, when did these changes take place? When did the two factions begin to define themselves and how far back, with the aid of the division lists, can this line of cleavage be traced? Was it a sudden break or was it the final stage in a disintegration that had been developing for a long time? There are some reasons to suppose that the break was long forecast. As Norman Gash says, Peel's administration was based on a party "deeply divided both on policy and personalities."[5] A number of circumstances of the history of the period suggest that the disruption of 1846 was the final outcome of a long growth of dissensions within the party and the product of tensions and disagreements that had been gathering momentum throughout Peel's ministry.

No attempt will be made in this paper to study men's motives or to explain why they voted as they did. For such a purpose it would be necessary to marshal the evidence in quite a different way: to correlate information on votes with other kinds of data about Members of Parliament such as their personal backgrounds or the kinds of constituencies they represented.[6] This paper, however, uses only the evidence of the division lists and attempts merely to show what the patterns of voting were, what were the principal lines of cleavage within the party, and how they were related to one another.

The study is based on a sample of 186 divisions selected from the total of 1,029 divisions that occurred during the lifetime of the Parliament of 1841-1847. The sample is small, only 18 per cent. It contains,

[4] G. Kitson Clark, "The Electorate and the Repeal of the Corn Laws," *Trans. Roy. Hist. Soc.*, 5th series, 1 (London, 1951), pp. 109-26; G. Kitson Clark, "The Repeal of the Corn Laws and the Politics of the Forties," *Economic History Review*, second series, IV (1951), pp. 1-13, hereinafter referred to as "Corn Laws and Politics"; Betty Kemp, "Reflections on the Repeal of the Corn Laws," *Victorian Studies*, Vol. 5, No. 3 (March 1962), pp. 189-204, hereinafter referred to as "Corn Laws"; Norman McCord, *The Anti-Corn Law League, 1838-1846* (London: Ruskin House, 1958), p. 22.

[5] Norman Gash, "Peel and the Party System, 1830-50," *Trans. Roy. Hist. Soc.*, 5th series, 1 (London, 1951), p. 62.

[6] I have worked a little on motivational questions along this line in another paper, "The Country Gentlemen and the Repeal of the Corn Laws," *English Historical Review*, Vol. 82, No. 322 (January 1967), pp. 47-60.

however, a much larger proportion of the 280 divisions in which 200 or more men (30 per cent of the House of Commons) participated: it includes 153 of these, or 55 per cent. Participation in voting in Parliament in the 1840s was extremely low, at least by twentieth-century standards, and the vast majority of divisions are tiny ones from which it is difficult to extract much information. The sample is really two samples: 84 items originally selected not by formal methods but on grounds of judgment of their importance and their relevance to certain problems; and an additional sample of 102 items, tabulated in the summer of 1968, designed to test some of the hypotheses that seemed to emerge from the earlier research, and selected by as orderly and as rigorous a procedure as the circumstances allowed. Although it proved possible to learn a good deal from the first 84 items, the addition of the 102 new items has done a great deal to amplify and clarify the original tentative inferences from the evidence, and has materially advanced the project.

The votes of all Members of Parliament, so far as they participated, in all of the 186 divisions have been punched. I have had fourfold tables prepared mechanically in which the votes of those positive or negative on each item were compared with the votes of those positive or negative on each of the 185 other items. The value of Yule's Q, which I have used as a searching statistic, was calculated for each paired comparison. I have also had a matrix of Q values made, suppressing those below an acceptable level. The level was, after some experimentation, set low, at 6.5; the information is limited, and I wanted to extract as much as I could from it. This produced a total of 17,205 fourfold tables, which seems like a good deal of material to look over. Actually the number of tables was three times this figure since these calculations were made not only for Parliament as a whole but also for each of the two main party groups separately. However, there are ways of managing such materials and, with the aid of the matrices and with certain other devices, it has proved possible to make some headway with them.

These data have been examined to find out on what items the two wings of the party were clearly opposed to each other, what scales could be made for the Conservatives alone and how these fitted the break in the party, and what differences could be found, both in subject matter and in date, between items statistically related to the break in the party over the Corn Laws and items not so related.

It should first be said, by way of background, that efforts to build scales for Parliament as a whole, regardless of party, have proved highly successful. Preliminary findings on this subject[7] have been confirmed and amplified by the additional information tabulated in the summer of 1968. Voting patterns in the Parliament of 1841-1847 turned out to be highly structured and extremely consistent, as can be shown if one attempts a multi-dimensional analysis instead of trying to fit everything into a single pattern. It has been possible to build, for Parliament as a whole, a number of scales which between them include 94 per cent of the items in the sample. Some of these scales are small, comprising only a few items, while others are more extensive. There is a certain amount of overlap between them since some items fit more than one dimension. The largest of these scales, which includes divisions on a variety of subjects, contains over half the items analyzed: 102 of the 186 if a threshold for Q of 6.5 is permitted; 94, still a considerable number, if the threshold for Q is set at 8.

This big scale was of particular interest in that it proved closely related to the party break. Items in it that divided the Liberals but on which Conservatives were unanimous or nearly unanimous appeared in the upper range, straight party items in the middle, while items on which Liberals were unanimous or nearly so but on which Conservatives divided appeared in the lower range. Thus it was possible, within certain limits, to predict a man's party affiliation from his vote on certain subjects, or to predict his vote from his party affiliation.

The big scale, however, was decidedly one sided. Of the 102 items it contained, 47 divided the Liberals, 47 were straight party votes, and only 9 divided the Conservatives. (One, which was counted twice, divided both parties.) Efforts to work into the scale more items on which Conservatives differed proved unavailing. The scale was useful mainly for studying disagreements among the Liberals or between the two parties. It contained the Corn Law divisions, so that it could be used to distinguish Peelites from Protectionists, but it gave few clues to dissensions within these two groups or to other lines of cleavage within the Conservative Party. In this respect it missed an important part of the story: the currents of opinion and the disagreements within the majority party that constituted three-fifths of the House of Commons and was in control of the government until June 1846.

It might be supposed that the reason for this was that, on the divisions analyzed, the Conservatives were generally united and had few differences of opinion. This, however, was far from being the case.

[7] W. O. Aydelotte, "Voting Patterns in the British House of Commons in the 1840s," *Comparative Studies in Society and History*, Vol. 5, No. 2 (January 1963), pp. 134-63; and "Parties and Issues."

Disagreements within the Conservative Party, even before 1846, were notorious. The information for the items in the sample is summarized in Table 1. A party has been counted as unanimous on an item if 90 per cent or more of those participating voted on one side; otherwise it is counted as divided. In these divisions, by this criterion, the Liberals were divided on 110 of the 186, 59 per cent and the Conservatives on 70, 38 per cent. The Conservatives disagreed less frequently than the Liberals but, even so, were divided on a large number of questions. Comparable figures for the two factions in the Conservative Party, the Peelites and the Protectionists, have also been included in the table. Percentages for these two groups have been calculated on the basis, not of the total number of items in the sample, but of the 70 items that split the Conservatives. The figures bring out that the Protectionist wing of the party, on which the big scale threw almost no light, was anything but a united body: the Protectionists were in fact, far more frequently divided than the Peelites.[8]

TABLE 1. EXTENT OF DISAGREEMENTS WITHIN BOTH PARTIES AND WITHIN THE TWO FACTIONS OF THE CONSERVATIVE PARTY, 1841-1847

	*Number of Divisions in Which Vote Was Unanimous**	*Number of Divisions in Which Vote Was Not Unanimous*	*Totals*
Liberals	76	110	186
Conservatives	116	70	186
Peelites	27	43	70
Protectionists	13	57	70
Percentages			
Liberals	41	59	
Conservatives	62	38	
Peelites	39	61	
Protectionists	19	81	

* A unanimous vote is defined as one in which 90 per cent or more of the group considered voted on the same side. Figures for Peelites and Protectionists include only the 70 divisions in which the Conservatives were not unanimous.

The present study of the Conservatives by themselves has made it clearer why dissensions in this party could, for the most part, not be

[8] If the percentages had been figured on the basis of the 186 items, the Peelites would prove to have been united on 77 per cent and the Protectionists on 69 per cent, a much less impressive difference.

fitted into the big scale and has brought out that the lines of disagreement among Conservatives were different in some interesting respects from those for Parliament as a whole or for the Liberals alone.

It is an important fact about the Conservatives, in the first place, that they voted unanimously (by the 90 per cent criterion) on 116 items, 62 per cent of those in the sample. Many of the most prominent topics of dispute in this Parliament did not divide the Conservatives at all, or hardly at all. There was no disagreement among them, for example, on divisions relating to political reform, public distress, the income tax (except for one ambiguous division that split both parties), the Irish question (with the single exception of the division on the second reading of the Irish Coercion Bill on 25 June 1846), and questions relating directly and obviously to the welfare of the landed interest. These matters were not subject to dispute within the Conservative Party and on them, in view of the clear Conservative majority in Parliament, the Liberal or Radical position had no hope of prevailing. Conservatives were also unanimous on the Corn Law question until 1846 and were unanimous on many, though not all, proposals relating to customs, religion, and the Poor Law.

The point is worth bringing out because it places in a more sharply defined context what Asa Briggs has described as "perhaps the most interesting exchange of political letters in the nineteenth century,"[9] the confidential letter of Richard Cobden to Sir Robert Peel and Peel's reply late in June 1846, just before the resignation of the government. Cobden wrote to Peel on 23 June urging him not to resign but to dissolve, calling attention to Peel's position in the opinion of the country as representing "the IDEA of the age," and arguing that differences of opinion on issues were no barrier to a fusion between Peelites and Whigs or Liberals which was already taking place in the country, and "must sooner or later take place in the House." The middle classes, Cobden argued, were not given to extreme or violent measures and were "not democratic," the Whig leaders were no more favorable than Peel to institutional changes, and: "Questions of organic reform have no vitality in the country, nor are they like to have any force in the House until your work is done." Peel, in his reply dated 24 June, not only referred to his own dislike of the duties of office and to the inadvisability of the political strategy Cobden proposed, but also gave a strong indication that the differences of opinion between himself and the Liberals could not easily be reconciled, and that even if he won an electoral victory on the Corn Law question he might fail to obtain

[9] Asa Briggs, *The Age of Improvement* (London: Longmans Green, 1959), p. 324.

a majority that would support his other policies. A minister, he said, is not justified in advising dissolution unless he is convinced it would produce "a majority based not on temporary personal sympathies, not on concurrence of sentiment on one branch of policy, however important that may be, but on general approval of his whole policy."[10]

The interest of Cobden's letter lies in the fact that it raised in provocative fashion the question of ideological differences between parties. It may also be said to have anticipated the future, since in the course of the next two decades important members of the Peelite group did move over to the other side of the House. It is clear in retrospect, however, that Cobden's immediate hopes were illusory and that his overture was doomed to failure from the start, not only because of the general parliamentary situation, but also because it was based on an incorrect appraisal of the differences of opinion between the principal political groups in Parliament. The evidence of the votes shows that substantial disagreements on important questions existed between the Peelites and the Whigs or Liberals, and that Peel sided with the rest of his party, and against the Liberals, on most subjects of special interest to Cobden with the single exception of free trade. It might be added that scholars now tend to regard Peel's handling of the Corn Law question not as a concession to the middle classes but as a skillful maneuver to protect the interests of the landed class,[11] though it was certainly not understood in this way by all those in Parliament at the time, either on the right or on the left.

Dissensions within the Conservative Party centered for the most part on matters different from those discussed above. Conservatives disagreed on, among other things, some free trade questions in 1846-1847, the Canada Wheat Bill of 1843, the Maynooth College grant of 1845, the Colleges (Ireland) Bill of 1845, the Health of Towns Bill of 1847, some religious questions, and some questions relating to factory legislation and to the Poor Law. On all these topics except free trade there was also occasional disagreement among the Liberals and on some of them, such as factory legislation and the Poor Law,

[10] Both letters are published in John Morley, *The Life of Richard Cobden* (2 vols.; London: Chapman & Hall, Limited, 1881), I, 390-401. The text of Peel's reply is also given in Charles Stuart Parker, ed., *Sir Robert Peel, From His Private Papers* (3 vols.; London: John Murray, 1891-99), III, 367-69. Peel wrote, in a memorandum which he enclosed in a letter he sent to the Duke of Wellington on 21 June 1846, regarding the possibility of a dissolution and a general election: "If we are to succeed, we shall succeed by an unnatural combination with those who agree with us in nothing but the principles of Free Trade. A short time only would pass before this combination would be dissolved, and we should be at the mercy of our new allies" (*ibid.*, p. 365).

[11] Kitson Clark, "Corn Laws and Politics"; Kemp, "Corn Laws."

frequent disagreement. Indeed, 42 of the 70 items dividing the Conservatives, 60 per cent, also divided the Liberals. Some of these items appear in the subsidiary scales for the whole Parliament but these in general are not extensive enough in range of P— values to yield a clear picture of what was happening within the Conservative Party.

Conservatives also differed from Liberals, or from Parliament as a whole, in the topics they associated together. The small scale that it has proved possible to build for Conservatives alone contains items on subjects that, for Parliament as a whole, belong to five different and largely unrelated dimensions: free trade, the Canada Wheat question, the Maynooth question, factory legislation, and the Poor Law. For Parliament as a whole, occasional items on some of these subjects will scale with the Corn Law division of 1846, but it proved impossible to get the majority of items on these matters into a single scale, and five separate scales had to be constructed to contain them.

There was also a difference between the two parties of another kind. It is true that, on a number of issues on which Peelites differed markedly from Protectionists, it was the Peelites who represented the point of view of the Liberal wing of Parliament while the Protectionists represented the opposite position. This was the case, for example, in the Corn Law divisions of 1846 and in the divisions on the Maynooth grant in 1845. This pattern, however, did not always obtain. On certain issues the structures of voting in the two main party groups were so different as to suggest an interesting reversal of values. On some topics the Peelites took a position directly opposed to that of the Liberals, while the Protectionists, or a section of them, joined the Liberals in opposing the government and, to some degree at least, came closer than the Peelites to approximating the Liberal view. The most famous example of this is the division on the second reading of Peel's Irish Coercion Bill on 25 June 1846. The bill was supported almost unanimously by the Peelites and opposed almost unanimously by the Liberals, while a large section of the Protectionists (74 out of the 190 who participated in the division) joined with the Liberal group to oppose the bill, and thus succeeded in overthrowing the government. Another case is the Canada Wheat Bill of 1843 which was supported unanimously or almost unanimously by the Peelites but opposed by the great majority of Liberals. A large segment of the Protectionists, 41 of the 135 who participated in the division of 26 May 1843, shown in Table 2, voted with the Liberals and against the government.

Variants of this pattern, also shown in Table 2, appear in divisions on the Poor Law and on factory legislation. On these two issues there was some disagreement among the Liberals, the Peelites inclined

TABLE 2. VOTES ON SOME ITEMS ON WHICH THE PROTECTIONISTS CAME CLOSER TO TAKING THE LIBERAL POSITION THAN THE PEELITES DID*

	Liberals		*Peelites*		*Protectionists*		*Other Conservatives*		*Totals*	
	+	−	+	−	+	−	+	−	+	−
3rd Reading of Corn Law Bill, 15 May 1846	235	10	114	0	0	241	0	0	349	251
3rd Reading of Maynooth Bill, 21 May 1845	169	35	79	18	55	119	16	14	319	186
2nd Reading of Irish Coercion Bill, 25 June 1846	6	239	110	4	116	74	12	1	244	318
Canada Wheat Bill, 26 May 1843	19	90	73	0	94	41	34	8	220	139
2nd Reading of Poor Law Bill, 17 June 1842	89	31	56	10	86	14	31	8	262	63
3rd Reading of Poor Law Bill, 22 July 1842	19	18	36	2	30	9	20	3	105	32
2nd Reading of Poor Law Bill 21 May 1847	120	11	39	3	56	29	5	1	220	44
3rd Reading of Poor Law Bill, 24 June 1847	69	14	21	1	15	21	2	1	107	37
Ten Hours, 22 March 1844	56	94	52	25	57	62	26	13	191	194
Ten Hours, 22 May 1846	78	74	75	8	47	111	5	3	205	196
Ten Hours, 3 March 1847	62	81	34	15	6	89	0	7	102	192

* The Corn Law and Maynooth divisions, on which Peelites and Liberals took the same line, are included for comparison. In the remaining divisions, votes for the Coercion Bill, for the Canada Wheat Bill, for the Poor Law, and against ten hours have been counted as positive.

strongly to one side while the Protectionists inclined, sometimes only slightly and sometimes strongly, to the opposite side. The Poor Law was ordinarily supported by all groups, Liberals, Peelites, and Protectionists, with substantial majorities. On the other hand, Peelites supported it more decidedly and more consistently than did either

Protectionists or Liberals, and such opposition as there was to the Poor Law in the Conservative Party came from the Protectionist wing. It did not always come even from this group. As appears from the table, the two factions in the Conservative Party supported the second reading of the Poor Law Bill of 1842 to almost exactly the same extent. On a number of divisions on the subject in 1841, 1842, and 1844 both factions in the party supported the Poor Law almost unanimously and the only opposition to it came from a few Liberals.

On the ten hours question the story is somewhat different. The Liberal group, though much divided, favored the proposal by a substantial majority in 1844, and by a somewhat smaller majority in 1847. Peelites were strong against it, approximately two to one, in 1844 and this opposition was clearly maintained and sometimes even increased in the divisions of 1846-1847. Protectionists, who were about equally divided on the question in 1844, supported it much more strongly in 1846 and supported it by an overwhelming majority in 1847. In other words, in the divisions on this question in 1846-1847 a large and increasing majority of the Protectionists joined a section of the Liberals, against the Peelites, to support a ten hours measure.

The information in Tables 2 and 3 has been arranged so as to correspond to these facts. Votes for the Coercion Bill, for the Canada Wheat Bill, for the Poor Law, and against ten hours or other factory reform proposals have all been counted as positive. On the same principle, positive values have been given to votes against J. A. Roebuck's motion on the Afghanistan War on 1 March 1843 and to votes for the motion of 28 June 1842 that John Walter attend and give evidence before the Select Committee on Election Proceedings. These assignments of plus and minus signs are not intended to indicate judgments on the merits of these questions. They are used merely to avoid negative correlations and to put the information in the tables in a form in which it can readily be grasped. In tabulating votes for Parliament as a whole, as it happens, the opposite notation was used, for various reasons, on all these items. The items have simply been reflected for the purpose of studying the Conservatives alone. It is necessary, however, to point out that these reflections have been made to make it clear that, on these questions, the Protectionists came closer than the Peelites to approximating the Liberal position.

What is intriguing about these findings is the suggestion of a pattern, or several slightly different patterns, of a combination of both ends against the middle, the extreme right and the left against the Peelites. Such a phenomenon could not be detected by scale analysis of Parliament as a whole since paired comparisons do not, in general, reveal an alliance of both extremes against the center. Clues leading to it did emerge, however, when the parties were scaled separately. The findings suggest that the notion of a Tory-Radical alliance, which has sometimes been suggested, may have some foundation in fact.

It seems doubtful, however, that much can be made of this. Tory-Radical collaboration developed on only a few topics, its extent was limited, and the circumstances in some cases were rather special. The only two issues, of those considered here, on which there appeared a clear collaboration between the extreme right and the Liberal wing of Parliament were the Canada Wheat Bill of 1843 and the Irish Coercion Bill of 1846. In neither case, however, did a clear majority of the Protectionists vote against the government, and Liberal opposition to both proposals was much stronger than Protectionist opposition. The Protectionist opposition to the second reading of the Irish Coercion Bill on 25 June 1846 had, notoriously, a factional basis. On the first reading, on 1 May 1846, Protectionists unanimously supported the government. The Canada Wheat Bill of 1843 was ambiguous and produced strange combinations. Its supporters in the division of 26 May 1843, shown in Table 2, included not only members of the government and other Conservatives like Sir Robert Inglis, Lord Ashley, and Lord George Bentinck but also prominent Radicals such as John Bowring, T. S. Duncombe, Joseph Hume, Joseph Brotherton, and W. S. Crawford. Its opponents included not only Disraeli and Sir William George Hylton Jolliffe but also Lord Palmerston and Lord John Russell. In this case, well-known Radicals were aligned with Peelites rather than Protectionists, and it would be difficult to push the Tory-Radical thesis very far.

Protectionist opposition to the Poor Law was limited. No group displayed a consistent or regular pattern of voting as a majority against the Poor Law. All that can be said is that Peelites supported the Poor Law more strongly than did either the Protectionists or the Liberals. On the ten hours question there was indeed a strong Protectionist majority for the measure in 1846, which had become an overwhelming one by 1847, while the Peelites were clearly on the other side. Liberals, though usually showing a majority for the cause, were heavily divided. Nor was the extreme or Radical left of the Liberal group more favorable to ten hours than were the moderate Whigs and Liberals; it was rather, so far as a difference existed, the other way round. The strong support of Protectionists for ten hours during the last year and a half of this Parliament has, of course, been used as ammunition for the thesis of Tory paternalism. The subject raises certain problems, however,[12] and is in any case too large a matter to digress upon here. There is also, as will appear from evidence to be advanced presently, the possibility of a different and simpler kind of explanation.

An attempt has been made, in these last several paragraphs, to show that the Conservatives were, to some extent, living in a world of their own in regard to issues and objectives. There was no dispute among them on many of the topics prominent in the discussions of this Parliament, they made associations between issues different from those made by the Liberals and, on certain questions and to varying degrees, right and left seem to have been reversed so that what was a conservative position for one party was a liberal position for the other. The Conservatives seem to have been operating on a set of assumptions somewhat different from those held by the Liberals with regard to the meaning and implications of some of these questions.

The following observations on voting patterns among the Conservatives are based only on the 70 items that divided the party: divisions in which not less than 11 per cent and not more than 89 per cent of the Conservatives participating voted on one side. Votes of 90 per cent or more of the Conservatives on the same side have been counted as unanimous and excluded from the analysis. Items with extreme marginals, on which the population studied was unanimous or nearly so, are not of much use for scaling. They may produce freak figures—in some cases the alteration of a single vote would change the value of Q from 10 to 0—and the results are not informative.

In examining the votes of Peelites and Protectionists it may be useful to begin with the two tests that were made for Liberals and Conservatives:[13] how far the members of each group were divided among themselves; and how far the votes of members of the two groups can be fitted into an ordinal scale in such a way that each group occupies a different segment of the scale.

1. As is clear from the figures already presented in Table 1, both factions of the Conservative Party were, like the two main party groups, much divided internally. Peelites voted unanimously, by the 90 per cent criterion, on only 27 of the 70 items, 39 per cent. The Pro-

[12] See David Roberts, "Tory Paternalism and Social Reform in Early Victorian England," *American Historical Review*, Vol. 63, No. 2 (March 1958), 323-37; Jenifer Hart, "Nineteenth-Century Social Reform: A Tory Interpretation of History," *Past and Present*, 31 (July 1965), pp. 39-61; Valerie Cromwell, "Interpretations of Nineteenth-Century Administration: An Analysis," *Victorian Studies*, Vol. 9, No. 3 (March 1966), pp. 245-55; and W. O. Aydelotte, "The Conservative and Radical Interpretations of Early Victorian Social Legislation," *Victorian Studies*, Vol. 11, No. 2 (December 1967), pp. 225-36.

[13] Aydelotte, "Parties and Issues," pp. 107-10.

tectionists were even more disunited and voted unanimously on only 13 items or 19 per cent. I have found only four "straight" votes in which 90 per cent or more of the Peelites were on one side and 90 per cent or more of the Protectionists on the other. These include three Corn Law divisions on 27 February, 27 March, and 15 May 1846—the last of these being, of course, the division used to define the two groups—and a division on a duty on cotton articles on 13 March 1846. It is sometimes said that certain other divisions reflected or prefigured the Corn Law division exactly, but this is not the case with those I have examined. In the vote on the second reading of the Irish Coercion Bill considerable Protectionist strength was certainly mustered against the government, but the majority of Protectionists who voted in this division supported Peel. Nor did the Maynooth divisions of 1845 exactly prefigure the Corn Law split, as has sometimes been supposed: a substantial proportion of those who had supported Peel on Maynooth in 1845 opposed him on the Corn Law question in 1846. The small proportion of straight votes between Peelites and Protectionists, 4 out of 70 or 6 per cent, stands in marked contrast to the relatively large proportion of straight votes between Liberals and Conservatives, which was 47 out of 186 or 25 per cent. By this test, the two factions seem ill defined.

2. It is possible, however, to make a further test, using the more refined technique of cumulative scaling, to find out whether the Peelite-Protectionist split has any relation to scales that can be worked out for the Conservative Party.

For this purpose it was necessary first to inquire what scale patterns appear among the 70 items dividing the Conservatives. The inquiry was commenced with topical scales: scales on each of the various subjects on which Conservatives disagreed. These worked out extremely well. On most topics, almost all the items fitted together into a scale. Of the 12 items on factory legislation, 11 formed a perfect scale, with which the 12th almost fitted. Of the 9 Poor Law items, 8 fitted a perfect scale, and the 9th one nearly did. (Q-matrices showing the relations between items on these two topics are presented in Table 8.) It proved possible to construct 13 topical scales containing, among them, 57 or 81 per cent of the 70 items. A number of the scales were small, some contained only two items, but this was to be expected in the distribution of a relatively small number of divisions among a relatively large number of subjects. The topical scales were, however, too narrow in range of P— values to provide an adequate test of the division in the party. For this purpose it was necessary to attempt to prepare a longer scale.

A number of the 13 topical scales were related to each other, and they could be brought together in any of several different ways so as to produce a smaller number of dimensions. The division on the third reading of the Corn Law Bill or, in other words, the Peelite-Protectionist split turned out to have a scale relation, shown by an acceptable value of Q in the paired comparison, with a large number of items in scales on other subjects. However, by no means all the items that scaled with the Corn Law division would also scale with each other, and it proved surprisingly difficult to build a scale of any length for the Conservatives alone. The lines of divergence in the party were complex and could not readily be fitted into a comprehensive pattern. The longest scale that could be constructed for the Conservatives, which is shown in Table 3, contained only 24 items. This assumes a threshold value for Q of 7; if the threshold were raised to 8, only 21 items could be included. Of the 24 items in the scale, 11 have been reflected: the 3 on the Canada Wheat Bill, the 1 on the Poor Law, and the 7 on factory legislation.

The figures in Table 3 make it clear that each of the two factions occupied or was principally concentrated in a different section of the ideological spectrum defined by this small scale. Items dividing Peelites, on which Protectionists were unanimous, appear in the upper part; straight items in the middle; and items dividing Protectionists, on which Peelites were unanimous or nearly so, in the lower part. The pattern is not quite so neat as that which it was possible to obtain in the comparison of Liberals and Conservatives. On some of the items in the lower part, for example, the Peelites were not quite unanimous by the 90 per cent criterion, though they were not badly divided either. On the whole the scale test, so far as it goes, seems successful. The two factions are clearly differentiated by their votes on the topics that appear in the scale, and they did differ substantially from each other in the range of causes that their members supported.

There is also another feature of the evidence that seems to point to the importance of the Corn Law break as a dividing line. The division on the third reading of the Corn Law Bill shows a scale relationship, by the Q test, not only with the 23 items that, with it, compose the scale just described, but also with 21 additional items that cannot be fitted into this scale. These 21 items could be fitted with the Corn Law division into other kinds of scales, presumably related to different general themes or to different political groupings. It would be tedious and would serve no useful purpose to describe in detail these additional possible scales. As a simpler way of presenting this information, Table 4 shows the number of items on each topic that fit the Conservative

TABLE 3. SCALE FOR CONSERVATIVE PARTY, SHOWING VOTES OF THE TWO FACTIONS

	Peelites		*Protectionists*	
	+	−	+	−
Ten Hours, 21 April 1847	10	8	2	52
Ten Hours, 17 February 1847	27	17	6	96
Hosiery Manufacturers Bill, 9 June 1847	8	3	7	49
Ten Hours, 3 March 1847	34	15	6	89
Ten Hours, 3 May 1847	27	8	7	78
Corn Law Bill, 2nd Reading, 27 March 1846	103	3	4	224
Corn Law Bill, 3rd Reading, 15 May 1846	114	0	0	241
Corn Laws, Motion for Committee, 27 February 1846	110	0	0	231
Duty on Cotton, 13 March 1846	63	1	3	100
Navigation Laws, Motion for Select Committee, 9 February 1847	29	2	8	60
Customs Bill, 26 March 1847	34	4	16	56
Maynooth Bill, 3 April 1845	60	9	35	89
Maynooth Bill, 3rd Reading, 21 May 1845	79	18	55	119
Fielden's Ten Hours Bill, 22 May 1846	75	8	47	111
Maynooth Bill, 2nd Reading, 18 April 1845	82	19	59	111
Lace Factories Bill, 20 May 1846	61	1	24	50
Maynooth Bill, 28 April 1845	68	11	36	70
Maynooth Bill, 2 May 1845	63	6	33	59
Poor Law Bill, 3rd Reading, 24 June 1847	21	1	46	65
Opposition to Miles's Proposal for Tax Relief for Agricultural Interest, 17 March 1845	69	1	15	21
Opposition to Miles's Proposal for Abatement of Tax to Farm Tenants, 10 March 1845	68	1	65	55
Canada Wheat Bill, 26 May 1843	73	0	94	41
Canada Wheat Bill, 3rd Reading, 15 June 1843	53	0	59	26
Canada Wheat Bill, 2nd Reading, 2 June 1843	72	0	87	39

scale, that do not fit it but have a scale relationship with the Corn Law division of some other kind, and that have no scale relationship with the Corn Law division.

It may seem puzzling to those who have not worked with these methods that an item, such as the Corn Law division, will fit into a scale with either of two other items, although these two other items will not fit into a scale with each other: that A will scale with either B or C, but B and C will not scale together. Such findings are, however, frequent in scale analysis. A given roll call may be multi-dimensional in the sense that it reflects more than one general question and,

TABLE 4. SCALE RELATIONSHIPS OF DIVISION ON THIRD READING OF CORN LAW BILL, 15 MAY 1846, TO THE OTHER 69 ITEMS DIVIDING THE CONSERVATIVES, ARRANGED BY TOPIC

	Items in Conservative Scale	*Other Items with Scale Relation to Corn Law Division*	*Items Unrelated to Corn Law Division*
Corn Law Bill	2		
Other Customs	3		2
Canada Wheat Bill	3		
Maynooth Bill	5		
Factory Legislation	7		5
Poor Law	1	3	5
Roman Catholic Relief		2	
Jewish Disabilities Bill		1	
Marriage with Deceased Wife's Sister			1
Ecclesiastical Courts Bill			1
Dissenters Chapels Bill		2	
Health of Towns Bill		6	
Irish Coercion Bill		1	
Prisons Bill		1	
Proposals of William Miles	2	1	
Colleges (Ireland) Bill		2	1
Mines and Collieries Bills		1	1
Disputed Elections			2
Railways Bill of 1844		1	
Bills to Establish Individual Railways			4
Drainage of Lands Bill			1
Roebuck's Motion on Afghanistan War			1
Masters and Servants Bill			1
TOTALS	23	21	25

when this is the case, it may prove possible to include it in any of two or more apparently unidimensional scales that, for the most part, are unrelated to one another. The Corn Law division is by no means the only multi-dimensional item that has appeared in this analysis; there will be occasion later to mention certain others.

The usual practice in scaling research is to disregard this feature of the evidence: to put an item into the scale where it falls first, or into which it fits best, and then not to consider it for inclusion in other scales. It would be impracticable to follow up all these connections, even with the aid of machines, in view of the amount of work that would be involved and the complexity of the ensuing findings. Following up these connections for a single item, however, is quite feasible particularly when, as in this case, the total number of items being analyzed is not large, and some brief consideration of them may throw additional light on the break in the party. It is an important point about the Corn Law division that it was related to a number of different attitude dimensions, not all of which were related to each other, and that in this sense it brought to a single focus a number of different and otherwise unrelated lines of controversy within the party.

The evidence presented so far suggests that, measured by the test of votes on other subjects, the break in the Conservative Party over the Corn Law question had considerable weight. Certain qualifications must, of course, be made. The break within the Conservative Party was not so sharply defined as the break between the two main party groups: there was a far smaller proportion of straight votes with the two factions voting unanimously, by the 90 per cent criterion, on opposite sides; and the two factions were in agreement with each other on many of the significant issues that came up during the course of this Parliament. Also, items on some topics on which Conservatives disagreed have no scale relation to the Corn Law division and, so far as the statistical evidence shows, were not connected with the party break. On the other hand, the scale test was reasonably successful, and the two factions fit not too badly into the upper and lower reaches of the spectrum defined by the scale. Also, the Corn Law division was related to a number of additional items that do not fit this scale. It was related, in a scale sense, to 44 or 64 per cent of the other 69 items that divided the Conservatives. This evidence is certainly consistent with the hypotheses that other issues besides the Corn Law question were involved in the party break, and that this break brought together to a single point several different lines of disagreement within the party.

This information, however, raises some questions. Although the situation can be described in statistical terms, it is harder to see what these results signify and what are the connections between these various subjects. A scale relationship between a set of roll calls does not, of course, imply that the scale is unidimensional in substantive content. On the contrary, this is exactly the inference that it is not permissible to draw from such evidence. The presence of two items in the same scale may have nothing to do with their subject matter. Other explanations, such as party discipline or political maneuver, are always possible and such alternatives are the more likely when, as here, the scale relationships have been empirically determined. On the other hand, scale findings are unquestionably consistent with the hypothesis of unidimensionality of content and, when this is plausible on other grounds, the existence of a scale may be regarded as supporting evidence. A case in point would be the topical scales described above. Items were selected that appeared to be similar in subject matter and, when it turned out that all or almost all the items on a topic fitted into a scale together, this seemed strong additional evidence for the existence of a single attitude dimension, which was represented by the items that fitted the pattern. Similarly, if a scale is developed empirically, such as the scale of 24 items for the Conservatives, and a conceptual scheme can then be developed that helps to explain these relationships, it would be possible to argue with more assurance that the scale is unidimensional in subject matter. If this cannot be done easily, however, it is natural to start casting around for a different explanation.

With regard to the present evidence there would seem to be some theoretical problems of this kind. It is hard to make sense of these findings in terms of subject matter or to understand the reasons why certain topics were statistically related to the Corn Law question while others were not. A principal feature of the results so far is their lack of intelligibility: the difficulty of hitting upon a rationale that will explain them.

The 24 items in the Conservative scale deal with diverse topics. The scale combines divisions on the Corn Laws, other customs, and the Canada Wheat Bill of 1843. These might all perhaps be regarded as having, to some extent, a common or related content. The votes on the two motions by William Miles regarding tax relief for agriculture might also be tied in, since a main theme of the Corn Law debate was the possible impact of repeal on the agricultural interest. It is less clear, however, what may have been the relationship between these proposals and the divisions on factory legislation, the Maynooth grant of 1845, and the Poor Law. It is hard to build a theory that comprises all these subjects or to identify a common denominator among them that would account for their being connected in a scale.

The 21 items not in this scale but showing a scale relationship to the Corn Law division of some other kind are also rather varied. One of them is another motion by Miles, in 1842, proposing that the duty on imported livestock be taken by weight, and this might be tied in with the free trade question. Another is the second reading of the Irish Coercion Bill: the connection of this division to the Corn Law division is fairly clear from the history of the period, but it is not a connection of substantive content. Other divisions showing a scale relationship to the Corn Law vote dealt with such matters as Jewish disabilities, Roman Catholic relief, the Colleges (Ireland) Bill, the Health of Towns Bill, the Poor Law, the Railways Bill of 1844, the Prisons Bill of 1847, and the Mines and Collieries Bill of 1842. For most of these matters it is hard to say with any degree of assurance what is the connection they might have with the Corn Law issue.

The subject matter of the 25 items unrelated to the Corn Law vote is roughly indicated in Table 4 and need not be recapitulated in the text. Presumably the break in the party was not related to any of these matters and, for most or all of them perhaps, one would not expect it, since there seems no obvious connection. It must be added, however, that there seems no obvious connection between the Corn Law question and some of the items it is statistically related to, either. One special puzzle is that on certain topics—notably customs, factory legislation, and the Poor Law—some items are related in a scale sense to the Corn Law division while others are not.

There would seem, then, to be considerable obstacles to the interpretation of the scale findings in terms of substantive content. The results do not seem altogether consistent with the evidence of the highly successful topical scales which appeared to give a strong indication that, in this Parliament, voting patterns were closely related to subject matter. It may be, of course, that something has been overlooked, that there is some underlying thematic unity in the items statistically related to the Corn Law division, some sense in which they could all be regarded as dealing with the same general question, which is not immediately apparent. Uncertainty on this point, however, may be somewhat relieved by the use of a different approach that has ultimately proved more fruitful.

The second general question raised at the outset was: how far back, by the evidence of the division lists, can the line of cleavage in the Conservative Party be traced? It seems useful to make clear, first, the chronological patterns of unanimity or division within the two main party groups and within the two factions of the Conservative Party. This information is presented in Table 5. To simplify the table the data have been given not for each year but for the three chronological periods that proved most clearly distinct from one another: 1841-1844, 1845-1846, and 1847. A unanimous vote has been counted, as before, as a vote in which 90 per cent or more of the group considered were on the same side. The percentages at the bottom of the table give the gist of the information.

During the six years of this Parliament, as has been pointed out already, Liberals disagreed on a considerably larger number of items than Conservatives did. However, as Table 5 shows, there was a chronological change. Conservatives were much more united in the early years of this Parliament than in the later years. They voted unanimously on three-fourths of the items in the sample for 1841-1844, on less than half of those for 1845-1846, and on less than a third of those for 1847. Liberals, on the other hand, tended to agree somewhat more frequently in the later years than in the early years, although the trend was much less marked. What it comes to is that Conservatives were much more united than Liberals in 1841-1844, about on a par with them in 1845-1846, and considerably less united in 1847.

TABLE 5. EXTENT OF DISAGREEMENTS WITHIN BOTH PARTIES AND WITHIN THE TWO FACTIONS OF THE CONSERVATIVE PARTY, SHOWN BY DATE

	Liberals		*Conservatives*		*Peelites**		*Protectionists*	
	Unanimous	*Not Unanimous*	*Unanimous*	*Not Unanimous*	*Unanimous*	*Not Unanimous*	*Unanimous*	*Not Unanimous*
1841-44	43	76	89	30	9	21	0	30
1845-46	20	18	18	20	14	6	4	16
1847	13	16	9	20	4	16	9	11
TOTALS	76	110	116	70	27	43	13	57
Percentages								
1841-44	36	64	75	25	30	70	0	100
1845-46	53	47	47	53	70	30	20	80
1847	45	55	32	68	20	80	45	55

* Figures for Peelites and Protectionists include only the 70 divisions in which the Conservatives were not unanimous.

Comparable figures for Peelites and Protectionists are shown on the right-hand side of Table 5. Both groups disagreed extensively right through the period of this Parliament, but here again there is a clear chronological trend. Peelites were extremely divided in the early years, much more united in 1845-1846, but heavily divided again in 1847. The Protectionists were, in the early years, even more divided than the Peelites. Actually, though the summary table does not bring this out, they did not vote unanimously, by the 90 per cent criterion, on a single one of the 42 items that divided the Conservatives in the years 1841-1845. It was only in 1846 that they first began to vote as a coherent group. By 1847 they were voting together more frequently than the Peelites.

It has already been shown that the break in the party over the Corn Laws corresponded exactly to a small number of other items and was related in a scale sense to many more. The question when the break in the party began to get under way can perhaps be answered, at least in part, by examining the dates of these other divisions with which the Corn Law vote was, statistically, so closely connected. This information is given in Table 6 which shows, for the same chronological periods that were used in the previous table, the dates of the 24 items in the Conservative scale (including the third reading of the Corn Law Bill), the 21 items not in this scale but having a scale relationship with the Corn Law division of some other kind, and the 25 items that have no scale relationship to the Corn Law division.

Table 6 clarifies the picture a good deal. Most of the divisions that fit the Conservative scale, 21 out of the 24, came in the last years of

TABLE 6. SCALE INFORMATION ON THE 70 ITEMS DIVIDING CONSERVATIVES, ARRANGED BY DATE

	Items in Conservative Scale	*Other Items with Scale Relation to Corn Law Division*	*Items Unrelated to Corn Law Division*
1841-44	3	7	20
1845-46	13	4	3
1847	8	10	2
TOTALS	24	21	25
Percentages			
1841-44	13	33	80
1845-46	54	19	12
1847	33	48	8

SUMMARY

	Items in Conservative Scale or Otherwise Related to Corn Law Division	*Items Unrelated to Corn Law Division*	*Items on Which Conservatives Unanimous*	*All Items in Sample*
1841-44	10	20	89	119
1845-47	35	5	27	67
TOTALS	45	25	116	186
Percentages				
1841-44	22	80	77	64
1845-47	78	20	23	36

this Parliament, 1845-1847. Divisions not in this scale but still having a scale relationship to the Corn Law division also tend strongly toward the later period: 14 out of the 21 occurred in 1845-1847. On the other hand, the vast majority of the divisions unrelated to the Corn Law vote by the Q test, 20 out of 25, took place in the early years of this Parliament, 1841-1844. The pattern appears more distinctly in the summary of the figures at the bottom of Table 6. Here, all items related to the Corn Law division, whether in the Conservative scale or not, have been thrown into a single category, and only two chronological divisions have been used, 1841-1844 and 1845-1847. There have been added for comparison the dates of the 116 items on which Conservatives were unanimous and the dates of the total of the 186 items in the sample. The summary shows the striking correspondence of the two categories with dates: of the items related to the Corn Law division, nearly four-fifths came in the years 1845-1847; of the items unrelated, exactly four-fifths came in the years 1841-1844. The unrelated items show a chronological pattern very similar to that of the 116 divisions in which Conservatives were unanimous.

The dates also help to explain why, for several topics, the Corn Law division has a scale relationship to some items but not to others.

TABLE 7. SCALE RELATIONSHIPS BETWEEN DIVISION ON THIRD READING OF CORN LAW BILL AND THE 69 OTHER ITEMS DIVIDING THE CONSERVATIVES, ARRANGED BY RELATIONSHIP, TOPIC, AND DATE

	Related		*Unrelated*	
	1841-44	*1845-47*	*1841-44*	*1845-47*
Corn Laws		2		
Other Customs		3	2	
Canada Wheat Bill	3			
Maynooth Bill		5		
Factory Legislation		7	5	
Poor Law	2	2	5	
Health of Towns Bill		6		
Colleges (Ireland) Bill		2		1
Miles's Motions	1	2		
Dissenters Chapels Bill	2			
Religion: Other		3	2	
Railways Bill of 1844	1			
Railways: Individual Lines			1	3
Mines and Collieries Bills	1			1
Other: Miscellaneous		2	5	
TOTALS	10	34	20	5

It turns out that, in most such cases, it is related to the late items but not to the early ones. The information is summarized in Table 7. The Corn Law division fits the three late customs divisions but not the two early ones. It fits all seven divisions on factory legislation in 1846-1847 but none of the five divisions on this subject in 1844. It fits both the two late Poor Law divisions but, of the seven early ones, it fits only two, and these badly, and has no scale relationship with the other five. This fact is the more striking since, for several of these topics, early and late divisions scale together. This is not true of the customs divisions, but it is true of the divisions on factory legislation and on the Poor Law. Matrices of Q values of items on these two topics are given in Table 8, with the Corn Law division added for comparison in the last column of each matrix. It will be observed that, on each topic, nearly all the items scale together regardless of date. To make a perfect scale one item would have to be omitted from each matrix but, even so, the fit of these slightly irregular items is not too bad. The relation of the Corn Law division to items on these other topics stands out so clearly from the table that it requires no further comment.

It might be pointed out that all the factory legislation divisions of 1846-1847 are multi-dimensional in the sense described earlier. They scale with the other divisions on this subject in 1844 and also with the Corn Law division, although the Corn Law division fits none of the factory legislation divisions of 1844. The Poor Law divisions of 1847 are multi-dimensional in the same way.

Although the trend of the figures is extremely strong, there are, of course, some exceptions to the pattern, as can be most conveniently observed from the summary at the bottom of Table 6. Of the 45 divisions related to the Corn Law division (including the Corn Law division itself), 10 came in the early period; while, of the 25 unrelated, 5 came in the later period. Some of these exceptions can perhaps be explained. As appears from Table 9, Conservative whips were used as tellers in almost all divisions in 1841-1846 that have a scale relationship to the Corn Law vote, the sole exception being the tiny division on Lord Ashley's Mines and Collieries Bill on 1 July 1842. Conservative whips were used much less frequently on the items in these years that proved unrelated to the Corn Law vote, perhaps because these matters were of less interest to the government. Other apparent irregularities might be explained in terms of subject matter. The ten early divisions that were related included the three Canada Wheat divisions of 1843 and a division of 1842 on a proposal by William Miles that duty on imported livestock be taken by weight. These matters

TABLE 8. Q-MATRIX OF ITEMS ON FACTORY LEGISLATION, WITH DIVISION ON THIRD READING OF CORN LAW BILL ADDED FOR COMPARISON: CONSERVATIVES ONLY

		1	*2*	*3*	*4*	*5*	*6*	*7*	*8*	*9*	*10*	*11*	*12*	*Division on Third Reading of Corn Law Bill*
1844	1		10	10	10	10	9	9	9	9	8	9	7	4
	2			10	10	10	9	9	9	9	8	9	7	4
	3				10	10	9	9	9	9	9	9	5	3
	4					10	9	9	9	9	9	9	5	3
	5						9	9	10	9	8	8	4	3
1846	6							10	10	10	10	10	9	9
	7								9	10	10	10	9	9
1847	8									10	10	9	9	9
	9										10	10	9	9
	10											10	8	9
	11												9	9
	12													8

Q-MATRIX OF ITEMS ON POOR LAW, WITH DIVISION ON THIRD READING OF CORN LAW BILL ADDED FOR COMPARISON: CONSERVATIVES ONLY

		1	*2*	*3*	*4*	*5*	*6*	*7*	*8*	*9*	*Division on Third Reading of Corn Law Bill*
1842	1		10	9	9	9	9	8	8	6	0
	2			10	9	10	10	9	9	8	6
	3				9	9	9	9	6	7	1
	4					9	9	9	7	4	3
	5						10	9	8	8	6
	6							9	8	8	3
1843	7								8	7	3
1847	8									10	7
	9										9

might be regarded as having some connection with the free trade question that finally broke up the party. The five late items that do not fit include three divisions on bills to establish individual railway lines, which scale with hardly any of the items in the entire sample; voting on these was apparently highly irregular.

TABLE 9. EXTENT TO WHICH THE CONSERVATIVE WHIPS WERE USED AS TELLERS ON THE 70 ITEMS DIVIDING THE CONSERVATIVES, ARRANGED BY SCALE RELATIONSHIP TO THIRD READING OF CORN LAW BILL, AND BY DATE

	Items in Conservative Scale or Otherwise Related to Corn Law Division		*Items Unrelated to Corn Law Division*	
	Conservative Whips Used	*Conservative Whips Not Used*	*Conservative Whips Used*	*Conservative Whips Not Used*
1841-44	9	1	12	8
1845-46	17	0	1	2
1847	0	18	0	2
TOTALS	26	19	13	12

These leads could be further pursued, and it is possible that a detailed study of the legislative history of some of these proposals would cast more light on the exceptions to the pattern. There is not space, however, to attempt this here and, in any case, the exceptions are relatively few. The general trend of the figures is so decided that, in spite of the small number of cases involved, it is not unimpressive.

This evidence, so far as it goes, suggests that the cleavage in the Conservative Party along the lines of the break of 1846 came late in the lifetime of this Parliament and was relatively sudden. It does not support the view that the break of 1846 was the final fruition or bringing to light of a division that had long existed. On the contrary, the break was not exactly prefigured by any vote before 1846, and even items related to this break in a scale sense began for the most part only in 1845, the year before the great disruption, when the Corn Law question was already coming to the fore. Though Conservatives unquestionably voted on a number of items in a scale pattern, this pattern began to emerge only in 1845, on the eve of the Corn Law struggle. The Peelites were not clearly defined by their votes in the divisions in this sample until 1845, the Protectionists not until 1846. There were frequent disagreements in the Conservative Party before 1845 but, for the most part, they were statistically unrelated to the Corn Law break, and this evidence gives no ground for supposing that they anticipated or forecast it. The division lists may not, of course, tell the whole story, and a break in the party might have been developing earlier without manifesting itself in open voting in the House of Commons, though this might seem surprising in view of the frequency with which members of Parliament in the 1840s voted against their own party leaders. In any case, this supposition cannot be tested by the limited evidence considered here. So far as the information of the division lists goes, it seems reasonable to conclude that the Conservative Party, despite its many internal disagreements, was not disintegrating until the last years of this Parliament.

The information on dates also bears on the question raised earlier, how far the Peelites and Protectionists could be clearly distinguished by their votes on subjects other than the Corn Law issue. It suggests the need for taking another look at the scale evidence and gives a strong hint, at least, as to how this evidence should be interpreted.

The situation might be summarized by saying that two different classes of evidence have been discovered that appear, at least superficially, to point in different directions. On the one hand, it is clear that, among the Conservatives in this Parliament, voting patterns were in general closely related to subject matter. Items on each topic, for the most part, scaled together extremely well regardless of date, and the presumption that these items reflected a single dimension of substantive content was vigorously confirmed by the statistical evidence. On the other hand, when the relations of the Corn Law question to other topics were examined, the situation turned out to be just the other way round. A strong chronological pattern suddenly appeared, and it proved that these connections followed date rather than subject matter.

These findings raise some question as to how far the disruption of the Conservative Party was related to disagreements on issues. There is no question, of course, that it was related to one issue at least. Indeed, the break in the party has been identified, for purposes of this analysis, in ideological terms, by men's votes on the Corn Law Bill, and rightly so, for this is one case where an issue was clearly involved in a major political episode. The notion of consensus, so popular today, would scarcely have seemed persuasive to the two bitterly opposed segments of the Conservative Party in 1846.

It is clear also that these two groups, so defined, did vote in a scale pattern in divisions on a considerable number of other questions. Not all these items scaled with each other so that, in this sense, the Corn Law vote reflected a number of different and sometimes unrelated lines of conflict within the party.

Yet there remains the question of what was the nature of the relation between the Corn Law vote and these other items that were statistically connected with it. The existence of a scale pattern, as has been explained, does not by itself demonstrate unidimensionality of content, though it may be admitted as supporting evidence if such a hypothesis is plausible on other grounds. These other grounds, however, are lacking in this case. The attempt to explain these configurations in terms of subject matter proved a failure except that it brought out, what was interesting, that this was difficult to do. The evidence of dates, on the other hand, provided a scheme that made the data at once fall into place but, in so doing, made the notion of substantive unidimensionality even more implausible. The facts that these scale connections developed late, that items related to the Corn Law vote clustered so closely around the period of the break, and that for some topics the Corn Law vote was related to the late items but not to the early ones make it difficult to believe that the connection of the Corn Law question with these other issues was exclusively one of content. By the same token, there would seem to be some question as to how far the disruption of the party can be ascribed to disagreements on the long range of items that were related to the Corn Law vote. Though the statistical relationship is undeniable, there might be legitimate doubt as to which is the independent variable. The fall of the government and the split of the party might have made a difference in men's attitudes on various questions. The argument need not be pushed too far, particularly since questions of causation are notoriously difficult to deal with. It should be stated, however, that the information on dates at least leaves the way open and perhaps points the way toward an alternative explanation of the scale evidence, couched less in ideological terms and more in strictly political terms.

The information on dates, then, raises some question as to how far the scale evidence can be accepted as proof of divergence on issues between the two factions. It appears to indicate that the ideological cleavage in the Conservative Party was less significant than, from the scale evidence, it originally seemed. Apart from the extremely important issue of free trade, the Peelites, as was suggested earlier in the discussion of the Cobden-Peel correspondence, actually had more in common, in their attitudes on issues, with the Protectionists than with the Liberals. The trend of the evidence seems clearly to be that the most significant ideological breaks were those between parties and not those between the two factions of a single party.

VIII

Expenditures in American Cities

J. ROGERS HOLLINGSWORTH AND

ELLEN JANE HOLLINGSWORTH

Introduction and Overview

The central concern of this study is with the following question: why did some American city governments spend more money than others at the beginning of the twentieth century?* Much of the analysis will be confined to an assessment of the influence of social and economic characteristics on public spending. Of course, the study of the social and economic basis of politics is not new in the literature of political science, as demonstrated by the writings of Aristotle, De Tocqueville, Marx, and Beard. But now that scholars have shifted their emphasis from particular institutions, defined in legalistic terms, research which analyzes the socio-economic basis of politics perhaps will come to have "universal implications" for the study of politics, whether the focus is at the local or national level.

During the past two decades, there have been a number of studies which examine the expenditures of state and local governments in contemporary America.[1] But there has been virtually no analysis of

* The Research Committee of the Graduate School of the University of Wisconsin, the American Council of Learned Societies, and the National Endowment for the Humanities have provided financial assistance for the project of which this essay is only a portion. To Professor Richard Dusenbury of Simpson College, we are indebted for his interest, criticism, and assistance in all phases of the project. Professors Michael Aiken and Leo Schnore of the University of Wisconsin provided helpful comments, as did Professors Charles Glaab of the University of Toledo and Robert Dykstra of the University of Iowa. We would also like to acknowledge the assistance of James Bruce Smith and Sue Goldberg of Social Systems Research Institute, University of Wisconsin.

[1] See Richard I. Hofferbert, "The Relation Between Public Policy and Some Structural and Environmental Variables in American States," *American Political Science Review*, 60 (March 1966), pp. 73-82; Solomon Fabricant, *The Trend of Government Activity in the United States Since 1900* (New York: National Bureau of Economic Research, 1952); Glenn W. Fischer, "Interstate Variation in State and Local Government Expenditures," *National Tax Journal*, 17 (March 1964), pp. 57-64, hereinafter referred to as "Interstate Variation"; Seymour Sacks and Robert Harris, "The Determinants of State and Local Government Expenditures and Intergovernmental Flow of Funds," *National Tax Journal*, 17 (March 1964), pp. 75-85, hereinafter referred to as "Flow of Funds"; Seymour Sacks and

expenditures for earlier periods of American history. And we have had very little attention devoted to the study of expenditures over time, aside from studies of changes in federal spending. Yet, the changing nature of technology and industrialization has significantly altered the nature and amount of governmental spending by small units. With these gaps in the literature in mind, this essay should be viewed only as a first step in the understanding of local expenditure patterns.

Unfortunately, it will be a difficult task to explain the changes which have taken place, for most of the existing studies vary not only in their units of analysis but also in their findings. Moreover, most of the studies are analyses of *combined* state and local spending.[2] There have been very few efforts to study expenditures at only the city level for the entire nation.[3] Indeed, there have been few studies of a statewide nature, as most have focused on single metropolitan areas.[4] One of the reasons for the dearth of nationwide studies is that comparisons of contemporary expenditures at only the state or the local level can be most difficult. For example, in one state, either the local or state government may perform functions which were performed by a different civil unit in another state. Moreover, many local governmental policies are not independent of state decisions because of the functional sharing between state and local governments. As a result, many scholars have proceeded on the assumption that a better research design is to study the combined per capita amount spent by state and local governments.

William F. Hellmuth, *Financing Government in a Metropolitan Area* (New York: Free Press of Glencoe, 1961), hereinafter referred to as *Financing*; Woo S. K. Kee, "Central City Expenditures and Metropolitan Areas," *National Tax Journal*, 18 (December 1965), pp. 337-53; Robert C. Wood, *1400 Governments* (Cambridge: Harvard Univ. Press, 1961), hereinafter referred to as *Governments*; Ira Sharkansky, *Spending in the American States* (Chicago: Rand McNally, 1968), hereinafter referred to as *Spending*; Thomas R. Dye, *Politics, Economics, and the Public: Policy Outcomes in the American States* (Chicago: Rand McNally, 1966), hereinafter referred to as *Politics*. Robert Lineberry and Ira Sharkansky, *Urban Politics and Public Policy* (New York: Harper & Row, Inc., 1971); Ira Sharkansky, ed., *Policy Analysis in Political Science* (Chicago: Markham Publishing Company, 1970); Richard I. Hofferbert and Ira Sharkansky, ed., *State and Urban Politics* (Boston: Little, Brown and Co., 1971); and James A. Riedel, ed., *New Perspectives in State and Local Politics* (Waltham, Mass.: Xerox College Publishing Co., 1971).

[2] See Sacks and Harris, "Flow of Funds," and Fischer, "Interstate Variation."

[3] For an example of such work, see Harvey E. Brazer, *City Expenditures in the United States* (New York: National Bureau of Economic Research, 1959), hereinafter referred to as *City Expenditures*.

[4] A statewide study is Stanley Scott and Edward L. Feder, *Factors Associated with Variations in Municipal Expenditures Levels* (Berkeley: Bureau of Public Administration, Univ. of California, 1957).

But even though the division of functions between state and local governments varies enormously, there are severe shortcomings to studies which combine local and state spending. Most importantly, this type of analysis masks decisions made by authorities in separate civil units. For example, some cities spend a great deal of money per capita; but the combined state and local expenditure levels appear to be low. And of course, this type of combined analysis makes it impossible to understand the discrete processes which might be operating at the state and local levels.[5]

In an effort to move beyond this kind of analysis, several scholars have recently concentrated on the influence of socio-economic and political phenomena on expenditures at only the state level.[6] But very few scholars have been willing to undertake a similar strategy with city governments in interstate comparisons. If we are to understand the discrete processes which are at work in local politics, however, we must focus on city outputs, as distinct from those of other governmental levels.

There appear to be two broad classes of comparative literature which attempt to explain why city governments vary in their policy outcomes. One body of literature is primarily concerned with discovering efficient predictors for given governmental policies. Using multiple regression analysis, some scholars have succeeded in explaining a high percentage of the variation in per capita local expenditures. The authors of studies of combined state and local spending generally agree that the following factors are the most important in generating governmental expenditures: per capita income, population density, per cent of population living in urban places, and per capita federal aid.[7]

While there have been very few efforts to study expenditures at only the city level for the entire nation, there was, until recently, an assumption among those who studied city expenditures that population size was a major factor influencing the level of per capita expenditure.[8] But in the last few years several scholars have argued

[5] Elliott R. Morss, "Some Thoughts on the Determinants of State and Local Government Expenditures," *National Tax Journal*, 19 (March 1966), pp. 95-103, hereinafter referred to as "Government Expenditures"; Sharkansky, *Spending*.

[6] Ira Sharkansky, "Government Expenditures and Public Services in the American States," *American Political Science Review*, 61 (December 1967), pp. 1066-77; Richard Dawson and James Robinson, "Interparty Competition, Economic Variables, and Welfare Policies in the American States," *Journal of Politics*, 25 (May 1963), pp. 265-89; Dye, *Politics*.

[7] See Morss, "Government Expenditures," pp. 95-103.

[8] See the discussion in Wood, *Governments*, and Henry J. Schmandt and G. Ross Stephens, "Local Government Expenditure Patterns in the United States," *Land Economics* (November 1963), pp. 397-406.

that there is no significant correlation between city expenditures and size of population when other variables are taken into account. For example, Harvey Brazer found city expenditures very much influenced by population density within the city but also by the population size of the entire *metropolitan area* in which the city was located.[9] Other studies have concluded that the economic resources of a community are far more important than population size or density in determining the level of per capita expenditures.[10] On the other hand, several studies do conclude that, though size may not be the most important determinant in explaining the variation in gross expenditures, it is strongly related to per capita expenditures for certain functional categories, such as police and fire protection.[11]

Unfortunately, this type of research does not necessarily permit the analyst to understand how the correlates of local governmental expenditures actually work on those who make decisions. Instead of explaining how processes work, many such studies appear to have as their goal "to explain" statistically the level of governmental expenditures merely by increasing the coefficient of determination over what other studies had done.

The other body of literature, differing more in degree than kind, is much more concerned with describing and analyzing the process underlying community outcomes rather than with finding efficient predictors. The analyst in this category might also use multiple regression analysis, but he is likely to accept a low coefficient of determination as long as he can satisfactorily account for the kind of process which produces policy outcomes. This body of literature is usually more theoretically oriented than the former, though implicit, if not explicit, theoretical guidelines are of course also operative in the choice of variables in the former type of literature. Or to phrase the matter another way, people working in the second vein are much more concerned with establishing the theoretical linkages between independent and dependent variables.[12]

[9] Brazer, *City Expenditures.*

[10] Seymour Sacks, *The Cleveland Metropolitan Area: A Fiscal Profile* (Cleveland: Cleveland Metropolitan Service Commission, 1958), hereinafter referred to as *Cleveland*; Sacks and Hellmuth, *Financing.*

[11] Brazer, *City Expenditures*; Sacks, *Cleveland*; John C. Bollens, ed., *Exploring the Metropolitan Community* (Berkeley: Univ. of California Press, 1961).

[12] Examples of literature emphasizing the process underlying community outcomes are Raymond Wolfinger and John Osgood Field, "Political Ethics and the Structure of City Government," *American Political Science Review*, 60 (June 1966), pp. 308-26; Amos H. Hawley, "Community Power Structure and Urban Renewal Success," *American Journal of Sociology*, 68 (January 1963), pp. 422-31,

The present study focuses only on expenditures at the city level and reflects the concerns and approaches of both bodies of literature discussed above. This is a study of governmental expenditures in American cities in 1903, cities ranging in size from 10,000 to 25,000 in population. There were 278 cities of that size. And in contrast with the period which was to follow, the states at the turn of the century were relatively uninvolved in matters affecting local expenditures. At that time, cities received very little assistance from state governments and virtually none from the federal government. For example, only 6.1 per cent of local revenue in 1902 came from the state governments, and much of that went to larger cities, not the middle-sized cities with which this project is concerned.[13] But in 1903, state and county governments engaged in very little sharing with local governments in providing local functions. True, state governments did have policies, varying from area to area, which attempted to restrict local spending; but at the turn of the century, the impact of these policies on middle-sized cities was relatively slight throughout the country.

In cities of this size range in 1903, there were few separate taxing and administrative districts. City governments operated their own school boards, sewer districts, etc. directly. State legislatures could set limits for indebtedness or deny municipalities the right to incur certain *kinds* of indebtedness. Such restrictions would be reflected in lower debt service charges and in lower expenditures for some governmental functions—i.e. a city which was not allowed to incur debt for schools would not be likely to spend large amounts on other instructional costs. Yet, these reservations were of limited applicability to middle-sized cities; usually, legislatures constrained the spending

hereinafter referred to as "Power Structure"; Terry N. Clark, "Community Structure, Decision Making, Budget Expenditures, and Urban Renewal in 51 American Communities," *American Sociological Review*, 33 (August 1968), pp. 576-93, hereinafter referred to as "Urban Renewal"; Michael Aiken and Robert Alford, "Community Structure and Mobilization: The Case of the War on Poverty" (Madison, Wisc.: Institute for Research on Poverty, Univ. of Wisconsin, 1969), hereinafter referred to as "Community Structure"; Terry Clark, ed., *Community Structure and Decision Making: Comparative Analyses* (San Francisco: Chandler Publishing Co., 1968), hereinafter referred to as *Decision Making*. Michael Aiken and Robert Alford, "Comparative Urban Research and Community Decision-Making," *The New Atlantis*, 1 (Winter 1970), pp. 85-110; Michael Aiken and Robert Alford, "Community Structure and Innovation: The Case of Public Housing," *American Political Science Review*, 64 (September 1970), pp. 843-64; Michael Aiken and Robert Alford, "Community Structure and Innovation: The Case of Urban Renewal," *American Sociological Review*, 35 (August 1970), pp. 650-65.

[13] James A. Maxwell, *Financing State and Local Governments* (Washington: Brookings Institution, 1965), pp. 14, 72, 126.

of larger urban units. Moreover, cities could and did appeal to legislatures for waivers on debt limits.[14]

The argument, then, is a simple one: to break municipal expenditures apart from state expenditures is both more feasible and more sensible for the turn of the century than for the present. This is not to argue that processes at work in middle-sized cities were discrete from processes elsewhere in the state, only that decisions taken in state capitals and Washington probably exercised minimal direct constraints on decisions about spending in the cities which we are studying. To judge the indirect effects of external civil units is impossible: that a skillful lobbyist might persuade the state or federal government to develop river and harbor facilities in his home town might have had extensive consequences. But such problems and situations lie beyond the scope of this study.

It is possible that relationships which exist between social and economic variables and governmental expenditures may be canceled out by situational variables reflecting the idiosyncrasies of particular communities: the personalities of particular leaders; the incidence of highly partisan local issues; unexpected events such as fire, tornado, or hideous crime. Unfortunately, comparative data do not exist to test the presence or importance of such situational factors, and we assume that the correlations reported below are only reduced and not reversed by such situational variables. Indeed, if situational variables account for most of the variation in governmental expenditures, consistent associations between expenditures and structural features of the community would not be expected to occur in statistical analysis. However, consistent relations do exist on a national basis.[15]

A second problem in this study deals with city size. Would inclusion of cities larger or smaller significantly affect the findings? Perhaps there are different sets of social processes in larger cities, or perhaps processes and structures vary in impact with different sized aggregations of people.

Using several devices, we have chosen to control for the size of these cities. First, the universe studied consists of cities of comparable size.

[14] For a summary description of the laws and constitution of each state and their relevance to local spending, see U.S. Census Bureau, *Wealth, Debt and Taxation*, Special Report (Washington: U.S. Govt. Printing Office, 1907). Also see Horace Secrist, *An Economic Analysis of the Constitutional Restrictions Upon Public Indebtedness in the United States* (Madison, Wis.: Univ. of Wisconsin Press, 1914).

[15] For an extended discussion which distinguishes situational from cultural and structural variables in urban analysis, see Robert Alford, "The Comparative Study of Urban Politics," in *Urban Research and Policy Planning*, ed. by Leo F. Schnore and Henry Fagin (Beverly Hills, Calif.: Sage Publications, 1967), pp. 263-302.

Second, variables have either been normed on a per capita basis or stated in terms of percentages, for there is some variation in the population of these cities (10,000 to 25,000). In a follow-up study, an assessment of the importance of size in shaping expenditures will be undertaken—at which time larger cities will be included in the analysis. Unfortunately, social scientists have not yet been very successful in specifying what they are holding constant when they control for size—whether it is resource availability, community heterogeneity, bureaucratic complexity, or frequency of elite interaction.[16]

The related problem of the implications of a hierarchy of cities for studying policy outputs has been grossly neglected by historians. (By hierarchy of cities, we mean a collection of cities varying by size as well as function.)[17] At the turn of the century, hierarchies of cities, especially in terms of size and of function, were in existence, and were characteristic of New England, Middle Atlantic, and the East North Central regions more so than elsewhere. Studying the relationship between hierarchies of cities and municipal expenditures seems promising and receives some attention below.

Even though an analysis of a system or hierarchy of cities is necessary to comprehend the social processes inherent in urban areas, this can most effectively be carried out by studying cities within particular regions. And yet, region is one of the most baffling concepts with which social scientists work. Because regions have different historical experiences, to study systems of cities within a region is to control not only for history but for all kinds of demographic, structural, and cultural variables as well. The strategy of this study is to examine the influence of selected socio-economic variables in shaping governmental expenditures for the nation as a whole. And because region

[16] For a discussion of size, see Herbert Jacob and Michael Lipsky, "An Analysis of Public Policies in Cities," *Journal of Politics*, 30 (May 1968), pp. 531-32; Aiken and Alford, "Community Structure"; Otis Dudley Duncan, "Optimum Size of Cities," in *Reader in Urban Sociology*, ed. by Paul K. Holt and Albert J. Reiss, Jr. (Glencoe, Ill.: Free Press, 1951), pp. 632-45; James Dahir, "What is the Best Size for a City?" *American City* (August 1951), pp. 104-05; Robert Lillibridge, "Urban Size: An Assessment," *Land Economics*, 27 (November 1952), pp. 341-52; William E. Ogburn and Otis Dudley Duncan, "City Size as a Sociological Variable," in *Urban Sociology*, ed. by Ernest W. Burgess and Donald J. Bogue (Chicago: Univ. of Chicago Press, 1967), pp. 58-76.

[17] For discussions of the concept "hierarchy of cities," see Otis Dudley Duncan, *et al., Metropolis and Region* (Baltimore: Johns Hopkins Press, 1960), Chaps. 1, 3, *passim*; Harold M. Mayer, "A Survey of Urban Geography," in *The Study of Urbanization*, ed. by Philip M. Hauser and Leo F. Schnore (New York: John Wiley & Sons, Inc., 1965), pp. 81-92; Brian J. L. Berry, "Research Frontiers in Urban Geography," in *ibid.*, pp. 403-15; Edward Ullman, "A Theory of Location for Cities," in *Readings in Urban Geography*, ed. by Harold M. Mayer and Clyde F. Kohn (Chicago: Univ. of Chicago Press, 1959), pp. 202-09.

is a surrogate for various kinds of historical process, its influence on governmental expenditures will be assessed.[18]

Of course there were intraregional variations for each of the variables in this study, and no doubt if cities were arranged by other regional groupings, the results would be somewhat different. However, there are historical and cultural processes which justify our particular regional arrangements of cities. (See Appendix B for our arrangement of cities by region.)[19]

It is important to emphasize that this is an exploratory study. Some of the concepts are drawn from recent literature on the problems of mobilizing community resources in contemporary American society, others from studies about the social and economic processes at the turn of the twentieth century. While concepts are employed which others have found useful in explaining why some cities were more successful than others in "mobilizing" community resources, the focus of the study is exclusively on the social and economic basis of politics. Clearly, there were other kinds of forces which help to account for the mobilization of community resources. For example, there is a substantial literature demonstrating that political structures are important in mobilizing the resources of a community. We are generally informed that mobilization is higher in cities that have a large number of councilmen, a mayor-council form of government, and ward elections which are partisan.[20] These are structures which facilitate access of groups into the political process. Hopefully, in a follow-up study,

[18] For a discussion of the difficulties of studying "region," see Harvey S. Perloff, *et al., Regions, Resources and Economic Growth* (Baltimore: Johns Hopkins Press, 1960), hereinafter referred to as *Regions*; Ira Sharkansky, "Regionalism, Economic Status and the Public Policies of American States," *The Southwestern Social Science Quarterly* (June 1968), pp. 9-26; Brian Berry, "Approaches to Regional Analysis: A Synthesis," *Annals of the Association of American Geographers*, 54 (March 1964), pp. 2-11; James R. McDonald, "The Region: Its Conception, Design and Limitations," *Annals of the Association of American Geographers*, 56 (September 1966), pp. 516-28.

[19] When the six regions used in this study are treated as dummy variables and are entered into a regression equation, they explain 20 per cent of the variation in local expenditures for all 278 cities ($R^2 = .20$).

When the same cities were arranged into larger regions (East, Midwest, South, Far West), region as a variable only explained 10 per cent of the variation in municipal expenditures ($R^2 = .10$).

[20] See Robert Alford and Eugene C. Lee, "Voting Turnout in American Cities," *American Political Science Review*, 62 (September 1968), pp. 796-813, hereinafter referred to as "Voting"; and Robert L. Lineberry and Edmund P. Fowler, "Reformism and Public Policies in American Cities," *ibid.*, 61 (September 1967), pp. 701-16, hereinafter referred to as "Reformism."

it will be possible to assess the impact of political structures on the ability of cities to mobilize their resources.

With these considerations in mind, we turn to the implications of different types of social and economic concepts and variables for understanding municipal expenditures.

Social Heterogeneity

The decisions which result in high or low per capita expenditures are an important measure of a city's capacity to mobilize its resources, both human and material, for collective action. In this connection, several scholars have argued that the degree of social heterogeneity in a city is a good indicator of its capability to mobilize resources. Unfortunately, there is no consensus among the scholars who have worked with this concept.

One group has argued that the more social heterogeneity, the more decentralized and loosely structured the city, the more successful it is in mobilizing its resources. The assumption in this literature is that the presence of a great deal of heterogeneity produces many political cleavages, which in turn create conflicting political demands among the citizenry, forcing political elites to increase the level of expenditures.

Another group of scholars makes the opposite assumption about policy consequences, though both groups agree that more social heterogeneity promotes greater decentralization. But in the latter group, there is the assumption that the more decentralized the structural arrangements within the city, the less successful the city is in mobilizing its resources. Interest groups, socially or ethnically defined, may so offset one another that elites need not be responsive to their constituents.[21]

Accordingly, the strategy of this study is to discover whether either body of literature is useful in understanding why some cities had high levels of expenditures per capita at the turn of the twentieth century. Because historians have recently interpreted much of American politics in ethno-cultural terms, there is an added incentive to measure the relationship between municipal expenditures and ethno-cultural variables in these cities.

The indicators of social heterogeneity are ethnic, racial, and religious diversity. To ascertain the degree to which each city was ethnically diverse, we have measured the percentage of the population

[21] For literature which discusses the relationship between policy outcomes and social heterogeneity, see Clark, "Urban Renewal," and *Decision Making*; Hawley, "Power Structure"; Aiken and Alford, "Community Structure."

which was foreign born or native born of foreign-born parents. As an indicator of religious diversity, data is presented on the percentage of the population which was Protestant in the county in which the city was located. And as a measure of racial diversity, the study relies on the per cent of the population which was non-white.

Stability of City

This concept is related to some of the assumptions underlying the concept of social heterogeneity. The age of American cities has been viewed by some scholars as an important indicator for the level of social and political differentiation within the city. Some literature suggests that the older the city and the less mobile its population, the greater the possibility that "centers of power" will have established and well-developed relations with each other, relations which facilitate the mobilization of community resources. If this view is valid for middle-sized American cities at the turn of the century, one would expect to find that older cities, with less mobile populations, assumed more municipal functions and spent more money per capita.

Newer cities presumably have fewer organized interest groups. And rapid growth, involving the turnover of large numbers of people weakly related to civic institutions, should mean lower expenditures.

There are only indirect measures of the age of each city, for some were villages or parts of other cities long before they were incorporated as cities. For example, New England cities were quite likely to have had several decades of municipal experience before reaching even a low population threshold. Despite the problems of measurement, the number of years since the city had a population of 2,500 has been chosen as an indicator of age.

Moreover, there are only indirect measures of the geographic mobility of a city's population—the percentage change in total population, 1890-1900 for each city. While better indicators are preferred, we justify the use of these on the grounds that they are the best available, and without using them, it would not be possible to make even preliminary inferences about the effects of stability on expenditures in American cities in 1903.[22]

Socio-Economic Status of a Community

The concept socio-economic status is included in the analysis as there are a number of studies which argue that communities of higher socio-

[22] For a discussion of the concept "stability," see Clark, *Decision Making*, p. 97; Alford and Lee, "Voting"; Aiken and Alford, "Community Structure."

economic status have large numbers of citizens who demand a variety of governmental services, who are more sophisticated in judging the quality of educational services, and who know how to make their demands felt in the political system. In contrast, communities with low S.E.S. have more people whose demands on local government are somewhat limited, who are less capable of judging the value of community services, and less able to mobilize political support.

The analyst encounters serious problems when he studies cities at the turn of the twentieth century, as data for most problems are simply not so complete as that which exists for later periods. Certain variables are thus used as indicators because the period under investigation is 1903, whereas if the analysis were conducted for American cities in 1960, different indicators would be used. For example, we use as indicators of the socio-economic status of a community certain variables which one may legitimately question—i.e. the percentage of dwellings owned by inhabitants, the per cent of school-age children attending school, the number of library books per capita, the per cent of wage earners in manufacturing who were children, and the number of high school graduates per 1,000 people. Reservations about these variables stem from a variety of sources, a few rather obvious: manufacturing employment for children was dependent on the existence of manufacturing facilities; the presence of a college or university frequently had inflationary effects on the number of books in a community. Even so, our knowledge of the period leads us to believe that these variables are reasonably reliable indicators of S.E.S. Moreover, a factor analysis of these cities resulted in a socio-economic status factor with high loadings for all of these variables, indicating that they are measures of the same phenomenon.

Several recent studies have reported that median family income and property value per person are the principal determinants of per capita expenditures, simply reflecting that communities spend what they can afford. For middle-sized cities in the early twentieth century, however, there is no data on the annual income of individuals. As a result, we have used as the best indicator of resource availability for these cities the total true value of personal and real property per capita in each city, computed from assessments for tax purposes. It is assumed that city governments were constrained in their spending if they had low levels of assessed valuation per capita, freer to spend if they had a high valuation level.

Though state and local laws provided for assessments at varying percentages of full value, the assessment figures have been standardized to full value. Even so, there may be some slippage in the data on this variable, for the efficiency and accuracy of tax assessments did vary across the country.[23]

Social and Economic Interaction with Environment

The more interaction a community has with its environment, the more services it is called upon to provide, not only for the immediate community but for people outside the city as well.[24] We also believe that the more economic activity the city has with its hinterland, the more capacity it has to respond to the demands for higher expenditures. There is an abundance of literature bearing on these points, much of it related to the delineation of zones, to the patterning of hierarchies of cities.

Suburb, a dummy variable, is used as an indicator of the interaction which a particular class of city had with its environment. The variable governmental center indicates whether a city was a state capital or a county seat. The presence of either of these seats of government means that the city had a higher level of interaction with its environment, had more demands placed on it for municipal services and, we hypothesize, generally responded with more expenditures per capita than other cities.

Presumably, the greater the density of the population in the environment of a city, the larger the number of people for whom it served as broker, trader, supplier. Of course, serving more people meant higher demands for services, but it also meant greater support in the forms of bank deposits subject to local taxes, business profits invested in taxable real estate—factors which influenced the level of municipal expenditures.

Along the same lines, the nature and amount of economic activity in the hinterland of a city influenced its behavior, and vice versa. Extensive literature has concerned itself with the relationship between center cities and hinterland zones, specifying their interaction. To test for the influence of the productivity of the hinterland, the study relies on the value of farm products per acre of the county in which the city

[23] For a discussion of the relation between high S.E.S. and policy outcomes, see Lineberry and Fowler, "Reformism," and Thomas R. Dye, "Governmental Structure, Urban Environment, and Educational Policy," *Midwest Journal of Politics*, 11 (August 1967), pp. 353-80.

Of course, the assessment policies of some communities may have operated in a circular fashion: that is, property valuation may have been shaped in response to tax or expenditure needs.

[24] See Brazer, *City Expenditures.*

was located. It must be allowed, of course, that marketing conditions, local and distant, affected such values, and that the size of the hinterland might also affect central city decisions.

Economic Activity

Much contemporary literature has pivoted around efforts to "type" cities according to labor force distribution, to indicate levels of service that may be expected according to labor force deployment. Having a large sector of the work force in primary activities (mining, lumbering, fishing) has generally been associated with low levels of community amenities. Conversely, communities with large numbers of professional people—because they are cities which are suburbs, educational centers, or state capitals—are more likely to have been characterized by generous civil spending.

The implications of widespread manufacturing employment are mixed and somewhat dependent upon whether manufacturing is predominantly processing or fabricating. Overall, emphasis on manufacturing serves as a depressant to municipal expenditure according to recent scholarship.

Although the variables employed in this study provide but an imperfect picture of economic activity carried on in a municipal unit, they serve as proxies for the distribution of the labor force into different sectors. In 1900, the Census Bureau did not report occupational data for cities with populations ranging between 10,000 and 25,000. However, data are available for the number of professionals, and for people engaged in manufacturing in these cities, from which it is possible to make some useful inferences about the total labor force.

In an effort to learn which cities had a sizeable population engaged in lumbering and mining, we have inferred that a city had a sizeable population engaged in lumbering if the county in which the city was located was a large producer of lumber. Spot checks of city directories and case studies of several dozen cities indicate that this assumption is legitimate. And we have assumed that a city had a sizeable population engaged in mining if it had a coal or iron ore mine within its city limits in 1890. Again, a random check of city directories has been consistent with this assumption. Unfortunately, more systematic data on employment for middle-sized cities throughout the nation were not available.[25]

[25] There is very little literature which assesses the relationship between economic activity in communities and their policy outcomes. For a brief discussion of the problem, however, see Lewis A. Froman, "An Analysis of Policies in Cities," *The Journal of Politics*, 24 (February 1967), pp. 94-108.

Findings

In most cases, several variables seem to index roughly the same phenomenon or process. Although dividing and specifying concepts, even descriptively, is both tedious and perilous, it does introduce some order in the explanatory scheme. Accordingly, for each concept described above we have used a cluster of variables. Factor analysis of a large number of social and economic variables was used to assist in discriminating variables into the most appropriate clusters. Working with clusters of variables which presume to index the same phenomenon, one is necessarily concerned with the problem of including duplicate measures of the same dimension. By working with stepwise regression and partial correlations, we have sought to eliminate and elucidate areas of overlap.

Overall, for 1903, variables reflecting social heterogeneity ("centers of power") do not afford much explanatory power for city expenditures as shown in Table 1. However, given the level of data available, it is difficult to distinguish in a region which of two phenomena was taking place: (1) religious and ethnic heterogeneity were not reflected in the existence of centers of power, or (2) centers of power existed, but had little consequence for policy outcomes. Perhaps both explanations are partially adequate—the presence of a large Negro population in the South, for example, did not mean the existence of an additional center of power. But in the Northeastern cities, there were merging centers of power reflecting ethnic and religious differences—but they apparently carried little weight in affecting city spending.

By controlling for size of city, we may be reducing the importance of heterogeneity as a source of explanation. Larger cities, with more formal and rationalized decision-making processes, are more likely to have demonstrated policy reflections of social heterogeneity, in that culturally distinct groups are less mixed together, more likely to react as enclaves to political culture processes. The smaller the city, the less likely that diverse groups were able to develop organizational structures capable of mobilizing support for their demands.

Yet, for the cities of the Eastern states, variables of heterogeneity carried different consequences. For example, the more Protestants there were in New England cities, the higher the expenditures per capita ($r = .15$), whereas the relationship was reversed in the Middle Atlantic states ($r = -.20$). Moreover, high expenditures were negatively associated with people having strong ethnic ties in New England cities, but a large ethnic population was positively related to expenditures in cities of the Middle Atlantic region. Thus, we are immediately

TABLE 1. RELATIONSHIPS BETWEEN MUNICIPAL EXPENDITURES PER CAPITA AND INDICATORS OF SOCIAL HETEROGENEITY*

	Zero Order Correlation Coefficient						Partial Correlation Coefficient					
Variable	*All Cities (N=278)*	*North-east (N=52)*	*Mid-Atlantic (N=68)*	*Lakes (N=78)*	*South (N=38)*	*Plains (N=28)*	*All Cities (N=278)*	*North-east (N=52)*	*Mid-Atlantic (N=68)*	*Lakes (N=78)*	*South (N=38)*	*Plains (N=28)*
Percentage of Population Consisting of Protestants (1)	–.27†	.15	–.20	–.03	.20	–.08	–.25	.06	–.11	–.06	.23	–.06
Per Cent Ethnic (2)	.09	–.30‡	.15	–.02	–.05	.07	–.05	–.27	.15	–.09	.10	–.03
Per Cent Non-White (3)	–.10	.12	.28‡	–.08	–.04	–.09	.02	.10	.34	–.10	.11	–.06
R^2	.08†	.10	.15‡	.01	.06	.01						

Variable number indicated in parentheses. See Appendix A.

* Throughout this study, no regional results are reported for cities of the Far West. The small number of cases (14) precluded this type of analysis.

† Significant at .01 level.

‡ Significant at .05 level.

confronted with one of the problems with research of this type. Hypotheses which explain activity in one region are not necessarily valid in another area.

"Ethnicity" and municipal expenditures were negatively related in Northeastern cities because most of the "ethnics" in those cities were foreign born, people who were not yet well integrated into the social structures of their communities and not yet able to mobilize effectively the resources of their cities. On the other hand, most of the population whom we have classified as "ethnics" in the Middle Atlantic cities were people who were native born of foreign-born parents. Being native Americans, they were better integrated into the social structure of their communities and were in a better position to mobilize their community resources.

Even though this cluster helps "to explain" the variation in spending in cities of the Northeast and the Middle Atlantic states, there was hardly any relationship between social heterogeneity and expenditures in the cities of the other three regions: the South, the Lakes, and the Plains.

Similarly, the relationships between our indicators of community stability and municipal expenditures reveal some of the difficulties in the type of analysis which we have undertaken, for it is now abundantly clear from Table 2 that the strength of our clusters varies on a regional basis. For example, the older the city, the higher the level of spending per capita in cities of the Northeast, the Middle Atlantic, and Southern states, while the relationship runs in the opposite direction for the cities of the Lakes and Plains regions. Moreover, there was a very strong relationship between spending and growth of cities in the Northeast and Middle Atlantic states, though the relationship was relatively weak elsewhere.

Table 3, a four cell table, presents the average expenditure per capita for four types of cities: (1) those which were old and growing rapidly, (2) new cities with rapid growth, (3) old but non-growing cities, and (4) new cities with rather stagnant rates of growth.[26] Significantly, younger cities had lower average expenditures than older cities, regardless of the rate of growth, thus adding strength to the hypothesis that social and economic groups in younger cities had not yet had the

[26] To categorize 278 cities as old or new, growing or not growing, we ranked all cities by age and by rate of population change between 1890 and 1900. The 139 (one-half of 278) cities which were oldest were categorized as the older cities, the remainder as the newer cities. Similarly, the 139 cities which had the highest rate of population growth during the nineties were listed as the growing cities.

TABLE 2. RELATIONSHIPS BETWEEN MUNICIPAL EXPENDITURES PER CAPITA AND INDICATORS OF STABILITY

	Zero Order Correlation Coefficient						*Partial Correlation Coefficient*					
Variable	*All Cities (N=278)*	*North-east (N=52)*	*Mid-Atlantic (N=68)*	*Lakes (N=78)*	*South (N=38)*	*Plains (N=28)*	*All Cities (N=278)*	*North-east (N=52)*	*Mid-Atlantic (N=68)*	*Lakes (N=78)*	*South (N=38)*	*Plains (N=28)*
Years Since City Reached 2,500 (4)	.18†	.12	.07	—.06	.13	—.25	.22	.26	.20	—.08	.14	—.32
Per Cent Population Change, 1890-1900 (5)	.07	.30‡	.35†	—.03	—.03	—.08	.15	.37	.39	—.06	.05	—.23
R^2	.05†	.15‡	.16†	.01	.02	.11						

Variable number indicated in parentheses. See Appendix A.

† Significant at .01 level.
‡ Significant at .05 level.

TABLE 3. EXPENDITURES OF 278 CITIES ACCORDING TO AGE AND RATE OF POPULATION GROWTH

Old Growing Cities	New Growing Cities
Average Annual Expenditure per capita $12.89	Average Annual Expenditure per capita $11.08
Old Cities, Not Growing	New Cities, Not Growing
Average Annual Expenditure per capita $11.19	Average Annual Expenditure per capita $10.12

opportunity to develop cohesion and effective communication, a process which aids in the mobilization of community resources. Conversely, old cities with high growth rates spent the most money per capita, a finding that is consistent with the literature which suggests that the older the city, the greater the probability that there are centers of power with established and well-developed relations with each other, relations which facilitate the mobilization of community resources.

There are both empirical and theoretical reasons for us to assume that newer cities had serious problems in discontinuities of leadership, with the consequence that after a certain state of development, many needs went unattended. On the other hand, newer, growing cities were more successful in mobilizing resources than new cities which were rather stagnant in their growth rates. Perhaps this resulted because new, growing cities had more needs than the new, non-growing ones.

Growth or mobility was usually a response to basic patterns of economic change—its absence usually meant greater stability bought at the cost of contracting resources, of local depression. In general, growth tended to imply higher expenditure levels, contrary to suggestions that it is stability which induces spending. Perhaps for middle-sized cities, one should expect growth and spending to be associated. Of course, different patterns may well have prevailed for larger units.

The cluster, socio-economic status of cities, has considerable explanatory power in aiding our understanding of municipal expenditures as Table 4 demonstrates.[27] One of the indicators of socio-economic status, wealth, or value of property per capita, is the most

[27] In an earlier stage of this study, a variable called "per cent of population not in private families" was included to see whether having a large number of social isolates, probably with few local loyalties, would tend to reduce spending. On the contrary, having more people not in private families was associated with greater spending. However, large numbers of people without families were located in areas of rapid economic growth, such as the Far West, where expenditures were also high.

TABLE 4. RELATIONSHIPS BETWEEN MUNICIPAL EXPENDITURES PER CAPITA AND INDICATORS OF SOCIO-ECONOMIC STATUS

	Zero Order Correlation Coefficient						*Partial Correlation Coefficient*					
Variable	*All Cities (N=278)*	*North-east (N=52)*	*Mid-Atlantic (N=68)*	*Lakes (N=78)*	*South (N=38)*	*Plains (N=28)*	*All Cities (N=278)*	*North-east (N=52)*	*Mid-Atlantic (N=68)*	*Lakes (N=78)*	*South (N=38)*	*Plains (N=28)*
Value of Property Per Capita (6)	.67†	.77†	.77†	.37†	.42†	.66†	.65	.75	.71	.30	.39	.64
Child Labor in Manufacturing (7)	—.23†	—.31‡	—.37†	—.31‡	.06	.02	—.13	—.09	—.13	—.26	—.09	—.03
Number of Library Books Per Capita (8)	.22†	.22	.08	.29‡	.21	—.02	.14	.10	.05	.22	.21	—.08
Per Cent of Children Attending School (9)	.31†	.51†	.40†	—.01	.01	.12	.19	.31	.17	.04	—.08	.07
Per Cent of Homes Owned by Inhabitants (10)	—.02	.24	.12	—.14	—.03	—.14	.02	.15	.15	—.09	—.00	—.14
Number of High School Graduates Per 1,000 People (11)	.16†	.38†	.03	.10	.32‡	.22	—.04	.16	—.09	—.05	.21	.06
R^2	.51†	.71†	.64†	.25†	.26	.46‡						

Variable number indicated in parentheses. See Appendix A.

† Significant at .01 level.
‡ Significant at .05 level.

powerful variable in the entire study, though its strength also varies considerably from region to region. It is interesting that the simple correlation between expenditures per capita and wealth is lowest in the cities of the Lakes region (r = 37). Perhaps cities of that region were least successful in mobilizing their resources, because many of the cities were lumber towns which were declining in size and wealth.

On the other hand, Southern cities, next to those of New England, were the wealthiest, and yet they too were relatively unsuccessful in mobilizing community wealth for governmental services. Southern cities were probably unsuccessful in mobilizing their resources since wealth was more concentrated among the upper classes than in cities elsewhere. Not only were there many poor whites in Southern cities but 35 per cent of the inhabitants were Negro—two sizeable groups doing very little to mobilize community resources.

Next to cities of the plains, those of the Middle Atlantic region had the lowest average per capita wealth in the country. Yet, the cities of the Middle Atlantic states were the most successful in mobilizing wealth for governmental expenditures (r = .77).

Elsewhere, high expenditures per capita were generally (1) inversely associated with a small percentage of wage earners in manufacturing who were children, and (2) positively associated with indicators of literacy and education—though the relationship runs weakly in the opposite direction for one or two of the regions.

Present-day literature supports the view that individuals without property are more inclined to support high municipal expenditures and that property owners desire relatively low expenditures. However, the data for these cities are inconclusive on this point. Unfortunately, we do not have data on individuals. But with aggregate data, there is a positive relationship between expenditures per capita and the per cent of homes owned by inhabitants for cities of the Northeast (r = .24) and the Middle Atlantic region (r = 12), but for cities in other regions the relationship runs in the opposite direction.

Just as recent scholars have found that high interaction with the environment is positively associated with higher expenditures per capita, there is considerable evidence that this was also the case at the turn of the century. It appears that increased activity with the immediate environment generally resulted in greater demands being made on the city government for municipal services, services which resulted in some benefit to those in surrounding areas as well as the residents of the community. Moreover, increased interaction with the environment generally produced wealthier communities. And since our indicators of interaction with the environment are positively related with wealth, and wealth is highly related to expenditures per capita, we believe that the positive relationship between expenditures per capita and the environment results because there was a tendency for most cities to spend money for government services if they could afford to do so.

With the cluster, interaction with the environment, as shown in Table 5, there is a modest association between governmental centers and expenditures per capita in cities of the South ($r = .17$), the Lakes area ($r = .14$), and the Plains region ($r = .36$), but there is hardly any relationship between these two variables for the cities in the two Eastern regions. This difference results in large part from the fact that many of the Southern and Lakes cities were governmental or administrative centers with relatively high levels of expenditure, whereas in the Eastern regions there were very few cities in this size range which were centers for governmental administration.

In this respect, the cities of the South are particularly interesting. Unlike cities of this size in other regions, Southern cities were major centers within the region—despite their relatively small size. Most of the Southern cities were either state capitals or regional centers within their state, and they provided many more social, economic, and political functions for their immediate environment than cities elsewhere of comparable size.

Knowing whether or not a city was a suburb is quite important in understanding the level of expenditure for cities in the East, but "suburb" as a variable offers very little explanatory power in the cities of the South, or the Lakes and the Plains regions. However, there were very few suburbs within this size range outside the Northeast and the Middle Atlantic areas. Important in this respect is the fact that the simple correlations between wealth and suburb were much stronger in cities of the Northeast ($r = .38$) and the Middle Atlantic ($r = .48$) than elsewhere—suggesting once again that the wealth of the community was a major variable for understanding its level of expenditures.

In the more settled areas of the country, agricultural production in the immediate hinterland of cities of this size was primarily truck farming, production which had a relatively high value per acre. And in most of the settled areas, the more truck farming, the greater the population density in the hinterland, the more the interaction with the city, and the greater the municipal expenditures per capita.

The indicators of economic activity have stronger explanatory power for municipal expenditures in the Lakes and the two Eastern regions than in cities of the South and the Plains (see Table 6). Significantly, the cities of the East and of the Lakes area are those which were more

TABLE 5. RELATIONSHIPS BETWEEN MUNICIPAL EXPENDITURES PER CAPITA AND INDICATORS OF SOCIAL AND ECONOMIC INTERACTION WITH ENVIRONMENT

	Zero Order Correlation Coefficient						*Partial Correlation Coefficient*					
Variable	*All Cities (N=278)*	*North-east (N=52)*	*Mid-Atlantic (N=68)*	*Lakes (N=78)*	*South (N=38)*	*Plains (N=28)*	*All Cities (N=278)*	*North-east (N=52)*	*Mid-Atlantic (N=68)*	*Lakes (N=78)*	*South (N=38)*	*Plains (N=28)*
Governmental Center (12)	—.03	—.00	—.09	.14	.17	.36	.05	.24	—.00	.16	.17	.32
Suburb (13)	.18†	.38†	.48†	.11	—.03	none	.19	.34	.49	.17	.03	none
Value of Farm Products in County (14)	.10	.23	.18	.10	.18	.03	.08	.10	.17	.27	—.01	.19
Population Density of County (15)	.10	.23	.09	—.21	.28	—.19	.04	.12	—.19	—.32	.21	—.20
R^2	.05†	.20	.27†	.15‡	.10	.17						

Variable number indicated in parentheses. See Appendix A.

† Significant at .01 level.
‡ Significant at .05 level.

Table 6. Relationships Between Municipal Expenditures Per Capita and Indicators of Economic Activity

Variable	*Zero Order Correlation Coefficient*						*Partial Correlation Coefficient*					
	All Cities (N=278)	*North-east (N=52)*	*Mid-Atlantic (N=68)*	*Lakes (N=78)*	*South (N=38)*	*Plains (N=28)*	*All Cities (N=278)*	*North-east (N=52)*	*Mid-Atlantic (N=68)*	*Lakes (N=78)*	*South (N=38)*	*Plains (N=28)*
Per Cent of Population Consisting of Professional People (16)	.05	.29†	—.06	.47‡	.26	.21	.05	.26	—.10	.51	.26	.16
Value of Timber Products (17)	.12†	.22	.19	.04	—.04	.07	.11	.15	.24	.23	.03	.03
Mining Activity (18)	—.28‡	none	—.39‡	—.12	—.05	—.24	—.28	none	—.47	—.03	—.08	—.16
Per Cent of Population in Manufacturing (19)	—.03	—.33†	—.12	—.06	—.01	—.08	—.07	—.25	—.21	.00	.00	.03
R^2	.10‡	.18†	.26‡	.27‡	.07	.08						

Variable number indicated in parentheses. See Appendix A.

† Significant at .05 level.
‡ Significant at .01 level.

integrated into a national economy. In other words, these particular variables of economic activity are ones which reflect integration into a national economy and such integration had predictive powers for municipal expenditures.

However, it is important to point out that there were other types of economic activity in these cities for which we lack systematic data. For example, retailing was an extremely important activity in the economies of cities of the South and the Plains, but there is no uniform data on retailing. And perhaps for this reason, the cluster, economic activity, is not as important in explaining municipal expenditures in cities of these two regions as in cities of the Lakes and the two Eastern regions.

By now it is apparent that these socio-economic concepts differ greatly in influencing the level of spending of American cities in 1903. As Table 7 indicates, the 19 socio-economic variables explain 64 per cent of the variation in governmental expenditures for all 278 cities, 84 per cent in the Northeast, 81 per cent in the Middle Atlantic, 49 per cent in the Lakes area, 52 per cent in the South, and 64 per cent in the Plains. However, it is apparent that some of these clusters, by their

TABLE 7. SUMMARY OF THE AMOUNT OF VARIANCE IN MUNICIPAL EXPENDITURES PER CAPITA EXPLAINED BY EACH SOCIAL ECONOMIC CLUSTER

	All Cities (N=278)	*North-east (N=52)*	*Mid-Atlantic (N=68)*	*Lakes (N=78)*	*South (N=38)*	*Plains (N=28)*
Indicators of Heterogeneity	.08†	.10	.15‡	.01	.06	.01
Indicators of Stability	.05†	.15‡	.16†	.01	.02	.11
Indicators of Socio-economic Status	.51†	.71†	.64†	.25†	.26	.46‡
Indicators of Interaction with Environment	.05†	.20	.27†	.15‡	.10	.17
Indicators of Economic Activity	.10†	.18‡	.26†	.27†	.07	.08
ALL CLUSTERS	.64†	.84†	.81†	.49	.52	.64

† Significant at .01 level.
‡ Significant at .05 level.

very nature, overlap or covary with other clusters. Our task now is to assess the unique relationship between each cluster of variables and municipal expenditures, a procedure most appropriate for a large number of observations.[28] The results are shown in Table 8.

In Table 8, we present in column one the amounts of variance explained by each cluster alone and by all five socio-economic clusters together for all cities. In column two, each of these per cents of variance is the amount of additional variance accounted for by each cluster after the other four have entered a regression equation. For example, the four clusters of economic activity, interaction with the environment, stability, and heterogeneity explain 29 per cent of the variation in expenditures for all 278 cities when the cluster socio-economic status is eliminated from the regression equation. But if socio-economic status is entered into a regression equation together with the other four clusters, the explained variance is raised to 64 per cent, an increase of 35 per cent of explained variance. In other words, with this set of variables, the socio-economic status of cities uniquely contributes 35 per cent of additionally explained variance.

TABLE 8. COMPARISON BETWEEN THE AMOUNT OF VARIANCE IN MUNICIPAL EXPENDITURES PER CAPITA EXPLAINED BY EACH CLUSTER ALONE AND THE AMOUNT OF VARIANCE UNIQUELY EXPLAINED BY EACH CLUSTER FOR 278 CITIES

	Per Cent of Variance Explained by Each Cluster Operating Alone	*Per Cent of Variance Uniquely Explained by Each Cluster*
Indicators of Heterogeneity	7.53	2.83
Indicators of Stability	5.43	.93
Indicators of Socio-economic Status	50.63	34.59
Indicators of Interaction with Environment	4.83	2.03
Indicators of Economic Activity	9.75	3.59
ALL ABOVE INDICATORS	63.56	

28 One must be particularly sensitive to the extent to which degrees of freedom are reduced by using several variables to explain a dependent variable. In other words, are high levels of statistical explanation the distorted result of using many variables? In an effort to address ourselves to this problem, significance tests for the R^2's are shown throughout the study.

At the same time, the socio-economic status variables can explain 51 per cent of the variation in municipal expenditures for all cities. This means that 16 per cent of the explained variation (the difference between 51 per cent and 35 per cent) is variance jointly explained with some, perhaps all, of the other four clusters. However, there is no way to apportion this jointly explained variance between the socio-economic status cluster and the variables in the other clusters. They are intricately bound together.

The other socio-economic clusters also make unique, though much more modest, contributions to the explanation of municipal expenditures for all 278 cities. Using the same method, the heterogeneity cluster uniquely explains 2.83 per cent of the variance in municipal expenditures, the environment cluster uniquely explains 2.03 per cent, and the economic activity cluster 3.59 per cent, while the stability cluster uniquely explains less than 1 per cent.

Because the variable wealth is clearly the most powerful indicator of the socio-economic status of a community, because the S.E.S. cluster explains uniquely so much more of the variance than any other single cluster, and because each of the other clusters uniquely explains so little in relation to what it explained when considered alone in its relationship with municipal expenditures, it is clear that the variable wealth has severely limited the unique power of explanation of each of the other clusters. There is, in other words, considerable covariance between wealth and other clusters. Obviously it is not surprising that economic activity, environmental interaction, and social stability would be reflected in community wealth, and that wealth is a surrogate for other socio-economic variables.

Any study of local expenditures must assess the relationship between local spending and external political systems (county, state, and federal governments). Otherwise, it is impossible to understand the extent to which a city is in a position to influence its own affairs. Studying recent state and local expenditures, scholars have found federal aid to states and to local governments to be strongly and positively related to per capita expenditures of state and local governments. In other words, the more external aid, the more the local spending. One scholar viewed this finding to be so obvious that he termed it as "rubbish." He commented,

> Inasmuch as states and localities must spend virtually all the . . . aid they receive, it is not surprising to find that aid and expenditures move together in a "statistically significant manner." Indeed, using aid to explain expenditures is analogous to using taxes to explain

> expenditures in the sense that both aid and taxes are sources of funds. The fact that these variables turn out to have substantial explanatory power serves as little more than verification of the quite obvious fact that government receipts and expenditures are closely related.[29]

While this may have been an obvious finding in the 1960s, the data reflect a contrary pattern for the turn of the century. For example, Table 9 reveals that receiving money from other civil divisions was inversely related to municipal expenditures per capita. The less money each city received from another civil division, the higher its municipal expenditures per capita. And unlike the 1960s, the state, county, and federal governments at the turn of the century contributed very small amounts to cities for local functions.

Excepting cities in the Plains region, Table 9 suggests spending by states was positively related to spending in local areas. The more the states spent, the more their cities spent, though the states were not making very significant contributions to local governmental functions. The relations between county and city spending are weak for the entire country, and the historical data reveal that counties assumed very few urban functions at the turn of the century.

It is true that many states had statutory and constitutional provisions limiting local spending, but most cities within our size range seldom had expenditures which reached that limit, suggesting that these provisions had very little effect on the local spending of middle-sized cities.

Conclusion

In comparison with municipal expenditures of the 1960s, the amounts middle-sized cities spent in 1903 seem quite small—the average expenditure was only $11.29 per capita. Still, state and county expenditures per person were even lower, $2.89 and $2.48 respectively. Education expenses were the largest component of almost every city's budget; the value of schools usually exceeded the value of other city possessions, for many cities did not own water, gas, or electric works.

Overall, it was the cities of the New England states that spent the most money per resident ($14.78), cities which were oldest, growing least rapidly, most inclined toward manufacturing, highest on education and literacy variables, most ethnic, most Catholic, most wealthy, and more suburban.

[29] Morss, "Government Expenditures," p. 97.

Table 9. Relationships Between Municipal Expenditures Per Capita and Indicators of Spending by External Political Systems

Variable	*Zero Order Correlation Coefficient*						*Partial Correlation Coefficient*					
	All Cities (N=278)	*North-east (N=52)*	*Mid-Atlantic (N=68)*	*Lakes (N=78)*	*South (N=38)*	*Plains (N=28)*	*All Cities (N=278)*	*North-east (N=52)*	*Mid-Atlantic (N=68)*	*Lakes (N=78)*	*South (N=38)*	*Plains (N=28)*
Contributions From Other Civil Divisions (20)	–.10	–.25	–.06	–.14	–.27	–.33	–.11	–.09	.14	–.20	–.29	–.35
State Spending Per Capita (21)	.47†	.34‡	.54†	.09	.10	–.04	.47	.27	.55	.18	.15	.11
County Spending Per Capita (22)	.05	.26‡	–.04	–.05	.03	.16	.09	.21	–.02	.09	–.03	.18
R^2	.23†	.17‡	.31†	.05	.10	.15						

Variable number indicated in parentheses. See Appendix A.

† Significant at .01 level.
‡ Significant at .05 level.

The cities of the Plains spent the least money. These cities were the youngest, the least involved with manufacturing, and the least wealthy. Even so, education-literacy levels were relatively high for the middle-sized cities of the Plains, as were levels of professional and/or administrative activity. In these cities, expenditures were $9.40 (see Appendix D).

That middle-sized cities of New England were located at the opposite end of the expenditure spectrum from those of the Plains is not unexpected. New England cities had flourishing commercial and civic institutions and had managed to retain their economic vitality despite the changes in the economy of the United States. Most had weathered changes in manufacturing emphasis: if the textile industry had declined, the boot and shoe business was flourishing. Wages might have been low, but a high percentage of the population was employed because labor-intensive manufacturing was characteristic. On the other hand, prospects for the middle-sized cities of the Plains were much less certain: the cattle drive, with its boom aspect, had declined. For some cities, the possibility of serving as a shipping point for grain or for processing offered bright prospects. But by 1900, prosperity was more a promise than a current reality.[30]

Cities in the Middle Atlantic, Lakes, and Southern states were quite similar in their expenditure levels ($10.47, $10.20, and $10.30 respectively). But rather different combinations of circumstances had contributed to roughly the same level of outcome.

Resources in the middle-sized cities of the Middle Atlantic region were in short supply: there were few wealthy suburbs, but many mining towns dependent on coal for community survival. Many old port cities were no longer involved in the prosperity syndrome of growth and shipping; even manufacturing activity was more monopolized by New York and Philadelphia in 1900 than had been the case a decade earlier.[31] Such resources as existed were mobilized, but the level of spending they could support was low.

Southern middle-sized cities were quite another story. There were not many large cities in the South; moreover, between 1860 and 1900, the large cities of the South dropped sharply in national population ranking. At the same time, middle-sized Southern cities, which served

[30] Robert Higgs, "Location Theory and the Growth of Cities in the Western Prairie Region, 1870-1900" (unpublished Ph.D. dissertation, Johns Hopkins University, 1968); Jeffrey Williamson and Joseph Swanson, "The Growth of Cities in the Northeast, 1820-1870," *Explorations in Entrepreneurial History*, 4 (Fall 1966), 2nd Series, Supplement.

[31] Allan R. Pred, *The Spatial Dynamics of U.S. Urban-Industrial Growth 1800-1914* (Cambridge: M.I.T. Press, 1966), pp. 12-85.

quite large areas, had grown very rapidly. They experienced a 45 per cent population increase from 1890 to 1900 alone, the fastest growth for any region other than the Far West. After 1900, they became both important and sizeable cities, as an inspection of Appendix E indicates. By 1900, they were carrying out commercial and retail functions for relatively large surrounding areas and populations, thereby enjoying the benefits of considerable activity that was not strictly local. Specifically, they were quite wealthy. But this wealth was not mobilized for political action. The figures for the South do not support what might seem an obvious explanation: that municipal expenditures were sharply curtailed when the percentage of the population which was Negro was high. Indeed, there was hardly any relationship between the percentage of the population which was Negro and municipal spending, or between wealth and per cent Negro.

It is always problematical to explain why things did not happen—why cities in the Southern states did not spend more money—but one is struck with the possibility that when over a third of the population was socially and economically non-participative, the leverage to mobilize wealth for civic purposes was greatly reduced. The Southern cities were enlarged by migrants from the farms, people who brought to the political process a minimal amount of experience. Moreover, the 35 per cent of the population that was Negro probably bore little influence. Wealth, then, was more concentrated in the South than in any other region and the levers for transmuting it into the public sector were fewer. It is interesting to note that of the monies spent, Southern cities were more inclined to spend for police than cities elsewhere in the country, less inclined to spend for public education. This social control orientation was not correlated with the per cent of the population that was Negro. From other evidence, we have reason to believe that police were a social control mechanism directed in large part toward whites.

The middle-sized cities of the Lakes states yield to an explanation that lies somewhere between that of the Middle Atlantic region and that of the South. Cities in the Lakes states were not so poor as those of Pennsylvania. Yet they did not serve as regional capitals to the same extent that Southern cities did. A few cities were administrative or educational centers: Lafayette, Indiana; Ann Arbor, Michigan; Madison, Wisconsin. Evanston was a bedroom suburb for Chicago. In general, however, 1900 was not an auspicious time for middle-sized cities in the Midwestern United States. And expenditure levels were circumscribed by two kinds of conditions, between which there was some overlap.

First, we know from other studies that the financial depression of the 1870s and 1880s had wrought havoc with the public finances of many Midwestern communities, especially newer cities. Committed to large debts, often unsecured, these cities were caught short by hard times. Even when economic recovery occurred, they remained reluctant to become locked in to aggressive expansion schemes if sizeable debt were involved. Willing to build schools, they remained chary of indebtedness for waterworks, electric plants, streetcar lines, etc. Fiscally conservative, the cities of the Lakes area lagged behind those of other regions in incurring debts in the 1890s, a decade characterized by very considerable debt increases elsewhere. This same hesitation is evident in municipal expenditures; tax effort was comparatively low, as cities did not tap available resources.

Second, for many cities of the Lakes states, economic problems were so severe at the turn of the century that efficient mobilization of resources was rendered unlikely. Over half the Lakes communities in this study were highly oriented toward extractive activity (mining or lumber). The wane of the lumber town is too familiar an episode to bear more than rather casual remark—by 1900 the value of lumber products, the number of board feet, had fallen precipitously in Michigan, greatly in Wisconsin. The hey days of cities like Menominee had passed, leaving a long period of economic adjustment to take its toll. As for the mining towns, they were not characterized by social or financial amenities. A few cities were feeders into the metropolitan growth in the region: by the turn of the century, Cleveland, Milwaukee, Detroit, and Chicago were industrial giants, centralizing unto themselves much of the manufacturing of the midwestern area. Pred's studies have shown that from 1870 to 1900 most counties in Illinois, Indiana, southern Michigan, and southern Wisconsin either underwent a decline in the percentage of the population employed in manufacturing, or had such a small percentage of people so employed that manufacturing was for all practical purposes trivial. In short, numerous Lakes cities were short of financial resources. Experiencing rather rapid growth, often resulting from the arrival of foreign immigrants, many cities were unable to mobilize their slender resources when they had to deal with demands, or needs, for spending. Paralyzed by economic decline, they made little effort to use the support sources that were available.

Two overarching problems, teasing in their inaccessibility, must be kept in mind, although their roles and ramifications cannot be fixed: the emergence of an effectively nationalized economy in the United States by 1900, and the existence of a national hierarchy of cities alongside and interconnected with regional hierarchies of cities. As yet, historians have not been able to recapture or simulate the data which would deal adequately with either problem, much less with the issue of how a national economy role or a place in a hierarchy would affect policy outcomes. Very broadly, the problem of a nationalized economy deals with what kinds of exchanges large or small regions made: whether they served as breadbaskets, fabricating specialists, labor suppliers, sources for emigration, locations for rapid increase of capital.[32] For the lumber cities of Minnesota and Wisconsin, the combination of forest depletion and the construction of transcontinental railroads for opening the Northwest spelled at best, rearrangement of resources, at worst, severe economic depression. In New England, some kinds of industries, however labor-intensive, could not continue to compete when the advantages of New York as a manufacturing center were accounted. It would be unrealistic to assume no relationship between municipal policy outcomes and the emergence of a nationwide economic system, but the tools for indicating the relationship have not been invented. Second, the problem of hierarchy, which has received considerable attention from historical geographers and economic historians, should be set alongside municipal outputs. The placement of a city in a hierarchy of size, or in a hierarchy of functions, should bear some influence on spending, as well as on growth and a host of other outcomes. As indicated above, in some states or regions, middle-sized cities were quite important in commerce, in retailing, even in manufacturing. But again, the specifics are not at hand for measurement, for assessing the role a city's place in a hierarchy or hierarchies has for its expenditures.

To turn this discussion in a different direction, one must also assess the overall adequacy of explanations hinged on the social and economic bases of decisions, or more broadly, of politics. Those concerned with decisions, specific or general, have long been inclined to emphasize the institutional and legal arrangements prevailing: the form of government, the method of choosing representation, the locus of veto power, the tenure of office-holders. And, more recently, this concern with the relatively formal circumstances presumably affecting decision-making has been greatly broadened into an effort to survey the political culture of civil entities, whether cities, states, or countries. Even with the best contemporary survey data complementing

[32] Perloff, *et al., Regions*, pp. 218-21; Harvey S. Perloff and Lowdon Wingo, Jr., "Natural Resource Endowment and Regional Economic Growth," in *Regional Development and Planning*, ed. by John Friedman and William Alonso (Cambridge: M.I.T. Press, 1964), pp. 215-39.

aggregate data, the dynamics of policy-making are difficult to assess with any precision: how does one weight demographic, ecological, structural, and psychological variables even if they are all available; how does one deal with the covariance among them? The historian is saved from some of these concerns, for the data available to him is of a narrower range. In another paper, we are addressing ourselves to the effects of political variables on expenditures, looking at the explanatory power unique to political variables in contrast to the explanatory power unique to social and economic variables. But for this essay, we leave moot the problem of the utility of using alternative concepts for explaining policy outcomes.

Even if we use systematic procedures (social and economic bases or political culture) for explaining municipal expenditures, we are unlikely to find wholly satisfactory results. To improve one's comprehension and explanation of municipal expenditures, one needs to turn to other essentially local variables which may affect policy outcomes.

Need for spending was not constant—communities differed in the incidence of problems posed by the nearness of rivers, the lack of water and power supplies, the shortage of adequate transportation facilities. Indeed, in the nineteenth century, one is struck over and over by the fact that climate and geography were vital forces in shaping spending, whether the immediate issue was yellow fever control in Baton Rouge, fire protection and bridges in Eau Claire, or railroads and canals in Green Bay.

The amounts and types of services obtained per dollar spent also varied from area to area. If labor costs were low, a city might have been able to maintain streets and highways with rather small sums; likewise, the availability of lumber in large quantities may have biased the cost-efficiency data on construction for areas of the Middle West. It cannot, in short, be assumed that a dollar spent in Galena, Kansas bought the same results that it did for Moline or Lockport.

There are other knotty problems: how to deal with the circularity of spending as both result and cause, how to determine the civil division to which demands were presented for solution. For the most part, dealing with these problems adequately has been beyond the grasp of contemporary political scientists, economists, and sociologists, even with the advantages of better data and "live" cases.

And, full circle, there are always situational variables that befog the picture of regularities: state legislatures that take over local administrations, city destruction by fire or flood, the decision to send high school students to private schools rather than to support public facilities for them. Evidence is wholly lacking which would allow us to make assumptions about the relative influence of situational variables in one region as opposed to another, although it is tempting to consider whether older cities, with more institutions and networks of relationships connected with each other might not have exhibited more regularity of behavior than newer communities, less locked into commitments of spending. After all, if a community had a long tradition of generous spending per capita, it was not so likely that the budget for 1903 would have been sharply lower, regardless of fires or squabbles over liquor licenses. Where spending patterns were less ingrained in residents because cities were new, or because residents were new, one would expect that personalities of leaders and circumstances of nature might have had a greater role in decision-making.

These are problems that we hope analysts will eventually be able to incorporate into their studies.

APPENDIX A

Variable Description and Notes

While this study concentrates on 1903, data were not always available for that particular year. Accordingly, data for years close to 1903 have frequently been used.

1. Per cent of population who were Protestant in the county in which the city was located. Bureau of the Census (Special Reports), *Religious Bodies: 1906*, Part 1, pp. 294-373.

2. Per cent of population which was foreign born or native-born white of foreign-born parents. *Note.* The Census Bureau reported on whether people had foreign-born parents only if they were white. *1900 Census*, Vol. 1, Part 1.

3. Per cent of the population which was non-white. *Note. 1900 Census*, Vol. 1, Part 1.

4. Number of years since census year in which city was first reported to have 2,500 residents. *Note.* A few cities had populations considerably in excess of 2,500 when they first appeared in the census as minor civil divisions; in those cases, the date of initial appearance was used. Federal census volumes were consulted, as well as local and county histories.

5. Per cent population change of city, 1890 to 1900. *Note. Statistics of Cities with Population 8,000 to 25,000*, Special Report of the Census Office, 1907; hereinafter referred to as *Bulletin 45; Statistics of Cities with Population over 25,000*, Special Report of the Census Office, 1907, hereinafter referred to as *Bulletin 20.*

6. True value of real and personal property per capita, 1903 (called wealth). *Note.* The true value of real and personal property was computed from the assessed value by using the percentages at which property was reported to have been assessed. *Bulletins 20, 45.*

7. Per cent of wage earners in manufacturing who were under sixteen years of age in 1900. *Note.* Data were missing for twelve cities. Estimated values were obtained through regression, using variables for which there were no missing data for any city. The means for cities of comparable size in small geographic regions were also computed and found to differ little from the regression estimation values. The means were then inserted. This procedure was used whenever data were missing for manufacturing. *1900 Census*, Vol. 7, Part 1; Vol. 8, Part 2.

8. Number of library books per capita. *Note. Report of the Commissioner of Education, 1899-1900.*

9. Per cent of children ages five to twenty who attended schools, private and public. *Note.* Data were missing for three cities, so the means for cities of comparable size in the small geographic regions in which they were located were inserted. *Report of the Commissioner of Education, 1899-1900.*

10. Per cent of homes owned or being purchased by inhabitants. *Note. 1900 Census,* Vol. 1, Part 2.

11. Number of students graduating from public and private high schools in 1900 per 1,000 population. *Note. Report of the Commissioner of Education, 1899-1900.*

12. Governmental center: whether city was county seat or state capital. *Note. Rand McNally Business Atlas, 1900.*

13. Whether city was suburb (dummy variable). *Note.* Central city was arbitrarily required to have population in excess of 125,000 before we classified a particular city as a suburb. *Rand McNally Business Atlas, 1900; 1900 Census,* Vol. 1, Part 1.

14. Value of farm products per square mile, of county in which city was located. *Note.* Plate #135, *Statistical Atlas of the 1900 Census.*

15. Population density per square mile of county within which city was located. *Note.* Plate #13 of *Statistical Atlas of the 1900 Census.*

16. Per cent of the population consisting of doctors, homeopaths, dentists, lawyers, business and normal school teachers, college and liberal arts teachers. *Note. Polk's Medical Register,* 1900; *Polk's Dental Register,* 1902; *Directory of the American Homeopathic Association,* 1900; *Martindale's American Legal Directory,* 1900-1901; *Report of the Commissioner of Education, 1897-1898, 1898-1899, 1899-1900, 1900-1901*; miscellaneous city directories (for suburbs).

17. Value of timber products per square mile, by county in which city was located. *Note.* Plate #196, *Statistical Atlas of the 1900 Census.*

18. Presence of coal and/or iron mining. *Note. Statistical Atlas of the 1890 Census,* Plate #58.

19. Per cent of the population employed in manufacturing, including hand trades and manufacturing incidental to merchandising. *Note.* Data were missing for eleven cities. For nine cities the per cent of the population employed as wage earners in manufacturing exclusive of hand trades and manufacturing incidental to merchandising was used. For two cities, the means of the variable for cities of comparable size in the appropriate small geographical regions were used. *1900 Census,* Vol. 7, Part 1; Vol. 8, Part 2; Special Report of the Census Office, *Manufactures,* Part 3, 1905.

20. Per cent of city's gross revenue received from other civil divisions, 1903. *Note. Bulletins 20, 45.*

21. Amount of money spent by state in which city was located (per capita, 1902). *Note.* Special Report of the Census Office, *Wealth, Debt, and Taxation,* 1907.

22. Amount of money spent by counties in state in which city was located (per capita, 1902). *Note.* Special Report of the Census Office, *Wealth, Debt, and Taxation,* 1907.

23. Municipal expenditures per capita, 1903. *Note.* In a few instances, schools were financed by counties rather than by cities. From other sources, city contributions to counties for education were obtained and the amounts were added to other municipal expenditures reported. This procedure was followed for three cities in Florida and for two in Maryland, as well as for Macon, Georgia, and Cripple Creek, Colorado. *Bulletins 20, 45; Report of the Commissioner of Education, 1899-1900.*

APPENDIX B

States by Geographical Regions

Northeast	*Middle Atlantic*	*Lakes*
52 cities	68 cities	78 cities
Maine	New York	Ohio
New Hampshire	New Jersey	Michigan
Vermont	Pennsylvania	Indiana
Massachusetts	Maryland	Illinois
Connecticut		Wisconsin
Rhode Island		

Plains	*South*	*West*
28 cities	38 cities	14 cities
Minnesota	Louisiana	Montana
Iowa	Mississippi	Colorado
South Dakota	Florida	Utah
Texas	Georgia	Wyoming
Denison	North Carolina	California
El Paso	South Carolina	Washington
Laredo	Virginia	
Sherman	West Virginia	
Oklahoma	Kentucky	
Kansas	Tennessee	
Arkansas	Texas	
Missouri	Austin	
	Waco	

APPENDIX C

GEOGRAPHICAL REGIONS USED FOR ESTIMATING DATA

Northeast	*Middle Atlantic*	*East North Central*	*West North Central*	*Mountain*
52 cities	68 cities	78 cities	12 cities	7 cities
Maine New Hampshire Vermont Massachusetts Connecticut Rhode Island	New York New Jersey Pennsylvania Maryland	Ohio Michigan Indiana Illinois Wisconsin	Minnesota Iowa South Dakota	Montana Colorado Utah Wyoming

Far West	*West Border*	*Deep South*	*East Border*
7 cities	20 cities	20 cities	14 cities
California Washington	Texas Oklahoma Kansas Arkansas Missouri	Louisiana Mississippi Florida Georgia North Carolina South Carolina	Virginia West Virginia Kentucky Tennessee

APPENDIX D

Policy Variable Means, by Region*

Variable	278 Cities	North-east (N=52)	Middle Atlantic (N=68)	Lakes (N=78)	South (N=38)	Plains (N=28)	West (N=14)
Municipal Expenditures, Excluding Capital Spending	$11.29	$14.78	$10.47	$10.20	$10.38	$ 9.40	$14.95
Police Expenditure	.71	.80	.61	.60	.94	.67	.96
Fire Expenditure	.96	1.06	.61	1.06	1.02	.96	1.45
Health Expenditure	.16	.22	.20	.13	.15	.08	.15
Highway Expenditure	2.06	2.93	1.91	1.75	1.85	1.58	2.85
Education Expenditure	3.60	4.37	3.53	3.77	1.87	3.32	3.53
Outlay Expenditure-Capital Spending Only	4.42	4.68	4.12	4.18	4.20	4.45	6.43
Capital Spending on Highways, Streets (outlay)	2.17	1.58	2.05	2.39	1.67	3.02	3.02
Indebtedness	30.18	40.81	30.60	21.30	35.94	23.94	35.06

* All figures reported are on a per capita basis and are reported in dollars.

APPENDIX E

List of 278 Cities in United States with Population of 10,000-25,000 in 1900

Northeast

Auburn, Maine
Augusta, Maine
Bangor, Maine
Bath, Maine
Biddeford, Maine
Lewiston, Maine
Concord, New Hampshire
Dover, New Hampshire
Nashua, New Hampshire
Portsmouth, New Hampshire
Burlington, Vermont
Rutland, Vermont
Adams, Massachusetts
Attleboro, Massachusetts
Beverly, Massachusetts
Brookline, Massachusetts
Chicopee, Massachusetts
Clinton, Massachusetts
Everett, Massachusetts
Framingham, Massachusetts
Gardner, Massachusetts
Hyde Park, Massachusetts
Leominster, Massachusetts
Marlboro, Massachusetts
Medford, Massachusetts
Melrose, Massachusetts
Milford, Massachusetts
Newburyport, Massachusetts
North Adams, Massachusetts
Northampton, Massachusetts
Peabody, Massachusetts
Pittsfield, Massachusetts
Quincy, Massachusetts
Revere, Massachusetts
Southbridge, Massachusetts
Waltham, Massachusetts
Westfield, Massachusetts
Weymouth, Massachusetts
Woburn, Massachusetts
Ansonia, Connecticut
Danbury, Connecticut
Manchester, Connecticut
Meriden, Connecticut
Naugatuck Bor., Connecticut
New London, Connecticut
Norwich, Connecticut
Stamford, Connecticut
Central Falls, Rhode Island
Cranston, Rhode Island
East Providence, Rhode Island
Newport, Rhode Island
Warwick, Rhode Island

Middle Atlantic

Amsterdam, New York
Cohoes, New York
Corning, New York
Dunkirk, New York
Geneva, New York
Glens Falls, New York
Gloversville, New York
Hornellsville, New York
Ithaca, New York
Jamestown, New York
Johnstown, New York
Kingston, New York
Little Falls, New York
Lockport, New York
Middletown, New York
Mt. Vernon, New York
Newburg, New York
New Rochelle, New York
Niagara Falls, New York
Ogdensburg, New York
Oswego, New York
Peekskill, New York
Poughkeepsie, New York
Rome, New York
Saratoga Springs, New York
Watertown, New York
Watervliet, New York
Bridgeton, New Jersey
East Orange, New Jersey
Harrison, New Jersey
Kearny, New Jersey
Millville, New Jersey
Montclair, New Jersey
Morristown, New Jersey
New Brunswick, New Jersey
Orange, New Jersey
Perth Amboy, New Jersey
Phillipsburg, New Jersey
Plainfield, New Jersey
Union, New Jersey
West Hoboken, New Jersey

Beaver Falls, Pennsylvania
Braddock, Pennsylvania
Bradford, Pennsylvania
Butler, Pennsylvania
Carbondale, Pennsylvania
Columbia, Pennsylvania
Dunmore, Pennsylvania
Hazleton, Pennsylvania
Homestead, Pennsylvania
Lebanon, Pennsylvania
Mahonoy City, Pennsylvania
Meadville, Pennsylvania
Mt. Carmel, Pennsylvania
Nanticoke, Pennsylvania
Norristown, Pennsylvania
Oil City, Pennsylvania
Pittston, Pennsylvania
Plymouth, Pennsylvania
Pottstown, Pennsylvania
Pottsville, Pennsylvania
Shamokin, Pennsylvania
Shenandoah, Pennsylvania
So. Bethlehem, Pennsylvania
Steelton, Pennsylvania
Wilkinsburg, Pennsylvania
Cumberland, Maryland
Hagerstown, Maryland

Lakes

Ashtabula, Ohio
Chillicothe, Ohio
East Liverpool, Ohio
Findlay, Ohio
Hamilton, Ohio
Ironton, Ohio
Lima, Ohio
Lorain, Ohio
Mansfield, Ohio
Marietta, Ohio
Marion, Ohio
Massillon, Ohio
Newark, Ohio
Piqua, Ohio
Portsmouth, Ohio
Sandusky, Ohio
Steubenville, Ohio
Tiffin, Ohio
Zanesville, Ohio
Anderson, Indiana
Elkhart, Indiana
Elwood, Indiana
Hammond, Indiana
Jeffersonville, Indiana
Kokomo, Indiana
Lafayette, Indiana
Logansport, Indiana
Marion, Indiana
Michigan City, Indiana
Muncie, Indiana
New Albany, Indiana
Richmond, Indiana
Vincennes, Indiana
Alton, Illinois
Aurora, Illinois
Belleville, Illinois
Bloomington, Illinois
Cairo, Illinois
Danville, Illinois
Decatur, Illinois
Elgin, Illinois
Evanston, Illinois
Freeport, Illinois
Galesburg, Illinois
Jacksonville, Illinois
Kankakee, Illinois
Lasalle, Illinois
Moline, Illinois
Ottawa, Illinois
Rock Island, Illinois
Streator, Illinois
Alpena, Michigan
Ann Arbor, Michigan
Battle Creek, Michigan
Flint, Michigan
Ishpeming, Michigan
Kalamazoo, Michigan
Lansing, Michigan
Manistee, Michigan
Marquette, Michigan
Menominee, Michigan
Muskegon, Michigan
Port Huron, Michigan
Sault Ste. Marie, Michigan
West Bay City, Michigan
Appleton, Wisconsin
Ashland, Wisconsin
Beloit, Wisconsin
Eau Claire, Wisconsin
Fond du Lac, Wisconsin
Green Bay, Wisconsin
Janesville, Wisconsin
Kenosha, Wisconsin
Madison, Wisconsin
Manitowoc, Wisconsin
Marinette, Wisconsin
Sheboygan, Wisconsin
Wausau, Wisconsin

Plains

Mankato, Minnesota
Stillwater, Minnesota
Winona, Minnesota
Burlington, Iowa
Clinton, Iowa
Fort Dodge, Iowa
Keokuk, Iowa
Marshalltown, Iowa
Muscatine, Iowa
Ottumwa, Iowa
Waterloo, Iowa
Sioux Falls, South Dakota
Hannibal, Missouri
Sedalia, Missouri
Springfield, Missouri
Atchison, Kansas
Fort Scott, Kansas
Galena, Kansas
Lawrence, Kansas
Leavenworth, Kansas
Pittsburg, Kansas
Wichita, Kansas
Guthrie, Oklahoma
Oklahoma City, Oklahoma
Denison, Texas
El Paso, Texas
Laredo, Texas
Sherman, Texas

South

Fort Smith, Arkansas
Pine Bluff, Arkansas
Baton Rouge, Louisiana
Shreveport, Louisiana
Meridian, Mississippi
Natchez, Mississippi
Vicksburg, Mississippi
Key West, Florida
Pensacola, Florida
Tampa, Florida
Athens, Georgia
Columbus, Georgia
Macon, Georgia
Asheville, North Carolina
Charlotte, North Carolina
Greensboro, North Carolina
Raleigh, North Carolina
Wilmington, North Carolina
Winston, North Carolina
Columbia, South Carolina
Greenville, South Carolina
Spartanburg, South Carolina
Alexandria, Virginia
Danville, Virginia
Lynchburg, Virginia
Newport News, Virginia
Petersburg, Virginia
Portsmouth, Virginia
Roanoke, Virginia
Charleston, West Virginia
Huntington, West Virginia
Parkersburg, West Virginia
Henderson, Kentucky
Owensboro, Kentucky
Paducah, Kentucky
Jackson, Tennessee
Austin, Texas
Waco, Texas

West

Great Falls, Montana
Helena, Montana
Colorado Springs, Colorado
Cripple Creek, Colorado
Leadville, Colorado
Ogden, Utah
Cheyenne, Wyoming
Alameda, California
Berkeley, California
Fresno, California
San Diego, California
San Jose, California
Stockton, California
Walla Walla, Washington

IX

The Efficiency Effects of Federal Land Policy, 1850-1900: A Report of Some Provisional Findings

ROBERT WILLIAM FOGEL AND

JACK L. RUTNER

THE HISTORIOGRAPHY of federal land policy has grown with great rapidity since the mid-1930s.* The bibliography to Paul W. Gates's prodigious new study of public land policy lists over 650 books and articles.[1] Two-thirds of these were published during the past 35 years. The main thrust of opinion in this literature with respect to the performance of the government is quite negative. The various criticisms can be divided into two categories—efficiency issues and equity issues.

The argument over efficiency turns on the effect of certain measures on the level of national income. Those who criticize federal land policy on this ground attempted to demonstrate that governmental decisions made national income lower than it would have been if an alternative set of policies had been pursued. The argument over equity is concerned with the effect of land policy on the distribution of income and wealth.

The paper is, for the most part, restricted to the consideration of the direct effect of land policy on economic efficiency. We do not deal with the broad array of equity issues. Nor do we attempt a general

* We have benefited from comments by Lee Benson, Allan Bogue, Lance Davis, Albert Fishlow, Paul Gates, Ronald W. Jones, Peter McClelland, Edward Nell, Malcolm Rohrbough, T. W. Schultz, Robert Solow, Robert Swierenga, and George Rogers Taylor as well as from a discussion of a still earlier version of this paper by J.R.T. Hughes, Harold Williamson, and the students in their graduate seminar in economic history.

The research on this paper was supported by grants from the Social Science Research Council, the Mathematical Social Science Board, and the University of Chicago.

[1] Paul W. Gates, *History of Public Land Law Development* (Washington: U.S. Govt. Printing Office, 1968). For a more comprehensive bibliography see Department of Interior, Bureau of Land Management, *Public Lands Bibliography* (Washington: U.S. Govt. Printing Office, 1962).

assessment of the consequences of changes in equity on efficiency. Our objective is rather to delineate the principal propositions in the literature which underlie the conclusion that federal land policy was inefficient. Since only one of these propositions involves the interaction between equity and efficiency in an essential way, consideration of the issue is limited to that point.

Our criticisms of conventional views involve both points of logic and fact. Much of our argument rests on the consistency between the accepted propositions and available aggregate data on productivity, profits, and other crucial variables. In this connection we rely heavily on recent estimates of national income, national wealth, factor shares, and other synthetic statistics. Because of limitations in the quality of these measures, and because of the complexities in adapting them to the evaluation of the issues raised by the debate over land policy, our findings are provisional.

Did Land Policy Induce Too Much Capital and Labor into Agriculture?

It is widely held that the federal government released land from the public domain too rapidly. This policy, it is argued, induced too much capital and labor into agriculture. Moreover, many of those who responded to the lure of the land bonanza were the wrong type—"misfits" who lacked the managerial skills and knowledge required for successful farming.[2] As a consequence, national income was lower than it would have been if the land had remained in the public domain for a longer period of time and if the labor and capital induced into agriculture had remained employed in manufacturing. The manifestation of the inefficiency within agriculture is said to have been the disastrous effect of land policy on the return to both labor and capital.[3]

[2] Theodore Saloutos, "Land Policy and its Relation to Agricultural Production and Distribution, 1862 to 1933," *Journal of Economic History*, 22 (December 1962), pp. 447-48, hereinafter referred to as "Land Policy."

[3] Thomas LeDuc, "Public Policy, Private Investment, and Land Use in American Agriculture, 1825-1875," *Agricultural History*, 37 (January 1963), pp. 3-9; Theodore Saloutos, "The Agricultural Problem and Nineteenth Century Industrialism," *Agricultural History*, 22 (July 1948), pp. 156-74, reprinted in *Economic Change in America*, ed. by Joseph T. Lambric and Richard V. Clemence (Harrisburg: The Stackpole Co., 1954), pp. 313-40, hereinafter referred to as "Industrialism"; Saloutos, "Land Policy," pp. 445-60.

LeDuc and Saloutos agree that too much money was spent on land. But while Saloutos holds that too much labor was induced to enter agriculture, LeDuc holds that there was not enough labor in agriculture, or at least in those areas where the government was distributing new lands most rapidly. LeDuc also argues that

The evidence presented to support this interpretation is meager indeed. Local studies of western Kansas and Nebraska—where many who began farming in the late seventies or early eighties failed in the late eighties or early nineties—are one of the principal pillars for the conventional position. The second principal pillar is the contention that the era of greatest land disposal during the nineteenth century, the three decades following the Civil War, was also an era of great agricultural depression. Proof of the depression is found not merely in the agrarian protests but also in the steady downward march of agricultural prices between 1864 and 1896.[4] The depression was the consequence of the persistent overproduction of farm products, an overproduction that was brought on by "policies that encouraged people to take to the land without regard for the fact that they accelerated agricultural production beyond all reasonable market demand."[5]

Unfortunately this type of evidence is much too frail to serve as a foundation for the edifice that has been erected on it. The failures of the late eighties in western Kansas and Nebraska are too special to be representative of the general effect of land policy on agriculture. Nor can the high rate of failure in this region, at this time, be taken as evidence that land policy drew into agriculture a disproportionately large number of "misfits." After all, "In God we trusted, in Kansas we busted" is not a confession of ineptitude but a lament about the

---

farmers should have increased the ratio of improved to unimproved land. We shall test the first two of these three efficiency issues. Data required to test the contention that the ratio of unimproved to improved land was too high are not now available. However, we examine this contention below and present prima-facie evidence which tends to contradict it.

Historians who have expressed views similar to those propounded by LeDuc are cited by Robert P. Swierenga in "Land Speculator 'Profits' Reconsidered: Central Iowa as a Test Case," *Journal of Economic History*, 26 (March 1966), p. 3, hereinafter referred to as "Land Speculator," and in *Pioneers and Profits: Land Speculation on the Iowa Frontier* (Ames: Iowa State Univ. Press, 1968), pp. 6, 218, hereinafter referred to as *Pioneers and Profits*. The interpretation put forth by Saloutos is also to be found in Solon J. Buck, *The Granger Movement* (Cambridge: Harvard Univ. Press, 1913) and John D. Hicks, *The Populist Revolt* (Minneapolis: Univ. of Minnesota Press, 1931). These arguments are repeated in such leading textbooks of economic history as Harold Underwood Faulkner, *American Economic History* (8th ed.; New York: Harper & Row, Inc., 1960); Herman E. Krooss, *American Economic Development* (2nd ed.; Englewood Cliffs, N.J.: Prentice-Hall, Inc., 1966); Ross M. Robertson, *History of the American Economy* (2nd ed.; New York: Harcourt, Brace and World, 1964), hereinafter referred to as *American Economy*.

[4] Ray Billington, *Westward Expansion* (New York: Macmillan Co., 1949), p. 723; Robertson, *American Economy*, pp. 260-64.

[5] Saloutos, "Industrialism," pp. 320-21.

fickleness of fate. In an era when authorities were uncertain about the extent of rainfall west of the hundredth meridian,[6] it was not difficult to mistake the long period (eight years) of above average rainfall which began at the end of the seventies, as a permanent shift in climatic conditions.[7]

The attempt to make land policy the cause of the "great agricultural depression" is also flawed. Proponents of this view have not only failed to establish the nexus between land policy and the depression, but even the existence of a thirty-year depression. There were, of course, two serious economic crises between 1866 and 1896 which affected not only agriculture but all economic activity. They were the depressions of 1873-1878 and 1892-1896. These two crises covered only eleven years of the period in question. Moreover, they were both followed by vigorous recoveries.[8]

The case for the proposition that the entire period from 1866 to 1896 was one of sustained depression rests on the steady decline in agricultural prices. Since the price level was also declining, the downward movement in agricultural prices does not necessarily imply a decline in the real prices of farm products. John Bowman[9] has recently pointed out that over the years from 1869 to 1900, the average rate of decline in the wholesale price index was more rapid than the rate of decline in both wheat and corn prices.[10] A more comprehensive measure is given in Table 1 which shows that the real price of agriculture output (col. 1-col. 2) remained constant or rose during each decade between 1849 and 1899, except that of the Civil War. On average the real price of agricultural goods increased at an annual rate of 0.2 per cent over the half-century.

But the conventional view is marred by more than an error in fact. It is wrong in supposing that a decline in the real price of agricultural output necessarily implies a decline in the real per capita in-

[6] Paul W. Gates, *The Farmer's Age* (New York: Holt, Rinehart and Winston, 1960), pp. 419-20, 434, hereinafter referred to as *Farmer's Age*.

[7] Thomas C. Cochran and William Miller, *The Age of Enterprise* (rev. ed.; New York: Harper & Row, Inc., 1961), p. 218.

[8] Edwin Frickey, *Production in the United States, 1860-1914* (Cambridge: Harvard Univ. Press, 1947), pp. 127, 128.

[9] John Bowman, "An Economic Analysis of Midwestern Farm Land Values and Farm Land Income, 1869-1900," *Yale Economic Essays*, Vol. 5, No. 2 (1965), p. 20, hereinafter referred to as "Farm Land Values."

[10] Similar points were made in Fred A. Shannon, *The Farmer's Last Frontier* (New York: Farrar and Rinehart, 1945) and C. F. Emerick, "An Analysis of Agricultural Discontent in the United States, III," *Political Science Quarterly*, 12 (March 1897), p. 106.

TABLE 1. THE ANNUAL RATES OF CHANGE IN INDEXES OF AGRICULTURAL PRICES (P_a), WHOLESALE PRICES (P_w), FARM CONSUMER PRICES (P_f), AND URBAN CONSUMER PRICES (P_u)
(*per cent*)

	1 P_a	2 P_w	3 P_f	4 P_u
1849-59	1.8	1.3	1.7	0.8
1859-69	3.9	4.3	3.6	3.9
1869-79	−3.8	−4.1	−2.5	−3.0
1879-89	−1.5	−1.5	−1.0	−0.4
1889-99	0.2	−0.3	−0.7	−1.0
1849-99	0.1	−0.1	0.2	0.0
1869-99	−1.7	−2.0	−1.4	−1.5

SOURCES AND NOTES: *Column 1.* Conference on Research in Income and Wealth, *American Economy*, p. 43.

Column 2. U.S. Bureau of the Census, *Historical Statistics of the United States, Colonial Times to 1957* (Washington: U.S. Govt. Printing Office, 1960), pp. 231-32. The price index for the census year is a weighted average of the index numbers for the two calendar years spanned by the census year. For example, the index for the census year 1849 is equal to 0.5833 times the index of calendar 1849 plus 0.4167 times the index of calendar 1850.

Column 3. P_f is a weighted average of the prices of food, housing, fuel and light, and clothing. All of these series except the last were taken from Conference on Research in Income and Wealth, *American Economy*, pp. 266, 291; clothing is from *ibid.*, pp. 142-43, and Albert Rees, *Real Wages in Manufacturing, 1890-1914* (Princeton: Princeton Univ. Press, 1961), Table 22. The weights were computed from W. C. Funk, "Value to Farm Families of Food, Fuel and Use of House," U.S. Department of Agriculture *Bulletin* No. 410 (1916), p. 2, and U.S. Department of Labor, *How American Buying Habits Change* (Washington: U.S. Govt. Printing Office, n.d.), p. 32.

Column 4. Conference on Research in Income and Wealth, *American Economy*, pp. 142, 162. The Hoover index begins with 1851. Hence the rates in lines 1 and 6 are for the years 1851-59 and 1851-99 respectively.

come of farmers.[11] If we approximate the aggregate demand function for agricultural output by

$$Q = D\left(\frac{P_a}{P_w}\right)^{-\varepsilon} \tag{1}$$

then

$$\overset{*}{Y}_a = \overset{*}{D} + (1-\varepsilon)\,(\overset{*}{P} - \overset{*}{P}_f) + \varepsilon\,(\overset{*}{P}_w - \overset{*}{P}_f) - \overset{*}{N} \tag{2}$$

[11] Since agriculture purchased few raw materials from the non-agricultural sector during the nineteenth century, we make no distinction here between gross income and value added. See Conference on Research in Income and Wealth, *Trends in the American Economy in the Nineteenth Century*, Studies in Income and Wealth, Vol. 24 (Princeton: Princeton Univ. Press, 1960), p. 48, hereinafter referred to as *American Economy in the Nineteenth Century.*

where

Q = an index of agricultural production
P_a = an index of the price of agricultural output
P_w = an index of the general price level
P_f = an index of farm consumer prices
$\overline{Y}_a$ = real gross agricultural income per capita
D = the shift term of the demand function and an index of the level of demand for agricultural output
N = farm population
ε = the elasticity of demand for agricultural output
$*$ = letters capped by asterisks stand for the rates of change of the uncapped variables.

It follows from equation (2) that a decline in the real price of agricultural output will lead to a decline in the average real income of farmers only when[12]

$$-(\overset{*}{P}_a - \overset{*}{P}_f) > \frac{\overset{*}{D} + \varepsilon(\overset{*}{P}_w - \overset{*}{P}_f) - \overset{*}{N}}{1 - \varepsilon} \qquad (3)$$

We can now see the precarious nature of, and the tenuous basis for confidence in, past attempts to infer the course of average real farm income merely from the movement of agricultural prices. Such inferences involved implicit assumptions not only about the rate of growth in the demand for agricultural output and the elasticity of that demand, but also assumptions about the rate of change in the purchasing-power parity index and in the ratio of the general price level to an index of farm consumer prices.

Fortunately, it is no longer necessary to speculate about the growth of real income in agriculture. Recent work on the construction of national income accounts makes it possible to estimate the rate of growth of this variable by decades between 1849 and 1899. As Table 2 indicates, there is no decade of that period during which the average real income of farmers declined. Over the half-century it rose at an average of 1.3 per cent per annum.[13] While this is certainly a respectable achievement, it still falls short of annual rate of increase in per capita income (1.6 per cent) for the nation as a whole over the same

[12] When $\varepsilon = 1$, a change in P_a has no effect on $\overline{Y}_a$. Then the inequality expressed in equation (3) does not exist.

[13] Using other evidence, Bogue, Bowman, and North have also concluded that average real income was rising during this period. Allan Bogue, *From Prairie to Cornbelt* (Chicago: Univ. of Chicago Press, 1963), hereinafter referred to as *Prairie*; Bowman, "Farm Land Values"; Douglass C. North, *Growth and Welfare in the American Past* (Englewood Cliffs, N.J.: Prentice-Hall, Inc., 1966).

period.[14] The gap becomes somewhat greater if the comparison is made with respect to the rate of growth in real income per worker. Then the agricultural and national averages become 1.0 and 1.4 respectively. One should not, however, leap from these discrepancies to the conclusion that land policy was at fault.

TABLE 2. THE AVERAGE ANNUAL RATE OF GROWTH IN AGRICULTURAL DEMAND, REAL PER CAPITA INCOME, LABOR, AND LAND IN FARMS
(*per cent*)

	1 Real Income Per Capita	2 *Real Income Per Worker*	3 *Demand*	4 *Land in Farms*	5 *Labor*
1849-59	2.0	2.0	4.4	3.3	2.4
1859-69	0.8	0.9	1.2	0.0	1.0
1869-79	0.8	0.3	4.4	2.8	2.4
1879-89	0.7	0.0	2.2	1.5	1.6
1889-99	2.2	2.1	2.2	3.0	0.7
1849-99	1.3	1.0	2.9	2.1	1.7
1869-99	1.2	0.7	2.9	2.4	1.6

SOURCES AND NOTES: *Column 1.* Computed from $\overset{*}{\bar{Y}} = \overset{*}{Q} + \overset{*}{P}_a - \overset{*}{N} - \overset{*}{P}_f$. Conference on Research in Income and Wealth, *American Economy*, p. 43; Morton S. Cooper, Glen T. Barton, and Albert Brodell, *Progress of Farm Mechanization*, U.S. Department of Agriculture, Misc. Pubs. No. 630 (1947), p. 5; Table 1 above.

Column 2. Computed from $\overset{*}{\bar{\bar{Y}}} = \overset{*}{Q} + \overset{*}{P}_a - \overset{*}{L}_a - \overset{*}{P}_f$, where L_a is the agricultural labor force. Conference on Research in Income and Wealth, *American Economy*, pp. 30, 43.

Column 3. Computed from $\overset{*}{D} = \overset{*}{Q} + \varepsilon (\overset{*}{P}_a - \overset{*}{P}_w)$ on the assumption that $\varepsilon =$ 0.5. Since $\overset{*}{P}_a - \overset{*}{P}_w$ averaged only 0.2, the assumed value of ε has little effect on the value of $\overset{*}{D}$. *Ibid.*, p. 43; Table 1 above.

Column 4. U.S. Bureau of the Census, *Twelfth Census of the United States: 1900*, Vol. 5: *Agriculture* (Washington: U.S. Govt. Printing Office, 1902), Part 1, p. xviii.

Column 5. Conference on Research in Income and Wealth, *American Economy*, p. 30.

[14] Conference on Research in Income and Wealth, *Output Employment and Productivity in the United States After 1800*, Studies in Income and Wealth, Vol. 30 (Princeton: Princeton Univ. Press, 1960), p. 26, hereinafter referred to as *Output Employment*; U.S. Bureau of the Census, *Historical Statistics of the United States, Colonial Times to 1957* (Washington: U.S. Govt. Printing Office, 1960), p. 7, hereinafter referred to as *Colonial Times*.

It must be remembered that lands in the western areas of the prairies and in the plains were much better substitutes for the wheat and other small grain lands of the North Central and North Atlantic states than for the cotton, sugar, rice, and tobacco lands of the South. Yet it is the poor performance of the South, not of the North, which explains almost all of the difference between the agricultural and national rates of growth in average real income. Table 3 shows that over the period from 1839 to 1899, income per worker in Southern agriculture grew at only 0.3 per cent per annum—less than a fourth of the national rate. The rest of agriculture virtually matched the national pace. And in the region where land was being distributed most rapidly—the North Central states and the West—the rise in agricultural income per worker exceeded the national rate by 25 per cent. In other words, the explanation for the gap between the performance of agriculture and that of

TABLE 3. THE GROWTH OF REAL AGRICULTURAL INCOME PER WORKER
(*annual rates, per cent*)

	North Atlantic	*North Central*	*South*	*United States Less South*	*United States Less South and North Atlantic*
1839-79	1.3	1.9	0.0	1.4	1.8
1879-99	0.2	1.5	0.9	1.2	1.5
1839-99	1.0	1.8	0.3	1.3	1.7

SOURCES AND NOTES: These regional estimates were constructed by applying Easterlin's state relatives (Conference on Research in Income and Wealth, *American Economy*, pp. 97-104) to Gallman's estimates of value added per worker (*ibid.*, p. 43) deflated by the wholesale price index (U.S. Bureau of the Census, *Historical Statistics of the United States, 1789-1945* [Washington: U. S. Govt. Printing Office, 1949], pp. 231-32).

The regions are defined as follows:

North Atlantic:	*North Central*	*South*
Maine	Ohio	Virginia
New Hampshire	Indiana	West Virginia
Vermont	Illinois	North Carolina
Massachusetts	Michigan	South Carolina
Rhode Island	Wisconsin	Georgia
Connecticut	Minnesota	Florida
New York	Iowa	Kentucky
New Jersey	Missouri	Tennessee
Pennsylvania	North Dakota	Alabama
	South Dakota	Mississippi
	Nebraska	Arkansas
	Kansas	Louisiana
		Oklahoma
		Texas

the rest of the economy appears to be lodged not so much in federal land policy as in conditions peculiar to the South.

While the argument thus far throws into doubt the proposition that there was a substantial and general overallocation of resources to agriculture, it does not preclude the possibility of a significant misallocation of particular factors. To evaluate that possibility it is necessary to compare the return to the factors employed in agriculture with alternative opportunities.

TABLE 4. REAL AVERAGE ANNUAL RATE OF RETURN ON ALL AGRICULTURAL CAPITAL
(*per cent*)

	A. UNITED STATES					
	1 *1859*	*2* *1869*	*3* *1879*	*4* *1889*	*5* *1899*	*6* *1899**
From Current Production	5.8	11.8	10.6	7.2	8.1	8.1
From Average Annual Real Capital Gain on Land	2.9	−2.0	3.1	3.0	−1.3	0.9
From Average Annual Real Capital Gain on Livestock	6.0	2.5	5.4	5.8	2.9	4.2
Weighted Sum of Previous Three Lines	8.5	10.1	13.4	10.0	7.7	9.3

	B. BY REGIONS				
	1 *North Atlantic*	*2* *North Central*	*3* *South Atlantic*	*4* *South Central*	*5* *Western*
From Current Production	6.4	5.8	10.9	10.4	20.3
From Average Annual Real Capital Gain on Land	−0.3	1.7	1.8	1.0	0.3
From Average Annual Real Capital Gain on Livestock	1.6	4.6	3.0	5.3	6.3
Weighted Sum of Three Previous Lines	6.4	7.6	12.4	12.1	21.9

NOTES TO PART A: The real rate of return in any given year is equal to the rate of return from current production plus the annual real rate of increase in the value of capital. In symbols,

$$i = \frac{\alpha_k Y_a}{K} + \left[\phi_1 \frac{dH}{H} + \phi_2 \frac{dP_t}{P_t} \right] \qquad (4A.\ 1)$$

where i = the real rate of return
α_k = the capital share in current production
Y_a = the value of current output
K = the current value of all farm assets

H = the real value of livestock
P_t = the real value of an acre of land
ϕ_1 = the ratio of the value of livestock to K in the base period
ϕ_2 = ratio of the value of farm land to K in the base period

In this equation, the first term on the right represents the rate of return on current production. The expression in brackets is the real return from capital gains and is a weighted average of the rate of capital gain from livestock and from the average value of farm land.

For each census year, the real capital gain was computed from the average annual rate of appreciation over the decade which ended in that year. However, for 1899 the real rate of capital gain was also computed for the 20 years ending in 1899. This result is given in column 6 which is headed "1899*." Columns 5 and 6 differ only in that the annual capital gain in the latter is a 20-year average, while in the former it is a 10-year average. Hence column 5 is comparable with the first four columns of Part A of the table, while column 6 is comparable with the columns in Part B.

The value of all farm assets (K) is from United States Bureau of the Census, *Twelfth Census of the United States: 1900*, Vol. 5: *Agriculture* (Washington: U.S. Govt. Printing Office, 1902), Part 1, p. xxiii. The value of buildings for 1849, 1879, and 1899 are from United States Bureau of the Census, *Colonial Times*, p. 151. For the years 1859 and 1869, the value of buildings was estimated by first finding the ratio of the value of buildings to K in 1849 and 1879 and then applying this ratio to the value of K in 1859 and 1869. The values of machinery, livestock, and acres in farms are from *ibid.*, and U.S. Bureau of the Census, *Twelfth Census of the United States: 1900*, Vol. 5: *Agriculture* (Washington: U.S. Govt. Printing Office, 1902), Part 1, pp. xviii, xxix, xxxii. The value of farm land is K less the value of buildings, livestock, and machinery. The Warren-Pearson price index was used as the deflator of asset values (Table 1 above). Aggregate farm income is from Conference on Research in Income and Wealth, *American Economy*, p. 43. The value of α_k is from *ibid.*, p. 383.

The argument in the text abstracts from the fact that mortgages on farms amounted to about 13 per cent of the total value of farms. U.S. Bureau of the Census, *Eleventh Census of the United States: 1890*, Vol. 12: *Report on Real Estate Mortgages in the United States* (Washington: U.S. Govt. Printing Office, 1902), p. 118. To the extent that the declining price level was unanticipated when these mortgages were signed, declining prices led to losses on mortgages that must be set off against capital gains. To take account of this effect, equation (4A. 1) should be rewritten as

$$i = \frac{\alpha_k Y_a}{K} + \left[\phi_1 \frac{dH}{H} + \phi_2 \frac{dP_t}{P_t} + \phi_3 \frac{d\overline{W}}{\overline{W}} \right] \qquad (4A.\ 2)$$

All of the symbols have been defined previously except

ϕ_3 = the ratio of the value of mortgages to the value of farms in the base period
$\overline{W}$ = the part of the rate of change in the Warren-Pearson wholesale price index that was unanticipated. Thus if

$$\frac{dW}{W}$$

is the actual rate of change in the Warren-Pearson index and

$$\frac{d\hat{W}}{\hat{W}}$$

is the anticipated rate of change, then

$$\frac{d\overline{W}}{\overline{W}} = \frac{dW}{W} - \frac{d\hat{W}}{\hat{W}}$$

The effect of the correction, if it could be made, would be to decrease the share of profit due to capital gains, and hence increase the share of profit originating in current production. The precise magnitude of the correction turns on the extent to which changes in the price level were unanticipated. Unfortunately, the data required to determine this are not available. However, it is possible to show that the correction would not be large in any case by recalculating the capital gain (or loss) on the extreme assumption that price changes were never anticipated. The following table shows that even on this assumption the failure to correct for losses on mortgages introduces an average error in the estimate of the capital gain of only 14 per cent. The upper limit on the error in the estimate of total profit is about 3 per cent.

Average Annual Capital Gain on Farms

	As Computed for Table 4	*Corrected for Loss on Mortgages*
1849-59	2.7	2.9
1859-69	−1.7	−1.1
1869-79	2.8	2.3
1879-89	2.8	2.6
1889-99	−0.4	−0.4

Notes to Part B: Income estimates by regions were obtained by the method and from the sources described in Table 3. Livestock, machinery, 1899 building values, and acres in farms are from U.S. Bureau of the Census, *Twelfth Census of the United States, 1900*, Vol. 5: *Agriculture* (Washington: U.S. Govt. Printing Office, 1902), Part 1, pp. xviii, xxix, xxxiii, and xxxvi. The value of buildings in 1879 was determined by applying the 1899 regional ratios of value of buildings to K (*ibid.*, p. xxxvi) against the 1879 regional values of K. Edward C. Budd's estimate of the capital share for 1899 was applied in each region (Conference on Research in Income and Wealth, *American Economy*, p. 382).

The regions are defined as follows:

North Atlantic	*South Atlantic*	*North Central*	*South Central*	*Western*
Maine	Delaware	Ohio	Kentucky	Montana
New Hampshire	Maryland	Indiana	Tennessee	Wyoming
Vermont	District of Columbia	Illinois	Alabama	Colorado
Massachusetts	Virginia	Michigan	Mississippi	New Mexico
Rhode Island	North Carolina	Minnesota	Louisiana	Arizona
New York	South Carolina	Iowa	Texas	Utah
New Jersey	Georgia	Missouri	Oklahoma (Indian Terr.)	Nevada
Pennsylvania	Florida	North Dakota	Arkansas	Idaho
		South Dakota		Washington
		Nebraska		Oregon
		Kansas		California

Part A of Table 4 gives the national average real rate of return on the investment in farm assets for the census years from 1859 to 1899.[15] Part B gives rates of return by regions for the year 1899. The entries in Table 4 do not support the contentions that land policy induced too much capital into agriculture and that land was overpriced. Quite the contrary, the rate of return from current production was high throughout the period. It compares quite favorably with the average yield on the common stock of manufacturing firms.[16] Table 4 also contradicts the frequent contention that farmers earned little if anything from current production and that farm investment was worthwhile only because of the capital gains from land.[17] This view both slights the return from current production and exaggerates the average rate of increase in the value of farmland. Table 4 shows that current production accounted for about 85 per cent (Part A, line 1 ÷ line 4) of the profit, while capital gains explain only 15 per cent.[18]

The large share of profit which originated in current production, the positive change in land values between 1849 and 1899, the moderate rate at which these land values increased—these facts collectively suggest that land was generally priced according to its value in production rather than on the basis of speculative manias. Of course, as conditions in the markets for agricultural products changed, farmers' expectations regarding the future productive value of land also changed. This accounts for the variation in the rate of capital gain from decade

[15] The rates of return are gross of depreciation. However only 20 per cent of the assets may have depreciated. If these assets depreciated at 2 per cent per annum, the adjustment for depreciation would reduce the rates shown in line one of Table 4, Part A, by only 2 per cent. Thus, for example, the entry in line 1, column 1, would be reduced from 5.8 to 5.7. We have not made this adjustment because we cannot separate residential structures from other buildings and because it is not clear that buildings actually depreciated in value. Buildings account for about 80 per cent of the potentially depreciable assets.

[16] U.S. Bureau of the Census, *Colonial Times*, p. 656.

[17] David Maldwyn Ellis, *Landlords and Farmers in the Hudson-Mohawk Region, 1790-1850* (New York: Octagon Books, 1967), p. 100, hereinafter referred to as *Landlords and Farmers*; Richard Hofstadter, *The Age of Reform* (New York: Vintage Books, 1960), p. 41; Robert D. Patton and Clinton Warne, *The Development of the American Economy* (Chicago: Scott, Foresman, 1963), pp. 214-15, hereinafter referred to as *Development*.

[18] As pointed out in the notes to Table 4, capital losses on mortgages due to unanticipated changes in the price level had only a slight effect on the average profit of farmers. This finding calls into question the widely held view that the declining price level hurt most farmers badly. Total farm mortgages represented only a small offset to total farm assets. Hence the debt to asset ratio was low (about 13 per cent) for most farmers. It was only the farmer with a high debt to asset ratio who was badly hurt by the declining price level. But such farmers were atypical. See notes to Table 4, above.

to decade. However, these variations are quite moderate, and they do not indicate that expectations diverged markedly from experience in the marketing of crops and livestock.

Part B of Table 4 contradicts still another aspect of the traditional position. It shows that the return was highest in the West, where land was being distributed most rapidly. This suggests that capital was not flowing into the West rapidly enough.

The most obvious test of the hypothesis that there was too much labor in agriculture is a comparison of the level of wages in agriculture and manufacturing. To perform such a test one must specify how large a wage differential is consistent with an efficient intersectoral distribution of labor. For one would expect wages in agriculture to be below those in manufacturing even when the distribution of labor between the sectors was optimal, because the average skill of labor in agriculture was below that of manufacturing and because the cost of living was less in rural than in urban areas.[19] The wage differential of the early 1850s may be taken as consistent with an optimum allocation of labor. This was a period of agricultural prosperity,[20] and the net outmigration of labor from agriculture, which has marked most of the past century, had not yet begun.[21]

The results of the test are reported in Table 5. Over the last half of the nineteenth century, agricultural wages grew at less than half the rate of those in manufacturing. This suggests that the agricultural labor force was expanding too rapidly. Precise measurement of the excess amount of labor requires more information on the demand and supply functions of both the manufacturing and agricultural sectors than is now available. One can roughly approximate the desired measure by making a series of simplifying, but not unreasonable, assumptions.[22] On this basis it appears that wages in agriculture would have kept pace with those of manufacturing if the average annual rate of growth of agricultural labor had been reduced from 1.7 per cent to

[19] D. Gale Johnson, "Comparability of Labor Capacity of Farm and Nonfarm Labor," *American Economic Review*, 43 (June 1953), pp. 296-313.

[20] Gates, *Farmer's Age*, p. 402.

[21] The rate of growth of the agricultural labor force was in excess of the natural increase in population between 1850 and 1860.

[22] The assumptions include the neglect of such secondary effects as the increase in demand for agricultural commodities resulting from the rise in income created by the more efficient allocation of labor. It is also assumed that the agricultural production function is Cobb-Douglas with constant returns to scale; that the output elasticity with respect to labor is given by labor's share; that the demand curve for agricultural output may be approximated by equation (1) above, with $\varepsilon = 0.5$; that the elasticity of P_f with respect to P is 0.7; and that wages in all regions within agriculture grew at the same rate.

1.5 per cent. Given such a decrease, the agricultural labor force would have reached only 90 per cent of the level that actually obtained in 1899. In other words there were about one million workers too many in agriculture in 1899, or at least in their particular agricultural occupations.

TABLE 5. GROWTH OF THE REAL WAGE IN MANUFACTURING AND AGRICULTURE, 1849-1899
(*annual rates, per cent*)

	1 *Manufacturing*	2 *Agriculture*	3 *Col. 1-Col. 2*
1849-59	0.5	1.2	−0.7
1859-69	0.7	−1.0	1.7
1869-79	0.5	0.0	0.4
1879-89	4.3	0.9	3.4
1889-99	−0.2	1.2	−1.4
1849-99	1.1	0.4	0.6

SOURCES AND NOTES:

Column 1. Computed from $\overset{*}{w}_m = \overset{*}{\alpha}_m + \overset{*}{Q}_m + \overset{*}{P}_m - \overset{*}{P}_u - \overset{*}{L}_m$. Data are from Conference on Research in Income and Wealth, *American Economy*, pp. 30, 43, 382; Table 1 above.

Column 2. Computed from $\overset{*}{w}_a = \overset{*}{\alpha}_a + \overset{*}{Q}_a + \overset{*}{P}_a - \overset{*}{P}_f - \overset{*}{L}_a$. *Ibid.*

Column 3. Col. 1-Col. 2 may not equal entry in Col. 3 because of rounding.

The last distinction is important. One of the assumptions of the calculation was that the distribution of labor within agriculture was optimal, i.e. that wages in all regions grew at the same rate. Table 6 shows that this assumption was false. Real wages in the South actually declined between 1840 and 1900, while in the rest of the nation they increased at 80 per cent of the manufacturing rate. And in the North Central and Western states the growth of real wages exceeded that of manufacturing by about 20 per cent. Thus a shift of labor from the South and the North Atlantic to the North Central and Western regions would have increased the growth of wages in agriculture as a whole and reduced the disparity between the performance of agriculture and manufacturing.

That the growth of wages in the Western and North Central states exceeded that of manufacturing militates against the contention that land policy induced too much labor into agriculture. For in those regions, where land was being brought into farms most rapidly, the

TABLE 6. THE CHANGE IN THE REAL WAGE OF AGRICULTURAL LABOR BY REGIONS
(*annual rates, per cent*)

	1 South	2 United States Less South	3 United States Less South and North Atlantic
1839-79	−0.7	0.7	1.2
1879-99	0.9	1.2	1.5
1839-99	−0.2	0.9	1.3

SOURCES AND NOTES: The entries are computed from

$$\overset{*}{w} = \overset{*}{\alpha}_a + \overset{*}{P}_a + \overset{*}{Q} - \overset{*}{L} - \overset{*}{P}_w$$

The regions are described in the notes to Table 3. The original values of

$$\overset{*}{P}_a + \overset{*}{Q} - \overset{*}{L} - \overset{*}{P}_w$$

are from Table 3. $\overset{*}{\alpha}$ was computed from Budd's data on factor shares (Conference on Research in Income and Wealth, *American Economy*, p. 382) with the further assumptions that the labor share remained constant from 1839 to 1849 and that there was no difference in the rate of change in this variable by regions.

labor force was not growing quickly enough. It was in the long-settled states of the Atlantic Coast that labor was redundant. To put the issue somewhat differently, the traditional position implies that the elasticity of the labor force with respect to land was an increasing function of the rate at which land was being brought into agriculture. This assumption is false. In the South Atlantic region that elasticity was 6.5, while in the Western and North Central regions it was less than one. The problem was not that land policy induced too much labor into agriculture but that labor in the East, especially the South Atlantic, was insufficiently mobile. This was due largely to the special circumstances of the South, to a failure of social and other economic policies rather than to land policy.[23]

THE RELATIONSHIP BETWEEN GAINS IN THE WEST AND LOSSES IN THE EAST

IT is frequently held that when assessing the change in national income caused by the release of land from the public domain, one ought to take into account the fact that increased competition from the West

[23] Cf. Stanley L. Engerman, "Economic Factors in Southern Backwardness in the Nineteenth Century," in *The State of Regional Economics*, ed. by John Cain and John R. Meyer (Cambridge: Harvard Univ. Press, 1971).

forced many Eastern farms out of business. More specifically it is said that one ought to subtract from the gain in national income attributable to the new lands the losses of income on the old lands.[24] In our opinion, this analysis is incorrect. It confuses equity issues with efficiency issues. The error can be demonstrated with the aid of Figure 1.

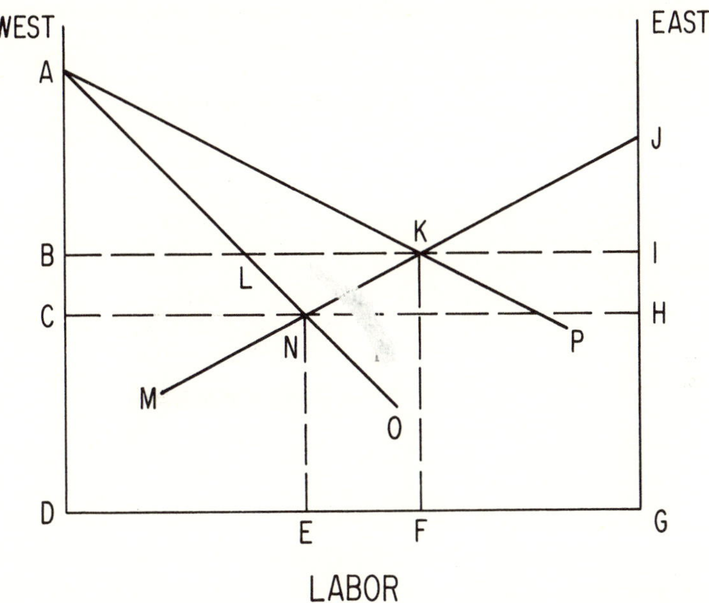

Fig. 1

The horizontal axis of Figure 1 represents the available supply of labor. The marginal product of labor in the West is represented by line AO and is read against the left axis. Line JM is the marginal product of Eastern labor and is read along the right axis. These lines are downward sloping because land is not homogeneous with respect to quality, and it is assumed that labor will be applied to the most productive land first. The distribution of labor and income between the two regions is determined by the intersection of the two curves at N, indicating that in equilibrium the marginal product of labor will be the same in both sectors.[25] National income is represented by the area

[24] Paul Cootner, review of *The Union Pacific Railroad*, by Robert W. Fogel, in *Journal of Economic History*, 21 (September 1961), pp. 404-06.

[25] We abstract from transportation costs. If these were taken into account, then in equilibrium, Western wages would exceed those of the East by the decapitalized value of the cost of moving.

under the marginal product curves between the vertical axes and their intersection—i.e. by the area ADGJNA. Before the release of new land from the public domain, the distribution of labor and income between the regions is given by the lines and areas summarized in columns 1 and 2 of Table 7, Part A.

TABLE 7. THE DISTRIBUTION OF LABOR AND INCOME BETWEEN THE EAST AND WEST

	A. Base-Period Labor Supply			
	Before the Release of the Land		*After the Release of the Land*	
	1 West	*2 East*	*3 West*	*4 East*
Labor	DE*	EG	DF	FG
Labor Income	CDEN	HGEN	BDFK	IGFK
Land Income	ACN	JHN	ABK	JIK

	B. End-Period Labor Supply			
	Before the Release of the Land		*After the Release of the Land*	
	1 West	*2 East*	*3 West*	*4 East*
Labor	DE′	E′G′	DF′	F′G′
Labor Income	C′DE′N′	H′G′E′N′	B′DF′K′	I′G′F′K′
Land Income	AC′N′	J′H′N′	AB′K′	J′I′K′

* Letters refer to areas in Figures 1 and 2.

If the land released from the public domain is in the West and has the same distribution of quality as that already in use in the region, the Western marginal product curve will pivot upward from its original position to the position given by AP.[26] The level of national income after the distribution of land is given by the area under the new Western marginal product curve and the corresponding Eastern curve, the area designated by ADGJKA. The increase in national income brought about by the release of the land is the triangle ANK. There is a loss of

[26] If the new land released from the public domain was of superior quality to that already in use (i.e. the best new land was superior to the best old land, etc.), curve AP would be above line AO at all points. For example, if each plot of new land was, when arrayed according to quality, 10 per cent more productive than each plot of the old land similarly arrayed, then AP would be 10 per cent higher than AO at all points.

income in the East. This is represented by the area KNEF. However, the loss to the East is not a loss to the nation. It is a transfer to the West which is associated with the migration of a part of the labor force (EF) from the East to the West.

Some further points are worth noting. While in this case there is a rise in the rental income on land in the West, the increase (ALK minus BCNL) is less than the rise in national income (ANK). Consequently, the change in Western rents may be regarded as a lower bound on the change in national income attributable to the release of land.[27] While Western rents rise, rental income in the East declines. In the nation as a whole there is a transfer of income from land owners to labor. The increase in labor income is represented by the rectangle BCHI. Only a fraction of this amount, the triangle LNK, is derived from the increase in national income. The balance is accounted for by a transfer to labor from land income. While in the West the transfer is more than offset by the gain in land income due to the new lands, the income of Eastern landowners declines not only relatively but absolutely.[28]

The argument thus far has not taken population change into account. With a growing population, one must decide whether to evaluate the effect of an introduction of new land with respect to the base-period or the end-period population. This is a common type of index number problem, and it poses no special difficulty with respect to the point at issue. If Figure 1 is taken to represent the base-period population, Figure 2 would represent the situation with the end-period population. Indeed Figure 2 is merely a stretched version of Figure 1. The labor force in the new diagram exceeds that of the old one by GG', or

27 We abstract from the Rybczynzki-Jones effect. See Ronald W. Jones, "The Structure of Simple General Equilibrium Models," *Journal of Political Economy*, 73 (December 1965), pp. 557-72, for a discussion of the circumstances under which this effect would hold. It appears unlikely that the elasticities of nineteenth-century America could have been of a magnitude that would falsify the statement in the text.

26 This preceding argument can be expressed algebraically as follows:

Define $Y_e = F(t_e, z_e)$ and $Y_w = G(t_w, z_w)$, where Y_i = output of i-th region, t_i is the land input in each region measured in efficiency units, and z_i is the input of all other factors; e = East and w = West. Assume that there is added in the West an amount of land equal to dt. We know that $dY = dY_e + dY_w = F_z dz_e + F_t dt_e + G_t dt_w + G_z dz_w$. Since $z = z_e + z_w$, and we have not affected the total quantity of z, we have $dz = 0$ and $dz_e = - dz_w$. Moreover $dt_e = 0$ and land is immobile, so that there is no interregional transfer of land. Hence $dY = (F_z - G_z)\, dz_e + G_t dt_w$. On the other hand, "z" is mobile and can be transferred. Given the mobility of goods and of z, we must have $F_z = G_z$. Hence $dY = G_t dt_w$ which is positive. Furthermore, since the last expression only involves the marginal product of land in the West, it indicates that dY is independent of the decline of land rent in the East.

approximately 25 per cent. Given the original quantity of land in the economy, national income is represented by the area ADG'J'N'A. After the release of new land, national income is represented by the area ADG'J'K'A. Now the change in national income due to the release of land from the public domain is given by the triangle AN'K'. Once again the decline of Eastern income induced by the new lands takes the form of a transfer to the West and is not a loss to the nation. Other distribution effects are summarized in Part B of Table 7.

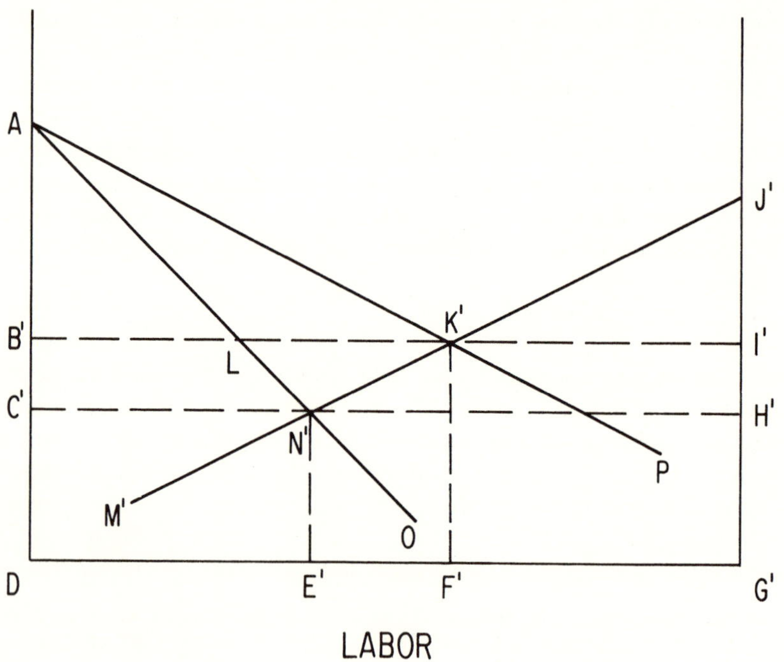

Fig. 2

Whether one ought to evaluate the income effect of new lands with respect to the base- or end-period population need not be resolved here. The answer depends on whether or not population growth was independent of land policy during the specific period under consideration. However, for those interested in using changes in land values to evaluate the effect of land policy, railroads, or other innovations on development in the West,[29] it is important to emphasize that when

[29] Cf. Albert Fishlow, *American Railroads and the Transformation of the Ante-bellum Economy* (Cambridge: Harvard Univ. Press, 1965); Robert W. Fogel,

population is changing, the change in Western land values will in part reflect this fact. This point may be shown by superimposing Figure 1 on Figure 2, as is done in Figure 3. It shows that AN'K' exceeds ANK by NN'K'K. Only the area ANK is due to the effect of land policy alone. The area NN'K'K reflects the interaction of land policy and population growth. In the diagram we have drawn, NN'K'K is small relative to ANK. In other cases it could be quite large. Consequently, to determine the pure land effect it is necessary to partition the interaction term.

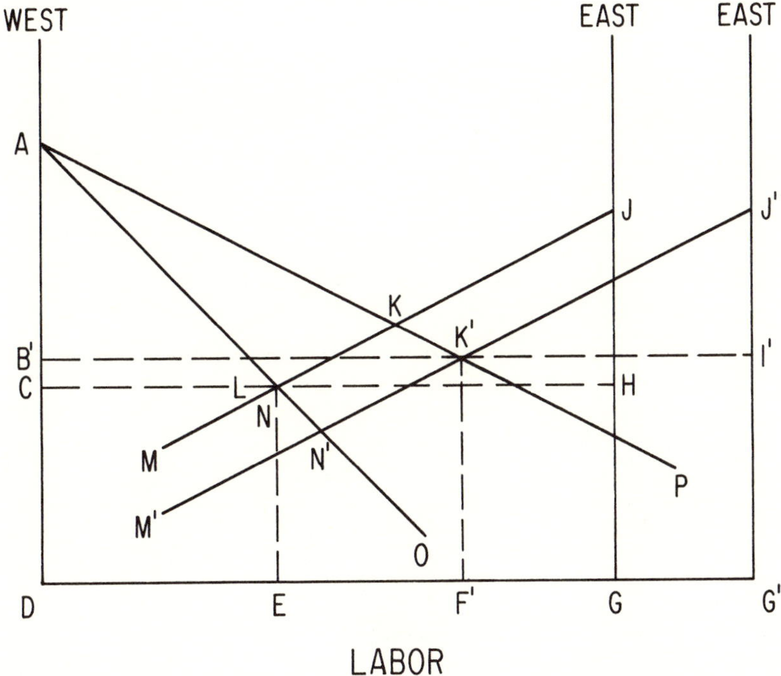

Fig. 3

So far we have assumed that a shift in the marginal product of labor in the West will have no effect on the marginal product of labor in the East. These curves need not be independent of each other. Indeed, it

Railroads and American Economic Growth: Essays in Econometric History (Baltimore: Johns Hopkins Press, 1964); Robert W. Fogel, *The Union Pacific Railroad: A Case in Premature Enterprise* (Baltimore: Johns Hopkins Press, 1960); Roger Ransom, "Canals and Development: A Discussion of the Issues," *American Economic Review*, 54 (May 1964), pp. 365-76.

has been argued the Western competition demoralized labor in the Northeast.[30] The effect is shown in Figure 4, where the release of land in the West not only shifts that region's marginal product curve upward to AP but simultaneously shifts the Eastern curve downward to J''M''. In this case the release of land takes national income from ADGJNA to ADGJ''K''A. And the net benefit of the new land is not the triangle ANK but AN''K'' minus JJ''K''KJ, which need not necessarily have a positive value. In other words, if demoralization did occur on a wide enough scale in the Northeast, the net effect of a release of new land may have been to reduce national income.

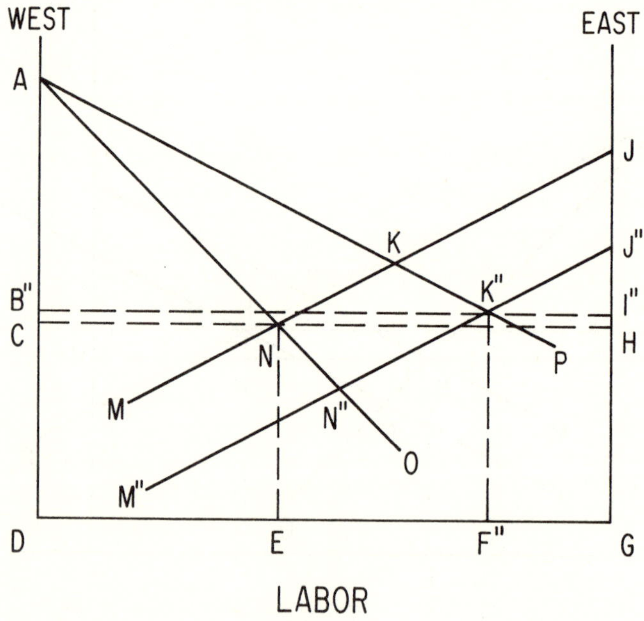

Fig. 4

However available aggregative evidence suggests that if there was demoralization in the farm sector of the North Atlantic region, it was too limited in scope and intensity to have had a measurable effect on the income of the region. From an economic standpoint, demoralization is equivalent to negative technological progress and would exhibit itself in a decline in total factor productivity. However between 1879

[30] Cf. Lee Benson, *Merchants, Farmers, and Railroads* (Cambridge: Harvard Univ. Press, 1955); James C. Malin, "Mobility and History: Reflections on the Agricultural Policies in Relation to a Mechanized World," *Agricultural History*, 17 (October 1943), pp. 177-91.

and 1899 total factor productivity rose at 0.3 per cent per annum.[31] This test is not conclusive since the North Atlantic exhibited a slower rate of increase in total factor productivity than the Western and North Central states. However the most probable explanation for the advantage of these regions is the decline in transportation costs which raised prices in the West relative to those in the East.[32]

The Efficiency Loss Due to Withholding of Land by Speculators

It has been argued frequently that federal land was released at too low a price. Because of the low price, it is said great amounts of land were purchased by large-scale speculators who kept out of production lands that would otherwise have been put to use in agriculture. If the facts have been correctly stated, such speculation must have reduced national income. The loss in efficiency does not depend, as is frequently assumed, on the proposition that the land withheld from production was, in general, superior to that actually in use. There would be a loss of income even if the distribution of the quality of the lands held by speculators was identical to that of land actually in use. This conclusion can be verified by referring to Figure 1. Let AO again represent the marginal product of labor on the lands farmed in Western agriculture. If the distribution of the quality of the lands held by speculators had been identical to that of land in use, release of these lands would cause the Western marginal product curve to pivot upward from AO to AP. The gain in national income is represented by the area ANK. The result is, of course, the same one obtained when we analyzed the effect of the withholding of land by the government. It is the fact that land is withheld from production, not the group which withholds it, that accounts for the inefficiency.

31 Computed from

$$\overset{*}{A} = \alpha_1 (\overset{*}{Q} - \overset{*}{L}) + \alpha_2 (\overset{*}{Q} - \overset{*}{T}),$$

with $\alpha_1 = 0.6$; $\alpha_2 = 0.4$. $\overset{*}{T}$ was computed from improved land which, because of the declining land input in the North Atlantic region, is more appropriate in this case than unimproved land. $\overset{*}{Q}$ was obtained by applying Easterlin's regional relatives to Gallman's estimate of the growth of real value added in agriculture (Conference on Research in Income and Wealth, *American Economy*, pp. 43, 99-104). The result is $\overset{*}{A} = 0.3$.

32 Over the period 1879-99 the price of corn in Chicago rose relative to the price of corn in New York at an annual rate of 0.6 per cent. Such a change in the average price of Western agricultural products alone would account for nearly all of the differences between the rate of growth of total factor productivity in the North Atlantic region and the rest of the nation.

The real issue, then, is the size of the loss in income attributable to land speculation. The traditional interpretation presumes a type of behavior by large speculators that led them to withhold land from production for long periods of time. Yet this proposition has not been supported either by theoretical arguments or empirical evidence. Indeed, theoretical considerations suggest that both of the two main types of land speculators identified in the literature—those who had superior information and those who were pure gamblers—would generally maximize profit if they resold the land in their possession quickly.

Figure 5 pertains to the speculator with superior information. The vertical axis is logarithmic and gives the price per acre of land. Time is the variable on the horizontal axis. The curve P_0, P_t represents the true course of the price of a particular quantity of land. The course of

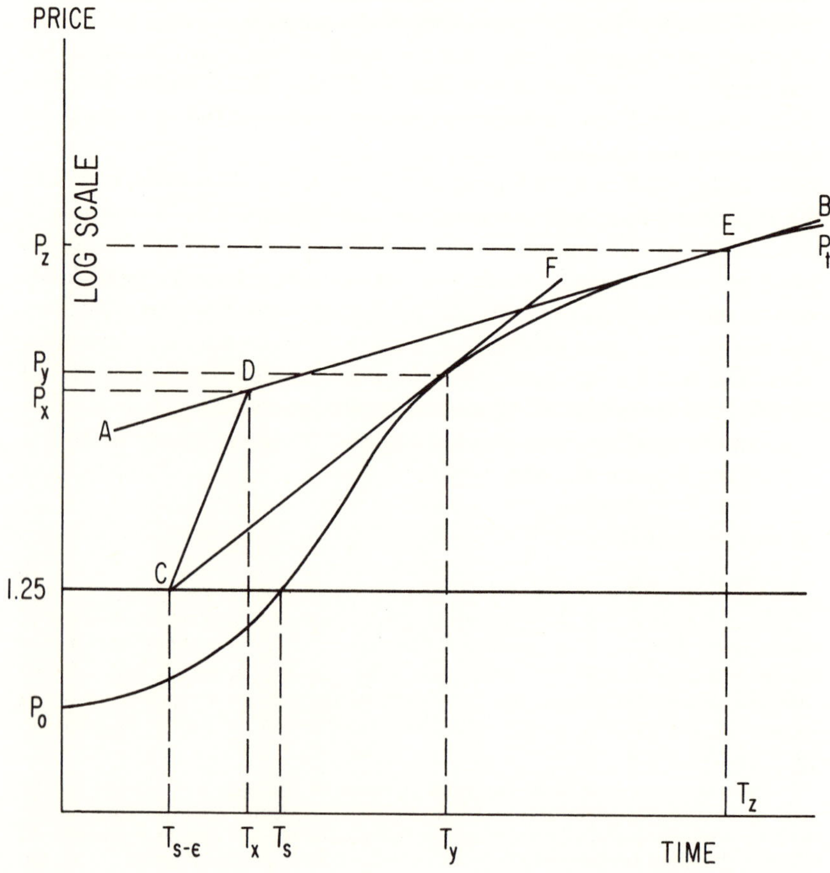

Fig. 5

the price of the land is assumed to be known by a speculator with superior knowledge, but not by others. The slope of this curve (or any other line) at any point gives the rate of growth of the price of land at that point. The slope of the line AB gives the mortgage rate of interest. The price at which this land can be obtained from the government is $1.25 per acre.

Those without superior knowledge would have bought the land at T_s when its value would have reached $1.25 per acre. However the informed speculator purchased the land at the government price at time $T_{s-\epsilon}$. The value of ϵ is determined by such factors as the speculator's estimate of the probability that others will discover what he knows and his alternate opportunities for investment. Having made the purchase, the speculator could merely sit tight and wait for T_y when the price of land will be at P_y. If the price of land followed the course given by P_0, P_t, a sale at time T_y would give the highest rate of return on his investment. This return is given by the slope of the line CF.

However, once the speculator has acquired the land it is clearly in his interest to convey to others in the land market his superior knowledge and to convince them that at time T_z this land will be worth P_z. For once he did that, the price of the land would immediately rise to the discounted present value of P_z. In other words, the path of the price of the land after the market accepted the speculator's information would be along the line AB. Thus, if by time T_x the market became convinced that the speculator's information was true, the speculator could sell the land at P_x. Then his rate of return would be given by the slope of the line CD, which is greater than the slope of CF.[33]

Figure 6 pertains to the speculator who is a pure gambler. Such a speculator has no superior information, but he realizes that there is variance in the market price of land. He hopes to make his profit by selling his land on some occasion when the market price deviates from the expected price. The axes of Figure 6 are defined as they were in Figure 5. The line P_0, P_0e^{rt} is the expected path of the price of land and is known by the general public. The actual price at any point in time will vary to either side of this line. The broken lines which parallel P_0, P_0e^{rt} are located two standard deviations from the line of expected price.[34] The slope of the line P_0, P_0e^{it} gives the mortgage rate of interest.

[33] The argument assumes that speculators could reinvest in land. We have abstracted from the problem of transaction costs since P_o, P_t may be defined as the value of land net of transaction costs.

[34] It will be noted that Figure 6 has the standard deviation of price increasing over time, since the standard deviation is a constant percentage of price. This as-

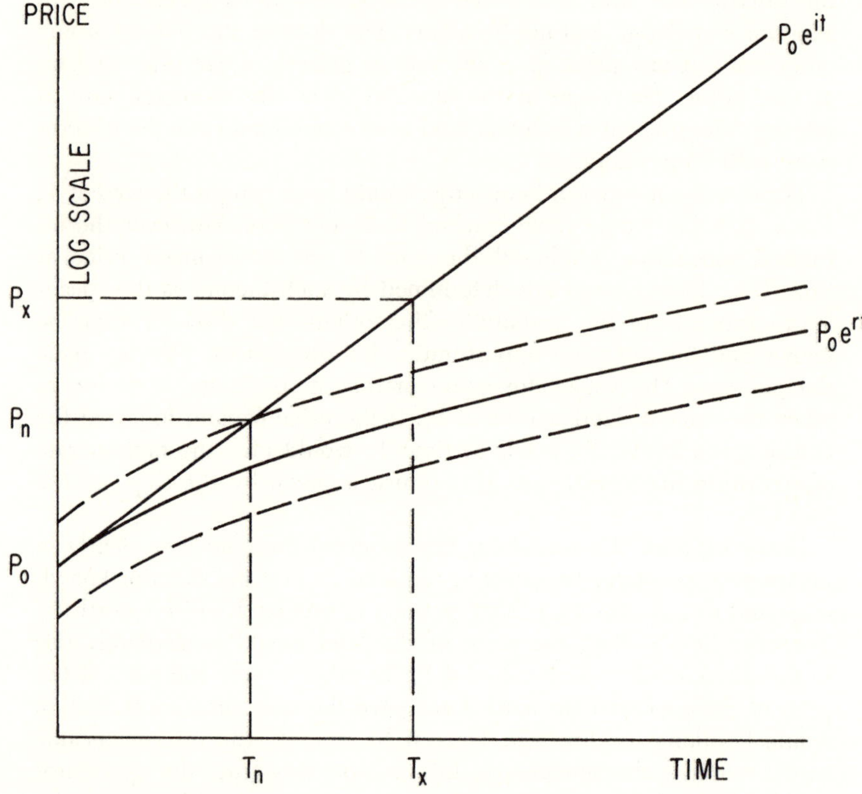

FIG. 6

Let us assume that the speculator buys a plot of land at time zero ($P_0 = \$1.25$) and that he plans to sell that land whenever its market price exceeds the expected price by an amount (say two standard deviations) that he considers to be a reasonable risk.

Figure 6 shows that the longer the speculator waits, the less probable it becomes that he will be able to sell the land at a price that will give him a rate of return equal to, or in excess of, the mortgage rate of interest. Indeed, after T_n even a price that is two standard deviations in excess of expected price would be inadequate to make the speculation profitable. And if he waits until T_x, it would take a deviation of market price in excess of 4 standard deviations (less than 1

sumption probably biases the argument in favor of the traditional interpretation. For one would expect the variance of price relative to actual price to decline as the characteristics of the land become better known, transportation improves, etc.

chance in 10,000) to yield a rate of return equal to the mortgage rate of interest.

We do not mean to suggest that speculators necessarily conformed to the behavior patterns characterized in Figures 5 and 6.[35] It was our aim merely to demonstrate that there are plausible alternatives to the assumption that speculators maximized profit by withholding land for long periods of time. Figures 5 and 6 show that whether a speculator had superior information or was a pure gambler, profit maximization might have led him to sell his land rather quickly. The only available body of empirical evidence against which one can test these theoretical arguments is that developed by Robert Swierenga.[36] Based on a study of land sales in an area covering one-third of the state of Iowa, his paper shows that the rate of return to large speculators (purchasers of 1,000 or more acres) was inversely correlated with the length of the time between a purchase and the resale. The average duration of this interval was about three years.

It is possible to estimate the loss in national income due to operations of large speculators by applying Swierenga's data to equation (4):

$$E_L = \frac{T\phi P_t iC}{Y} \qquad (4)$$

where

E_L = the loss in Gross National Product (GNP) due to the action of large speculators in withholding land from production, expressed as a proportion of GNP

T = the quantity of land released by the federal government in any given year

ϕ = the share of T taken by large speculators

P_t = the average price of land on resale

i = the rate of return on farm capital

C = the average number of years between purchase and resale

Y = Gross National Product

Swierenga's data indicate that the values of ϕ, P_t, and C were 0.32, \$3.10, and 3.2 years respectively.[37] The average amount of land re-

[35] The actual behavior of speculators probably reflected various mixtures of the "pure types" defined by Figures 5 and 6. It is worth noting that the decision rule which maximizes profit for the speculator characterized by Figure 6 is quite complex.

[36] Swierenga, "Land Speculator"; and Swierenga, *Pioneers and Profits.*

[37] The figure used for C, 3.2 years, is the average duration between purchase and resale for the 10 largest buyers in each county. It is not published in *ibid.* or Swierenga, "Land Speculator," but reported by Professor Swierenga at the 1969 MSSB Conference referred to in the introduction to this volume above. It is

leased annually between 1851 and 1860 was approximately 9.5 million acres;[38] and Table 4 above indicates that 0.1 is a reasonable estimate of the rate of return on farm capital. According to Gallman,[39] GNP was $2.3 billion in 1850 and $4.2 billion in 1860; the average of these two figures is $3.25 billion. Substituting into equation (4) we find that the value of E_L is 0.0009 or 0.09 per cent of GNP. This is the amount of national output produced in 1850 during three hours of economic activity.

Even this small number is probably an exaggeration of the efficiency loss due to speculators, for our calculation assumed that none of the land held by speculators was put to productive use between the initial purchase and the resale. Yet according to Swierenga, between 35 and 72 per cent of the land covered by his study was purchased under the time-entry system and involved farmers who were working or improving the land to an undetermined extent.[40] Moreover, to get at the efficiency loss, one must subtract from $E_L \times$ GNP the extra cost of administering an alternative system of land distribution. This alternative cost includes not only such extra direct expenditures as the salaries of government officials but also the foregone income attributable to any addition to the span between the time that land was open to public acquisition and the time a sale was effected. Thus Hibbard's proposal for improving the efficiency of the land distribution by raising the government's minimum price to $4.00 can hardly be called an improvement.[41] Such a price would have kept more land out of production than was withheld by large-scale speculators.

Not only has the traditional interpretation exaggerated the magnitude of the inefficiency induced by speculators, it has also exaggerated the ubiquity of the practice of withholding land from production. It has been charged that virtually every farmer was also a petty speculator who purchased more land than he could use. One of the main foundations for this position are census statistics which show that for

---

slightly larger than the figure of 2.8 years reported in Swierenga, *Pioneers and Profits*, p. 200. Neither figure is fully appropriate for our calculation. We have chosen the larger figure since we prefer to err in the direction of an overestimate of E_L. In any case, the difference in results obtained by using 3.2 instead of 2.8 is trivial.

[38] Paul W. Gates, "Charts of Public Land Sales and Entries," *Journal of Economic History*, 24 (March 1964), p. 28.

[39] Conference on Research in Income and Wealth, *Output Employment*, p. 26.

[40] Swierenga, *Pioneers and Profits*, p. 120. Moreover, some of the land held by speculators was no doubt exploited for grazing and other purposes by neighboring farmers, with or without the authorization of the owners.

[41] Benjamin Horace Hibbard, *A History of the Public Land Policies* (Madison, Wisc.: Univ. of Wisconsin Press, 1965), p. 555.

the nation as a whole the average farm size declined from 203 to 147 acres between 1850 and 1900.[42] Another foundation is the relatively large percentage of land in farms which was unimproved in 1850. Census data indicate that nearly 60 per cent of all farmland in the North Central states was unimproved in the middle of the century. By the end of the century the share of farmland that was unimproved stood at only 30 per cent.[43] To many writers, these facts have suggested that farmers initially had more land than they could use.

Such an inference is unwarranted for two reasons. First, almost all of the decline in the average national farm size is explained by the breakup of the large plantations after the Civil War. In the South Atlantic states, for example, average farm size declined by over 70 per cent between 1850 and 1900, from 376 to 108 acres. On the other hand, over the same period the average farm size in the North Central states showed no decline at all; indeed the average farm size actually rose slightly, going from 143 to 145 acres per farm.[44]

But more important, the fact that land prices rose relative to the price of labor as time progressed for one-time frontier areas, is by itself sufficient not only to explain a decline in the average number of acres per farmer, but also a rise in the ratio of improved to unimproved acres. For when land is cheap relative to labor, efficiency dictates the use of land-intensive methods of production—such as reliance on mast feeding in the raising of hogs and use of pasturage for cattle. But as the relative price of land rises, efficiency dictates a shift to such labor-intensive methods of agriculture as corn feeding. Thus the large share of unimproved land does not necessarily imply that farmers held more land than they could use in 1850. Unimproved is not a synonym for unexploited. There is abundant evidence which shows that the unimproved farm lands of the 1850s were in fact employed for agricultural production.[45] But these lands were employed in a different way in the middle of the nineteenth century than at the end of it. Moreover, the change in the manner of land employment—the shift from unimproved to improved land, from land-intensive to labor- and capital-intensive techniques of animal husbandry—is pre-

[42] U.S. Bureau of the Census, *Twelfth Census of the United States: 1900*, Vol. 5: *Agriculture* (Washington: U.S. Govt. Printing Office, 1902), Part 1, p. xxi.

[43] *Ibid.*, p. xviii.

[44] Patton and Warne, *Development*, p. xxi. There was a decline of 15 per cent in the average size of North Central farms between 1850 and 1880. But this trend was reversed during the next two decades.

[45] Bogue, *Prairie*, pp. 108-09; Gates, *Farmer's Age*, pp. 193, 217-18; Eugene D. Genovese, "Livestock in the Slave Economy of the Old South: A Revised View," *Agricultural History*, 36 (July 1962), pp. 145, 147.

cisely the response that farms attempting to minimize their cost of production should have had to the rise in the price of land relative to the price of labor and capital.[46]

Finally, the traditional interpretation of land policy reflects a certain schizophrenia. The federal government is simultaneously condemned by some writers both for encouraging speculation and for discouraging land ownership—that is, for causing an increasing share of farmers to rent rather than to own land. However there was no way to divorce land ownership from land speculation. A farmer who purchased the land on which he worked was of necessity engaged in a speculation on the future course of land values. The only way by which an agriculturalist could divorce farming from land speculation was by renting his farm for a fixed sum.[47] Viewed in this perspective, some of the criticism of federal land policy comes down to a condemnation of the government for failing to have found a way that permitted the farmer to enjoy the benefits of land ownership without having to have borne its risks.

In closing we wish to repeat the caveat set forth at the beginning of our paper. The weaknesses in present estimates of national income and related variables make the findings that we have set forth provisional. Better data could reverse certain of our conclusions. But pending the development of improved information, writers concerned with the efficiency of federal land policy ought to be at least more tentative, if not more sanguine, in their judgments.

[46] Some writers are critical of the regimen of frontier husbandry under which livestock were permitted to run free in woods, fields, and swamps. The result was a leaner, tougher, and to some, less tasty meat than was obtained by penning and intensive feeding. The appropriateness of these criticisms of the frontier farmer is open to question. Just because relatively high land prices in the East during the 1850s and 1860s, and in the prairies at later dates, led farmers to switch from land-intensive to labor- and capital-intensive methods of husbandry does not mean that frontier farmers were backward. The epitome of good practice under one set of relative prices might well lead to bankruptcy under another. The skill and acumen of the frontier farmers should be evaluated with respect to the particular economic conditions under which they labored rather than by the standards of other regions or later generations.

[47] Share cropping is a means of dividing the risk from land speculation between the farmer and the land owner.

Appendix

To assist in the preparation of this volume, MSSB organized two conferences. The first was held at Harvard University during June 13-16, 1966. At this meeting the contributors to the volume presented preliminary versions of their papers to a small group of social scientists and statisticians for criticisms and suggestions. The meeting was timed to be held late enough so that those preparing the papers would have a clear conception of the substantive and technical issues that confronted them, but early enough so that they could take full advantage of suggestions that arose from the discussion, even those that required massive revisions.

The participants in the 1966 meeting were:

Name	*Department or Field*	*University Affiliation*
William O. Aydelotte	History	Iowa (Iowa City)
Samuel Beer	Government	Harvard
Lee Benson	History	Pennsylvania
Allan G. Bogue	History	Wisconsin
Robert William Fogel	Economics	Chicago
John Gilbert	Statistics	Harvard
William Kruskal	Statistics	Chicago
Thomas Kurtz	Statistics	Dartmouth
Richard Link	Statistics	Princeton
Douglas K. Price	Government	Harvard
Robert Riffenbergh	Statistics	Connecticut
Richard Rosett	Economics	Rochester
Barbara Solow	Economics	Brandeis
Robert Solow	Economics	M.I.T.
Lawrence Stone	History	Princeton
Stephan Thernstrom	History	Harvard
Charles Tilly	Sociology	Harvard
Sasha Weitman	Sociology	Johns Hopkins

The second conference was held at the University of Chicago during June 4-7, 1969. It brought together 61 historians, social scientists, and statisticians for an initial discussion of the penultimate versions of the papers. The program and participants (with their institutional affiliations at the time) in the 1969 meeting were:

Conference on the Application of Quantitative Methods to Political, Social and Economic History

Sponsored by the Mathematical Social Science Board

June 4-7, 1969

University of Chicago

Center for Continuing Education

June 4: Reception

June 5

Chairman: Stephan Thernstrom

Allan G. Bogue: "Voting Patterns, 'Power' and Individual Deviancy in the Thirty-Seventh Senate."
Discussants: John McCarthy, Duncan MacRae

Lee Benson & *Alan Oslick*: "The Uses and Abuses of Statistical Methods in Studies of Legislative Behavior: 1836 Congressional Gag Rule Decision as Test Case."
Discussants: Douglas Price, Joel Silbey

William O. Aydelotte: "The Dimensions of Early Victorian Politics."
Discussants: H. S. Hanham, Duncan MacRae, David Roberts

Gerald Kramer & *Susan Lepper*: "Congressional Elections During the 20th Century."
Discussants: Richard Jensen, Douglas K. Price

June 6

Chairman: William O. Aydelotte

Gilbert Shapiro & *Philip Dawson*: "Social Mobility and Political Radicalism: the Case of the French Revolution."
Discussants: Alan B. Spitzer, Stephen Fienberg

Charles Tilly: "How Protest Modernized in France, 1845-1855."
Discussants: Peter Amann, Leo Loubere

Lawrence Stone: "Countryhouse Building and Changes of Ownership in Hertfordshire 1500-1880."
Discussants: J. H. Hexter, Donald N. McCloskey

Robert W. Fogel & *Jack L. Rutner*: "The Efficiency Effects of Federal

Land Policy during the Nineteenth Century: Some Preliminary Findings."
Discussants: Robert Swierenga, Paul Gates, Albert Fishlow

June 7

Chairman: Allan G. Bogue

Stephan Thernstrom: "Social Mobility in Boston."
Discussants: Leo Schnore, Arthur Mann, Donald Bogue

J. Rogers Hollingsworth & *Ellen J. Hollingsworth*: "Exploring Expenditures in American Cities, 1903."
Discussants: Robert R. Dykstra, Charles N. Glaab, Leo F. Schnore

Participants

Name	*Department or Field*	*University or Other Affiliation*
Thomas B. Alexander	History	Alabama
Peter Amann	History	Michigan
Ralph Austen	History	Chicago
William O. Aydelotte	History	Iowa (Iowa City)
Keith Baker	History	Chicago
Thomas Barnes	History	California (Berkeley)
Lee Benson	History	Pennsylvania
S. Bhattacharyya	History	Chicago
Allan G. Bogue	History	Wisconsin
Donald Bogue	Sociology	Chicago
Vernon Carstensen	History	Washington (Seattle)
Terry Clark	History	Chicago
Jerome Clubb	History	Michigan
Bernard Cohn	History/ Anthropology	Chicago
Thomas Condon	American Council of Learned Societies	
Georges Dupeux	History	Kent State (Bordeaux)
Robert R. Dykstra	History	Iowa (Iowa City)
Stephen Fienberg	Statistics	Chicago
Albert Fishlow	Economics	California (Berkeley)
Robert William Fogel	Economics/ History	Chicago/Rochester
Paul Gates	History	Wisconsin/Cornell
Charles Glaab	History	Ohio

Name	*Department or Field*	*University or Other Affiliation*
Louis Gottschalk	History	Chicago
H. J. Hanham	History	Harvard
Richard Hellie	History	Chicago
J. H. Hexter	History	Yale
Ellen Jane Hollingsworth	History	Wisconsin
J. Rogers Hollingsworth	History	Wisconsin
Richard Jensen	History	Washington (St. Louis)
Harry G. Johnson	Economics	Chicago
Herbert Klein	History	Chicago
Gerald Kramer	Political Science	Yale
Susan Lepper	Economics	Yale
Lester Little	History	Chicago
Leo Loubere	History	State University of New York (Buffalo)
Duncan MacRae	Political Science and Sociology	Chicago
Arthur Mann	History	Chicago
John McCarthy	History	Yale
Donald McCloskey	Economics	Chicago
William McQuire	Psychology	California (San Diego)
Bo Öhngren	Historiska Institutionen	Uppsala (Sweden)
Alan Oslick	History	Pennsylvania
Douglas Price	Government	Harvard
Theodore Rabb	History	Princeton
Martin Ridge	History	Indiana
David Roberts	History	Dartmouth
Malcolm Rohrbough	History	Iowa (Iowa City)
Jack L. Rutner	Economics	Chicago
Leo Schnore	Sociology	Wisconsin
T. W. Schultz	Economics	Chicago
Donald Scott	History	Chicago
William Sewell	History	Chicago
Gilbert Shapiro	Sociology	Pittsburgh
Joel Silbey	History	Cornell
Alan B. Spitzer	History	Iowa (Iowa City)
Lawrence Stone	History	Princeton
Robert Swierenga	History	Kent
Stephan Thernstrom	History	Brandeis

Name	*Department or Field*	*University or Other Affiliation*
Charles Tilly	Sociology	Toronto
Robert K. Webb	History	American Historical Review
E. A. Wrigley	History	Cambridge (England)

The Contributors

William O. Aydelotte has been professor of history at the University of Iowa since 1947. He received his Ph.D. from the University of Cambridge and taught previously at Trinity College and Princeton University. In addition to being chairman of Iowa's Department of History for fifteen years, he was a member of the Board of Directors of the Social Science Research Council from 1965 through 1970 and is currently a member of the American History Association's Committee on Quantitative Data and chairman of its subcommittee on European Quantitative Data. Aydelotte's previous publications include *Bismarck and British Colonial Policy* (1970) and *Quantification in History* (1971). He was awarded an honorary O.B.E. by Queen Elizabeth II in 1961.

Allan G. Bogue is the F. J. Turner Professor of History at the University of Wisconsin where he has taught since 1964. He received his Ph.D. in history from Cornell University and taught previously at the University of Western Ontario and the State University of Iowa. Bogue was the President of the Agricultural History Society in 1964 and is currently a member of the editorial boards of the *Journal of American History*, the *Journal of Interdisciplinary History*, *Civil War History*, and *Behavioral Scientist*. His previous publications include *From Prairie to Corn Belt: Farming on the Illinois and Iowa Prairies in the Nineteenth Century* (1963) and "Bloc and Party in the United States Senate: 1861-1863," *Civil War History* (1967).

Philip Dawson is associate professor of History at Stanford University. He received his Ph.D. in history from Harvard University in 1961. His previous publications include *Provincial Magistrates and Revolutionary Politics in France, 1789-1795* (1971).

Robert William Fogel is professor of economics and history at the University of Chicago and professor of economics at the University of Rochester. He received his Ph.D. in economics from the Johns Hopkins University in 1963. His previous publications include *Railroads and American Economic Growth* (1963) and (with Stanley L. Engerman and others) *The Reinterpretation of American Economic History* (1971). He was awarded the Arthur H. Cole Prize in 1968 and the Joseph A. Schumpeter Prize in 1971.

Ellen Jane Hollingsworth is Research Associate at the Institute for Research on Poverty at the University of Wisconsin where she is studying for a Ph.D. in sociology. Her previous publications include (with Joel Handler) *The "Deserving Poor"* (1971).

J. Rogers Hollingsworth is professor of history at the University of Wisconsin where he has taught since 1964. He received his Ph.D. in history from the University of Chicago in 1960 and taught previously at the University of Illinois. Hollingsworth is the Planner and Coordinator of the International Conference on History and Theory which will be held at the University of Michigan in 1972. His publications include *The Whirligig of Politics: The Democracy of Cleveland and Bryan* (1963) and *The Politics of Nation and State Building: The American Experience* (1971).

Gerald H. Kramer is associate professor of political science and a staff member of the Cowles Foundation for Research in Economics at Yale University. He received his Ph.D. in political science from the Massachusetts Institute of Technology in 1965. Before coming to Yale, he taught at the University of Rochester. His publications include "The Effect of Precinct-Level Canvassing on Voter Behavior," *The Public Opinion Quarterly* (1970-1971). Kramer received the Pi Sigma Alpha Award in 1968.

Susan Jewett Lepper is Research Associate and Lecturer in Economics as well as the Assistant Director of the Cowles Foundation for Research in Economics at Yale University. She received her Ph.D. from Yale in 1963. She has previously published "The Effects of Alternative Tax Structures on Individuals' Holdings of Financial Assets," in *Risk Aversion and Portfolio Choice*, Donald Hester and James Tobin, eds., Cowles Foundation Monograph No. 19 (1967).

Jack L. Rutner is an assistant professor of economics at the Illinois State University. He is currently working toward his Ph.D. in economics from the University of Chicago.

Gilbert Shapiro is professor of sociology and history at the University of Pittsburgh. He received his Ph.D. in sociology from Cornell in 1954 and taught previously at Washington State University and Boston College. He is a member of the editorial boards of the *Historical Methods Newsletter* and the *Journal of Social History*. His previous publications include (with Charles Winick) *Trends in Human Relations Research* (1955) and "The Many Lives of Georges Lefebvre," *American Historical Review* (1967).

Lawrence Stone is the Dodge Professor of History at Princeton University and Director of the Shelby Cullom Davis Center for Historical Studies. He studied at the Sorbonne and at Christ Church, Oxford. He was a Fellow of Wadham College, Oxford, from 1950 until 1962.

His previous publications include *The Crisis of the Aristocracy, 1558-1641* (1965), *An Elizabethan: Sir Horatio Palavicino* (1956), *Britain: the Middle Ages* (1955), and *The Causes of the English Revolution* (1972). He is a member of the editorial board of *Past and Present.*

Jeanne C. Fawtier Stone studied at Bordeaux University and Somerville College, Oxford, and worked as research assistant in the British Political Warfare Executive, 1941-1946. She is now a historical research assistant, specializing in data processing for the computer.

Stephan Thernstrom is professor of history at the University of California, Los Angeles. He received his Ph.D. in the History of American Civilization from Harvard University in 1962. He taught previously at Harvard and Brandeis universities and is currently on the editorial boards of *Labor History* and the *Journal of Interdisciplinary History.* His previous publications include *Poverty and Progress: Social Mobility in a Nineteenth-Century City* (1964) and (with Richard Sennett and others) *Nineteenth-Century Cities: Essays in the New Urban History* (1969).

Charles Tilly is professor of sociology and history at the University of Michigan. He received his Ph.D. in sociology from Harvard in 1958. In addition to having taught at Harvard University and the University of Toronto, he was a Fellow of the Center for Advanced Study in the Behavioral Sciences (1968-1969) and a member of the Institute for Advanced Study (1970-1971). Tilly was co-chairman of the History Panel of the Behavioral and the Social Sciences of the Social Science Research Council and National Academy of Sciences. His previous publications include *The Vendée* (1964) and (with David S. Landes and others) *History as Social Science* (1971).

Index